Cybersecurity Incident Response System

by

Matt Dean

ISBN: 978-1-7750957-2-9

Published by Matthew Dean © 2025

Dedication

To the diligent cybersecurity professionals, the vigilant incident responders, the strategic IT managers, the keen security analysts, and the prepared emergency management personnel who stand on the front lines of our digital defense. Your unwavering commitment to protecting our interconnected world, often in the face of overwhelming challenges, is the bedrock upon which our digital security is built. This book is a testament to your dedication, offering a structured approach to enhance your capabilities and resilience in an ever-evolving threat landscape. May this work serve as a valuable tool in your critical mission to safeguard critical information, systems, and the trust placed in your expertise. Your efforts are not only appreciated but are essential to the stability and progress of our modern society.

The digital realm, once a nascent frontier, has rapidly transformed into the primary arena for commerce, communication, and critical infrastructure. With this pervasive digitization comes an ever-escalating array of sophisticated cyber threats. Organizations, regardless of size or sector, are increasingly vulnerable to attacks that can cripple operations, erode public trust, and inflict significant financial and reputational damage. Traditional incident response models, often reactive and ad-hoc, are proving insufficient against the persistent and advanced nature of these threats. This book addresses this critical gap by advocating for and detailing the adaptation of the proven Incident Command System (ICS) framework to the unique challenges of cybersecurity incident response. ICS, originally developed for emergency management, offers a standardized, scalable, and flexible structure that can bring much-needed order, clarity, and efficiency to the chaotic environment of a cyberattack. We aim to provide cybersecurity professionals, IT managers, and emergency responders with a practical guide to implementing and leveraging ICS principles, transforming their incident response capabilities from reactive measures to proactive, well-orchestrated defenses. Through real-world examples and actionable advice, this book seeks to equip you with the knowledge and tools necessary to build a robust and resilient cybersecurity incident response program.

1

The digital realm is in a perpetual state of flux, a vibrant ecosystem constantly reshaped by innovation, economic pressures, and human ingenuity. Within this dynamic environment, cybersecurity threats have evolved from a niche concern for IT departments to a pervasive, existential risk for organizations of all sizes and sectors. The adversaries we face are no longer simply script-kiddies or opportunistic hackers; they are increasingly sophisticated, well-resourced, and highly motivated actors, ranging from organized criminal syndicates driven by financial gain to nation-states wielding cyber capabilities as a strategic weapon. This evolving threat landscape demands more than just reactive defense; it necessitates a proactive, structured, and adaptable approach to incident response that can effectively manage the inevitable disruptions.

The sheer volume and velocity of cyberattacks have escalated dramatically. What once might have been a trickle of isolated incidents has now become a torrent, overwhelming traditional security measures and overwhelming unprepared organizations. This increase in frequency is mirrored by a significant leap in sophistication. Attackers are no longer content with brute-force methods or exploiting well-known vulnerabilities. Instead, they employ advanced techniques that are stealthy, persistent, and tailored to evade detection. This is where the concept of Advanced Persistent Threats (APTs) becomes critically important. APTs are characterized by their prolonged presence within a target network, their stealthy reconnaissance, and their ability to adapt their methods to avoid detection. These are not smash-and-grab operations; they are meticulous, long-term campaigns designed to exfiltrate sensitive data, disrupt operations, or establish a persistent foothold for future attacks. APT actors often possess significant resources, including highly skilled personnel and substantial funding, allowing them to develop custom malware, conduct intricate social engineering campaigns, and maintain access for months or even years before being discovered. The WannaCry ransomware attack in 2017, which rapidly spread across the globe exploiting a Windows vulnerability, serves as a stark reminder of how quickly even sophisticated threats can proliferate. While WannaCry had elements of widespread infection, the underlying vulnerabilities exploited were known, and patches existed. The true danger of APTs lies in their ability to leverage unknown vulnerabilities or to remain undetected for extended periods, making them a formidable challenge.

A significant driver of this escalating sophistication is the emergence and increasing prevalence of zero-day exploits. A zero-day exploit targets a previously unknown vulnerability in software or hardware, meaning that no patch or defense exists at the time of the attack. Attackers who discover or acquire access to a zero-day vulnerability can use it to compromise systems with a very high probability of success, as defenders are essentially blind to the threat. The discovery and weaponization of zero-days represent a critical inflection point in the cybersecurity arms race. Organizations are in a perpetual race to patch known vulnerabilities, but the existence of zero-days means that even the most diligently patched systems can remain at risk. The implications of a zero-day exploit being used in a widespread attack are profound, potentially leading to rapid compromise of critical systems and widespread disruption before any defensive measures can be effectively deployed. The SolarWinds supply chain attack, which came to light in late 2020, exemplified the devastating impact of sophisticated attacks that leverage subtle entry points and sophisticated techniques. While not solely a zero-day exploit in its initial vector, the attack demonstrated the power of stealthy, long-term infiltration, where malicious code was embedded in legitimate software updates, allowing attackers to gain access to numerous high-profile organizations for an extended period without detection. This incident highlighted the vulnerability of supply chains and the immense challenge of defending against threats that operate with such a high degree of sophistication and stealth.

Furthermore, the rapid advancements in Artificial Intelligence (AI) and Machine Learning (ML) are profoundly reshaping the cybersecurity landscape, presenting a double-edged sword. On one hand, these technologies offer unprecedented capabilities for defense, enabling the development of more intelligent intrusion detection systems, automated threat analysis, and predictive security measures. AI can process vast amounts of data, identify subtle anomalies, and respond to threats at machine speed, augmenting human capabilities and improving overall security posture. However, the same AI and ML technologies are also being weaponized by threat actors. Adversaries are leveraging AI to develop more sophisticated and evasive malware, to automate reconnaissance and vulnerability exploitation, and to craft highly personalized and convincing phishing campaigns. AI-powered social engineering, for instance, can analyze vast amounts of public data about individuals to create tailored messages that are far more likely to elicit a desired response. This arms race, where AI is used for both attack and defense, escalates the complexity and urgency of cybersecurity challenges. The implications are that defenses must become smarter, faster, and more adaptive, while attackers will become more agile, stealthy, and capable of launching highly personalized and effective attacks. The need for a structured response framework becomes even more pronounced in this AI-driven era, as manual response efforts may struggle to keep pace with the speed and sophistication of AI-enhanced attacks.

The implications of this evolving threat landscape are stark. Organizations are no longer simply facing the risk of data loss or financial theft; they are contending with threats that can cripple critical infrastructure, disrupt essential services, compromise national security, and erode public trust. The interconnectedness of our digital world means that a successful cyberattack on one organization can have cascading effects, impacting supply chains, partners, and even entire industries. Consider the impact of ransomware attacks on healthcare systems. These attacks can lead to the cancellation of surgeries, the inability to access patient records, and a direct threat to patient safety and well-being. Similarly, attacks on energy grids or financial institutions can have far-reaching economic and societal consequences. The frequency and sophistication of these incidents underscore a critical realization: traditional, ad-hoc, or purely reactive approaches to cybersecurity incident response are no longer sufficient. The sheer scale and complexity of modern cyber threats demand a more robust, structured, and inherently scalable approach. This is precisely why the principles of the Incident

Command System (ICS), originally developed for managing large-scale physical disasters, are gaining traction as a model for modern cybersecurity incident response. ICS provides a standardized framework for organizing resources, coordinating efforts, and managing complex incidents, offering a proven methodology for bringing order to chaos. By adapting and applying these principles, organizations can enhance their resilience, minimize the impact of cyberattacks, and ensure a more effective and coordinated response when incidents inevitably occur. The adoption of such a framework is not merely a technical imperative; it is a strategic necessity for survival and sustained operation in the face of an increasingly hostile digital environment.

The sheer diversity of threats necessitates a flexible and adaptive response. The landscape is not static; it is a constantly shifting battleground where new attack vectors emerge with alarming regularity. For instance, the rise of the Internet of Things (IoT) has introduced a vast new attack surface. Billions of interconnected devices, often with limited built-in security, represent potential entry points for attackers. From smart home devices to industrial control systems, these IoT devices can be compromised and used to launch attacks, disrupt operations, or serve as pivot points into more secure networks. The proliferation of these devices, coupled with often inadequate security practices for their deployment and management, creates a fertile ground for opportunistic and sophisticated attacks. The Mirai botnet, which in 2016 leveraged thousands of compromised IoT devices to launch massive Distributed Denial of Service (DDoS) attacks, demonstrated the potential for these seemingly innocuous devices to be weaponized on a global scale.

This expanded attack surface complicates incident response efforts significantly, requiring organizations to not only defend their traditional IT infrastructure but also to monitor and secure a sprawling ecosystem of connected devices.

Another significant trend is the increasing professionalization and monetization of cybercrime. What began as a hobby for many has evolved into a highly organized and profitable industry. Cybercriminal operations are now structured like legitimate businesses, with specialized roles, clear hierarchies, and sophisticated business models. Ransomware-as-a-Service (RaaS) platforms, for example, allow less technically skilled individuals to launch ransomware attacks by purchasing the necessary tools and infrastructure from established criminal groups. This lowers the barrier to entry for cybercrime, leading to an explosion in the number of attacks. These criminal enterprises are driven by profit, constantly innovating to find new ways to extort money from their victims. They invest heavily in research and development, developing new malware variants, finding new exploitation techniques, and refining their extortion tactics. The financial motivation behind these attacks makes them relentless and highly persistent, as long as the profits continue to flow. This industrialization of cybercrime means that organizations are no longer just fighting individual hackers but entire criminal syndicates with significant resources and a business-driven approach to attacks.

The geopolitical dimension of cyber threats also continues to escalate. Nation-states are increasingly using cyber capabilities for espionage, sabotage, and information warfare. These state-sponsored actors often possess advanced technical capabilities, significant resources, and a strategic objective, making them among the most dangerous adversaries. They can target critical infrastructure, engage in intellectual property theft, and conduct sophisticated disinformation campaigns to destabilize adversaries or influence political outcomes. The Stuxnet worm, which targeted Iran's nuclear program, is a prime example of a state-sponsored cyber weapon capable of causing physical damage. The attribution of such attacks can be challenging, often involving complex investigations and geopolitical considerations. However, the intent is clear: to leverage cyberspace as a domain of conflict and competition. This threat requires a different level of response, often involving collaboration with national security agencies and a focus on resilience against state-level attacks. The increasing blurring of lines between criminal activity and state-sponsored operations further complicates the threat landscape, as it can be difficult to discern the true motives and origins of an attack.

The growing reliance on cloud computing and distributed systems introduces further complexities. While cloud services offer numerous benefits in terms of scalability and flexibility, they also create new challenges for cybersecurity. Misconfigurations in cloud environments are a leading cause of data breaches, as attackers exploit weak access controls or exposed storage buckets. Furthermore, the shared responsibility model in cloud security means that organizations must understand where their security obligations end and the cloud provider's begin. Incident response in cloud environments requires specialized skills and tools to effectively monitor, investigate, and contain threats across distributed infrastructure. The dynamic nature of cloud deployments, with resources being spun up and down rapidly, adds another layer of complexity to tracking and analyzing security events. This means that incident response plans must be adapted to account for the unique characteristics of cloud and hybrid environments, ensuring that visibility and control are maintained across all deployed assets.

The human element remains a critical vulnerability and a frequent target. Social engineering, in its myriad forms, continues to be one of the most effective methods for attackers to gain initial access to systems. Phishing emails, spear-phishing attacks, vishing (voice phishing), and smishing (SMS phishing) prey on human psychology, exploiting trust, fear, or greed to trick individuals into revealing credentials, downloading malware, or transferring funds. The rise of AI-powered tools has made these social engineering tactics even more sophisticated and personalized. Attackers can craft highly convincing messages that are tailored to individual recipients, making them increasingly difficult to detect. This underscores the importance of ongoing security awareness training for all employees, not just IT personnel. A well-trained workforce can act as the first line of defense, identifying and reporting suspicious activities, thereby preventing many incidents before they can escalate. The effectiveness of incident response is directly tied to the organization's ability to foster a security-conscious culture where every individual understands their role in protecting the organization.

The increasing sophistication and prevalence of these threats have underscored a fundamental truth: a reactive approach to cybersecurity is no longer viable.

Organizations must shift from a posture of simply responding to incidents after they occur to one of proactive resilience, built upon a framework that can effectively manage and coordinate response efforts when the inevitable happens. The dynamic nature of cyber threats, characterized by their increasing sophistication, frequency, and the introduction of new attack vectors like AI-driven attacks and IoT vulnerabilities, necessitates a robust and scalable incident response framework. Such a framework must be capable of adapting to novel threats, coordinating diverse response teams, and ensuring that an organization can minimize impact and recover swiftly. This is the core rationale for adopting and adapting established command and control structures, like the Incident Command System (ICS), to the unique challenges of the cybersecurity domain. The goal is to transform incident response from a chaotic, fragmented effort into a well-orchestrated operation, ensuring that an organization can not only withstand but also effectively manage and recover from the inevitable cyber disruptions of the modern era. The lessons learned from major global incidents—from the widespread disruption caused by ransomware to the subtle infiltration of supply chain attacks—all point towards the urgent need for a structured, scalable, and universally understood approach to managing these complex events. This is the foundation upon which resilient cybersecurity operations are built.

A cybersecurity incident is not a monolithic event; rather, it is a broad classification encompassing a wide spectrum of unwanted or unauthorized actions within an organization's digital infrastructure. At its most basic level, an incident can be as seemingly minor as a single workstation becoming infected with a common virus or a user accidentally clicking on a malicious link. However, the scope quickly expands to include more pervasive and damaging events. This can manifest as the unauthorized access or exfiltration of sensitive data, which forms the basis of most data breaches. It can also involve the disruption of critical services, such as a denial-of-service (DoS) or distributed denial-of-service (DDoS) attack that renders websites or internal systems inaccessible to legitimate users. Furthermore, the compromise of critical systems, leading to their malfunction or complete shutdown, such as the catastrophic consequences of a destructive malware attack or a sophisticated sabotage operation, also falls under the umbrella of cybersecurity incidents. Even the accidental exposure of confidential information due to human error or misconfiguration can be classified as an incident, as it carries potential negative ramifications.

The spectrum of impact is equally vast, mirroring the diversity of incident types. The most immediate and often quantifiable impact is financial loss. This can stem from direct costs associated with the incident, such as the ransom payments demanded in a ransomware attack, the expenses incurred for forensic investigation and system recovery, legal fees, and the cost of notifying affected parties. Beyond these direct expenditures, there are the often-hidden costs of business disruption. When systems are down, employees cannot perform their duties, production halts, and revenue streams are interrupted. The longer the downtime, the more significant these financial losses become. Consider a retail company experiencing a ransomware attack during a peak shopping season; the lost sales and the cost of restoring systems could be crippling.

Beyond financial considerations, reputational damage can be one of the most insidious and long-lasting consequences of a cybersecurity incident. In today's hyper-connected world, news of a data breach or significant system compromise can spread like wildfire through social media and news outlets. Customers, partners, and investors place a high degree of trust in organizations to protect their data and maintain operational integrity. A breach of this trust can lead to a significant erosion of customer loyalty, a decline in market share, and difficulty in attracting new business. For instance, a healthcare provider experiencing a breach of patient records not only faces regulatory penalties but also the profound loss of trust from individuals who have entrusted them with their most sensitive personal information. Rebuilding this trust can take years, if it is possible at all.

Operational disruption is another critical impact that can have far-reaching consequences. A successful cyberattack can cripple an organization's ability to function, impacting everything from daily operations to critical service delivery. This is particularly true for organizations in sectors like healthcare, finance, and critical infrastructure. An attack on a hospital's IT systems, for example, can lead to canceled surgeries, delays in patient care, and an inability to access vital medical records, directly endangering lives. Similarly, an attack on a financial institution could disrupt trading, halt transactions, and undermine confidence in the broader financial system. The interconnected nature of modern economies means that the operational disruption experienced by one organization can have cascading effects on its partners, suppliers, and even the wider public.

Legal and regulatory liabilities represent another significant consequence of cybersecurity incidents. Depending on the nature of the data compromised and the jurisdictions in which the organization operates, breaches can trigger a host of legal obligations and penalties. Regulations such as the General Data Protection Regulation (GDPR) in Europe, the California Consumer Privacy Act (CCPA) in the United States, and numerous others worldwide impose strict requirements for data protection and breach notification. Failure to comply can result in substantial fines, costly lawsuits, and intense regulatory scrutiny. For example, a breach involving the personal data of European citizens could expose an organization to fines of up to 4% of its annual global turnover under GDPR, a figure that could be devastating for many businesses.

The loss of intellectual property and competitive advantage is also a critical concern. For many organizations, their intellectual property—patents, trade secrets, proprietary algorithms, and strategic plans—is their most valuable asset. A sophisticated attacker, particularly a state-sponsored actor or a competitor, might target an organization specifically to steal this information. Such a theft can not only result in immediate financial losses due to lost market opportunities but can also severely undermine an organization's long-term viability and competitive standing. The economic espionage carried out by some nation-states, aiming to gain an advantage in key industries, highlights the strategic importance of protecting intellectual property in the digital age.

Furthermore, the impact of cybersecurity incidents extends to the loss of public trust and confidence. This is particularly relevant for government agencies, public utilities, and organizations that provide essential services. When a government agency suffers a breach, it can erode citizens' trust in their ability to protect sensitive information and maintain essential services. This can lead to public outcry, political pressure, and a general decline in faith in institutions. Similarly, for organizations that rely heavily on consumer trust, such as social media platforms or e-commerce sites, a significant security failure can lead to a mass exodus of users, making recovery extremely difficult. The trust of individuals is a hard-won asset that can be lost in an instant through a single, significant cybersecurity lapse.

The scale of an organization, whether it's a small startup or a multinational corporation, significantly influences the nature and severity of these impacts. A small business might be completely obliterated by a ransomware attack that cripples its operations and depletes its limited financial reserves. A large enterprise, while potentially better equipped to absorb some financial losses, might face immense reputational damage and regulatory penalties due to the sheer volume of data compromised. The interconnectedness of modern business ecosystems also means that an incident affecting one entity can have ripple effects throughout its supply chain, impacting partners and customers alike. For example, a breach in a critical software supplier could compromise the security of dozens or even hundreds of downstream businesses.

Considering the diverse range of potential cybersecurity incidents and their multifaceted, often devastating, impacts, the imperative for a well-defined and robust incident response strategy becomes unequivocally clear. This strategy is not merely a technical safeguard; it is a fundamental business necessity. It serves as the blueprint for how an organization will detect, contain, eradicate, and recover from the inevitable security events that will occur. Without such a strategy, organizations are left to react in a chaotic and piecemeal fashion during a crisis, exacerbating the damage and increasing the likelihood of long-term harm. A proactive, structured approach to incident response is therefore essential for any organization seeking to build resilience, protect its assets, and maintain the confidence of its stakeholders in the face of an ever-evolving threat landscape. The ability to effectively manage and mitigate these incidents is a critical determinant of an organization's survival and success in the digital age. It transforms a potential catastrophe into a manageable challenge, allowing for swift recovery and continued operation.

The landscape of cybersecurity threats has evolved dramatically, far outpacing the capabilities of many traditional incident response (IR) models. These established approaches, often developed in an era of less sophisticated and pervasive threats, are increasingly showing their limitations. While they may have served adequately in the past, the sheer volume, velocity, and sophistication of today's cyberattacks expose significant gaps in their effectiveness. A critical examination of these conventional methodologies reveals several common pitfalls that, if left unaddressed, can lead to prolonged breaches, increased damage, and greater long-term repercussions for an organization.

One of the most persistent and debilitating issues with many traditional IR frameworks is the breakdown in communication. In the heat of a security incident, clear, timely, and accurate communication is paramount. However, outdated models often lack defined communication channels or protocols. This can result in information silos, where different teams or individuals possess critical pieces of intelligence but fail to share them effectively. For instance, the technical team might be aware of the extent of a network compromise, while the legal team is unaware of the type of data potentially affected, leading to incorrect legal advice or delayed notification procedures. Conversely, management might receive incomplete or sensationalized information, leading to rash decisions that exacerbate the situation. The absence of a centralized, real-time communication hub or a lack of pre-defined communication trees can turn a potentially contained incident into a widespread crisis as misinformation spreads and collaborative efforts are hindered. This lack of synchronized communication can also manifest in a reactive rather than proactive approach, with teams scrambling to understand the situation as it unfolds, rather than having a structured flow of information enabling informed, strategic decision-making. The consequences are often significant: missed critical windows for containment, wasted resources on redundant efforts, and an overall increase in the duration and impact of the incident.

Compounding the communication challenges is the frequent lack of clearly defined roles and responsibilities. Traditional IR models often assume a level of organizational maturity and clarity that simply doesn't exist in many environments. When an incident strikes, a common outcome is confusion over who is in charge, who is responsible for specific actions, and who has the authority to make crucial decisions. This ambiguity can lead to paralysis, where no one takes ownership of critical tasks, or to conflicting actions, where different individuals or teams pursue independent, and sometimes contradictory, strategies. For example, in a traditional setup, it might be unclear whether the IT security team or the IT operations team is primarily responsible for isolating compromised systems, or if the legal department or the public relations team should lead external communications. This "handoff" problem, or worse, the complete absence of a defined handoff, can create significant delays. During a fast-moving attack, such as a ransomware campaign that encrypts systems rapidly, every minute of indecision translates into more data being lost or corrupted, more systems becoming inaccessible, and a greater financial and operational toll. Without a pre-assigned incident commander and clearly delineated responsibilities for areas like forensics, containment, eradication, and recovery, organizations often find themselves in a state of reactive chaos, with valuable time and resources frittered away on internal debates and a lack of coordinated action. This can also lead to burnout among individuals who end up shouldering responsibilities beyond their defined roles, without proper support or recognition, while critical tasks fall through the cracks.

Another significant limitation of conventional IR approaches is their inherent inconsistency. Many organizations have not formalized their incident response processes, leading to ad-hoc, reactive measures that vary wildly from one incident to another. What might have worked for a minor virus outbreak in the past might be entirely inadequate for a sophisticated targeted attack involving advanced persistent threats (APTs). This lack of standardization means that lessons learned from previous incidents are often not institutionalized, and each new event is essentially treated as a novel problem, requiring a fresh, and often suboptimal, approach. For instance, an organization might have a checklist for responding to a phishing email, but no defined procedure for handling a distributed denial-of-service (DDoS) attack or a data exfiltration event. This inconsistency extends to the tools and techniques used, the documentation maintained, and the post-incident analysis conducted. Without a standardized play-book or a well-documented procedural framework, responders are more prone to making mistakes, overlooking critical steps, or employing inefficient methods. The absence of consistent procedures also makes it difficult to train new personnel effectively or to conduct realistic simulations and exercises, further perpetuating the cycle of ad-hoc responses. This inconsistency can be particularly detrimental when dealing with regulatory compliance, as inconsistent handling of incidents can lead to non-compliance and significant penalties.

The inability to scale responses effectively to match the magnitude of an incident is a further, and often critical, failing of traditional IR models. These models are frequently designed with a "one-size-fits-all" mentality, which is wholly inappropriate for the diverse range of cyber threats an organization faces. A minor malware infection might be handled by a small IT team, but a sophisticated nation-state attack or a widespread ransomware outbreak could require the mobilization of hundreds of personnel, specialized external consultants, legal experts, and crisis communication professionals. Traditional frameworks often lack the mechanisms to rapidly scale up resources, personnel, and communication channels to meet such demands. When an incident exceeds the predefined scope or complexity, these models tend to buckle under the pressure. This can lead to overwhelmed teams, insufficient resources allocated to critical tasks, and a prolonged period of disruption. For example, an organization that has only prepared for localized phishing attacks might find itself completely unprepared for a zero-day exploit that compromises a critical enterprise system. The response would likely be slow, disjointed, and ultimately ineffective, as the existing resources and procedures are simply not equipped to handle the scale and sophistication of the threat. This lack of scalability can turn a manageable incident into a catastrophic event, as the organization's response capabilities are outstripped by the incident's scope and impact. The reliance on pre-existing, often limited, internal resources without a clear plan for augmenting them during a crisis is a recipe for disaster in today's interconnected and complex threat environment.

Furthermore, many traditional IR models suffer from a reactive rather than proactive stance. They are often designed to address incidents *after* they have occurred, focusing on detection and recovery rather than on continuous threat hunting, vulnerability management, and proactive defense. This "firefighting" mentality means that organizations are constantly playing catch-up, responding to threats that have already bypassed their defenses. The underlying assumption in these models is that incidents are exceptional events, rather than an inevitable part of operating in a digital landscape. This approach overlooks the significant gains that can be achieved through proactive measures, such as regular security assessments, penetration testing, and the continuous monitoring of network traffic for anomalous behavior. Without a proactive element, organizations are essentially waiting for the next breach to happen, rather than actively working to prevent it or to minimize its potential impact. This can also lead to a lack of investment in preventative technologies and practices, as the focus remains on the cost of response rather than the cost of prevention. The evolving nature of threats means that a purely reactive strategy is destined to fail, as attackers are constantly developing new techniques that will inevitably circumvent static defenses.

The complexity of modern IT environments also presents a significant challenge for traditional IR models. Organizations today operate with a vast array of technologies, including cloud services, mobile devices, IoT endpoints, and complex interconnected systems. Many older IR frameworks were developed in simpler times, when IT infrastructures were more monolithic and easier to manage. These frameworks often lack the granularity to effectively map, understand, and respond to incidents across such distributed and heterogeneous environments. For instance, a traditional model might struggle to identify the source of an attack that spans on-premises servers, multiple cloud platforms, and a fleet of remote employee laptops. The lack of a comprehensive asset inventory, coupled with poor visibility across different technology stacks, can render the incident response team effectively blind. Without the ability to gain a holistic view of the IT landscape, containment and eradication efforts become significantly more difficult, and the risk of overlooking critical components of the breach increases substantially. The challenge is amplified by the dynamic nature of cloud environments, where resources can be provisioned and de-provisioned rapidly, making it difficult for static IR plans to remain relevant and effective.

Another significant deficiency lies in the insufficient focus on post-incident analysis and continuous improvement. While some traditional models may include a phase for reviewing what happened, this is often superficial or performed inconsistently. The true value of incident response lies not just in mitigating the immediate damage, but in learning from the experience to strengthen defenses and improve future responses. Without a rigorous post-incident review process, organizations risk repeating the same mistakes. This review should go beyond identifying the technical cause of the incident; it should critically assess the effectiveness of the response itself, including communication, decision-making, and the application of procedures. It should also identify systemic weaknesses and recommend concrete improvements to policies, technologies, and training. Many traditional models, however, are so focused on "getting back to business" that the crucial learning phase is rushed or skipped altogether. This leads to a stagnant security posture, where the organization remains vulnerable to the same types of attacks in the future. The absence of a feedback loop for continuous improvement means that the incident response capability never truly matures, leaving it perpetually a step behind the evolving threat landscape.

Finally, a pervasive issue is the lack of integration between incident response and other critical business functions, such as legal, compliance, risk management, and public relations. Traditional IR models often operate in isolation within the IT or security department. This siloed approach can lead to significant problems during an incident. For example, the IR team might take actions that inadvertently violate regulatory requirements or create legal liabilities, simply because they were not aware of these constraints. Conversely, legal or PR teams might issue statements or make decisions that hinder the technical investigation or containment efforts. Effective incident response requires a coordinated effort involving multiple stakeholders across the organization. When these functions are not integrated into the IR planning and execution process, the organization's ability to manage the incident comprehensively—addressing technical, legal, reputational, and business continuity aspects simultaneously—is severely compromised. This lack of cross-functional collaboration results in a fragmented response, where different parts of the organization are working at cross-purposes, rather than in a unified effort to protect the organization's assets and interests. The consequence is a significantly higher risk of cascading failures, increased damage, and a more protracted recovery period.

The fundamental challenge in navigating the increasingly complex and volatile landscape of cybersecurity incidents lies in establishing a structured, adaptable, and scalable framework for response. While traditional incident response methodologies have historically focused on technical remediation, they often fall short when confronted with the sheer magnitude, interconnectedness, and dynamic nature of modern cyber threats. The limitations highlighted in the previous discussion – communication breakdowns, undefined roles, inconsistency, lack of scalability, reactivity, IT complexity, and poor cross-functional integration – all point to an urgent need for a more robust and universally applicable system. It is within this critical context that the Incident Command System (ICS) emerges not merely as a useful tool, but as a foundational philosophy for effective crisis management, adaptable to the unique demands of cybersecurity.

The Incident Command System, often abbreviated as ICS, is a standardized, on-scene, all-hazard incident management concept. Its origins are not rooted in the digital realm, but rather in the demanding and often chaotic environments of large-scale emergency management, particularly wildfire suppression. The genesis of ICS can be traced back to the late 1960s in California, following a series of devastating wildfires that exposed significant coordination and communication failures among various responding agencies. Firefighters, law enforcement, emergency medical services, and governmental bodies, each with their own protocols and jargon, struggled to work together effectively. This lack of a unified command structure led to duplicated efforts, conflicting directives, delayed responses, and ultimately, an inability to manage the crises efficiently, resulting in greater loss of life and property. Recognizing these critical shortcomings, a collaborative effort involving federal, state, and local fire and emergency management agencies led to the development of a system designed to overcome these inherent organizational and communication barriers. The initial goal was to create a system that could be implemented consistently across different jurisdictions and agencies, ensuring that all responders understood their roles, reported to a single point of command, and communicated in a standardized manner, regardless of their specific agency affiliation.

At its core, ICS is built upon a set of key principles and features that enable its remarkable adaptability and scalability. These principles are not abstract concepts; they are practical, operational imperatives designed to bring order to chaos. Firstly,

Common Terminology is paramount. ICS mandates the use of common organizational functions, titles, and resource descriptions to ensure clear communication. Instead of referring to a "tech lead," an "IT manager," or a "network administrator" with potentially different understandings of their roles, ICS uses standardized terms like "Incident Commander," "Operations Section Chief," or "Logistics Section Chief." This linguistic uniformity eliminates ambiguity and allows personnel from diverse backgrounds and organizations to understand each other instantaneously, a critical advantage in high-pressure situations.

Secondly, **Modular Organization** is a cornerstone. ICS is designed to be flexible, allowing the organizational structure to expand or contract based on the size and complexity of the incident. It employs a top-down structure that grows in a modular fashion. Common functions are established as needed, and the span of control is managed effectively. This means that for a small incident, only a few key roles might be activated, while for a major catastrophe, the full hierarchical structure can be deployed. This modularity ensures that resources are used efficiently and that the command structure remains manageable, regardless of scale.

Thirdly, **Integrated Communications** is a non-negotiable component. ICS emphasizes the development and implementation of a communications plan that integrates all incident-related communications, including voice and data. This involves establishing clear communication channels, protocols, and frequencies, ensuring that information flows smoothly and reliably between all levels and elements of the incident management organization. This prevents the information silos that plague many conventional response efforts. Fourthly, **Unified Command** or **Incident Command** is the guiding principle for authority. In Unified Command, representatives from multiple agencies with jurisdictional or functional responsibility come together to form a single management team. This ensures that all agencies with a role in the incident have a voice and that decisions are made collaboratively, preventing conflicting directives and optimizing resource allocation. In situations where only one agency has lead responsibility, a single Incident Commander is designated. This clear locus of authority ensures decisive leadership.

Fifthly, **Actionable Plans** are developed. ICS requires the development of a written Incident Action Plan (IAP) for each operational period, typically 12 or 24 hours. The IAP details objectives, strategies, tactics, and resource assignments for the upcoming period, ensuring that all responders are working towards the same goals and understand their specific roles and responsibilities in achieving them. This proactive planning contrasts sharply with reactive, ad-hoc responses.

Sixthly, **Manageable Span of Control** is maintained. Typically, a span of control ranging from three to seven subordinates reporting to a single supervisor is considered optimal to ensure effective supervision and communication. ICS structures are designed to maintain this manageable span. Seventhly, **Designated Incident Facilities** are established. These include the Incident Command Post (ICP), Staging Areas, Bases, Camps, and Helibases, all of which serve specific logistical and operational support functions and are clearly identified and organized.

The adaptability of ICS is best illustrated by its successful deployment beyond its initial wildfire applications. Over time, the system proved its mettle in a wide array of emergency situations. For instance, during major natural disasters like hurricanes, earthquakes, and floods, ICS has been instrumental in coordinating the efforts of federal, state, local, and non-governmental organizations. Think of the aftermath of a major hurricane; response efforts involve FEMA, the National Guard, state emergency management agencies, local police and fire departments, the Red Cross, and countless other volunteer groups. Without a system like ICS to provide a common operating picture, standardized roles, and a unified command structure, the response would descend into chaos. Each entity, with its own operational protocols and communication systems, would struggle to coordinate effectively, leading to immense inefficiency and potentially life-threatening delays in delivering aid and restoring essential services. The ability of ICS to integrate these diverse elements into a cohesive response mechanism is its defining characteristic.

Consider the Great California Wildfires, a series of devastating fires that burned across California in 2018. These were not isolated incidents but complex, multi-jurisdictional events requiring the coordinated efforts of hundreds of fire departments, law enforcement agencies, and utility companies. The scale of these fires necessitated the activation of ICS at multiple levels, from local fire engines to national disaster response coordination centers. The system allowed for the rapid deployment and management of thousands of personnel and hundreds of pieces of equipment across vast geographical areas. The structure facilitated communication between incident commanders on the ground and strategic leaders in command centers, ensuring that resources were allocated effectively to contain the fires and protect communities. Without the standardized procedures and clear lines of authority provided by ICS, the coordination of such a massive and complex response would have been nearly impossible, leading to greater destruction and loss.

Another compelling example is the response to the Deepwater Horizon oil spill in the Gulf of Mexico in 2010. This environmental disaster presented a unique set of challenges, involving multiple federal agencies (including the Coast Guard, EPA, NOAA), state governments, and the responsible private entity. The sheer scale of the spill, its widespread environmental impact, and the complex legal and regulatory frameworks involved demanded an extraordinary level of interagency coordination. ICS provided the essential framework for the Unified Command established to manage the response. It enabled the Coast Guard, as the lead federal agency, to integrate efforts with other federal departments, state authorities, and BP (the responsible party) to coordinate containment, cleanup, and assessment operations. The system facilitated the communication of crucial information regarding environmental impact, resource availability, and operational progress, allowing for strategic decision-making in a rapidly evolving and highly scrutinized situation. The ability to establish clear roles, responsibilities, and communication pathways amidst such a complex, multi-stakeholder environment was a testament to the adaptability of the ICS framework, proving its effectiveness not only in immediate life-saving scenarios but also in prolonged, technically complex environmental crises.

These historical applications, deeply rooted in the physical world of disaster and emergency response, underscore the fundamental strengths of ICS: its ability to impose order on chaos, facilitate clear communication among disparate groups, define roles and responsibilities, and scale resources dynamically to meet the demands of an incident. These are precisely the attributes that are critically needed in the realm of cybersecurity, where incidents can evolve with alarming speed and affect interconnected systems across an organization and beyond. The principles of common terminology, modular organization, integrated communications, unified command, and actionable planning are not merely theoretical constructs; they are proven mechanisms for effective management under pressure. The transition from physical disasters to digital crises is not as great a leap as it might initially appear, as the core challenges of coordination, communication, and command remain remarkably similar. The proven effectiveness of ICS in large-scale, multi-agency, and complex scenarios provides a strong foundation for its adoption and adaptation within the cybersecurity domain, offering a pathway to overcome many of the deficiencies inherent in traditional, often ad-hoc, cyber incident response approaches. The robustness and tested nature of ICS in high-stakes, real-world scenarios make it an ideal candidate to bring structure and command to the often-unpredictable world of cyber threats. Its foundational principles, honed through decades of practical application in emergency management, offer a logical and effective model for building resilient and responsive cybersecurity incident handling capabilities.

The core rationale for adapting the Incident Command System (ICS) to the domain of cybersecurity hinges on a fundamental alignment between the challenges inherent in cyber incidents and the strengths of the ICS framework. While ICS was forged in the crucible of physical disaster response, the chaotic, interconnected, and rapidly evolving nature of modern cyberattacks presents analogous, and in some ways amplified, demands for structured management. Traditional cybersecurity incident response, often characterized by its technical focus and siloed operational teams, frequently struggles with the very issues that ICS is designed to address: fragmented communication, undefined leadership, inconsistent execution, and an inability to scale effectively under pressure. The adoption of ICS offers a proven, albeit adapted, methodology to inject order, clarity, and efficiency into these often-overwhelmed cyber response efforts, ensuring that organizational objectives and stakeholder trust are preserved amidst digital crises.

Cyber incidents rarely manifest as isolated technical events; they are complex occurrences that ripple through an organization's entire operational fabric, impacting business continuity, reputation, and financial stability. The very attributes that make ICS successful in large-scale emergencies—its modularity, common terminology, and integrated communications—are precisely what cyber incident response teams need to navigate the complexities of the digital battlefield. The inherent chaos of a significant cyberattack, whether it's a ransomware outbreak paralyzing critical systems, a data breach exposing sensitive customer information, or a sophisticated persistent threat compromising intellectual property, mirrors the disarray of a natural disaster. In such scenarios, IT security teams, legal departments, public relations, executive leadership, and potentially external forensic investigators and law enforcement must collaborate seamlessly. Without a unifying framework like ICS, the response can quickly devolve into a reactive scramble, with teams operating in parallel yet disconnected efforts, wasting valuable time and resources, and potentially exacerbating the damage.

The structured hierarchy of ICS provides a critical advantage in establishing clear lines of authority and accountability, which are often blurred in cybersecurity response. In a typical cyber incident, multiple individuals or teams might possess technical expertise relevant to the attack, but determining who is ultimately in charge of the overall response, who makes critical decisions, and who communicates with stakeholders can be a significant bottleneck. ICS mandates a singular Incident Commander or a Unified Command structure comprising representatives from all relevant entities. This centralized or collaborative leadership ensures that decisions are made decisively and strategically, rather than through a fragmented and time-consuming consensus-building process. For instance, during a widespread ransomware attack that encrypts vital servers, the Incident Commander, supported by Section Chiefs for Operations (responsible for containment and eradication), Logistics (securing resources like backup systems and external expertise), and Planning (developing the incident action plan), can direct the collective effort. This contrasts sharply with a scenario where the network security team, the server administration team, and the backup and recovery team operate independently, potentially issuing conflicting instructions or duplicating efforts, thereby prolonging the downtime and increasing the financial impact.

Furthermore, the principle of "Common Terminology" within ICS is profoundly relevant to cybersecurity. The IT and cybersecurity fields are replete with jargon and acronyms that can be opaque to individuals outside of technical specializations. An Incident Commander accustomed to terms like "SIEM," "IOC," "EDR," or "zero-day exploit" might struggle to effectively communicate with legal counsel concerned about regulatory compliance or with executives focused on public perception and business continuity. ICS standardizes roles and functions, allowing a "Security Operations Center (SOC) Lead" to be clearly understood within the "Operations Section," and their reports to the "Incident Commander" to be unambiguous. This shared lexicon facilitates efficient communication across organizational boundaries and between different functional areas, a critical factor when the integrity of an organization's operations, not just its digital assets, is at stake. Imagine a data exfiltration incident; the technical team might describe the "exfiltration vector," while the legal team needs to understand the "scope of data compromised" for breach notification purposes, and the communications team needs to formulate a "public statement." ICS provides the common ground for these diverse perspectives to be integrated into a cohesive response strategy.

The "Modular Organization" principle of ICS is exceptionally well-suited to the dynamic nature of cyber incidents. Cyberattacks can start small and escalate rapidly, or they can be part of a larger, coordinated campaign involving multiple attack vectors. ICS allows the response structure to expand or contract as needed. A minor phishing incident might only require the activation of a few basic ICS roles, perhaps a single Incident Commander and a representative from IT support. However, a sophisticated nation-state-level cyberattack targeting critical infrastructure would necessitate the full deployment of ICS, with multiple sections, branches, and task forces established to manage the complexity. This scalability ensures that resources are not over-allocated for minor incidents, nor are they insufficient for major ones. The ability to scale up the command structure and delegate responsibilities effectively is paramount when dealing with attacks that can evolve within minutes or hours, potentially compromising entire networks before a traditional, static organizational structure can even react. For example, a "zero-day" exploit targeting a widely used software application could quickly morph from a localized alert to a global crisis, requiring rapid expansion of the incident response team and its command structure to manage the cascading effects across an enterprise.

"Integrated Communications," a cornerstone of ICS, directly addresses the notorious communication silos that plague many cybersecurity incident responses. In the heat of a cyber crisis, information often gets trapped within specific teams—the network security team might have critical telemetry, the endpoint security team might have logs indicating compromise, and the forensics team might be uncovering the attacker's TTPs (Tactics, Techniques, and Procedures). Without a plan for integrating this information, response efforts can be inefficient, leading to missed opportunities for early detection or containment. ICS mandates a comprehensive communications plan, ensuring that information flows seamlessly between different functional areas and levels of the organization. This includes establishing clear protocols for reporting, information sharing, and decision-making. For instance, when responding to a Distributed Denial-of-Service (DDoS) attack, effective communication between the network operations center (NOC) monitoring traffic, the security operations center (SOC) analyzing attack patterns, and the Internet Service Provider (ISP) or Content Delivery Network (CDN) provider is crucial for mitigation. ICS provides the structure to ensure these communications are not only happening but are integrated into a unified strategic effort.

The development of an "Incident Action Plan" (IAP) under ICS is a proactive measure that can significantly enhance cybersecurity incident response. Instead of a reactive, ad-hoc approach, the IAP provides a clear, time-bound roadmap for the response. It outlines objectives, strategies, and specific actions for a defined operational period, typically 12 or 24 hours. This ensures that all team members are working towards common goals with a clear understanding of their roles and responsibilities. For a data breach investigation, the IAP might detail objectives such as identifying the source of the breach, determining the scope of compromised data, implementing containment measures, and preparing for regulatory reporting. This structured planning contrasts with a scenario where teams might be working on different aspects of the incident without a unified plan, leading to confusion and inefficiencies. The IAP also serves as a vital tool for documenting the response, providing a clear audit trail for post-incident analysis and lessons learned, which is crucial for improving future preparedness.

The principle of "Manageable Span of Control" in ICS is also highly relevant to cybersecurity teams, which can often become overwhelmed with too many direct reports or too many disparate tasks. By ensuring that no individual is responsible for more than a manageable number of subordinates or functions, ICS prevents the burnout and cognitive overload that can impair decision-making during high-stress incidents. This is particularly important in cybersecurity, where the technical complexity and the constant influx of alerts and data can be overwhelming. A well-defined span of control ensures that supervisors can effectively oversee their teams, provide guidance, and make informed decisions without being bogged down by an unmanageable workload. This leads to more focused and effective execution of response tasks.

Finally, the adaptability of ICS, proven across a multitude of physical disaster scenarios, strongly suggests its potential for the cybersecurity domain. Just as ICS evolved from wildfire response to manage hurricanes, earthquakes, and terrorist attacks, it can be similarly adapted to the nuances of cyber threats. The underlying principles of command, control, communication, and coordination are universal to crisis management. The core challenges in responding to a massive data breach are not fundamentally different in terms of organizational management from responding to a major industrial accident: both require clear leadership, coordinated efforts from diverse expertise, effective communication, and strategic allocation of resources under immense pressure. By leveraging the established, tested, and scalable framework of ICS, organizations can move beyond the limitations of fragmented and reactive cyber incident response, building a more resilient, efficient, and ultimately more effective defense against the ever-evolving landscape of cyber threats. The investment in adapting ICS is an investment in the organization's ability to withstand and recover from digital crises, safeguarding its assets, reputation, and operational integrity.

The Incident Command System (ICS) is not a rigid, prescriptive set of rules but rather a flexible framework built upon a foundation of universally applicable principles. These core tenets are the very essence of why ICS proves so effective in managing complex, chaotic events, and their adaptation to cybersecurity necessitates a clear understanding of their individual contributions to the overall system. At its heart, ICS is designed to ensure that response efforts are organized, coordinated, and effective, regardless of the size or nature of the incident, or the number of agencies involved. The power of ICS lies in its ability to impose order and structure on inherently disordered situations, fostering clarity in leadership, communication, and operational execution.

One of the most foundational and critical principles of ICS is **Common Terminology**. In any large-scale or multi-agency response, the potential for miscommunication due to differing jargon, acronyms, or organizational-specific language is immense. This principle mandates the use of standardized names for organizational functions, resources, and incident facilities. For example, instead of one agency calling a critical data repository a "server farm" and another referring to it as a "compute cluster," ICS establishes a standardized term like "Resource Unit" or a more specific descriptor within the context of the incident. In cybersecurity, this translates to the adoption of agreed-upon terms for threats, vulnerabilities, tools, and response actions. For instance, rather than relying on a cacophony of internal security tool names or highly technical, often proprietary, nomenclature, ICS encourages the use of terms like "malware," "phishing attempt," "unauthorized access," or "data exfiltration." This shared vocabulary ensures that everyone involved, from the frontline analyst to the executive leadership, understands what is being communicated. When the Incident Commander states, "We need to isolate the affected systems to prevent further propagation," all members of the response team, regardless of their specific technical background or department affiliation, grasp the immediate objective. This eliminates the need for constant translation and clarification, saving precious time during a rapidly unfolding cyber event. This principle also extends to the naming of individuals in command and general staff positions. Designations such as "Incident Commander," "Operations Section Chief," "Planning Section Chief," "Logistics Section Chief," and "Finance/Administration Section Chief" are universally understood within the ICS framework. This clarity removes ambiguity about roles and responsibilities, preventing situations where individuals might hesitate to take action due to uncertainty about their authority or the authority of others. The adoption of common terminology is not merely about using the same words; it is about ensuring a shared understanding of concepts, objectives, and roles, thereby creating a unified operational picture. This is especially vital in cybersecurity where the technical intricacies can often create an information asymmetry that hinders effective decision-making for non-technical stakeholders. By providing a common lexicon, ICS bridges these gaps, enabling more informed and collaborative responses.

The principle of **Modular Organization** is ICS's answer to scalability and adaptability. This principle dictates that the ICS organizational structure should be formed from the top down, based on the incident's complexity and needs. Instead of having a fixed, hierarchical structure, ICS allows for the creation of functional sections—Operations, Planning, Logistics, and Finance/Administration—and the staffing of these sections as required. For smaller incidents, the Incident Commander might directly manage a few key personnel. As the incident escalates, specific sections are activated, and branches, divisions, groups, and units are established within those sections to manage specific tasks or geographic areas. In a cybersecurity context, this means that a minor phishing incident might only necessitate the activation of a basic Incident Command and a few IT security personnel working in an "Operations" capacity. However, a nation-state-sponsored attack targeting critical infrastructure would require the full deployment of all ICS sections, with multiple branches and groups dedicated to analyzing the attack vector, containing lateral movement, restoring systems, and managing public relations. The modularity ensures that the response organization can grow or shrink organically to match the demands of the incident. It prevents the system from becoming overly cumbersome for minor events and ensures that it can adequately encompass the complexity of major crises. This flexibility is paramount in cybersecurity, where an initial alert can rapidly escalate into a full-blown crisis impacting multiple systems, business units, and potentially external partners. The ability to scale the response organization efficiently, without the need to re-engineer the entire structure, is a significant advantage. For instance, if a ransomware attack begins to spread across a network, the Operations Section Chief can quickly establish a "Containment Group" and an "Eradication Group," each with its own manager and assigned personnel, all reporting up through the established ICS structure. This allows for specialized efforts to be managed effectively without overwhelming a single point of command. The modular approach ensures that the response is always appropriately resourced and structured for the task at hand, fostering efficiency and reducing the likelihood of critical functions being overlooked due to a lack of organizational capacity.

Management by Objectives is the guiding principle that ensures all actions taken during an incident are aligned with the overall goals of the response. ICS requires that objectives be clearly defined, measurable, achievable, relevant, and time-bound (SMART). These objectives are then documented in the Incident Action Plan (IAP). In cybersecurity, this means that instead of simply reacting to alerts, the response team focuses on achieving specific outcomes. For example, a cybersecurity incident might have objectives such as: "Contain the spread of the malware to all critical servers within 4 hours," "Identify the initial point of compromise within 12 hours," or "Restore affected user accounts to full operational status by the end of the business day." This principle shifts the focus from tactical firefighting to strategic resolution. It provides direction and purpose to the efforts of the response team, ensuring that resources are utilized effectively and that progress can be tracked. Without clear objectives, response efforts can become fragmented and inefficient, with teams working at cross-purposes or addressing symptoms rather than root causes. The "Manageability" aspect of these objectives is crucial; they must be realistic given the available resources and the nature of the threat. For a data breach, objectives might be geared towards forensic investigation, legal notification requirements, and public communication, ensuring that the response addresses all facets of the crisis. By defining and pursuing specific objectives, ICS helps to maintain focus and accountability, ensuring that the response is not only active but also purposeful and effective in mitigating the incident and returning the organization to normal operations.

Directly linked to Management by Objectives is the **Incident Action Plan (IAP)**. The IAP is the formal document that outlines the objectives, strategies, tactics, and resource assignments for a specific operational period, typically 12 or 24 hours. It is the roadmap for the response, providing a clear and concise plan of action for everyone involved. In cybersecurity, the IAP serves as a critical communication and coordination tool. It ensures that all team members understand the current situation, the goals for the next operational period, and their specific roles in achieving those goals. A well-developed IAP might include sections on: Situation Summary (current status of the incident), Objectives (what needs to be accomplished), Strategies and Tactics (how objectives will be met), Organizational Structure (who is responsible for what), Resource Assignments (personnel, equipment, and information needed), Communications Plan (how information will be shared), and Safety and Health Information. For a sophisticated phishing campaign targeting an organization, the IAP might detail objectives like: "Block all malicious email domains and IP addresses within 1 hour," "Remediate all compromised user accounts and endpoints within 6 hours," and "Communicate incident status to executive leadership every 4 hours." The IAP is a dynamic document, reviewed and updated at the beginning of each operational period to reflect the progress made, any changes in the incident's nature, and new objectives. This iterative planning process ensures that the response remains agile and responsive to the evolving threat landscape. The IAP also serves as a vital tool for documentation, providing a clear record of the response efforts, which is invaluable for post-incident analysis, lessons learned, and potentially for legal or regulatory purposes. Without a formal IAP, response efforts can become chaotic and uncoordinated, leading to missed opportunities, duplicated efforts, and a general lack of direction. The IAP transforms a potentially ad-hoc reaction into a structured, strategic, and accountable response.

The principle of **Manageable Span of Control** is fundamental to ensuring that supervisors can effectively manage their teams and that responders do not become overwhelmed. ICS generally dictates that a supervisor should not have more than five subordinates reporting directly to them. This limit is not absolute but serves as a guideline to ensure effective supervision, communication, and management. In the high-pressure environment of a cybersecurity incident, where information overload and stress are common, maintaining a manageable span of control is crucial for optimal performance. When a supervisor has too many direct reports or is responsible for too many disparate tasks, their ability to provide clear direction, monitor progress, and make timely decisions is compromised. This can lead to errors, missed critical details, and burnout among team members. In a cybersecurity response, a "unit" might be a group of analysts investigating a particular type of malware, a "division" might oversee all endpoint remediation efforts, and a "section" might manage all operational aspects of the incident. By adhering to a manageable span of control, ICS ensures that each level of the organization is appropriately staffed and that supervisors are empowered to effectively lead their teams. This principle also supports the efficient flow of information up and down the command chain. With fewer direct reports, supervisors can more effectively gather and synthesize information from their teams before passing it up to higher levels, and they can more clearly communicate directives down to their subordinates. This prevents information bottlenecks and ensures that critical updates and decisions are disseminated promptly and accurately. The application of this principle in cybersecurity means that the Incident Commander is not inundated with individual status reports from dozens of analysts but receives consolidated updates from Section Chiefs, who in turn receive updates from their direct reports. This structured approach to management is essential for maintaining clarity and effectiveness in what can often be a highly complex and demanding operational environment.

Finally, the principle of **Unity of Command** ensures that each individual reports to only one supervisor at a time. This prevents conflicting orders and confusion, which can be detrimental to an effective response. While "Unified Command" allows multiple agencies or disciplines to share command responsibilities, Unity of Command ensures that within a specific reporting structure, an individual has a single point of accountability. In cybersecurity, this means that an analyst working on malware analysis reports to their team lead, who reports to the Operations Section Chief, who reports to the Incident Commander. This clear reporting chain eliminates ambiguity about who to follow and who is responsible for assigning tasks. It fosters discipline and ensures that orders are received and executed without question or confusion, a critical element when swift and coordinated action is required. When applied consistently, these core principles of ICS create a robust and adaptable framework that can be effectively applied to the unique challenges of cybersecurity incident response, providing a standardized and systematic approach to managing even the most complex digital crises.

The effectiveness of any incident response framework hinges on its ability to foster clear, unambiguous communication and facilitate coordinated action, especially when multiple entities are involved. In the realm of cybersecurity, where threats can emerge from anywhere and impact a wide array of systems and stakeholders, this need for clarity and coordination is amplified. This section delves into two foundational pillars of the Incident Command System (ICS) that are particularly critical for successful cybersecurity incident management: Common Terminology and Unified Command.

Common Terminology: Building a Shared Lexicon for Cyber Response

The principle of **Common Terminology** within ICS is a cornerstone for ensuring that all participants in an incident response effort, regardless of their organizational affiliation, functional role, or technical expertise, share a mutual understanding of critical information. In the fast-paced, high-stakes environment of a cybersecurity incident, where seconds can make the difference between containment and catastrophic data loss or system compromise, the absence of a shared vocabulary can lead to devastating delays, misunderstandings, and misallocated resources. This principle mandates the use of standardized names for organizational functions, resources, incident facilities, and key personnel. It's not merely about adopting a few buzzwords; it's about establishing a robust, universally understood language that transcends the specific jargon, acronyms, and internal nomenclature that often plague complex organizations and interagency operations.

Consider a scenario where a sophisticated distributed denial-of-service (DDoS) attack is overwhelming an organization's public-facing web servers. Without common terminology, one team might refer to the affected infrastructure as the "front-end farm," another as the "web tier," and a third as the "customer access layer." The Incident Commander, needing to direct resources to bolster defenses, might issue an order to "reinforce the perimeter." This seemingly straightforward instruction could lead to confusion: which perimeter? The network perimeter? The application perimeter? Or perhaps the perimeter of the specific server cluster under attack? Each interpretation might lead responders to focus on different aspects of the problem, potentially neglecting the most critical areas and allowing the attack to persist or escalate.

ICS, by adhering to common terminology, dictates that such resources would be consistently identified. For instance, the affected infrastructure might be designated as the "Internet-facing Web Servers" or a more specific identifier within the ICS organizational structure, such as a "Resource Unit" within the Operations Section. The command to reinforce defenses would then be precise: "Increase bandwidth allocation and deploy additional mitigation appliances to the Internet-facing Web Servers." This clarity ensures that all teams understand precisely which assets are under threat and where efforts need to be concentrated. This principle extends to the naming of key ICS positions. Titles such as Incident Commander, Operations Section Chief, Planning Section Chief, Logistics Section Chief, and Finance/Administration Section Chief are universally recognized and understood within the ICS framework. This eliminates any ambiguity regarding roles, responsibilities, and lines of authority, preventing situations where individuals might hesitate to act due to uncertainty about their designated authority or the authority of others.

In the context of cybersecurity, common terminology is particularly vital because of the inherent complexity and specialized nature of the field. Technical terms, vendor-specific product names, and the rapid evolution of threat actors and their techniques can create significant barriers to understanding for those outside of the immediate technical response teams, including executive leadership, legal counsel, public relations, and even other departments within the same organization. For example, the difference between "command and control (C2) traffic," "lateral movement," and "data exfiltration" might be starkly clear to a seasoned security analyst, but a company executive might conflate these terms or fail to grasp the immediate severity and implications of each. ICS promotes the use of standardized descriptors for threats, vulnerabilities, and response actions that are understandable across different levels of technical proficiency. This might involve using terms like "malware intrusion," "unauthorized access," "phishing campaign," "credential stuffing," or "system compromise." When the Incident Commander states, "We are experiencing an unauthorized data exfiltration event impacting the customer database," all stakeholders, from the IT security team to the Chief Legal Officer, grasp the critical nature of the event and the immediate need to prevent further data loss.

Furthermore, common terminology applies to the classification of incident severity and impact. Instead of ad-hoc descriptions like "big problem" or "major outage," ICS encourages a standardized rating system, perhaps based on factors such as the criticality of affected systems, the volume of data compromised, the duration of the disruption, and the potential legal or reputational ramifications. This allows for consistent reporting and prioritization of response efforts. When a common set of terms is used to describe the incident's status, impact, and required actions, it creates a unified operational picture. This picture is essential for making informed decisions, allocating resources effectively, and maintaining stakeholder confidence. The adoption of common terminology is not a mere stylistic choice; it is a functional imperative that underpins the entire ICS structure, ensuring that every individual involved speaks the same operational language, thereby minimizing confusion, maximizing efficiency, and fostering a cohesive and effective response to cyber incidents.

Unified Command: Orchestrating Multi-Jurisdictional Cyber Responses

The principle of **Unified Command** addresses one of the most persistent challenges in managing complex incidents: the involvement of multiple agencies, organizations, or jurisdictions, each with its own mandates, authorities, and operational procedures. In traditional incident management, especially in physical disasters, this often means law enforcement, fire departments, emergency medical services, and public works collaborating. In the cybersecurity domain, the landscape of involved parties can be even more diffuse and complex. A significant cyberattack might involve the organization's internal IT security team, specialized incident response firms, law enforcement agencies (such as the FBI or its international equivalents), national cybersecurity agencies (like CISA in the US), regulatory bodies, and potentially even vendors of security software or cloud service providers. Each of these entities may have distinct legal authorities, reporting requirements, and operational objectives.

Unified Command provides a structure to manage these diverse interests and capabilities effectively. It is a system where key stakeholders with jurisdictional or functional responsibility for an incident come together to establish a common set of objectives and strategies, and to develop and execute a single Incident Action Plan (IAP). Instead of each entity operating in a silo, or competing for control, Unified Command allows for a single, integrated command structure to be established. This is achieved by having representatives from each key agency or organization jointly manage the incident. They collectively define incident objectives, determine strategies, assign responsibilities, and approve resource requests. The Incident Commander's role might be filled by a single individual from the lead agency, or the command function itself can be shared among representatives of the primary organizations involved, forming a Unified Command group.

The benefits of Unified Command are profound, particularly in cybersecurity. Firstly, it ensures **interoperability** and **coordination**. Without Unified Command, a situation could arise where the organization's internal security team is focused on eradicating malware, while a law enforcement agency is focused on preserving digital evidence for prosecution, and a regulatory body is focused on ensuring compliance with data breach notification laws. These objectives, while not necessarily conflicting, could be pursued in ways that hinder each other. For example, aggressive eradication by the internal team might inadvertently destroy crucial forensic evidence that law enforcement needs. Unified Command brings all these stakeholders to the table to agree on priorities and sequencing, ensuring that all objectives are addressed in a coordinated manner that maximizes overall effectiveness.

Secondly, Unified Command provides **clarity of authority and responsibility**. When multiple agencies are involved, there can be significant ambiguity about who has the ultimate decision-making authority, who is responsible for which tasks, and who has the legal standing to compel certain actions. Unified Command resolves this by clearly defining roles and responsibilities within the joint command structure. Representatives of each agency work together, leveraging their respective expertise and authorities, to manage the incident. This avoids duplication of effort, prevents conflicting directives, and ensures that all necessary functions are covered.

Thirdly, Unified Command facilitates **resource sharing and efficient allocation**. In a large-scale cyber incident, resources – whether they be highly specialized forensic analysts, sophisticated threat intelligence platforms, or legal experts in data privacy – are often finite. Unified Command allows for a holistic view of available resources across all involved entities. This enables the command group to allocate these resources to where they are most needed, rather than each agency hoarding its own resources or competing for external support. For instance, if a national cybersecurity agency has access to advanced tools for analyzing command-and-control infrastructure that the affected organization does not possess, Unified Command ensures that these tools can be brought to bear on the incident in a coordinated fashion.

Consider a scenario involving a ransomware attack that has encrypted critical data across multiple networked systems, potentially impacting sensitive personal information or operational technology (OT) systems in an industrial control environment. The affected organization's IT department will want to restore data and systems. The legal department will be concerned with data breach notification requirements. Law enforcement may need to investigate the perpetrators. If the affected data includes personal health information (PHI) or financial data, regulatory bodies like the HHS (for HIPAA) or SEC might become involved, each with its own investigation and reporting mandates.

Without Unified Command, the organization might be dealing with separate requests from each of these entities, potentially leading to conflicting demands on IT resources, delays in communication, and an incomplete or disjointed response. With Unified Command, representatives from the organization's incident response team, the relevant law enforcement agencies, and applicable regulatory bodies would form the Unified Command group. They would collectively agree on objectives, such as: 1. Contain the ransomware spread. 2. Eradicate the malware. 3. Restore affected systems and data. 4. Preserve forensic evidence. 5. Comply with all legal and regulatory notification requirements. 6. Investigate the source and attribution of the attack. The IAP would then detail how these objectives will be met, who is responsible for each task, and how resources will be shared. For example, the IT team might lead eradication and restoration, while a specialized forensic unit from law enforcement handles evidence preservation, and the legal department coordinates with regulatory bodies on notification timelines.

The establishment of Unified Command is particularly crucial when a cyber incident transcends organizational boundaries. This can occur in several ways:

Supply Chain Attacks: Where a compromise in a third-party vendor's systems impacts multiple downstream clients. The vendor, its clients, and potentially cybersecurity agencies may all need to collaborate.

Critical Infrastructure Attacks: Where an attack on a sector like energy, finance, or healthcare can have cascading effects across multiple organizations and potentially national security implications. Agencies responsible for sector-specific security and national security will be heavily involved.

Cross-Border Incidents: Where an attack originates in one country but targets systems or data in another, requiring coordination between national law enforcement and cybersecurity agencies of multiple nations.

Complex Data Breaches: Where the compromised data belongs to multiple entities or individuals, triggering responsibilities and investigations from various data protection authorities.

In such scenarios, Unified Command provides the framework to bring these disparate parties together under a common leadership structure. It ensures that the response is not fragmented but rather a cohesive effort driven by shared goals and a coordinated strategy. The success of Unified Command relies on mutual respect, a willingness to share information and resources, and a shared commitment to resolving the incident. It transforms what could be a chaotic, multi-agency quagmire into a focused, integrated, and effective response. This collaborative approach is indispensable for tackling the increasingly complex and interconnected nature of modern cyber threats. The common terminology principle ensures everyone speaks the same language, while Unified Command ensures everyone is working towards the same goals, under a singular, albeit jointly managed, operational banner. Together, these ICS principles provide a robust foundation for managing cybersecurity incidents that extend beyond the boundaries of a single organization or jurisdiction.

The effectiveness of any incident response framework hinges on its ability to foster clear, unambiguous communication and facilitate coordinated action, especially when multiple entities are involved. In the realm of cybersecurity, where threats can emerge from anywhere and impact a wide array of systems and stakeholders, this need for clarity and coordination is amplified. This section delves into two foundational pillars of the Incident Command System (ICS) that are particularly critical for successful cybersecurity incident management: Common Terminology and Unified Command.

Common Terminology: Building a Shared Lexicon for Cyber Response

The principle of **Common Terminology** within ICS is a cornerstone for ensuring that all participants in an incident response effort, regardless of their organizational affiliation, functional role, or technical expertise, share a mutual understanding of critical information. In the fast-paced, high-stakes environment of a cybersecurity incident, where seconds can make the difference between containment and catastrophic data loss or system compromise, the absence of a shared vocabulary can lead to devastating delays, misunderstandings, and misallocated resources. This principle mandates the use of standardized names for organizational functions, resources, incident facilities, and key personnel. It's not merely about adopting a few buzzwords; it's about establishing a robust, universally understood language that transcends the specific jargon, acronyms, and internal nomenclature that often plague complex organizations and interagency operations.

Consider a scenario where a sophisticated distributed denial-of-service (DDoS) attack is overwhelming an organization's public-facing web servers. Without common terminology, one team might refer to the affected infrastructure as the "front-end farm," another as the "web tier," and a third as the "customer access layer." The Incident Commander, needing to direct resources to bolster defenses, might issue an order to "reinforce the perimeter." This seemingly straightforward instruction could lead to confusion: which perimeter? The network perimeter? The application perimeter? Or perhaps the perimeter of the specific server cluster under attack? Each interpretation might lead responders to focus on different aspects of the problem, potentially neglecting the most critical areas and allowing the attack to persist or escalate.

ICS, by adhering to common terminology, dictates that such resources would be consistently identified. For instance, the affected infrastructure might be designated as the "Internet-facing Web Servers" or a more specific identifier within the ICS organizational structure, such as a "Resource Unit" within the Operations Section. The command to reinforce defenses would then be precise: "Increase bandwidth allocation and deploy additional mitigation appliances to the Internet-facing Web Servers." This clarity ensures that all teams understand precisely which assets are under threat and where efforts need to be concentrated. This principle extends to the naming of key ICS positions. Titles such as Incident Commander, Operations Section Chief, Planning Section Chief, Logistics Section Chief, and Finance/Administration Section Chief are universally recognized and understood within the ICS framework. This eliminates any ambiguity regarding roles, responsibilities, and lines of authority, preventing situations where individuals might hesitate to act due to uncertainty about their designated authority or the authority of others.

In the context of cybersecurity, common terminology is particularly vital because of the inherent complexity and specialized nature of the field. Technical terms, vendor-specific product names, and the rapid evolution of threat actors and their techniques can create significant barriers to understanding for those outside of the immediate technical response teams, including executive leadership, legal counsel, public relations, and even other departments within the same organization. For example, the difference between "command and control (C2) traffic," "lateral movement," and "data exfiltration" might be starkly clear to a seasoned security analyst, but a company executive might conflate these terms or fail to grasp the immediate severity and implications of each. ICS promotes the use of standardized descriptors for threats, vulnerabilities, and response actions that are understandable across different levels of technical proficiency. This might involve using terms like "malware intrusion," "unauthorized access," "phishing campaign," "credential stuffing," or "system compromise." When the Incident Commander states, "We are experiencing an unauthorized data exfiltration event impacting the customer database," all stakeholders, from the IT security team to the Chief Legal Officer, grasp the critical nature of the event and the immediate need to prevent further data loss.

Furthermore, common terminology applies to the classification of incident severity and impact. Instead of ad-hoc descriptions like "big problem" or "major outage," ICS encourages a standardized rating system, perhaps based on factors such as the criticality of affected systems, the volume of data compromised, the duration of the disruption, and the potential legal or reputational ramifications. This allows for consistent reporting and prioritization of response efforts. When a common set of terms is used to describe the incident's status, impact, and required actions, it creates a unified operational picture. This picture is essential for making informed decisions, allocating resources effectively, and maintaining stakeholder confidence. The adoption of common terminology is not a mere stylistic choice; it is a functional imperative that underpins the entire ICS structure, ensuring that every individual involved speaks the same operational language, thereby minimizing confusion, maximizing efficiency, and fostering a cohesive and effective response to cyber incidents.

Unified Command: Orchestrating Multi-Jurisdictional Cyber Responses

The principle of **Unified Command** addresses one of the most persistent challenges in managing complex incidents: the involvement of multiple agencies, organizations, or jurisdictions, each with its own mandates, authorities, and operational procedures. In traditional incident management, especially in physical disasters, this often means law enforcement, fire departments, emergency medical services, and public works collaborating. In the cybersecurity domain, the landscape of involved parties can be even more diffuse and complex. A significant cyberattack might involve the organization's internal IT security team, specialized incident response firms, law enforcement agencies (such as the FBI or its international equivalents), national cybersecurity agencies (like CISA in the US), regulatory bodies, and potentially even vendors of security software or cloud service providers. Each of these entities may have distinct legal authorities, reporting requirements, and operational objectives.

Unified Command provides a structure to manage these diverse interests and capabilities effectively. It is a system where key stakeholders with jurisdictional or functional responsibility for an incident come together to establish a common set of objectives and strategies, and to develop and execute a single Incident Action Plan (IAP). Instead of each entity operating in a silo, or competing for control, Unified Command allows for a single, integrated command structure to be established. This is achieved by having representatives from each key agency or organization jointly manage the incident. They collectively define incident objectives, determine strategies, assign responsibilities, and approve resource requests. The Incident Commander's role might be filled by a single individual from the lead agency, or the command function itself can be shared among representatives of the primary organizations involved, forming a Unified Command group.

The benefits of Unified Command are profound, particularly in cybersecurity. Firstly, it ensures **interoperability** and **coordination**. Without Unified Command, a situation could arise where the organization's internal security team is focused on eradicating malware, while a law enforcement agency is focused on preserving digital evidence for prosecution, and a regulatory body is focused on ensuring compliance with data breach notification laws. These objectives, while not necessarily conflicting, could be pursued in ways that hinder each other. For example, aggressive eradication by the internal team might inadvertently destroy crucial forensic evidence that law enforcement needs. Unified Command brings all these stakeholders to the table to agree on priorities and sequencing, ensuring that all objectives are addressed in a coordinated manner that maximizes overall effectiveness.

Secondly, Unified Command provides **clarity of authority and responsibility**. When multiple agencies are involved, there can be significant ambiguity about who has the ultimate decision-making authority, who is responsible for which tasks, and who has the legal standing to compel certain actions. Unified Command resolves this by clearly defining roles and responsibilities within the joint command structure. Representatives of each agency work together, leveraging their respective expertise and authorities, to manage the incident. This avoids duplication of effort, prevents conflicting directives, and ensures that all necessary functions are covered.

Thirdly, Unified Command facilitates **resource sharing and efficient allocation**. In a large-scale cyber incident, resources – whether they be highly specialized forensic analysts, sophisticated threat intelligence platforms, or legal experts in data privacy – are often finite. Unified Command allows for a holistic view of available resources across all involved entities. This enables the command group to allocate these resources to where they are most needed, rather than each agency hoarding its own resources or competing for external support. For instance, if a national cybersecurity agency has access to advanced tools for analyzing command-and-control infrastructure that the affected organization does not possess, Unified Command ensures that these tools can be brought to bear on the incident in a coordinated fashion.

Consider a scenario involving a ransomware attack that has encrypted critical data across multiple networked systems, potentially impacting sensitive personal information or operational technology (OT) systems in an industrial control environment. The affected organization's IT department will want to restore data and systems. The legal department will be concerned with data breach notification requirements.

Law enforcement may need to investigate the perpetrators. If the affected data includes personal health information (PHI) or financial data, regulatory bodies like the HHS (for HIPAA) or SEC might become involved, each with its own investigation and reporting mandates.

Without Unified Command, the organization might be dealing with separate requests from each of these entities, potentially leading to conflicting demands on IT resources, delays in communication, and an incomplete or disjointed response. With Unified Command, representatives from the organization's incident response team, the relevant law enforcement agencies, and applicable regulatory bodies would form the Unified Command group. They would collectively agree on objectives, such as: 1. Contain the ransomware spread. 2. Eradicate the malware. 3. Restore affected systems and data. 4. Preserve forensic evidence. 5. Comply with all legal and regulatory notification requirements. 6. Investigate the source and attribution of the attack. The IAP would then detail how these objectives will be met, who is responsible for each task, and how resources will be shared. For example, the IT team might lead eradication and restoration, while a specialized forensic unit from law enforcement handles evidence preservation, and the legal department coordinates with regulatory bodies on notification timelines.

The establishment of Unified Command is particularly crucial when a cyber incident transcends organizational boundaries. This can occur in several ways:

Supply Chain Attacks: Where a compromise in a third-party vendor's systems impacts multiple downstream clients. The vendor, its clients, and potentially cybersecurity agencies may all need to collaborate.

Critical Infrastructure Attacks: Where an attack on a sector like energy, finance, or healthcare can have cascading effects across multiple organizations and potentially national security implications. Agencies responsible for sector-specific security and national security will be heavily involved.

Cross-Border Incidents: Where an attack originates in one country but targets systems or data in another, requiring coordination between national law enforcement and cybersecurity agencies of multiple nations.

Complex Data Breaches: Where the compromised data belongs to multiple entities or individuals, triggering responsibilities and investigations from various data protection authorities.

In such scenarios, Unified Command provides the framework to bring these disparate parties together under a common leadership structure. It ensures that the response is not fragmented but rather a cohesive effort driven by shared goals and a coordinated strategy. The success of Unified Command relies on mutual respect, a willingness to share information and resources, and a shared commitment to resolving the incident. It transforms what could be a chaotic, multi-agency quagmire into a focused, integrated, and effective response. This collaborative approach is indispensable for tackling the increasingly complex and interconnected nature of modern cyber threats.

The common terminology principle ensures everyone speaks the same language, while Unified Command ensures everyone is working towards the same goals, under a singular, albeit jointly managed, operational banner. Together, these ICS principles provide a robust foundation for managing cybersecurity incidents that extend beyond the boundaries of a single organization or jurisdiction.

Modular Organization and Scalability of the Incident Command System

The Incident Command System (ICS) is fundamentally designed with a modular approach, allowing its organizational structure to be established and expanded in direct proportion to the needs of a specific incident. This inherent flexibility ensures that the framework is equally effective whether dealing with a minor security alert that requires minimal intervention or a full-blown national cyber crisis that stretches resources to their absolute limits. The principle is simple yet profoundly powerful: you build the organization you need, when you need it, and dismantle it or scale it down just as efficiently when the incident subsides. This adaptability is a cornerstone of effective incident management, particularly in the dynamic and often unpredictable landscape of cybersecurity.

The modular nature of ICS means that the organizational structure can grow organically, either from the top down or by rolling up from the bottom up. In a top-down approach, the Incident Commander, upon being appointed, establishes the core command structure, typically including the Section Chiefs for Operations, Planning, Logistics, and

Finance/Administration, as these are often the foundational roles required for any significant event. As the incident unfolds and its scope becomes clearer, these sections can then be further subdivided into branches, divisions, groups, and units, each with specific responsibilities and reporting lines. For example, a large-scale data breach might necessitate the Operations Section Chief to establish a "Digital Forensics Branch" to handle evidence collection and analysis, an "Eradication Branch" to remove malware and secure compromised systems, and a "Recovery Branch" to restore services and data. Each of these branches would then be further populated with specialized groups or units, such as a "Malware Analysis Unit" within the Eradication Branch or a "Database Restoration Group" within the Recovery Branch.

Conversely, the ICS structure can also be built from the bottom up. This often occurs when a localized security event is detected by a specific team or individual. For instance, an intrusion detection system might flag unusual network activity in a particular server segment. The initial response might be from a small IT security team. As the scope and severity of the alert are investigated, if it escalates, the incident can be "rolled up" into the ICS structure. The individual or team identifying the issue might form the initial "Unit" or "Group," which then reports to a "Division" or "Branch" chief within the Operations Section. This reporting chain continues upward until it reaches the Incident Commander, who then formalizes the structure and assigns resources as needed. This bottom-up approach ensures that even the smallest alerts are managed systematically and can be rapidly scaled if the situation warrants it.

The scalability of ICS is what truly distinguishes it as a robust incident management system. Scalability in this context refers to the ability of the framework to adapt its size and complexity to match the magnitude of the incident. For a minor security incident, such as a single employee falling victim to a phishing attempt that results in a compromised account, the ICS structure might consist of just the Incident Commander and perhaps a single Incident Action Officer or a small team within the Operations Section. The response would be swift, focused, and involve a limited number of personnel and resources. The Incident Commander might be the CISO or a senior security manager, the Operations Section might simply be the core incident response team, and the Planning Section might only involve a single individual documenting the event.

As the incident grows in complexity and impact, so too does the ICS organization. A widespread malware outbreak across a significant portion of an organization's network would necessitate a more elaborate structure. The Operations Section might need to be divided into multiple branches or divisions, perhaps one for network infrastructure, another for endpoints, and a third for critical applications. The Planning Section would become more robust, with distinct teams dedicated to documenting all actions, tracking resources, assessing damage, and developing future action plans. The Logistics Section would be crucial for acquiring and distributing necessary hardware, software, and specialized personnel, while the Finance/Administration Section would manage costs, track personnel time, and handle any contractual obligations with third-party vendors.

Consider the impact of a nation-state sponsored cyberattack targeting critical infrastructure. Such an event would demand the full realization of ICS scalability. The Incident Commander might be a high-ranking government official or a designated leader from a national cybersecurity agency. The ICS organization would likely encompass multiple levels of branches, divisions, groups, and units, potentially involving hundreds or even thousands of personnel from various government agencies, private sector entities, and international partners. The Planning Section would be a complex entity, meticulously forecasting the cascading effects of the attack, coordinating intelligence gathering from numerous sources, and developing multi-phase recovery strategies. The Logistics Section would be tasked with procuring and deploying highly specialized resources, potentially including advanced cyber-defense tools, secure communication networks, and personnel with unique skill sets. The Finance/Administration Section would manage an enormous budget, track costs associated with mitigation, recovery, and potential legal liabilities, and ensure compliance with numerous governmental and international regulations.

The scalability of ICS is not merely about adding more people; it's about adding the *right* people in the *right* organizational structure to manage the incident effectively. The modular design ensures that reporting relationships remain clear and manageable, even as the organization expands. Each module – whether it's a section, branch, division, group, or unit – has clearly defined responsibilities and interfaces with other modules. This hierarchical yet adaptable structure prevents the organization from becoming unwieldy or chaotic, even under immense pressure.

In cybersecurity, the ability to scale rapidly is paramount. A threat that initially appears contained can, through sophisticated techniques like lateral movement or exploitation of zero-day vulnerabilities, spread with alarming speed and impact. An ICS framework that can seamlessly expand its organizational components – adding more incident responders, forensic analysts, communication specialists, legal counsel, and public relations experts as needed – provides the agility required to keep pace with the evolving threat. This means that an organization can have a pre-defined, yet flexible, plan for how its incident response structure will grow. For instance, a company might have a tiered response plan where specific triggers or thresholds of an incident (e.g., number of affected systems, type of data compromised, duration of outage) automatically initiate the activation of additional ICS roles and organizational branches.

The scalability also extends to the Incident Action Plan (IAP). As the ICS organization grows to meet the demands of a larger incident, the IAP becomes more detailed and comprehensive. For minor incidents, a simple one-page plan might suffice. For major crises, the IAP can evolve into a multi-document package, detailing objectives, strategies, tactical assignments, resource allocation, and communication protocols for all activated organizational elements. The Planning Section is responsible for developing and disseminating these plans, ensuring that everyone involved has a clear understanding of the current situation and their assigned tasks.

Furthermore, the scalability of ICS allows for the effective management of multiple, concurrent incidents. If an organization is facing several distinct security events simultaneously, ICS principles can be applied to establish separate command structures for each incident, or a single, overarching command structure can be established with multiple Incident Commanders or a Unified Command overseeing all events. The modularity ensures that resources can be strategically allocated across these different incidents based on their respective priorities and severity.

The concept of scalability also touches upon the temporal aspect of incident response. As an incident progresses from initial detection and containment through eradication and recovery, the needs of the incident response team change. In the early stages, the focus might be on rapid containment and information gathering, requiring a more operational and analytical structure. As recovery efforts commence, the emphasis shifts towards restoration, testing, and validation, necessitating a greater role for the Logistics and Planning Sections in coordinating these activities. The ability of ICS to adapt its organizational focus and scale up or down specific functional areas in response to these shifting needs is a critical component of its overall effectiveness.

In essence, the modular organization and scalability of ICS provide a robust and adaptable framework for cybersecurity incident management. It ensures that the response can be tailored precisely to the incident's scope and severity, preventing over- or under-resourcing. This principle allows organizations to manage a spectrum of cyber threats, from minor security breaches to catastrophic cyberattacks, with a consistent and proven methodology. The ability to "grow" or "shrink" the incident response organization on demand, while maintaining clear lines of authority, communication, and accountability, is a powerful asset in the ongoing battle against cyber adversaries. It provides a structured approach to chaos, ensuring that even in the most challenging circumstances, a coordinated and effective response can be mounted.

The cornerstone of an effective cybersecurity incident response lies in establishing clear, actionable objectives and meticulously documenting them within a formalized Incident Action Plan (IAP). This plan serves not merely as a record, but as a dynamic, living document that guides the entire response effort, ensuring coherence, accountability, and a shared understanding of goals among all involved parties. For any incident, whether it's a localized malware infection or a sophisticated nation-state attack, the process begins with defining what success looks like. These objectives must be SMART: Specific, Measurable, Achievable, Relevant, and Time-bound. Without this foundational step, response efforts can become disjointed, inefficient, and ultimately, ineffective.

In the context of cybersecurity, the establishment of objectives within an IAP typically revolves around the core phases of incident response: containment, eradication, and recovery. For containment, objectives might include specific targets for isolating compromised systems, blocking malicious network traffic, or preventing further unauthorized access to sensitive data. For example, an objective could be: "Contain the spread of the WannaCry ransomware to all critical servers within the financial services division within four hours of incident declaration." This is specific, measurable (through network monitoring and system status checks), achievable with dedicated resources, relevant to preventing financial loss and operational disruption, and time-bound. Similarly, eradication objectives might focus on the complete removal of malware, the disabling of malicious command-and-control infrastructure, or the remediation of exploited vulnerabilities. A measurable objective here could be: "Achieve 100% eradication of the Conficker worm from all active endpoints on the corporate network by the end of business day tomorrow, verified by endpoint detection and response (EDR) scans."

Recovery objectives are equally critical and often the longest phase of incident response. These objectives are geared towards restoring affected systems and services to their pre-incident state, or an acceptable operational baseline, while ensuring that the threat has been neutralized and vulnerabilities addressed. Examples include: "Restore critical customer-facing applications to full operational capacity within 48 hours, ensuring data integrity through validated backups," or "Re-image and redeploy 95% of compromised workstations with the latest security patches by the end of the week." These objectives are designed to bring the organization back to a state of normalcy, minimizing the business impact of the incident.

The Incident Action Plan is the primary vehicle for communicating these objectives, along with the strategies and tactics to achieve them. It acts as a force multiplier, ensuring that all responders, regardless of their specific roles or teams, are working towards the same overarching goals. The IAP typically includes several key components:

Incident Objectives: These are the overarching goals for the incident, derived from the SMART principles discussed earlier. They provide the strategic direction for the entire response effort.

Strategies and Tactics: Strategies are the broad approaches to achieving the objectives, while tactics are the specific actions taken to implement those strategies. For instance, a strategy for containment might be network segmentation, with tactics including the configuration of firewall rules, the disabling of specific network ports, and the rerouting of network traffic. For eradication, a strategy could be system sanitization, implemented through tactics such as forensic imaging, malware removal tools, and secure wiping procedures.

Organizational Structure: The IAP will often reiterate the established ICS organizational structure for the incident, including the key personnel assigned to command and general staff positions, and any expanded organizational elements like branches, divisions, or groups. This reinforces lines of authority and communication.

Resource Assignments: A critical component of the IAP is the listing of required resources, including personnel, equipment, supplies, and facilities. This section details who is responsible for what, and what resources they have been allocated or need to request. For instance, it might specify that the "Digital Forensics Unit" has been assigned two senior forensic analysts and is authorized to deploy specialized imaging hardware.

Communication Plan: The IAP will often outline the communication protocols, including who reports to whom, how often status updates will be provided, and the designated channels for internal and external communication. This ensures a consistent flow of information and prevents communication breakdowns.

Safety Plan: While often a separate document, the IAP may reference specific safety considerations relevant to the incident response, particularly if there are physical risks involved in accessing compromised areas or handling potentially hazardous materials or equipment.

For cybersecurity incidents, the IAP is especially vital due to the often-invisible nature of the threat and the rapid pace at which it can evolve. A well-structured IAP provides a tangible framework for managing an inherently fluid and complex situation. It moves the response from a reactive scramble to a proactive, planned operation.

Consider a scenario where an organization detects a sophisticated phishing campaign that has successfully compromised a significant number of user credentials, leading to unauthorized access to sensitive customer data. The initial response might involve a flurry of activity from the IT security team. However, without a formalized IAP, their efforts could be fragmented. Some might focus on blocking sender domains, others on resetting passwords, and yet others on investigating the extent of the breach. This is where the IAP becomes indispensable.

The Incident Commander, or the Unified Command group, would convene to define the core objectives. These might include:

1. **Containment:** Prevent further unauthorized access to customer databases and other sensitive systems within 12 hours.

2. **Eradication:** Remove all traces of the phishing malware and associated malicious tools from affected systems within 24 hours.

3. **Recovery:** Restore compromised user accounts and implement enhanced security measures for access to sensitive data within 72 hours.

4. **Forensics:** Preserve all relevant logs and artifacts to support investigation and attribution within 48 hours.

5. **Notification:** Comply with all legal and regulatory data breach notification requirements within specified timelines.

Once these objectives are established, the IAP would detail the strategies and tactics to achieve them. For containment, strategies might include immediate password resets for all potentially compromised accounts, network isolation of identified infected systems, and enhanced monitoring of critical data repositories. Tactics would involve IT administrators systematically working through the list of affected users, deploying endpoint detection and response (EDR) tools to identify and isolate machines, and configuring firewall rules to restrict access to sensitive network segments.

The IAP would then assign specific responsibilities. The Operations Section Chief might be tasked with overseeing the containment and eradication efforts, assigning teams to conduct password resets and system isolations. The Planning Section Chief would be responsible for tracking the progress against the defined objectives, documenting all actions taken, and updating the IAP as necessary. The Logistics Section Chief would ensure that the necessary tools – such as remote administration software, forensic imaging kits, and additional security software licenses – are available. The Finance/Administration Section Chief would track any overtime incurred by staff or costs associated with engaging external incident response firms.

Crucially, the IAP provides a mechanism for reporting and accountability. Regular status updates, as outlined in the communication plan within the IAP, ensure that leadership and other stakeholders are kept informed of the incident's progress, any emerging challenges, and the effectiveness of the response efforts. This transparency is vital for maintaining confidence and facilitating informed decision-making. If, for example, the password reset process is proving slower than anticipated due to unforeseen technical issues, the IAP mechanism allows this to be flagged early, prompting a reassessment of tactics or resource allocation.

The dynamic nature of cybersecurity threats means that the IAP is not a static document. As the incident evolves, new information emerges, or the situation changes, the IAP must be updated to reflect these developments. This might involve revising objectives, adapting strategies, reassigning resources, or adding new tactical steps. The Planning Section, through its role in documenting and analyzing the incident, is typically responsible for managing these updates, ensuring that any changes are communicated effectively to all relevant parties. This iterative process of planning, executing, and re-planning is fundamental to successful incident management.

For instance, during the eradication phase of the phishing incident, investigators might discover that the attackers used a zero-day exploit to gain initial access, rather than just relying on compromised credentials. This new information would necessitate an update to the IAP. The objectives might need to be revised to include patching this zero-day vulnerability. New strategies and tactics would be developed, potentially involving collaboration with the vendor of the affected software or the deployment of specific security patches. The resource assignments would be adjusted accordingly, perhaps bringing in specialized vulnerability management teams.

Furthermore, the IAP plays a critical role in post-incident review and analysis. Once the incident is resolved, the IAP, along with all its updates and associated documentation, provides a comprehensive record of the response. This documentation is invaluable for conducting a thorough after-action review, identifying lessons learned, and improving future incident response capabilities. It allows for a systematic evaluation of what worked well, what could have been done better, and how organizational policies, procedures, and technical defenses can be enhanced to prevent similar incidents or mitigate their impact in the future.

The inclusion of specific performance metrics within the IAP's objectives further enhances its utility. By setting measurable targets, responders are provided with clear benchmarks against which to gauge their effectiveness. This not only drives performance but also facilitates objective assessment during the incident and in the post-incident review. For example, if an objective was to "isolate 90% of identified compromised systems within 12 hours," the ability to track the actual percentage achieved provides direct evidence of performance and identifies areas needing immediate attention if targets are not being met.

In complex, multi-jurisdictional cyber incidents, the IAP, developed under Unified Command, becomes an even more critical tool. It ensures that disparate organizations, each with its own priorities and reporting structures, are aligned under a common set of goals and a coordinated strategy. The IAP effectively translates the collective will of the Unified Command group into actionable steps that can be executed by the various entities involved. Without this document, a response involving multiple agencies could devolve into a series of uncoordinated, and potentially conflicting, actions, severely undermining the overall effectiveness of the response.

The process of developing an IAP is an exercise in collaborative problem-solving and strategic thinking. It requires input from various functional areas, including technical experts, legal counsel, communications specialists, and leadership. This cross-functional collaboration, facilitated by the structured framework of ICS and the IAP, helps to ensure that all potential implications of the incident and the response are considered, from technical feasibility and resource availability to legal compliance and public perception.

Ultimately, the Incident Action Plan is more than just a bureaucratic requirement; it is the operational blueprint for navigating the chaos of a cybersecurity incident. By defining clear objectives, outlining strategies and tactics, assigning responsibilities, and establishing communication protocols, the IAP transforms a potentially overwhelming situation into a manageable and coordinated response. It ensures that every action taken is purposeful, aligned with overarching goals, and contributes to the ultimate objective of mitigating damage, restoring operations, and protecting the organization. The discipline of developing and adhering to an IAP instills a sense of order and direction that is indispensable in the face of evolving and sophisticated cyber threats. It provides a clear path forward, guiding responders through the complexities of containment, eradication, and recovery with a unified purpose and a shared vision of success. This systematic approach, codified in the IAP, is a critical differentiator between a chaotic, damaging incident and a well-managed, controlled response that minimizes adverse outcomes and strengthens organizational resilience.

The effective management of any incident, particularly a complex cybersecurity event, hinges on the clear definition of reporting structures and the distribution of responsibilities. A fundamental principle guiding this structure is the **span of control**. This concept, borrowed from classical management theory and deeply embedded within the Incident Command System (ICS), dictates that each supervisor or manager should have a manageable number of subordinates or direct reports. For cybersecurity incidents, where the pace can be frantic and decisions need to be made rapidly, maintaining an appropriate span of control is paramount to preventing bottlenecks, ensuring clear communication, and avoiding overburdening key personnel. An overly wide span of control can lead to supervisors being unable to provide adequate guidance, support, or oversight to their teams, resulting in errors, delays, and a decrease in overall response effectiveness. Conversely, an excessively narrow span of control can lead to an unwieldy hierarchy, with too many layers of management, increasing the time it takes for decisions to be made and communicated. In the context of a cyber incident, this might translate to ensuring that a lead forensic analyst is not directly supervising more than five or six junior analysts, or that a section chief is not responsible for coordinating more than seven or eight distinct teams or functional units. This principle ensures that supervisory efforts are focused, that information flows efficiently up and down the chain of command, and that individuals receiving direction have a clear point of contact for guidance and support. When a cyber incident escalates, requiring the mobilization of numerous individuals and teams, the adherence to the span of control principle becomes even more critical. It allows for the scaling of the response effort without sacrificing the clarity and efficiency of command and coordination. For example, if a major data breach is underway, the Incident Commander might delegate oversight of specific technical mitigation efforts to a single Operations Section Chief. This Chief, in turn, would ensure that any subordinate managers or team leads also adhere to the span of control principle when assigning tasks and managing their respective teams involved in, for instance, isolating compromised servers, blocking malicious IP addresses, or analyzing network traffic for further indicators of compromise. This tiered approach, grounded in the principle of span of control, ensures that the overall response remains coordinated and manageable, even amidst significant complexity and high stakes.

Integral to the successful application of the span of control principle and the overall organization of an incident response is the establishment of distinct **functional areas** within the ICS framework. These functional areas provide a structured approach to managing all aspects of an incident, ensuring that no critical area is overlooked and that resources are allocated effectively. For cybersecurity incidents, these five ICS functional areas offer a robust blueprint for organizing the response effort: Command, Operations, Planning, Logistics, and Finance/Administration.

The **Command** functional area is the bedrock of the entire incident response structure. It is responsible for overall management and strategic direction. The Incident Commander (IC), or the Unified Command group if multiple agencies or organizations are involved, holds ultimate authority and responsibility for the incident. In a cybersecurity context, the Incident Commander might be the CISO, a senior IT security director, or a designated lead for incident response. Their role is not to be the technical expert in every facet of the cyber attack, but rather to ensure that the response is effectively managed, objectives are being met, and resources are being utilized appropriately. The Command staff, which can include Public Information Officers, Safety Officers, and Liaison Officers, directly support the Incident Commander. For instance, a Public Information Officer would be crucial in managing external communications about a data breach to regulatory bodies, affected customers, and the media, ensuring that information released is accurate, timely, and consistent with the overall incident strategy. The Safety Officer would focus on identifying and mitigating any safety risks associated with the response, which in a cyber incident might seem less immediate than in a physical disaster, but could still involve risks related to physical security of IT infrastructure, personnel well-being under extreme stress, or even the potential for secondary attacks targeting responders. The Liaison Officer facilitates communication and coordination with external agencies or organizations that may have an interest in or responsibility for the incident.

The **Operations** functional area is where the "hands-on" work of incident response takes place. This section is responsible for implementing the tactical objectives defined in the Incident Action Plan (IAP). In a cybersecurity incident, the Operations Section would typically include teams responsible for containment, eradication, and recovery activities. This might involve network security engineers actively isolating compromised segments of the network, system administrators deploying patches to vulnerable systems, forensic investigators collecting digital evidence, and cybersecurity analysts monitoring for ongoing malicious activity. The Chief of Operations reports directly to the Incident Commander and is responsible for managing all personnel and resources assigned to direct incident mitigation. For a ransomware attack, the Operations Section would be tasked with identifying infected systems, containing the spread of the malware, eradicating the ransomware from affected systems, and overseeing the restoration of data from backups. The success of the Operations Section is directly tied to the clear articulation of tactical objectives and the availability of the necessary technical skills and tools. If the

Operations Section identifies that a particular tactic is not yielding the desired results – for example, if malware removal tools are failing to fully clean infected endpoints – they would report this to the Incident Commander and the Planning Section, triggering a reassessment of strategies and tactics. The Chief of Operations must therefore maintain a keen awareness of the operational challenges and effectively communicate these back to the Command and Planning Sections to ensure the response remains agile and effective. The size and complexity of the Operations Section will scale directly with the severity and scope of the cyber incident. In a large-scale distributed denial-of-service (DDoS) attack, the Operations Section might comprise multiple teams dedicated to traffic analysis, firewall rule management, and coordination with internet service providers.

The **Planning** functional area is responsible for gathering, evaluating, and disseminating information about the incident and the response. This section plays a critical role in developing the Incident Action Plan (IAP), which outlines the incident objectives, strategies, and tactical assignments for operational periods. The Planning Section Chief works closely with the Incident Commander and the Operations Section Chief to ensure that the IAP is realistic, achievable, and aligned with the overall incident objectives. This section is also responsible for tracking the progress of the response, documenting all actions taken, and anticipating future needs. In a cybersecurity incident, the Planning Section would analyze threat intelligence, review logs for indicators of compromise, assess the impact of the attack, and project the resource requirements for ongoing mitigation and recovery efforts. They are the keepers of situational awareness, constantly updating the incident picture for the Incident Commander and the rest of the response organization. For example, if an intrusion detection system (IDS) alerts to a new, previously unknown malware variant, the Planning Section would be tasked with gathering information on this new threat, assessing its potential impact, and recommending changes to the response strategy. This section also plays a crucial role in the post-incident review, analyzing the effectiveness of the response and identifying lessons learned. The documentation generated by the Planning Section, including the IAP itself and all subsequent updates and situation reports, serves as a vital historical record of the incident and the response. This ensures accountability, facilitates continuous improvement, and provides valuable data for future training exercises and preparedness efforts. The intelligence gathering and analytical capabilities of the Planning Section are paramount in understanding the evolving nature of cyber threats, allowing the response to remain proactive rather than purely reactive.

The **Logistics** functional area is responsible for providing all the necessary resources and support for the incident response effort. This includes personnel, equipment, supplies, facilities, and services. The Logistics Section Chief works to ensure that responders have what they need, when they need it, to effectively carry out their assigned tasks. In a cybersecurity incident, this could involve procuring specialized forensic software licenses, setting up secure communication channels, arranging for off-site backup storage facilities, or even providing catering and accommodation for round-the-clock response teams. This section is the backbone that supports the operational and planning efforts, ensuring that the technical teams are not hampered by a lack of essential tools or infrastructure. For instance, if the Operations Section requires additional high-performance workstations for malware analysis, or specialized network taps for traffic monitoring, the Logistics Section would be responsible for acquiring and deploying these resources. They also manage the maintenance and repair of equipment, the ordering and distribution of supplies, and the provision of transportation if needed for personnel or equipment. The proactive identification of resource needs by the Planning Section is crucial for the Logistics Section to function efficiently. Without adequate planning, the Logistics Section might struggle to procure critical items quickly, leading to delays in the response. The effective management of these support functions by the Logistics Section is vital to maintaining the momentum of the incident response and preventing operational effectiveness from being compromised by a lack of resources. This can also extend to managing external vendors and contractors, ensuring that they are integrated smoothly into the response effort and adhere to organizational security policies.

Finally, the **Finance/Administration** functional area is responsible for tracking all costs associated with the incident response. This includes managing personnel costs, equipment purchases, contracted services, and any other expenses incurred during the response. The Finance/Administration Section Chief ensures that all financial aspects of the incident are properly documented, accounted for, and reported. In a large-scale cyber incident, the costs can quickly escalate, involving overtime pay, procurement of new security tools, potential legal fees, and engagement of external cybersecurity firms. Accurate cost tracking is essential for budget management, resource allocation decisions, and post-incident financial review. This section also handles administrative tasks such as timekeeping, procurement procedures, and claims management. For example, if a cybersecurity firm is brought in to assist with the investigation and recovery, the Finance/Administration Section would be responsible for negotiating contracts, approving invoices, and ensuring that payments are made in a timely manner. They also play a role in ensuring compliance with financial regulations and organizational policies related to emergency expenditures. While often perceived as less critical than the technical aspects of incident response, the meticulous financial management by this section is vital for the long-term sustainability and accountability of the response effort. It provides leadership with a clear understanding of the financial impact of cyber incidents and helps inform future investments in cybersecurity defenses and incident response capabilities. The ability to accurately attribute costs to specific response activities also aids in post-incident analysis, allowing for a more comprehensive understanding of the total cost of an incident.

The interdependency of these five functional areas is a hallmark of the ICS. The Command Section sets the overall direction, the Operations Section executes the tactical actions, the Planning Section provides the strategic framework and situational awareness, the Logistics Section supplies the necessary resources, and the Finance/Administration Section manages the financial implications. Each functional area relies on the others to effectively manage a cybersecurity incident. For instance, the Operations Section cannot execute its tasks without the resources provided by Logistics, nor can it operate effectively without the strategic guidance and planning developed by the Planning Section under the direction of Command. This integrated structure ensures that all facets of a cyber incident are addressed systematically, from the initial detection and assessment to containment, eradication, recovery, and post-incident analysis. The clear delineation of roles and responsibilities within these functional areas, coupled with adherence to the span of control principle, creates a robust and adaptable framework for navigating the complexities of even the most challenging cybersecurity events. This organizational clarity is not just about efficiency; it is about ensuring that the right people are in the right roles, making the right decisions, at the right time, to effectively protect the organization.

The initial hours following the detection of a significant cybersecurity incident are often characterized by a whirlwind of activity, driven by a pressing need to understand the scope of the compromise and to initiate containment measures. Amidst this urgent environment, the establishment of a dedicated Incident Command Post (ICP) serves as a critical anchor, providing a central point for coordination, decision-making, and resource management. The ICP is more than just a location; it is the operational hub from which the entire incident response effort is directed and managed. Its successful establishment directly impacts the speed, efficiency, and overall effectiveness of the organization's ability to mitigate the incident and restore normal operations.

The nature of the ICP can vary significantly depending on the organization's size, resources, and the specific characteristics of the incident. In some cases, particularly for smaller organizations or less severe incidents, the ICP might be a designated physical location within the office – perhaps a conference room or an underutilized office space that can be rapidly provisioned. This physical ICP should ideally be equipped with robust communication infrastructure, access to relevant network diagrams, up-to-date contact lists, and a secure environment for sensitive discussions. Essential elements would include multiple redundant internet connections, reliable power sources, and sufficient workspace for the core response team. However, in today's increasingly distributed work environments and for incidents that may compromise physical office spaces or deem them unsafe, a virtual ICP has become equally, if not more, prevalent. A virtual ICP leverages secure cloud-based collaboration tools, video conferencing platforms, and dedicated incident response management software to create a functional command center accessible from various remote locations. Regardless of whether it is physical or virtual, the paramount consideration is that it provides a dedicated, secure, and functional space where the incident response team can operate with minimal distractions and maximum efficiency. The choice between a physical and virtual ICP, or a hybrid approach, must be pre-determined and tested through regular exercises to ensure seamless activation when an incident occurs. For instance, an organization might designate a primary physical ICP and a secondary virtual ICP, with protocols in place for rapidly shifting to the virtual environment if the physical location becomes compromised or inaccessible due to the nature of the attack, such as a widespread power outage affecting the corporate network or a physical threat.

Critical to the functioning of any ICP, whether physical or virtual, is the availability of robust and redundant communication tools. In a cybersecurity incident, communication channels can become targets themselves, making resilience a key design principle. This includes not only standard tools like email and instant messaging but also secure, out-of-band communication methods that are less susceptible to compromise. This might involve dedicated satellite phones, encrypted voice-over-IP (VoIP) services, or even pre-arranged communication protocols with external agencies or vendors that utilize independent networks. The ICP must be equipped with multiple, diverse communication pathways to ensure that information can flow freely between the Incident

Commander, the various functional sections, and external stakeholders, even if primary communication infrastructure is degraded or unavailable. For example, during a sophisticated distributed denial-of-service (DDoS) attack that overwhelms network bandwidth, the ability to switch to an encrypted messaging application running over a cellular network or a pre-established satellite link becomes invaluable for critical coordination. The ICP team should have access to up-to-date contact information for all essential personnel, including backup contacts, and clear protocols for how and when each communication method should be employed. Furthermore, the ICP should facilitate secure information sharing, perhaps through a dedicated, segmented network or a secure cloud portal, where sensitive logs, forensic data, and strategic documents can be accessed and updated by authorized personnel. The sheer volume of data generated during a cyber incident necessitates an ICP that can support the ingestion, analysis, and dissemination of this information effectively, often requiring dedicated displays and processing capabilities.

The initial establishment of the Incident Command System (ICS) structure within the ICP is a foundational step that dictates the flow of authority, responsibility, and information throughout the response. The most critical initial action is the formal designation of the **Incident Commander (IC)**. This individual, typically a senior leader with a deep understanding of the organization's operations, risk appetite, and decision-making authority, is ultimately responsible for the entire incident response effort. In a cybersecurity context, this could be the Chief Information Security Officer (CISO), a Director of IT Security, or a designated incident response lead. The IC's role is not necessarily to be the deepest technical expert but to provide strategic direction, ensure that objectives are being met, and manage the allocation of resources effectively. They are the ultimate decision-maker, tasked with authorizing significant actions, communicating with executive leadership and external parties, and ensuring that the response aligns with the organization's overall business continuity and resilience objectives. The selection of the IC must be pre-defined in incident response plans and exercises, ensuring that there is no ambiguity or delay in appointing this crucial role when an incident occurs. This appointment must be communicated clearly to all involved parties, establishing a single point of accountability for the response.

Working directly under the Incident Commander are the core members of the **Command Staff**. These individuals are appointed by the IC to provide specialized support and advice, and they play a vital role in extending the IC's reach and ensuring that critical functions are managed effectively. For cybersecurity incidents, the most common and crucial members of the Command Staff are the **Public Information Officer (PIO)**, the **Safety Officer (SO)**, and the **Liaison Officer (LO)**. The PIO is responsible for developing and disseminating accurate, timely, and consistent information to the public, media, employees, and other stakeholders. In a data breach scenario, for example, the PIO works closely with legal counsel and the IC to craft statements that inform affected individuals without compromising the integrity of the ongoing investigation or admitting undue liability. They manage media inquiries, social media monitoring, and ensure that all external communications are aligned with the overall incident strategy. The Safety Officer, while perhaps less immediately obvious in a cyber incident than in a physical disaster, is nonetheless critical. Their focus is on identifying and mitigating any risks to the safety and health of response personnel and the organization's assets. This could include ensuring that response teams are not overexposed to stress, that physical security of critical IT infrastructure is maintained during a crisis, or that remote workers have secure and safe environments from which to operate. They also monitor for any potential secondary physical impacts or risks arising from the cyber incident. The Liaison Officer is responsible for coordinating with external agencies, partners, and other organizations that may be involved in or affected by the incident. This could include law enforcement agencies, regulatory bodies, industry peers, or third-party vendors. Establishing clear lines of communication and collaboration with these external entities is essential for a coordinated and effective response, especially in complex incidents that span multiple jurisdictions or involve interconnected systems. The effective functioning of these staff roles ensures that the IC is not overwhelmed and that specialized aspects of the response are managed with appropriate expertise and focus.

Following the appointment of the Incident Commander and the core Command Staff, the next critical step is to establish the initial **functional sections** based on the nature of the reported incident. This involves identifying the individuals who will lead the Operations, Planning, Logistics, and Finance/Administration sections. The **Operations Section Chief** is typically appointed next, as this is where the direct tactical response to the incident will be managed. This individual will be responsible for leading the teams that will perform containment, eradication, and recovery actions. For a ransomware attack, the Operations Chief would oversee efforts to isolate infected systems, deploy endpoint detection and response (EDR) tools, and manage the process of restoring data from backups. Their focus is on executing the hands-on technical work required to mitigate the immediate threat. The **Planning Section Chief** is crucial for developing the strategic framework of the response. This individual is responsible for gathering and analyzing information about the incident, assessing its impact, and developing the Incident Action Plan (IAP) that guides the tactical efforts. In a cyber incident, the Planning Section would be analyzing threat intelligence, correlating log data, and forecasting resource needs. They maintain situational awareness and ensure that the response remains on track and adaptable to evolving threats. The **Logistics Section Chief** is responsible for ensuring that all necessary resources – personnel, equipment, supplies, and services – are available to support the response effort. This could involve procuring specialized software, setting up secure communication channels, or arranging for off-site data storage. They are the enablers, ensuring that the technical teams have what they need to perform their duties. Finally, the **Finance/Administration Section Chief** is tasked with tracking all costs associated with the incident response. This includes managing overtime, equipment purchases, and any external services procured. Accurate financial tracking is essential for budget management and post-incident review.

The initial assignment of personnel to these roles should be based on pre-defined incident response plans and the skills and experience of available personnel. For a less severe incident, the IC might initially fulfill some of these roles themselves, or one individual might temporarily cover multiple responsibilities. However, as the incident escalates in complexity or scope, it becomes essential to fill these roles with dedicated individuals to maintain an appropriate span of control and ensure that no critical area of the response is neglected. The selection of these initial leaders is a strategic decision that sets the tone for the entire response. They must be competent, decisive, and capable of working effectively under pressure. For instance, if the initial report indicates a widespread phishing campaign leading to credential compromise, the IC might immediately appoint a seasoned network security manager as the Operations Chief, a senior threat intelligence analyst as the Planning Chief, an IT procurement specialist as the Logistics Chief, and a finance department representative as the Finance/Administration Chief. Clear briefings must be provided to these newly appointed leaders, outlining the known facts of the incident, the initial objectives, and their immediate responsibilities within the ICS framework. This initial structuring within the ICP ensures that the response begins in an organized and systematic manner, laying the groundwork for effective containment, eradication, and recovery. The success of the incident response hinges on the clarity of these initial roles and responsibilities, ensuring that every member of the team understands their purpose and how they contribute to the overall mission of protecting the organization.

Establishing the ICP and its initial organizational structure is not merely a procedural step; it is a strategic imperative that underpins the entire incident response capability. It provides the framework for clear communication, effective decision-making, and efficient resource allocation. The physical or virtual nature of the ICP, the robustness of its communication systems, and the precise appointment of the Incident Commander and functional section chiefs all contribute to an organization's ability to weather the storm of a cybersecurity attack. Without this foundational structure, even the most technically proficient response teams can find themselves operating in chaos, leading to delayed containment, increased damage, and prolonged recovery periods. The selection of the right individuals for these critical roles, based on their expertise, leadership qualities, and understanding of the organization's operational landscape, is paramount. This initial setup ensures that as more information becomes available and the incident evolves, the response can scale effectively, with clear lines of authority and responsibility always maintained. It transforms a potentially chaotic situation into a managed operation, where every action is deliberate, coordinated, and aimed at achieving the overarching goal of incident resolution and organizational resilience. The ICP, therefore, is the nerve center of the response, and its proper establishment is the first, and arguably one of the most vital, steps in navigating the complex terrain of a cybersecurity incident. This initial phase sets the stage for the subsequent development of comprehensive incident action plans and the mobilization of all necessary resources. It's about creating an organized and controlled environment from which to launch a proactive and effective defense against digital threats.

The effective management of a cybersecurity incident hinges on a well-defined organizational structure, and the Incident Command System (ICS) provides a standardized framework for achieving this. Within the Incident Command Post (ICP), each key position carries specific duties and authorities, ensuring that the response is coordinated, efficient, and comprehensive. While the previous context established the foundational importance of the ICP and the initial appointment of the Incident Commander, a deeper dive into the specific roles and responsibilities of the core ICS positions is essential for a robust understanding of incident management in a cybersecurity context. This detailed examination will illuminate how each position contributes to the overall success of the incident response lifecycle, from initial detection through to recovery and post-incident review.

The **Incident Commander (IC)** stands at the apex of the ICS structure, holding ultimate authority and responsibility for the incident response. This individual is the central figure responsible for setting objectives, developing strategies, and making critical decisions that guide the entire operation. In a cybersecurity scenario, the IC's background is crucial; they are typically a senior leader, such as a Chief Information Security Officer (CISO), a VP of IT, or a similarly empowered executive, who possesses a comprehensive understanding of the organization's risk tolerance, business objectives, and operational capabilities. Their primary mandate is to ensure that the response is aligned with these broader organizational goals, rather than getting lost in the technical minutiae of the incident itself. The IC must delegate effectively, trust their appointed staff and section chiefs, and maintain a clear line of sight on the incident's impact on the business. Their responsibilities include approving the Incident Action Plan (IAP), authorizing resource allocation, serving as the primary point of contact for executive leadership, and potentially for external agencies depending on the incident's nature and regulatory requirements. For instance, during a widespread data breach affecting customer personally identifiable information (PII), the IC would be the one to authorize the engagement of external forensic investigators, approve the public notification strategy, and liaise with the legal department to ensure compliance with data protection laws like GDPR or CCPA. The IC's role is not about technical execution but about strategic leadership and ensuring the right actions are taken, by the right people, at the right time. This requires strong leadership skills, the ability to remain calm under pressure, and a profound understanding of the organization's critical assets and dependencies. They must also ensure that all response activities are conducted in a manner that minimizes further damage and supports the organization's long-term resilience. A critical aspect of the IC's responsibility is to foster an environment of trust and clear communication within the response team, ensuring that information flows freely and that decisions are made based on the best available intelligence.

Complementing the Incident Commander is the **Deputy Incident Commander**. This individual serves as the IC's principal assistant, ready to assume command of the incident if the IC becomes unavailable or incapacitated. The Deputy is often chosen for their complementary skill set or in-depth knowledge of specific areas of the organization's operations or IT infrastructure. They work closely with the IC, providing support, managing specific tasks as delegated, and acting as a sounding board for strategic decisions. In a complex, multi-faceted cyber attack, the Deputy IC might be tasked with overseeing the day-to-day operational aspects of the response, allowing the IC to focus on strategic oversight and external communications. For example, if the IC is heavily engaged in briefings with the board of directors, the Deputy IC might be responsible for ensuring that containment efforts are progressing as planned and that the Planning Section is producing updated situational reports on schedule. This role is crucial for ensuring continuity of command and maintaining momentum during an incident, particularly during extended operations where the IC may require periods of rest or be engaged in high-level external meetings. The Deputy IC also plays a vital role in facilitating communication between the IC and the various functional sections, ensuring that the IC's directives are clearly understood and implemented, and that the IC is kept abreast of the progress and challenges faced by each section. Their proactive engagement can help anticipate potential roadblocks and ensure that the response team remains agile and responsive to the evolving threat landscape.

The **Public Information Officer (PIO)** is a critical component of the Command Staff, responsible for managing all communications related to the incident intended for the public and other external stakeholders. In the digital realm, where information can spread instantaneously and often inaccurately through social media and news outlets, the PIO's role is paramount in maintaining organizational reputation, providing accurate situational awareness, and managing public perception. The PIO works under the direct supervision of the IC, but their responsibilities are specialized and require distinct expertise in communications, media relations, and crisis communication. Their primary tasks include developing, coordinating, and disseminating accurate and timely information about the incident, its impact, and the response efforts. This involves crafting press releases, preparing statements for media interviews, managing the organization's official social media channels, and ensuring that internal stakeholders (employees) are also kept informed. For a ransomware attack that has encrypted critical business systems, the PIO would be responsible for communicating with affected customers, partners, and the general public about the disruption, while carefully coordinating messaging with legal counsel to avoid any implications of liability or premature disclosure of sensitive operational details. They must also monitor media coverage and social media sentiment to identify and address misinformation or rumors. A key challenge for the PIO in cybersecurity incidents is balancing the need for transparency with the imperative to protect sensitive investigation details, operational security, and proprietary information. This requires a close working relationship with the Planning Section to understand the factual basis for communications and with the Legal department to ensure compliance with all relevant regulations and legal obligations. The PIO acts as the organization's voice during a crisis, ensuring that the narrative is controlled, credible, and consistent with the overall incident response strategy.

The **Safety Officer (SO)**, while sometimes perceived as less critical in a virtual or cyber-centric incident compared to a physical disaster, plays a vital role in ensuring the well-being of response personnel and the integrity of organizational assets. The SO is responsible for monitoring and assessing all operational safety and incident hazards, developing measures to mitigate risks, and ensuring that safety considerations are integrated into the Incident Action Plan. In a cybersecurity context, this role extends beyond physical safety. It encompasses the well-being of the incident response team itself, who can experience significant stress and burnout due to the intense pressure and long hours often associated with major cyber incidents. The SO might implement protocols for regular breaks, ensure adequate staffing levels to prevent fatigue-related errors, and monitor for signs of stress or burnout among team members. Furthermore, the SO is responsible for ensuring the safety and security of the physical infrastructure supporting the response, such as ensuring that the ICP has adequate power, cooling, and physical security, especially if it is a designated physical location. They also assess risks associated with the incident itself, such as potential for cascading failures in critical systems, the risk of further compromise of sensitive data, or the potential for physical security threats to arise as a consequence of the cyber attack (e.g., if a compromised system controls physical access to a facility). For example, during a sophisticated attack that aims to disrupt industrial control systems (ICS) in a manufacturing plant, the Safety Officer would be instrumental in evaluating the risks of operational changes on personnel safety and environmental impact, and in coordinating with plant operations to ensure that any containment or remediation actions do not inadvertently create hazardous conditions. The SO has the authority to stop or suspend any activity that poses an unacceptable risk to personnel or organizational assets, a power that must be respected by all other ICS positions. Their proactive approach helps prevent accidents and ensures that the response can be conducted in a secure and sustainable manner.

The **Liaison Officer (LO)** is responsible for coordinating the incident response activities with external agencies, organizations, and stakeholders who are not directly part of the responding organization but have a vested interest or role in the incident. This role is crucial for ensuring a cohesive and unified response, particularly in complex incidents that may involve multiple jurisdictions, regulatory bodies, or interdependent entities. The LO acts as the primary point of contact for representatives from outside organizations, facilitating information sharing, coordination of efforts, and ensuring that the response aligns with the requirements and expectations of these external parties. In a cybersecurity incident, this could include liaising with law enforcement agencies (e.g., FBI, Interpol), regulatory bodies (e.g., data protection authorities, financial regulators), cybersecurity insurance providers, external forensic firms, critical infrastructure partners, or even neighboring organizations if the incident has a potential for lateral spread. For instance, if a critical infrastructure organization experiences a cyber attack that threatens the stability of a regional power grid, the LO would be responsible for communicating with government agencies responsible for critical infrastructure protection, utility companies, and emergency management services to ensure a coordinated response and minimize impact. The LO must possess strong interpersonal skills, negotiation abilities, and a thorough understanding of the regulatory and legal frameworks governing the organization and the incident. They serve as the "bridge" between the internal incident response team and the external landscape, ensuring that communication is effective, that information requests from external parties are managed appropriately, and that the organization's actions are understood and supported by relevant stakeholders. This role is vital for navigating the complexities of inter-agency cooperation and ensuring that the incident response is not hindered by a lack of coordination or understanding between different entities.

Beyond the Command Staff, the ICS structure is further elaborated through functional sections, each led by a Chief responsible for specific operational areas. While the previous context touched upon the initial appointment of section chiefs, a more granular examination of their roles and responsibilities is beneficial. The **Operations Section Chief** is directly responsible for managing all tactical operations to resolve the incident. This includes implementing the strategies and objectives outlined in the Incident Action Plan, directing the efforts of response teams in containment, eradication, and recovery activities. For a denial-of-service (DoS) attack, the Operations Chief would lead the teams responsible for traffic analysis, implementing mitigation strategies such as IP blocking or rate limiting, and coordinating with internet service providers (ISPs). In a malware outbreak, they would direct the deployment of anti-malware tools, manage the isolation of infected systems, and oversee the process of system cleanup and restoration. The Operations Chief must have a strong technical background in cybersecurity and incident response, as well as excellent leadership and team management skills. Their focus is on the "doing" – executing the hands-on tasks required to neutralize the threat and restore services. They receive assignments from the IC and ensure they are carried out efficiently and effectively, reporting back on progress, challenges, and resource needs.

The **Planning Section Chief** plays a pivotal role in developing the strategic direction of the incident response. This section is responsible for gathering and analyzing information about the incident, assessing its impact, developing and maintaining the Incident Action Plan (IAP), and forecasting future needs. The Planning Section is crucial for maintaining situational awareness, tracking the evolution of the incident, and ensuring that the response remains adaptable and effective. In a phishing campaign that has led to widespread credential compromise, the Planning Section would be analyzing the scope of compromised accounts, identifying the affected systems and data, and projecting the potential for further lateral movement. They work closely with the Operations Section to understand the tactical challenges and with the Logistics Section to identify resource requirements. The Planning Section Chief must be adept at information analysis, strategic thinking, and documentation. They are responsible for producing regular situation reports, tracking resources, and developing the IAP, which is the cornerstone document that outlines incident objectives, strategies, tactics, and resource assignments for a specific operational period. This section essentially provides the "brains" behind the response, ensuring that actions are deliberate, informed, and aligned with overall incident objectives.

The **Logistics Section Chief** is responsible for ensuring that all resources—personnel, equipment, supplies, and services—are available and provided to support the incident response effort. This section handles the practical aspects of equipping and sustaining the response teams. In a cybersecurity incident, this could involve procuring specialized security software licenses, ensuring that response team members have access to secure workstations and communication tools, arranging for off-site or cloud-based recovery environments, or securing necessary consulting services from third-party experts. For example, if a significant portion of an organization's data center is rendered inaccessible due to a cyber attack, the Logistics Section Chief would be responsible for sourcing and setting up alternative computing resources, ensuring redundant network connectivity, and procuring any necessary hardware or software for recovery. They must anticipate the needs of the Operations and Planning Sections and proactively procure or arrange for these resources. This requires a strong understanding of procurement processes, vendor management, and resource management. The Logistics Section ensures that the tactical and strategic efforts are not hindered by a lack of essential tools, facilities, or support.

Finally, the **Finance/Administration Section Chief** is responsible for managing all financial aspects of the incident response. This includes tracking costs, processing reimbursements, managing claims, and maintaining financial records related to the incident. In a large-scale cybersecurity event, the costs can escalate rapidly due to overtime pay, equipment purchases, procurement of specialized services, and potential legal fees or regulatory fines. The Finance/Administration Section ensures that all expenditures are properly documented, authorized, and aligned with organizational policies and incident response budgets. This role is crucial for post-incident analysis, insurance claims, and demonstrating fiscal responsibility. For instance, after a ransomware attack where external negotiators and decryption specialists were engaged, the Finance/Administration Section would be responsible for verifying and processing all associated invoices and ensuring accurate financial reporting. While often less visible than the Operations or Planning sections, this role is critical for the financial accountability and long-term impact assessment of the incident response.

The effective interplay between these key ICS positions—the Incident Commander, Deputy IC, Command Staff (PIO, SO, LO), and the functional section chiefs (Operations, Planning, Logistics, Finance/Administration)—creates a structured and authoritative framework for managing cybersecurity incidents. Each role is distinct, with defined responsibilities and clear lines of authority, ensuring that no critical aspect of the response is overlooked. This standardized approach, when implemented and practiced regularly, empowers organizations to respond to cyber threats with agility, precision, and a clear focus on achieving resolution and restoring operational resilience. The success of any incident response is, therefore, deeply rooted in the precise understanding and diligent execution of these roles and responsibilities, transforming potential chaos into a controlled and effective operation.

The Operations Section, under the leadership of its Chief, is the dynamic engine that drives the practical execution of the cybersecurity incident response. This is where the strategies and objectives formulated by the Incident Commander and the Planning Section are translated into tangible actions. The core mandate of the Operations Section is to directly confront and neutralize the threat, thereby mitigating its impact and facilitating the organization's return to normal operational status. This involves a broad spectrum of activities, from the immediate containment of a breach to the meticulous eradication of malicious elements and the comprehensive restoration of compromised systems and services. The effectiveness of the Operations Section is paramount; it is the frontline force that battles the cyber adversary, and its proficiency directly dictates the speed and success of the overall incident resolution.

At the heart of the Operations Section's responsibilities lies the concept of **containment**. This is the crucial first step in preventing the incident from spreading further and causing more damage. In the context of a cybersecurity incident, containment involves a range of tactical measures designed to isolate affected systems and networks. For instance, in the event of a widespread malware outbreak, the Operations team would immediately work to disconnect infected machines from the network. This might involve physically unplugging network cables, disabling network interface cards (NICs), or implementing network segmentation policies to create barriers that prevent the malware from propagating to other parts of the infrastructure. The goal is to create a "containment zone" around the compromised assets, effectively quarantining the threat. This isolation must be done strategically; for example, isolating a critical server too aggressively might halt essential business operations, so the Operations Chief must work closely with the Planning Section to understand the business impact and prioritize containment actions accordingly. Another critical containment strategy involves blocking malicious IP addresses, domains, or Uniform Resource Locators (URLs) at the network perimeter, firewalls, or intrusion prevention systems (IPS). This is particularly relevant in cases of distributed denial-of-service (DDoS) attacks or command-and-control (C2) communication channels used by advanced persistent threats (APTs). The Operations team would continuously monitor network traffic for indicators of compromise (IoCs) and rapidly update security devices to block any identified malicious sources. This requires real-time analysis and a deep understanding of network protocols and traffic patterns. For phishing campaigns that have led to credential compromise, containment might involve rapidly disabling compromised user accounts, forcing password resets for affected individuals, and blocking access to any systems or data that the compromised credentials could have been used to access. The speed of these actions is critical, as attackers often attempt to leverage stolen credentials for lateral movement within the network. The decision on the type and scope of containment actions is informed by the initial assessment of the incident's severity and the potential for further damage, a process heavily reliant on intelligence provided by the Planning Section and strategic direction from the Incident Commander.

Following containment, the Operations Section focuses on **eradication**. This phase is about completely removing the threat from the environment. This is a more involved process than simply isolating the affected systems, as it requires identifying and eliminating the root cause of the incident. For a malware infection, eradication might involve not only removing the malicious files from infected systems but also patching vulnerabilities that allowed the malware to enter in the first place. This could mean applying security updates to operating systems and applications, reconfiguring vulnerable services, or implementing more robust security controls. In the case of a sophisticated intrusion by an APT, eradication can be a complex and time-consuming undertaking. It may involve identifying and removing all backdoors, rootkits, and other persistent mechanisms that the attacker may have installed to maintain access. This often requires deep forensic analysis to uncover hidden malicious components. The Operations team might be tasked with rebuilding compromised systems from trusted backups or reimaging affected machines to ensure a clean state. The eradication process must be thorough to prevent re-infection or recurrence of the incident. For instance, if an attacker has exploited a zero-day vulnerability, the Operations team, guided by security researchers and intelligence from the Planning Section, would work to apply vendor patches as soon as they become available or implement temporary workarounds to mitigate the risk until a permanent solution can be deployed. The eradication of malicious code or unauthorized access requires meticulous attention to detail and a systematic approach to ensure that no trace of the adversary remains. This might involve scanning systems with multiple anti-malware engines, conducting integrity checks of critical system files, and verifying that all unauthorized accounts or configurations have been removed.

Once the threat has been eradicated, the Operations Section shifts its focus to **recovery**. This is the phase where normal operations are restored. This involves bringing systems back online, restoring data from backups, and verifying that all services are functioning correctly and securely. The recovery process must be carefully planned and executed to minimize downtime and ensure that the organization's critical business functions are resumed as quickly and efficiently as possible. The Operations team would work to bring the contained and cleaned systems back into the production environment, often in a phased approach. For example, after a ransomware attack, the recovery process would involve restoring encrypted data from clean backups, ensuring that the restored data is uncorrupted and that the systems are free of any residual malware. This might require significant effort in data validation and integrity checks. The Operations Section would also be responsible for bringing services back online in a prioritized order, based on business criticality as determined by the Planning Section and the Incident Commander. For instance, critical customer-facing applications might be restored before internal administrative tools. The recovery phase also involves re-establishing network connectivity for the restored systems and ensuring that security controls are functioning as intended. This could include reconfiguring firewalls, re-enabling security monitoring tools, and conducting post-recovery vulnerability scans to ensure that no new weaknesses have been introduced. The goal of recovery is not just to return to the pre-incident state, but to do so in a manner that enhances the organization's resilience and security posture. This might involve implementing new security technologies, refining security policies, or conducting additional training for staff. For example, after a successful social engineering attack that led to unauthorized access, the recovery phase might include mandatory security awareness training for all employees to reinforce best practices for identifying and reporting phishing attempts. The Operations Section plays a pivotal role in validating the effectiveness of the recovery efforts, ensuring that systems are not only operational but also secure and resilient against future attacks.

The Operations Section's activities are highly dependent on the **type of cyber incident** being managed. Different threats require different tactical approaches. For instance, in the case of a **malware outbreak**, the Operations team would prioritize swift identification of the malware variant, its propagation methods, and its payload. Containment would involve network segmentation and endpoint isolation. Eradication would focus on signature-based and heuristic scanning, manual removal of malicious files, and registry modifications. Recovery would involve restoring systems from clean backups and ensuring that endpoint protection solutions are updated and functioning. Patching vulnerabilities that facilitated the initial infection would be a critical component of preventing recurrence.

For **Advanced Persistent Threats (APTs)**, the Operations Section faces a more complex and sophisticated adversary. Containment strategies need to be highly stealthy to avoid tipping off the attackers. This might involve subtle network traffic redirection, disabling suspicious accounts, or creating "honeypots" to lure attackers away from critical assets. Eradication in APT scenarios is notoriously difficult, as attackers often employ advanced evasion techniques and maintain multiple backdoors. It requires deep forensic analysis to identify and remove all persistence mechanisms, which might involve significant system rebuilding or reimaging. Recovery from APTs often involves a comprehensive security posture review and the implementation of enhanced monitoring and threat hunting capabilities to detect any residual presence or future attempts. The Operations team would likely need to work closely with threat intelligence providers and external forensic experts to effectively combat APTs.

In response to **Distributed Denial-of-Service (DDoS) attacks**, the Operations Section would focus on mitigating the overwhelming volume of malicious traffic. Containment involves rapid implementation of traffic filtering rules at the network edge, utilizing specialized DDoS mitigation services, and collaborating with Internet Service Providers (ISPs) to block traffic at upstream points. Eradication in this context is less about removing malware and more about resiliently filtering traffic to allow legitimate users access to services while dropping malicious packets. Recovery involves ensuring that the affected services can handle legitimate traffic loads and that the mitigation measures are robust enough to withstand future attacks. This might involve scaling up network bandwidth or investing in advanced traffic scrubbing services.

When dealing with **insider threats**, the Operations Section's role becomes more nuanced and requires close collaboration with Human Resources and Legal departments. Containment might involve revoking access privileges, monitoring user activity more closely, and potentially securing physical access to sensitive areas or systems. Eradication would focus on removing unauthorized access, revoking malicious configurations, and ensuring that no data has been exfiltrated or compromised. Recovery would involve re-establishing trust, implementing stricter access controls, and potentially conducting data integrity checks to ensure no data loss or tampering has occurred. The sensitive nature of insider threats often requires a delicate balance between robust response actions and preserving employee privacy rights, necessitating clear guidance from legal counsel.

The Operations Section is also responsible for **managing and deploying response tools**. This includes a wide array of software and hardware solutions. These might include forensic analysis tools for collecting and examining digital evidence, malware analysis sandboxes for safely studying malicious code, network traffic analyzers for detecting anomalies, endpoint detection and response (EDR) solutions for monitoring and controlling individual devices, and security information and event management (SIEM) systems for aggregating and analyzing log data from various sources. The Operations Chief must ensure that these tools are readily available, properly configured, and that the team members are proficient in their use. This often involves ongoing training and development to keep pace with evolving technologies and threat landscapes. For example, deploying and configuring EDR agents across a large fleet of endpoints requires careful planning to minimize disruption to end-users. Similarly, ensuring that SIEM systems are ingesting the correct log sources and are configured with relevant detection rules is a continuous task.

Furthermore, the Operations Section is responsible for **documentation of actions taken**. While the Planning Section is responsible for the overall Incident Action

Plan, the Operations Section must meticulously document all actions performed during the incident response. This includes records of system changes, configuration modifications, IP addresses blocked, accounts disabled, data restored, and any other significant actions taken. This detailed record-keeping is crucial for several reasons. Firstly, it provides an audit trail for post-incident analysis, helping to identify what worked well and what could be improved in future responses. Secondly, it is essential for legal and regulatory compliance, particularly in cases of data breaches where detailed documentation of response efforts may be required by authorities or for insurance claims. Thirdly, it helps in understanding the timeline of events and the impact of specific actions, which can be vital for communicating with stakeholders and potentially for pursuing legal action against perpetrators. The Operations team might use ticketing systems, incident response platforms, or even detailed logbooks to capture these actions, ensuring that the information is accurate, timestamped, and easily retrievable.

The Operations Section also plays a vital role in **resource management**, albeit in coordination with the Logistics Section. While Logistics procures and provides resources, Operations identifies the specific needs and ensures their effective utilization. This can involve requesting additional personnel with specialized skills, procuring licenses for security software on an emergency basis, or securing access to cloud-based resources for analysis or recovery. The Operations Chief must constantly assess the resource requirements of the ongoing response and communicate these needs clearly and promptly to the Logistics Chief. For instance, if a network intrusion requires extensive log analysis, the Operations team might need additional analysts and access to a more powerful SIEM instance, which Logistics would then facilitate. Effective resource allocation is critical to ensuring that the response remains agile and capable of addressing the evolving threat.

Finally, the Operations Section Chief, in collaboration with other section chiefs and under the direction of the Incident Commander, contributes to the **development and refinement of the Incident Action Plan (IAP)**. While the Planning Section is primarily responsible for authoring the IAP, the Operations Section provides critical ground-truth information about the feasibility of proposed tactics, the availability of resources, and the potential operational impact of different strategies. This feedback loop ensures that the IAP is not just a theoretical document but a practical and actionable roadmap for the incident response. The Operations team's experience in executing tactical actions provides invaluable insights into what is achievable in the dynamic and often chaotic environment of a cyber incident. This collaborative approach ensures that the entire incident response framework, from strategic planning to tactical execution, operates in a cohesive and effective manner, ultimately leading to a more successful resolution of the cybersecurity incident.

The Planning Section is the strategic compass and foresight of the incident response effort, dedicated to understanding the "what," "why," "how," and "what next" of a cyber incident. Unlike the immediate, hands-on remediation carried out by the Operations Section, Planning operates at a higher altitude, synthesizing information to guide the overall response. Its primary function is to gather, analyze, and disseminate all pertinent information, ensuring that the Incident Commander and other sections have the situational awareness necessary to make sound decisions and adapt to the ever-changing landscape of a cyber attack. This involves a multifaceted approach, encompassing the diligent collection of threat intelligence, the thorough assessment of an incident's scope and potential impact, the development of comprehensive situational awareness reports, and the critical forecasting of future developments and potential adversary actions. Without the rigorous and continuous efforts of the Planning Section, the incident response would be akin to navigating treacherous waters without a map or a sextant, relying solely on instinct and reacting haphazardly to emerging threats rather than proactively shaping the response.

At the forefront of the Planning Section's mandate is the acquisition and interpretation of **threat intelligence**. This is not merely about collecting raw data, but about transforming that data into actionable insights. Threat intelligence can originate from a multitude of sources, both internal and external to the organization. Internally, logs from security devices such as firewalls, intrusion detection/prevention systems (IDPS), Security Information and Event Management (SIEM) systems, and Endpoint Detection and Response (EDR) solutions provide a wealth of information about network activity, system events, and user behavior. Forensic analysis of compromised systems can also yield valuable intelligence regarding the tools, techniques, and procedures (TTPs) employed by the adversary. Externally, organizations can leverage a wide array of sources, including commercial threat intelligence feeds, open-source intelligence (OSINT) platforms, government cybersecurity advisories, industry-specific information sharing groups, and even direct communication with law enforcement agencies or cybersecurity vendors. The Planning Section is responsible for curating these diverse sources, identifying reliable and relevant intelligence, and integrating it into the broader understanding of the incident. For instance, if an organization detects a new strain of ransomware, the Planning Section would immediately seek out any available intelligence on its origin, propagation methods, known vulnerabilities it exploits, and any associated indicators of compromise (IoCs) such as specific file hashes, registry keys, or network communication patterns. This intelligence can then be shared with the Operations Section to inform containment and eradication strategies, or with the Public Information Officer (PIO) to craft appropriate external communications. The quality and timeliness of threat intelligence directly influence the effectiveness of the entire response; outdated or inaccurate intelligence can lead to misguided efforts and wasted resources. Therefore, a robust intelligence-gathering and analysis capability is a cornerstone of effective incident response planning.

Beyond intelligence gathering, a critical function of the Planning Section is the **assessment of the incident's scope and impact**. This involves a deep dive into understanding not just what happened, but the extent of the damage and the potential consequences for the organization. Scope assessment focuses on identifying which systems, networks, data, and user accounts have been affected by the incident. This requires close collaboration with the Operations Section, which is executing the technical response. For example, if malware has been detected, the Planning Section, with input from Operations, would work to determine how many machines are infected, which network segments are compromised, and whether the malware has attempted to move laterally to other parts of the infrastructure. This mapping of the incident's reach is crucial for prioritizing response efforts and allocating resources effectively. The impact assessment, on the other hand, delves into the business implications of the incident. This includes evaluating the potential financial losses (e.g., lost revenue due to system downtime, costs of remediation), reputational damage (e.g., loss of customer trust, negative media coverage), legal and regulatory ramifications (e.g., violations of data privacy laws like GDPR or CCPA), and operational disruptions (e.g., inability to perform critical business functions). A ransomware attack that encrypts customer databases, for instance, would have a far greater impact than one that only affects a few non-critical workstations. The Planning Section must quantify these impacts as accurately as possible to inform the Incident Commander's decision-making, particularly regarding the severity of the incident and the level of organizational resources that should be dedicated to its resolution. This impact assessment is an ongoing process, as the full ramifications of an incident may not be immediately apparent and can evolve as the investigation progresses. For instance, initial assessments might focus on data exfiltration, but further investigation by the Planning Section could reveal that the exfiltrated data includes sensitive intellectual property, significantly escalating the perceived impact and the urgency of recovery efforts.

A tangible output of the Planning Section's work is the development of **situational awareness reports**. These reports serve as a vital communication tool, providing a consolidated and easily digestible overview of the incident's status to all relevant stakeholders, including the Incident Commander, section chiefs, and potentially executive leadership. A well-crafted situational awareness report synthesizes the gathered intelligence, the scope and impact assessments, the progress of response actions by the Operations Section, and any emerging trends or risks. The frequency and format of these reports are typically determined by the Incident Commander and the nature of the incident. In a rapidly evolving crisis, daily or even hourly updates might be necessary, whereas for a less severe incident, weekly summaries might suffice. These reports should be concise, objective, and focused on providing the most critical information. They often include sections such as: a summary of the current incident, key findings and intelligence updates, status of containment and eradication efforts, known impacts (technical and business), identified risks and vulnerabilities, and planned next steps. For example, a situational awareness report following a phishing campaign might highlight the number of compromised accounts, the types of data potentially accessed, the ongoing efforts to revoke access and reset passwords, and the increased vigilance required to detect further phishing attempts. The Planning Section's ability to translate complex technical details into clear, understandable language is paramount for ensuring that all stakeholders, regardless of their technical expertise, can grasp the situation and support the response effectively. Moreover, these reports form the basis for post-incident reviews, providing a historical record of the event and the response.

Perhaps the most forward-looking and critical function of the Planning Section is **forecasting potential**

future developments. This aspect of planning involves anticipating the adversary's next moves, identifying potential escalation paths for the incident, and proactively developing strategies to address these contingencies. This requires a sophisticated understanding of attacker motivations, TTPs, and the broader threat landscape. For instance, if an attacker has successfully breached a network, the Planning Section would consider what their likely objectives are. Are they seeking to steal data, disrupt operations, establish persistent access for future attacks, or extort money? Understanding these potential objectives allows the response team to prepare for various scenarios. If the intelligence suggests the attacker is seeking to establish persistence, the Planning Section might advise the Operations Section to focus on identifying and removing any backdoors or rootkits, and to implement enhanced monitoring for unusual outbound network traffic. If the incident involves a nation-state actor, the Planning Section would consider the geopolitical context and potential for widespread, state-sponsored attacks. This predictive analysis extends to anticipating the impact of planned response actions. For example, if the Operations Section plans to take a critical system offline for forensic analysis, the Planning Section would assess the business impact of that downtime and work with the Incident Commander to ensure that the decision is justified and that any necessary business continuity measures are in place. This forward-thinking approach allows the incident response to be agile and adaptive, moving from a reactive posture to a more proactive one. It involves conducting "what-if" scenarios, red-teaming exercises within the response itself, and continuously updating the understanding of the threat based on new intelligence and observations. For instance, in the aftermath of a data exfiltration event, the Planning Section would consider the potential for the attacker to release the stolen data publicly and advise on communication strategies and legal recourse. This predictive capability is what elevates an incident response from simply managing a crisis to effectively controlling and resolving it.

The success of the Planning Section is intrinsically linked to its ability to foster **collaboration and information sharing** across all response teams and with external entities. No single individual or team possesses all the necessary information or expertise to manage a complex cyber incident. The Planning Section acts as a central hub, facilitating the flow of information between different functional areas. This involves establishing clear communication channels, ensuring that information is disseminated in a timely and accessible manner, and actively seeking input from all parties. For instance, the Planning Section might organize regular inter-section briefings where the Operations Section provides updates on technical findings, the Logistics Section reports on resource availability, and the Finance Section outlines any budgetary implications. This cross-pollination of information ensures that all parts of the response are working in concert and are aware of each other's activities and challenges. Furthermore, the Planning Section is often the point of contact for external stakeholders, such as law enforcement, regulatory bodies, and specialized cybersecurity firms. Facilitating secure and effective communication with these entities is crucial for coordinating efforts, sharing evidence, and leveraging external expertise. For example, if the incident involves potential criminal activity, the Planning Section would liaunt with law enforcement to ensure that evidence is collected and preserved in a forensically sound manner, meeting legal requirements for prosecution. The ability of the Planning Section to build trust and facilitate open communication is fundamental to the overall effectiveness and efficiency of the incident response.

Within the Planning Section itself, specific roles and responsibilities are often delineated to manage the workload and ensure comprehensive coverage. While the exact structure may vary based on the size and complexity of the incident, key functions typically include:

Intelligence Analyst: This role is dedicated to the continuous gathering, processing, and analysis of threat intelligence from all available sources. The Intelligence Analyst is responsible for identifying trends, correlating disparate pieces of information, and producing intelligence reports that inform the broader planning effort. They often possess deep technical knowledge of malware, attack vectors, and adversary TTPs, as well as strong analytical and research skills. For example, an Intelligence Analyst might spend hours sifting through dark web forums, monitoring security mailing lists, and analyzing network traffic for signs of sophisticated reconnaissance activities.

Requirements Analyst: This role focuses on defining and documenting the requirements for the incident response, based on the assessed scope and impact of the incident. The Requirements Analyst works to translate the strategic objectives set by the Incident Commander into specific, measurable, achievable, relevant, and time-bound (SMART) tasks for the Operations Section and other support functions. They also help to identify resource needs and potential gaps in capability. For instance, after a critical system breach, the Requirements Analyst might define the need for specific forensic tools, additional skilled personnel, and accelerated procurement of security software licenses.

Situational Awareness Specialist: This individual is responsible for synthesizing information from all sources into clear and concise situational awareness reports. They ensure that the reports are accurate, up-to-date, and tailored to the needs of the intended audience. This role requires strong communication and writing skills, as well as the ability to distill complex technical information into understandable summaries. The Situational Awareness Specialist acts as the primary editor and curator of information that is disseminated to the Incident Commander and other leadership.

Technical Writer/Documentarian: While intelligence analysts and situational awareness specialists focus on the content, the Technical Writer is responsible for the format, structure, and overall presentation of planning documents, including the Incident Action Plan (IAP) itself. They ensure that the documentation is clear, consistent, and adheres to established templates and standards. This role is crucial for maintaining order and ensuring that all critical information is captured and communicated effectively. They may also be responsible for managing the repository of all planning documents.

Forecasting/Liaison Specialist: This role, or set of responsibilities, is focused on looking ahead. The Forecasting Specialist anticipates future threats, adversary actions, and potential escalation scenarios. They might conduct "what-if" analyses and contribute to the development of contingency plans. The Liaison Specialist, on the other hand, manages communication and coordination with external agencies and partners, ensuring that information is exchanged effectively and that organizational interests are represented. In some structures, these roles might be combined or distributed among senior planning staff.

The effective integration of these roles ensures that the Planning Section can provide the Incident Commander with the intelligence, foresight, and situational awareness required to navigate the complexities of a cyber incident. It is through their meticulous work that the response team can move beyond simply reacting to threats and begin to proactively shape the outcome of the incident, minimizing damage and accelerating the return to normal operations. The Planning Section is not a static entity; it is a dynamic and evolving component of the incident response framework, constantly adapting to new information and challenges, and ensuring that the organization is as prepared as possible for whatever the adversary might throw at it next. This continuous cycle of information gathering, analysis, reporting, and forecasting is what empowers the entire incident response team to act with confidence and precision.

The Logistics Section is the operational backbone of any incident response effort, focusing on the critical task of ensuring that all personnel, equipment, technology, facilities, and supplies necessary for a successful response are readily available and effectively managed. In the fast-paced and often chaotic environment of a cyber incident, the ability to rapidly procure, deploy, and maintain these essential resources can be the difference between a swift resolution and a prolonged, damaging event. This section operates on the principle that even the most brilliant plans and the most skilled personnel are rendered ineffective if they lack the tools, infrastructure, or basic support needed to execute their duties. Therefore, the Logistics Section is dedicated to anticipating and fulfilling the material and support requirements of the entire incident response team, ensuring seamless operations from the moment an incident is declared until its full resolution and recovery.

In the context of a cyber incident, the scope of logistical support extends beyond traditional physical resources. While securing and providing adequate shelter, food, and basic communication for on-site personnel remains important, the primary focus shifts towards the specialized technological and informational resources that are vital for digital forensics, containment, eradication, and recovery. This involves a proactive approach to identifying potential needs and establishing robust mechanisms for acquiring them, often under extreme time pressure. The Logistics Section works closely with the Planning Section to understand the evolving requirements of the response, translating strategic needs into concrete resource requests. It also collaborates with the Operations Section to ensure that deployed resources are functioning optimally and are accessible to the teams that need them. This intricate coordination ensures that the response team can operate with the necessary tools and infrastructure, unhindered by resource constraints.

One of the most fundamental aspects of the Logistics Section's role is managing **personnel resources**. While the Incident Commander assigns individuals to various sections and tasks, Logistics is responsible for ensuring those individuals have what they need to perform their roles. This can encompass a wide range of support, from ensuring response team members have adequate rest and sustenance, especially during extended operations, to facilitating the rapid onboarding of external subject matter experts or augmenting staff. For instance, if a critical system needs immediate forensic examination, and the internal team is overwhelmed, Logistics might be tasked with identifying and bringing in external digital forensic specialists, ensuring they have the necessary credentials, secure access, and workspace. This also extends to providing specialized training or equipment if existing personnel require it for a specific incident. In the digital realm, this might involve ensuring that personnel have access to secure remote work capabilities, including VPNs, multi-factor authentication, and encrypted communication tools, especially if the response effort requires individuals to work from home or different geographical locations due to facility access restrictions or safety concerns. The availability of personnel with the right skills, at the right time, and with the right support is a cornerstone of effective incident response, and Logistics plays a crucial role in enabling this.

Beyond personnel, the acquisition and management of **equipment and technology** form a significant portion of the Logistics Section's responsibilities in a cyber incident. This can include a vast array of items, from high-performance workstations and servers for data analysis to specialized hardware for network forensics.

When an incident involves a massive data breach, for example, the Operations Section might require additional storage capacity or enhanced processing power to sift through terabytes of log data. The Logistics Section would be responsible for procuring or provisioning these resources, whether through internal IT departments, external vendors, or cloud service providers. This also extends to procuring specialized software licenses for forensic tools, malware analysis platforms, or incident response management systems. In scenarios where existing infrastructure is compromised or insufficient, Logistics might need to arrange for the rapid deployment of temporary network hardware, including routers, switches, and firewalls, to establish isolated forensic environments or to segment compromised networks. The timely availability of reliable and secure technology is paramount. For instance, if an organization is hit with a ransomware attack, and the Operations Section needs to perform disk imaging of multiple affected systems, Logistics must ensure that sufficient imaging hardware (e.g., write-blockers, forensic imaging devices) and storage media are available and delivered to the response teams without delay. This might involve expedited shipping, on-site delivery, or even establishing temporary staging areas for equipment deployment. The security of this equipment is also a key concern; Logistics must ensure that all procured hardware and software meet the organization's security standards and are deployed in a manner that does not introduce new vulnerabilities.

The provision and management of **facilities and supplies** are also critical components managed by the Logistics Section. For significant cyber incidents, it may be necessary to establish a dedicated Incident

Response Center (IRC) or a Command Post. Logistics is responsible for identifying suitable locations, ensuring they are secure, equipped with the necessary power, cooling, and network connectivity, and furnished with all required amenities. This could range from a designated room within the organization's premises to off-site facilities if the primary location is compromised or inaccessible. Beyond physical spaces, Logistics manages the procurement and distribution of essential supplies. In a cyber context, this can include items like secure storage media for evidence collection (e.g., hard drives, USB drives), temporary signage to cordon off sensitive areas, whiteboards and markers for collaboration, and basic office supplies. Crucially, for prolonged incidents, it also extends to ensuring the well-being of the response team through provisions like catering, hydration, and access to rest areas. For example, if a major breach requires round-the-clock work for several days, the Logistics Section would arrange for continuous food and beverage services, comfortable resting facilities, and any necessary personal protective equipment if the incident response involves physical access to potentially contaminated or hazardous environments (though less common in pure cyber incidents, it can occur in hybrid scenarios). The aim is to create an environment where the response team can focus entirely on their critical tasks without being distracted by basic needs or a lack of essential materials.

Furthermore, the Logistics Section plays a vital role in managing **communication and information flow infrastructure**. While the Planning Section synthesizes information and the Operations Section executes tasks, the ability to communicate effectively and securely underpins the entire response. Logistics is responsible for ensuring that the incident response team has access to reliable and secure communication channels. This can include setting up dedicated phone lines, secure chat platforms, video conferencing capabilities, and ensuring adequate network bandwidth for large data transfers or real-time collaboration. If the organization's primary network is compromised or unavailable, Logistics must be able to rapidly deploy alternative communication solutions. This might involve procuring satellite phones, setting up temporary Wi-Fi hotspots in secure locations, or coordinating with external communication providers. For instance, in the event of a distributed denial-of-service (DDoS) attack that overwhelms an organization's internet connectivity, Logistics would work with internet service providers (ISPs) or cloud-based DDoS mitigation services to restore or augment network capacity. They would also ensure that secure channels are established for sensitive communications, such as sharing forensic findings or discussing containment strategies, to prevent further compromise. This involves understanding the security requirements of different communication streams and ensuring that the deployed solutions meet those requirements, potentially through encryption, authentication, and access controls. The efficiency and security of these communication channels are directly managed and supported by the Logistics Section, ensuring that information can be shared rapidly and safely among all response team members and relevant stakeholders.

The procurement and management of **specialized services** also fall under the purview of the Logistics Section. Cyber incidents often require expertise that may not be readily available within the organization.

This could include engaging external cybersecurity consulting firms for specialized forensics, threat hunting, legal counsel specializing in cyber law, or public relations firms to manage external communications and reputational damage. Logistics is responsible for identifying the need for such services (often in conjunction with Planning and the Incident Commander), vetting potential providers, negotiating contracts, and ensuring that these external resources are integrated seamlessly into the response effort. This involves handling the administrative and financial aspects of engaging these third parties, such as issuing purchase orders, processing invoices, and ensuring that their access to organizational systems and information is appropriately managed and secured. For example, if a state-sponsored attack is suspected, Logistics might be tasked with onboarding a specialized threat intelligence firm or engaging with national cybersecurity agencies. This requires understanding contractual obligations, service level agreements (SLAs), and ensuring that all external parties adhere to the organization's security policies and procedures. The timely and effective engagement of these specialized services, facilitated by Logistics, can significantly bolster the response team's capabilities and accelerate the resolution of complex incidents.

A critical, albeit often overlooked, aspect of Logistics in a cyber incident response is **evidence handling and chain of custody support**. While the technical execution of evidence collection falls to the Operations Section, Logistics provides the foundational support for ensuring this process is conducted correctly and compliantly. This includes procuring tamper-evident evidence bags, secure storage containers for digital media, and specialized labeling materials. Logistics ensures that these supplies are readily available to forensic investigators and that procedures for their use are understood. They may also be involved in establishing secure evidence storage areas, controlling access to these areas, and maintaining logs of who accesses the evidence and when. For digital evidence, this translates to ensuring that the forensic media used for imaging drives or capturing network traffic is properly formatted, acquired from trusted sources, and handled in a manner that preserves its integrity. For example, if the Operations Section needs to collect volatile memory from a server for analysis, Logistics would ensure that the appropriate tools, such as USB drives with specific write-blocking capabilities or specialized memory acquisition hardware, are procured and available. The meticulous management of these seemingly minor details, facilitated by Logistics, is crucial for maintaining the legal and forensic defensibility of the evidence collected, which can be vital for subsequent legal proceedings, regulatory investigations, or internal post-incident analysis.

The Logistics Section must also be adept at **risk management and contingency planning** related to resources. What happens if a critical piece of equipment fails? What if a key vendor cannot deliver within the promised timeframe? Logistics anticipates these potential disruptions and develops contingency plans. This might involve identifying backup vendors, maintaining a cache of critical spare parts or equipment, or establishing pre-negotiated emergency procurement agreements with key suppliers. For instance, if the primary forensic lab is unavailable due to a power outage, Logistics might have pre-identified alternative secure facilities with the necessary infrastructure and equipment. Similarly, if a key cybersecurity tool provider experiences an outage, Logistics would have a list of alternative solutions or workarounds. This proactive approach to resource-related risks ensures that the incident response is not derailed by unforeseen circumstances. It involves understanding the dependencies within the response effort and having mitigation strategies in place for each critical resource. This might also extend to personnel availability; for example, identifying individuals who can be rapidly deployed to support the response if key team members become unavailable due to illness or other unforeseen circumstances.

The effective functioning of the Logistics Section is underpinned by strong **vendor management and procurement processes**. In a cyber incident, speed and reliability are paramount. Logistics must have established relationships with trusted vendors for hardware, software, and specialized services. They need to have streamlined procurement processes that can handle urgent requests, often bypassing standard bureaucratic procedures when necessary, while still maintaining an audit trail. This can involve pre-approved vendor lists, blanket purchase agreements for common incident response needs, and clear authorization workflows for emergency expenditures. For example, if a new variant of malware requires a specific, expensive analysis tool that the organization does not currently possess, Logistics needs to be able to quickly identify a vendor, obtain a quote, and secure approval for purchase and delivery within hours, not days or weeks. This requires a deep understanding of the procurement landscape for cybersecurity-related resources and the ability to navigate contractual and legal complexities rapidly. The relationships built and the processes established by Logistics before an incident even occurs are what enable rapid and effective resource mobilization when it is most critical.

Finally, the Logistics Section's role continues beyond the immediate containment and eradication phases. During the **recovery and remediation** stages, Logistics is essential for procuring any necessary hardware or software upgrades, facilitating the re-imaging or rebuilding of systems, and ensuring that the response team has the resources needed to test and validate the restored environment. This could involve coordinating the delivery of new servers, securing licenses for updated security software, or arranging for the secure disposal of compromised hardware. As the incident winds down, Logistics also plays a role in the demobilization of the response team, ensuring that all deployed equipment is accounted for, returned to its proper location, or disposed of according to policy. This thoroughness ensures that resources are not lost, that evidence is properly handled, and that the organization is prepared for future incidents. The transition from an active response to a return to normal operations requires sustained logistical support, ensuring that the recovery efforts are adequately resourced and executed efficiently. The Logistics Section, therefore, is not merely a support function but a critical enabler of the entire incident response lifecycle, ensuring that the organization has the capacity, capability, and resilience to navigate and recover from even the most challenging cyber threats.

The Finance and Administration Section is indispensable in ensuring the fiscal accountability and operational efficiency of any cybersecurity incident response. While the technical teams are focused on containment, eradication, and recovery, this section meticulously tracks and manages all financial expenditures related to the incident. This encompasses a broad spectrum of costs, from the direct expenses incurred during the active response phase to the indirect costs that may manifest long after the immediate threat has been neutralized. Effective financial management is not merely an administrative task; it is a critical component that supports budgetary oversight, facilitates insurance claims, informs post-incident analysis, and ultimately ensures transparency and accountability in the allocation of organizational resources during a high-pressure crisis. The rigor applied by the Finance and Administration Section directly impacts the organization's ability to understand the true cost of a cyber incident, to recover financially where possible, and to strengthen its defenses against future events by learning from the financial implications of past responses.

One of the primary responsibilities of the Finance and Administration Section is the meticulous tracking of all costs associated with the incident response. This begins with documenting personnel-related expenses. During a cyber incident, internal staff may be required to work extended hours, weekends, or holidays. The Finance and Administration Section is responsible for accurately recording all overtime hours worked by incident response team members, ensuring that these are properly authorized and compensated according to company policy and applicable labor laws. Furthermore, if external subject matter experts or temporary staff are brought in to bolster the response team, their contracts, billing rates, and hours worked must be meticulously documented. This includes specialists in digital forensics, malware analysis, incident management, or even legal counsel and public relations professionals. The Section ensures that all invoices from these external resources are reviewed for accuracy against their contracts and promptly processed for payment. Beyond personnel, the procurement of necessary equipment and technology represents a significant cost. This can range from specialized hardware such as forensic workstations, network taps, or high-capacity storage devices, to software licenses for advanced analytical tools, threat intelligence platforms, or incident response management systems. Each purchase order, invoice, and delivery confirmation must be carefully logged and reconciled. The Finance and Administration Section must ensure that all such acquisitions are properly authorized, align with the needs identified by the Planning and Operations Sections, and are recorded against the incident's budget. This detailed record-keeping is essential not only for internal financial controls but also for substantiating claims for reimbursement, whether from insurance providers or, in certain regulatory contexts, from government bodies.

The financial impact of a cyber incident can be substantial and multifaceted, extending far beyond the immediate costs of investigation and remediation. The Finance and Administration Section plays a crucial role in identifying, categorizing, and tracking these diverse expenses. This involves a systematic approach to financial record-keeping that ensures no cost goes undocumented. Key categories of expenses that require rigorous tracking include:

Personnel Costs: This is often the largest component of incident response expenditure. It encompasses:

Overtime Pay: As mentioned, internal staff working beyond their regular hours. Accurate timekeeping and authorization are paramount.

Temporary Staffing: Engaging external consultants, contractors, or augmenting existing teams with specialized skill sets not available internally. This includes their hourly or project rates, as well as any associated administrative or onboarding costs.

Travel and Per Diem: If response team members are required to travel to a different location, be it to a secure facility or to assist a remote office, all travel expenses (airfare, accommodation, meals, local transportation) must be tracked.

Training and Certification: In some cases, immediate upskilling or certification for personnel might be necessary, and these costs must be attributed to the incident.

Technology and Equipment Costs: This category covers the tangible and intangible assets acquired or utilized for the response:

Hardware Procurement: Purchasing new workstations, servers, network devices, storage media, forensic imaging hardware, or mobile device acquisition tools.

Software Licenses: Acquiring licenses for specialized forensic software, malware analysis tools, endpoint detection and response (EDR) solutions, security information and event management (SIEM) systems, or incident response platforms. This can also include temporary or emergency licenses.

Cloud Services: Subscriptions to cloud-based security solutions, storage for forensic data, or processing power for analysis.

Maintenance and Support: Costs associated with expedited maintenance or support contracts for critical systems or newly procured equipment during the incident.

External Service Provider Fees: Engaging third-party experts is often unavoidable. The Finance and Administration Section is responsible for managing and tracking:

Forensic Investigators: Fees charged by external digital forensics firms.

Legal Counsel: Costs associated with specialized cybersecurity lawyers, including advice on regulatory compliance, breach notification laws, and potential litigation.

Public Relations and Communications Firms: Fees for managing external communications, media relations, and reputational damage control.

Cyber Insurance Providers: While not a cost to be tracked in the same way, understanding the policy and working with the insurer is a key administrative function.

Threat Intelligence Services: Subscription costs for specialized threat intelligence feeds or consulting services.

Operational and Administrative Costs: These are the supporting expenses that facilitate the response:

Facility Usage: Costs associated with setting up and maintaining a dedicated incident response center, including rental fees, utilities, and setup costs if an external facility is used.

Supplies: Procurement of office supplies, evidence bags, secure storage media, labeling materials, and other physical items needed for the response.

Communication Expenses: Costs related to setting up temporary communication lines, satellite phones, or enhanced internet connectivity.

Evidence Handling and Storage: Costs associated with secure evidence transportation, storage lockers, and specialized handling equipment.

Potential Legal and Regulatory Costs: These are often difficult to quantify upfront but must be accounted for:

Fines and Penalties: Potential fines levied by regulatory bodies (e.g., GDPR, CCPA) due to data breaches or non-compliance.

Legal Settlements: Costs associated with class-action lawsuits or settlements with affected individuals or entities.

Notification Costs: Expenses related to notifying affected individuals or regulatory bodies about the breach, which can include mailings, call centers, and credit monitoring services.

The Finance and Administration Section's role extends to establishing clear procedures for authorizing expenditures related to the incident. This involves defining who has the authority to approve purchases, what documentation is required for each type of expenditure, and how emergency procurements will be handled. In a crisis, traditional procurement processes may need to be expedited, but this must be done with appropriate oversight to prevent fraud or waste. This might involve establishing pre-approved lists of vendors for critical services or creating emergency procurement authorization forms.

A critical aspect of the Finance and Administration Section's work is to maintain detailed and accurate financial records for the entire duration of the incident and beyond. This involves not only tracking expenditures but also reconciling these costs against allocated budgets. If a dedicated incident response budget has been established, the Section monitors spending against this budget and flags any significant deviations. In the absence of a specific budget, costs are often drawn from departmental budgets or a contingency fund. The Section ensures that all expenditures are properly coded and attributed to the incident, allowing for a clear understanding of the financial burden. This detailed documentation is also essential for auditing purposes. Both internal and external auditors will scrutinize the financial records related to the incident response to ensure compliance with financial policies and regulations.

Furthermore, the Finance and Administration Section is pivotal in the process of filing insurance claims. Many organizations carry cyber insurance policies that can help offset some of the costs associated with a breach. The Section is responsible for gathering all the necessary documentation to support these claims, including invoices, purchase orders, contracts, and proof of payment. They must work closely with the insurance provider, providing them with the required financial information and ensuring that the claim is processed efficiently and effectively. This often involves a deep understanding of the insurance policy's terms and conditions, including deductibles, coverage limits, and required reporting procedures. The accurate and comprehensive financial data collected by the Finance and Administration Section is indispensable for maximizing the benefits of cyber insurance.

Beyond immediate cost tracking and insurance claims, the Finance and Administration Section plays a crucial role in post-incident analysis. By providing a detailed breakdown of all incurred costs, the Section enables the organization to understand the true financial impact of the cyber incident. This information is invaluable for:

Budgeting and Financial Planning: Understanding the actual costs incurred helps in future budgeting for cybersecurity defenses, incident response preparedness, and risk mitigation strategies.

Return on Investment (ROI) Analysis: Evaluating the effectiveness of the incident response by comparing the costs incurred against the potential losses that were averted.

Risk Assessment Refinement: Quantifying the financial risks associated with various types of cyber threats can inform strategic decision-making regarding security investments.

Lessons Learned: Identifying areas where costs were unexpectedly high or where efficiencies could be improved can lead to more effective and cost-efficient incident response planning in the future.

The Finance and Administration Section's commitment to transparency and accountability is paramount. In the midst of a crisis, where emotions can run high and resources may be strained, a clear and well-documented financial picture provides a stable anchor. It ensures that all stakeholders, from the executive leadership to the incident response team members, have confidence in the management of financial resources. This section ensures that every dollar spent is justified, documented, and aligned with the overarching goal of effectively managing and resolving the cybersecurity incident. Without this diligent financial stewardship, an organization risks not only incurring uncontrolled expenses but also facing regulatory scrutiny, reputational damage, and a lack of preparedness for future security challenges. The financial discipline enforced by this section is as vital to a successful response as the technical expertise of the operations team.

The process of tracking costs requires a robust system for documentation and reporting. The Finance and Administration Section typically establishes a dedicated incident cost tracking log or utilizes specialized incident management software that integrates financial tracking capabilities. This log should capture, at a minimum, the date of the expenditure, the nature of the cost, the vendor or individual paid, the amount, the method of payment, and the authorization for the expenditure. For larger organizations, this might involve creating a specific cost center or project code for the incident to segregate expenses within the accounting system. Cross-referencing with purchase requisitions, invoices, and payment records is essential to ensure accuracy and completeness. The Section must also be prepared to provide regular financial status reports to the Incident Commander and other key stakeholders, offering a clear overview of the cumulative costs incurred to date and projections for future expenses. This continuous communication allows for informed decision-making regarding resource allocation and strategic adjustments to the response effort.

Moreover, the Finance and Administration Section must be adept at navigating the complexities of procurement under duress. When essential equipment or services are needed immediately, standard procurement cycles may be too slow. This necessitates the establishment of pre-negotiated contracts with key vendors, the development of emergency procurement protocols that bypass some of the usual bureaucratic hurdles while maintaining necessary oversight, and the empowerment of designated personnel to make rapid purchasing decisions within defined financial limits. For instance, if the Operations Section identifies an urgent need for specialized forensic analysis hardware, Logistics might initiate an expedited purchase process, with Finance and Administration ensuring proper documentation and authorization are retroactively applied or concurrently managed. The ability to swiftly acquire necessary resources without compromising financial controls is a hallmark of an effective response.

The financial implications of a cyber incident can also extend to reputational damage and loss of customer trust, which, while not directly quantifiable as line-item expenses, can have profound long-term economic consequences. The Finance and Administration Section, by ensuring a well-managed and transparent response, contributes to mitigating these indirect costs. A controlled and documented response demonstrates organizational competence and responsibility, which can help to preserve stakeholder confidence during and after a crisis. Conversely, financial mismanagement or a lack of transparency during an incident can exacerbate reputational damage, leading to greater long-term financial harm.

Ultimately, the Finance and Administration Section acts as the financial guardian of the incident response effort. Their meticulous tracking of costs, diligent management of claims, and rigorous documentation practices ensure that the organization not only navigates the immediate financial challenges of a cybersecurity incident but also gains valuable insights for future preparedness and resilience. This function is a critical, though often unseen, pillar supporting the entire incident response framework, ensuring that the organization can recover effectively and learn from the experience in a financially sound manner.

The effective integration of specialized technical teams into the Incident Command System (ICS) structure is a critical determinant of a swift and successful cybersecurity incident response. While the overarching ICS framework provides a standardized, hierarchical approach to managing any incident, the unique demands of cyber threats necessitate a nuanced application of this structure to harness the full potential of technical expertise. These teams, encompassing disciplines such as digital forensics, network security analysis, malware reverse engineering, endpoint detection and response (EDR) specialists, and threat intelligence analysts, possess the deep, specialized knowledge required to understand, contain, and eradicate sophisticated cyber intrusions. Their seamless incorporation into the ICS is not merely about assigning tasks; it is about establishing robust communication channels, defining clear roles and responsibilities within the established hierarchy, and ensuring that their technical insights directly inform strategic decision-making.

The primary challenge in integrating these technical units lies in balancing the need for centralized command and control inherent in ICS with the often distributed, iterative, and specialized nature of technical work. Technical specialists frequently operate in environments that require a high degree of autonomy for in-depth analysis, experimentation, and rapid iteration on solutions. Forcing them into rigid, overly bureaucratic reporting structures can stifle their agility, delay critical findings, and lead to suboptimal technical outcomes. Conversely, allowing them to operate entirely outside the ICS structure can result in fragmented efforts, misaligned priorities, and a lack of cohesive strategic direction. The goal, therefore, is to find the optimal point of integration where their specialized capabilities are leveraged efficiently within the broader incident response orchestration.

Within the ICS framework, the Operations Section and the Planning Section are the most logical and common placements for specialized technical teams. The Operations Section is directly responsible for the tactical execution of response activities, including containment, eradication, and recovery. Technical teams can be assigned to specific sub-units within Operations, focused on distinct aspects of the response effort. For example, a Digital Forensics Unit might be established within Operations to collect, preserve, and analyze digital evidence, providing crucial insights into the incident's origin, scope, and impact. Similarly, a Network Security Monitoring Unit, also reporting within Operations, could be tasked with real-time traffic analysis, identifying malicious network activity, and implementing containment measures like firewall rule adjustments or network segmentation. A Malware Analysis Unit could focus on dissecting and understanding the behavior of malicious code, informing defensive strategies and eradication efforts.

The Planning Section, on the other hand, is responsible for gathering and analyzing information, developing incident action plans, and anticipating future issues. Technical teams can contribute significantly to Planning by providing detailed technical assessments and forecasts. A Threat Intelligence Unit, for instance, could reside within Planning, synthesizing information from various sources to provide context on the attackers' motivations, tactics, techniques, and procedures (TTPs), and predicting potential future actions. This intelligence is vital for developing proactive defense strategies and updating incident action plans. Furthermore, technical subject matter experts can be assigned as technical advisors to the Planning Section Chief, offering specialized perspectives on the feasibility of proposed response strategies, the potential technical implications of different courses of action, and the identification of critical technical vulnerabilities.

Regardless of whether a technical team is assigned to Operations or Planning, maintaining clear lines of communication and reporting is paramount. The ICS structure provides a defined chain of command, and technical teams must adhere to this. This means that team leaders or assigned points of contact within the technical units will report to their designated supervisor within the ICS structure (e.g., a Branch Director, Division Supervisor, or Group Supervisor). This ensures that information flows effectively up and down the chain of command, allowing the Incident Commander to have a comprehensive overview of the situation and to issue clear directives. However, this adherence to structure should not come at the expense of direct, fluid communication between technical specialists and their peers or other relevant functional areas.

A common and effective model is to establish technical teams as functional groups or units that report up through the Operations Section. For instance, the Digital Forensics Unit, led by a Digital Forensics Lead, would report to a specialized supervisor within the Operations Section, perhaps a "Technical Operations Supervisor" or a "Special Operations Group Supervisor." This supervisor would then integrate the findings and needs of the Digital Forensics Unit into the broader operational plan. Similarly, the Malware Analysis Unit and Network Security Analysis Unit would be organized and report within Operations. This organizational approach ensures that the technical teams' findings are directly translated into actionable containment and eradication tasks.

The integration into the Planning Section offers a different but equally valuable perspective. A Threat Intelligence Unit, for example, could be part of the Intelligence/Information Section, which often operates under the Planning Section Chief. This unit would focus on synthesizing open-source intelligence, internal telemetry, and external threat feeds to provide a strategic understanding of the adversary. This information would then be used by the Planning Section to develop longer-term strategies and anticipate next steps of the attack. Technical specialists can also be embedded as advisors to the Planning Section's Documentation Unit, ensuring that technical details are accurately recorded in incident reports and action plans.

Crucially, the integration must preserve the technical autonomy and specialized workflows that these teams require. Digital forensics, for example, follows a rigorous process of evidence acquisition, preservation, examination, and reporting, often involving specialized tools and methodologies that cannot be rushed or subjected to standard operational procedures. Similarly, malware reverse engineering requires dedicated environments and time for in-depth analysis. While these teams operate *within* the ICS structure, their internal processes should not be dictated by the ICS hierarchy in a way that compromises the integrity or efficiency of their technical work. This means that the team leader or point of contact within the ICS structure must be empowered to protect their team's workflow and ensure they have the necessary resources and time to perform their specialized tasks effectively.

To facilitate this, clear definitions of roles and responsibilities are essential. Before an incident occurs, organizations should clearly define which technical teams exist, what their core competencies are, and how they will be activated and integrated into the ICS. This includes pre-designating team leads or points of contact who are familiar with both the technical discipline and the ICS principles. These individuals will act as the crucial interface between the technical team and the broader ICS structure, translating operational needs into technical requirements and technical findings into actionable intelligence for the Incident Commander.

Furthermore, fostering a culture of collaboration and mutual understanding between technical specialists and the broader incident response management team is vital. This can be achieved through cross-training initiatives, joint exercises, and the use of common operational language and terminology. Technical teams need to understand the strategic objectives of the incident response, and the management team needs to appreciate the complexities and requirements of technical investigations. For instance, the Operations Section Chief should understand that digital forensics requires careful handling of evidence to maintain its integrity, and the Digital Forensics Lead should understand that the Operations Section needs timely findings to implement effective containment.

Effective communication protocols are the lifeblood of this integration. While hierarchical reporting is important for structure and accountability, ad-hoc communication channels are often necessary for technical problem-solving. This can involve establishing secure chat channels for technical teams to collaborate, holding regular technical sync-up meetings, and ensuring that technical leads have direct access to relevant members of the Planning and Operations Sections. The Incident Commander should encourage and enable these direct communication pathways, as long as they are managed efficiently and do not bypass critical decision-making points.

Consider the scenario of a ransomware attack. The Network Security Analysis Unit, reporting to Operations, might identify the initial point of compromise and the affected network segments. Simultaneously, the Malware Analysis Unit, also within Operations, could be dissecting the ransomware sample to understand its encryption mechanisms and propagation vectors. The Digital Forensics Unit would be tasked with recovering encrypted files, preserving the infected systems for analysis, and potentially identifying the initial intrusion vector by examining endpoint logs. All these findings need to be synthesized and fed back to the Operations Section Chief to guide containment and eradication efforts. The Planning Section, in parallel, would leverage the Threat Intelligence Unit's assessment of the threat actor to anticipate subsequent attack phases and develop broader defensive strategies.

The liaison between these technical units and the Incident Command Post (ICP) is another critical element. Designated liaisons from key technical teams, or the technical team leads themselves, should have direct access to the ICP or maintain constant communication with the Incident Commander or their

Chief of Staff. This ensures that the Incident Commander is continuously updated on the technical situation and can make informed decisions based on the latest technical intelligence. These liaisons also serve to translate the Incident Commander's strategic objectives into specific technical tasks for their respective teams.

The concept of "Technical Working Groups" (TWGs) can be particularly effective. These groups, often formed under the umbrella of the Operations or Planning Section, bring together specialists from different technical disciplines to collaborate on specific aspects of the response. For example, a TWG focused on "Network Containment" might include members from Network Security Analysis, Endpoint Response, and Incident Response Coordination, all working together to implement and verify containment measures. These TWGs operate within the broader ICS structure but allow for a more fluid, interdisciplinary approach to problem-solving.

Moreover, the role of the Incident Commander and their senior staff (Chief of Staff, Operations Section Chief, Planning Section Chief) is crucial in ensuring that technical expertise is valued and effectively utilized. They must be comfortable engaging with technical specialists, asking probing questions, and understanding the implications of technical findings. A strong leadership team will proactively seek out technical input, rather than waiting for it to be formally delivered through prescribed channels. They should foster an environment where technical teams feel empowered to raise concerns, highlight critical findings, and even challenge proposed courses of action based on their technical expertise, knowing that their input will be respected and seriously considered.

The integration of technical teams also necessitates careful consideration of resource management. Specialized technical tools, software licenses, dedicated analysis environments, and highly skilled personnel are all finite resources. The ICS structure, particularly through the Logistics Section and under the direction of the Incident Commander, is responsible for ensuring that these resources are requested, procured, and allocated efficiently to the technical teams that need them most. The Finance and Administration Section, as previously discussed, plays a vital role in tracking the significant costs associated with these specialized resources, but the initial identification and prioritization of needs falls to the technical teams and their integration within the operational and planning frameworks.

For very large-scale or prolonged incidents, it may be beneficial to establish a dedicated "Technical Directorate" or "Technical Operations Branch" within the ICS structure. This would consolidate various technical teams under a single, senior-level manager who reports directly to the Incident Commander or the Operations Section Chief. This formalized structure can enhance coordination, streamline resource allocation, and ensure that technical efforts are fully aligned with the overall incident response strategy. However, for most cybersecurity incidents, integrating technical teams as functional units or specialized groups within the existing Operations and Planning Sections is typically sufficient and more agile.

The success of integrating technical teams hinges on preparation and practice. Incident response plans should explicitly detail how technical capabilities will be deployed and managed within the ICS framework. Regular tabletop exercises, functional drills, and full-scale simulations that involve these technical teams are essential to test and refine these integration strategies. These exercises provide invaluable opportunities to identify communication breakdowns, clarify roles, and improve the overall effectiveness of the technical response within the structured environment of ICS. Without this deliberate planning and consistent practice, the integration of specialized technical talent can become a point of friction rather than a force multiplier during a critical cybersecurity incident.

In essence, the process is one of strategic placement and clear communication. Technical teams are not appendages to be bolted onto the ICS structure; they are integral components whose expertise must be woven into the fabric of incident management. By assigning them to functional areas like Operations or Planning, establishing defined reporting lines, ensuring robust communication pathways, and respecting their technical workflows, organizations can maximize the effectiveness of their specialized cybersecurity talent, leading to more efficient containment, thorough analysis, and successful remediation of cyber incidents. This thoughtful integration ensures that the collective intelligence and capabilities of the technical workforce are harnessed in a coordinated and strategic manner, directly supporting the Incident Commander's mission to protect the organization. The challenge is to maintain the agility and depth of specialized technical work while operating within the clear, command-and-control principles of ICS, a balance that requires ongoing attention to planning, training, and inter-team communication.

The operational effectiveness of any cybersecurity incident response hinges not only on the technical prowess of its teams but also on the robustness of its communication protocols and the clarity of information flow. Once specialized technical units are integrated into the Incident Command System (ICS) framework, as discussed previously, the next critical step is to define precisely how information will move within this structure, to whom it will be reported, and through which channels. This subsection delves into the intricate details of establishing and maintaining these vital communication lifelines, ensuring that every piece of crucial data reaches the right eyes at the right time, without compromise.

At the core of successful incident response communication is the establishment of clear, pre-defined protocols. These protocols are not just suggestions; they are operational mandates designed to ensure predictability, efficiency, and accuracy, especially under the immense pressure of a live cyber event. This begins with identifying primary and, crucially, backup communication methods. In the chaotic environment of a cybersecurity incident, primary communication channels—such as enterprise-grade secure instant messaging platforms, dedicated incident response conference bridges, or secure VoIP services—can become overwhelmed, targeted, or simply rendered inoperable due to the very nature of the attack. Therefore, a comprehensive plan must include alternative methods. This might involve leveraging out-of-band communication channels, such as pre-arranged satellite phones for key personnel, secure encrypted email for less time-sensitive updates, or even a callback tree using personal mobile numbers for critical personnel if corporate networks are compromised. The selection of these methods must consider the potential impact of the incident itself on the infrastructure that supports them. For instance, if the incident involves a denial-of-service attack targeting the organization's primary network, relying solely on IP-based communication systems would be a critical failure. Redundancy and resilience are the watchwords here, ensuring that communication can persist even when the organization's digital infrastructure is under duress.

Reporting frequencies are another cornerstone of effective communication protocols. For technical teams deeply embedded within the incident response, regular, scheduled updates are essential. These updates provide the Incident Commander and other ICS leadership with a consistent pulse on the evolving situation. For operational teams like Network Security Analysis or Endpoint Detection and Response (EDR), hourly or bi-hourly sync-ups might be necessary during the active containment and eradication phases. These sync-ups are not exhaustive debriefs but rather concise summaries of key findings, actions taken, and immediate challenges. For analytical teams, such as those involved in digital forensics or malware reverse engineering, reporting might be tied to the completion of specific milestones or the generation of critical insights. The key is to strike a balance between providing timely information to guide decision-making and allowing technical specialists the uninterrupted time required for in-depth analysis. Overly frequent reporting can disrupt deep work, while infrequent updates can lead to strategic missteps based on outdated information. Incident action plans (IAPs) themselves often dictate reporting requirements, and the planning section plays a pivotal role in collating these needs and ensuring they are met.

The dissemination of information requires equally precise protocols. Who needs to know what, and when? This is a complex question, but the ICS framework, with its defined sections and roles, provides a structure for answering it. Technical findings from teams within Operations, for example, must be relayed to the Planning Section for incorporation into updated IAPs and to the Incident Commander for strategic decision-making. Similarly, intelligence gathered by teams within Planning, such as threat actor profiling from a Threat Intelligence Unit, needs to be communicated back to Operations to inform tactical execution and to the Communications or Public Information Officer (PIO) if external messaging is required. The ICS structure mandates reporting up the chain of command, but effective incident response also requires lateral and downward communication. Technical teams may need to communicate directly with other technical teams, even if they report through different ICS branches, to resolve complex issues. The Incident Commander or their designated chief of staff must ensure that these cross-functional communications are facilitated and that critical information is then funneled back into the formal reporting structure to maintain situational awareness for all relevant parties. This often involves establishing clear points of contact within each section or branch who are responsible for gathering and disseminating information to and from their respective units.

Security of communication channels and the data transmitted through them is a non-negotiable imperative in cybersecurity incident response. The very nature of an incident often means that highly sensitive information is being discussed: details of vulnerabilities, the extent of data breaches, the identity of attackers, and the organization's defensive strategies. If these communications are intercepted, they could be exploited by adversaries to further their attack, evade detection, or gain strategic advantage. Therefore, all communication channels used for incident response must be secured, preferably employing end-to-end encryption. This applies not only to digital platforms but also to any verbal communications. For instance, conference calls should be conducted over secure, authenticated lines, and sensitive discussions should not occur over unsecured public Wi-Fi. A key consideration is the classification of information. Sensitive technical findings or intelligence related to an active threat might be classified as "Confidential" or "Restricted," dictating the level of security required for its transmission and storage. This might involve using dedicated, air-gapped systems for analysis and communication, or employing secure data transfer protocols that are resistant to eavesdropping. The Principle of Least Privilege should also extend to communication access, ensuring that only authorized personnel can participate in or access incident-related communications.

The need for a single, unified point of contact for all external communications, particularly with stakeholders outside the immediate incident response team, cannot be overstated. This role is typically fulfilled by the Public Information Officer (PIO), who operates under the direction of the Incident

Commander and often within the Public Information function of the Planning Section. For cybersecurity incidents, this external communication function extends beyond traditional media relations. It includes communicating with:

Law Enforcement Agencies: Providing them with requested information and coordinating investigative efforts.

Regulatory Bodies: Informing them of breaches and compliance requirements.

Affected Customers or Partners: Communicating the nature of the incident, its impact, and steps being taken to mitigate further risks.

Third-Party Forensic or Security Vendors: Coordinating efforts and sharing necessary information securely.

Cyber Insurance Providers: Initiating claims and providing required documentation.

Having a single, designated spokesperson ensures that the organization presents a consistent, accurate, and controlled message to the outside world. This prevents conflicting information from being released, which can damage credibility, create confusion, or even inadvertently tip off adversaries. The PIO, working closely with the Incident Commander, Operations, and Planning Sections, will craft messaging that is truthful, timely, and appropriate to the audience, while safeguarding sensitive internal details of the response. This individual acts as a crucial gatekeeper, ensuring that all outward-facing communications are vetted and aligned with the overall incident response strategy.

The technical teams themselves should be instructed not to communicate directly with external parties regarding the incident unless specifically authorized and briefed by the PIO or Incident Commander. This protocol protects both the integrity of the investigation and the organization's public image.

Furthermore, the process of information flow extends to the documentation and archiving of incident-related communications. All significant communications, decisions, and findings should be logged. This serves multiple purposes: it creates an audit trail for post-incident review, aids in legal or regulatory inquiries, and provides a knowledge base for future incident preparedness. Secure and organized storage of these records is paramount, ensuring that they can be accessed when needed but remain protected from unauthorized disclosure. The Documentation Unit within the Planning Section plays a critical role here, but the responsibility for capturing information often begins with the individuals and teams generating it. This reinforces the need for clear guidelines on what needs to be logged and how.

The integration of communication protocols is an ongoing process. It requires regular review, updates based on lessons learned from exercises or actual incidents, and continuous training for all personnel involved in incident response. The technology landscape evolves rapidly, and so too must the methods and tools used for communication. What is considered secure and reliable today might be obsolete or vulnerable tomorrow. Therefore, organizations must invest in maintaining and updating their incident response communication infrastructure and training programs. This proactive approach ensures that when a cyber incident strikes, the communication channels are not an afterthought, but a well-oiled, resilient, and secure mechanism that supports the swift and effective resolution of the crisis. The establishment of these robust communication protocols is not merely a procedural step; it is a strategic imperative that underpins the entire incident response capability, enabling seamless coordination, informed decision-making, and ultimately, a more successful defense against sophisticated cyber threats.

The role of the Safety Officer, traditionally focused on physical well-being and workplace hazards, takes on a critical, albeit less visible, dimension within the realm of cybersecurity incident response. While the immediate focus of an incident response effort is understandably on containing and eradicating the cyber threat, the human element remains paramount. The Safety Officer's mandate is to ensure that the personnel engaged in this high-stress, technically demanding, and often protracted endeavor are protected from undue harm, both physical and psychological, and that their actions do not introduce secondary risks. This involves a proactive and continuous assessment of the operational environment and the well-being of the individuals operating within it.

One of the primary responsibilities of the Safety Officer in a cyber incident context is the identification and mitigation of risks related to personnel fatigue and burnout. Cyber incidents can be protracted affairs, demanding long hours, intense concentration, and the constant processing of alarming information. Teams may be required to work around the clock for days, even weeks, to restore systems, investigate the breach, and implement remediation measures. This relentless pressure can lead to exhaustion, impaired judgment, increased error rates, and significant psychological distress. The Safety Officer must therefore advocate for structured rest periods, encourage rotation of duties where feasible, and monitor team members for signs of extreme fatigue. This might involve working with the Incident Commander and the Planning Section to ensure realistic work schedules are established and adhered to, promoting breaks and encouraging team leaders to actively check on the welfare of their staff. The psychological toll of dealing with breaches, potential data loss, and the feeling of being under siege can be immense. The Safety Officer, in collaboration with HR or mental health professionals, can help ensure that support mechanisms are available and communicated to the response team, normalizing the discussion around mental well-being during stressful operational periods.

Beyond burnout, the Safety Officer also addresses the risks associated with exposure to sensitive and potentially harmful information. During a cyber investigation, responders may encounter personally identifiable information (PII), protected health information (PHI), financial data, or proprietary intellectual property that has been compromised or is being handled during the response. The Safety Officer ensures that personnel are adequately trained on data handling protocols and the principle of least privilege, particularly concerning their access to this sensitive data. This minimizes the risk of accidental disclosure or mishandling, which could lead to further breaches, regulatory violations, or legal liability for the individuals involved and the organization. The Safety Officer can audit access logs, review data handling procedures, and ensure that secure disposal methods are employed for any transient data generated during the response. This oversight is crucial in preventing what might be termed "secondary breaches" stemming from the response activities themselves.

Furthermore, the Safety Officer plays a vital role in safeguarding personnel against potential legal repercussions. In the aftermath of a significant cyber incident, investigations by regulatory bodies, law enforcement, or even civil litigation are common. Individuals involved in the response may be called upon to provide testimony or evidence regarding their actions. The Safety Officer, working closely with legal counsel and the Incident Commander, ensures that all response activities are documented appropriately and that personnel understand the importance of adhering to established protocols and legal advice. This includes advising responders on what they can and cannot discuss externally, especially with parties not directly involved in the response effort, and ensuring that all communications and actions are aligned with legal guidance provided. This protective role is essential for building a robust defense against potential future claims and ensuring that the organization and its employees can navigate the complex legal landscape that often follows a major security event.

A critical aspect of the Safety Officer's function in a cyber incident is to ensure that the response activities themselves do not inadvertently create new security vulnerabilities or operational hazards. For instance, hastily implemented temporary fixes or workarounds designed to restore functionality might introduce new weaknesses that could be exploited by adversaries. The Safety Officer scrutinizes proposed technical solutions and operational changes to identify any potential security trade-offs or unintended consequences. This might involve reviewing network configuration changes, access control modifications, or the deployment of new tools to ensure they do not compromise the overall security posture. Similarly, if the incident response involves physical aspects, such as securing data center access or managing equipment, the Safety Officer ensures that these physical security measures are maintained and that no new physical hazards are introduced. This requires a close working relationship with the technical teams in Operations and the analytical teams in Planning to understand the technical implications of their actions and to provide a safety and security-focused perspective.

The Safety Officer's involvement also extends to ensuring that the incident response process adheres to all relevant legal and regulatory requirements. Depending on the nature of the organization and the type of data involved, specific laws such as GDPR, CCPA, HIPAA, or PCI DSS may come into play. A cyber incident can trigger reporting obligations, data breach notification requirements, and specific timelines for remediation. The Safety Officer, in coordination with legal and compliance departments, ensures that the response team is aware of these obligations and that their actions are consistent with meeting them. This might involve confirming that notification timelines are being met, that evidence preservation adheres to legal standards, and that any required third-party notifications or engagements are properly managed. This proactive engagement helps prevent compliance failures that could exacerbate the impact of the incident and lead to further penalties.

Furthermore, the Safety Officer is instrumental in ensuring that the incident response plan itself is safe and effective. This involves reviewing the plan for any inherent risks or omissions that could endanger personnel or compromise the response. During exercises and simulations, the Safety Officer observes how the plan is executed, identifying areas where safety protocols might be inadequate or where procedures could lead to undue risk for responders. Lessons learned from these exercises, as well as from actual incidents, are then fed back into the planning process to refine and improve the safety aspects of the incident response framework. This continuous improvement cycle is vital for maintaining a resilient and safe incident response capability.

The Safety Officer also acts as an advocate for the well-being of the incident response team by ensuring that adequate resources are available to support their efforts safely. This could range from ensuring that personnel have access to necessary personal protective equipment if physical interventions are required, to providing adequate and secure workspaces that are conducive to focused work and minimize distractions or potential hazards. In a remote or hybrid incident response scenario, the Safety Officer might also address the ergonomics of home workstations, the security of home networks used for critical tasks, and the potential for isolation or blurred work-life boundaries that can contribute to stress and burnout. Ensuring access to proper nutrition, hydration, and even basic amenities during prolonged operations is also within the purview of the Safety Officer's concern, as these factors significantly impact performance and well-being under duress.

The principle of "do no harm" extends not just to the organization's data and systems, but crucially, to the people tasked with defending them. The Safety Officer ensures that the ethical considerations inherent in cybersecurity incident response are addressed. This includes ensuring that data collected during an investigation is handled with respect for privacy, that the response does not disproportionately impact certain groups within the organization or its customer base, and that transparency is maintained where appropriate and safe to do so. The Safety Officer acts as a conscience for the response, ensuring that the pursuit of technical resolution does not come at an unacceptable human cost or ethical compromise.

In essence, the Safety Officer in a cyber incident scenario is a multifaceted role that bridges the gap between technical execution and human welfare. They are the guardians of the responders, ensuring that while the organization fights off digital threats, its most valuable asset – its people – are protected from harm. Their proactive identification and mitigation of risks, whether related to fatigue, data exposure, legal liabilities, or secondary vulnerabilities, are indispensable to the overall success and sustainability of any incident response effort. By integrating safety considerations into the very fabric of the incident response framework, the Safety Officer contributes significantly to maintaining operational effectiveness, preserving organizational reputation, and upholding ethical standards during times of crisis. This often-understated role is, therefore, a cornerstone of a mature and resilient cybersecurity incident response capability.

The Liaison Officer plays a pivotal role in extending the reach of an incident response team beyond the confines of the organization. In the intricate and often rapidly evolving landscape of cybersecurity incidents, the ability to effectively communicate and coordinate with external agencies is not merely advantageous, it is frequently essential for a successful resolution. This subsection delves into the multifaceted responsibilities of the Liaison Officer, emphasizing their function as the primary conduit for interactions with a diverse array of external stakeholders. These stakeholders can encompass a broad spectrum, including law enforcement agencies (LEAs) such as the FBI, Interpol, or national cybercrime units; regulatory bodies responsible for enforcing data protection and privacy laws like the ICO in the UK or the FTC in the US; industry-specific information sharing and analysis centers (ISACs); and other governmental or non-governmental organizations that may possess relevant expertise or jurisdiction.

The proactive establishment of these liaisons is a cornerstone of effective incident response planning. Before an incident even occurs, the Liaison Officer, or the team responsible for this function, should identify key external partners, understand their roles and responsibilities, and pre-establish communication channels. This pre-existing relationship-building fosters an environment of trust and mutual understanding, which can significantly expedite crucial processes during a crisis. When a cyber incident strikes, especially one that is complex, widespread, or involves cross-jurisdictional elements, the ability to quickly engage these external entities can mean the difference between a contained event and a catastrophic breach. For instance, a ransomware attack that encrypts critical data might necessitate collaboration with LEAs to track down the perpetrators and potentially assist in decryption if a viable solution is offered. Similarly, a data breach involving personally identifiable information (PII) will almost certainly trigger obligations to notify relevant data protection authorities, making early engagement with those regulatory bodies paramount.

The scope of the Liaison Officer's responsibilities extends to facilitating the seamless flow of information. During an incident, different entities will possess pieces of a larger puzzle. Law enforcement may have intelligence on threat actor methodologies or infrastructure, while regulatory bodies will provide guidance on legal and compliance requirements. Industry partners might share threat intelligence that helps identify the scope or origin of an attack. The Liaison Officer acts as the central point for gathering this disparate information, ensuring it is disseminated appropriately to the internal incident response team, and relaying approved organizational information back to external parties. This requires a keen understanding of information classification, confidentiality agreements, and the legal ramifications of sharing sensitive data. The officer must be adept at translating technical jargon into language understandable by non-technical stakeholders and vice versa, ensuring that communication is both accurate and efficient.

Moreover, the Liaison Officer is instrumental in requesting and coordinating the deployment of external resources. Cyber incidents can quickly overwhelm an organization's internal capabilities. LEAs might be called upon for forensic investigations, digital evidence collection, or even to assist in the disruption of attacker infrastructure. Regulatory bodies may offer guidance on notification procedures or provide expertise on specific compliance frameworks. In some cases, specialized government agencies or international organizations might possess unique capabilities for tracking advanced persistent threats (APTs) or mitigating nation-state sponsored attacks. The Liaison Officer is responsible for articulating the organization's needs clearly to these external agencies, navigating their intake processes, and coordinating the logistical aspects of their involvement, ensuring that external support is integrated effectively into the overall response strategy without creating additional chaos or security risks.

The cultivation of trust and the presentation of a unified front are intangible yet critical outcomes facilitated by the Liaison Officer. When an organization demonstrates a willingness to cooperate with external agencies, share relevant information responsibly, and adhere to regulatory guidance, it builds credibility. This is particularly important in the aftermath of a significant incident, where public perception, investor confidence, and regulatory scrutiny can be intense. A well-managed relationship with external partners, spearheaded by the Liaison Officer, can help to mitigate negative publicity, demonstrate responsible crisis management, and potentially lead to more favorable outcomes from regulatory investigations or legal proceedings. Conversely, a lack of cooperation or a breakdown in communication can exacerbate an already dire situation, leading to increased penalties, reputational damage, and prolonged recovery times.

The Liaison Officer's role is not static; it is a dynamic function that requires continuous engagement and adaptation. This involves not only responding to immediate incident needs but also participating in ongoing dialogues, exercises, and policy discussions with external bodies. For instance, participating in joint cyber exercises with LEAs or regulatory agencies can help to refine communication protocols, identify potential bottlenecks, and strengthen collaborative response capabilities for future events. Building and maintaining these relationships requires consistent effort, including attending industry forums, participating in working groups, and providing feedback on proposed regulations or best practices. This proactive engagement ensures that the organization remains informed about evolving threat landscapes, emerging legal requirements, and the capabilities of its external partners, thereby enhancing its overall resilience.

Consider a scenario where a sophisticated supply chain attack compromises a critical software used by numerous organizations. The Liaison Officer within the affected organization would be the point person for coordinating with the software vendor's incident response team, potentially other affected customers (through industry ISACs), and relevant cybersecurity agencies. This cross-organizational coordination is vital to understand the full scope of the compromise, share indicators of compromise (IOCs), and develop unified remediation strategies. Without a dedicated liaison, fragmented communication could lead to delayed patching, inconsistent containment efforts, and a greater overall risk to the ecosystem of users. The Liaison Officer acts as the conductor of this complex orchestra of external entities, ensuring that each plays their part effectively and in harmony with the others.

Furthermore, the Liaison Officer must possess a nuanced understanding of the legal frameworks governing cyber incidents in different jurisdictions. A data breach might involve customers in multiple countries, each with its own set of data protection laws and reporting requirements. The Liaison Officer, in conjunction with legal counsel, must navigate these complexities, ensuring that notifications are made to the correct authorities within the stipulated timeframes. This could involve working with international law enforcement agencies if the threat actors are located abroad, or engaging with foreign data protection authorities if personal data of their citizens has been compromised. The ability to bridge legal and cultural divides is a crucial aspect of this role, ensuring that the organization acts in compliance with all applicable laws and regulations.

The Liaison Officer also serves as a vital bridge for knowledge transfer. External agencies often possess insights into emerging threats, advanced adversary tactics, and innovative defensive techniques that may not yet be widely known or understood within a particular organization. By engaging with these bodies, the Liaison Officer can bring this valuable external knowledge back into the organization, informing threat intelligence efforts, security awareness training, and the refinement of incident response plans. Similarly, the organization's experiences and lessons learned from an incident can be valuable to external partners, contributing to the collective understanding of cyber threats and the development of more effective countermeasures. This reciprocal exchange of information is a key benefit of strong external liaison.

The effectiveness of the Liaison Officer is intrinsically linked to their ability to manage expectations and communicate limitations. While external agencies can provide invaluable support, they also have their own priorities, resource constraints, and legal mandates. The Liaison Officer must be adept at articulating what is feasible and what is not, managing the expectations of both internal stakeholders regarding external support and external agencies regarding the organization's capabilities and constraints. This involves transparent communication about the nature of the incident, the steps already taken, and the information that can be shared, always within the bounds of security and legal considerations.

In essence, the Liaison Officer is the external face of the incident response effort. They are the architects of collaboration, the translators of complex information, and the navigators of intricate legal and jurisdictional landscapes. Their proactive cultivation of relationships, their adeptness at facilitating communication and information sharing, and their ability to coordinate the deployment of external resources are indispensable for organizations facing the multifaceted challenges of modern cyber threats. In an era where cyber incidents rarely respect organizational or national boundaries, the Liaison Officer's role in fostering cooperation and presenting a unified defense is more critical than ever before. Their work ensures that the organization is not isolated in its fight against cyber adversaries but is instead part of a broader, coordinated effort, maximizing the chances of a swift and effective resolution while minimizing potential collateral damage and legal repercussions. This function, though often operating behind the scenes, is a fundamental pillar of a robust and resilient incident response capability.

The officer's mandate also includes the critical task of managing external perceptions during a crisis. When an incident occurs, stakeholders such as customers, partners, investors, and the media will be looking for information and reassurance. The Liaison Officer, working in close coordination with the communications team, ensures that consistent, accurate, and timely information is provided to external parties. This avoids conflicting messages, prevents the spread of misinformation, and helps to maintain confidence in the organization's ability to manage the situation. The tone and content of these external communications are carefully managed, often involving legal review to ensure compliance with disclosure obligations and to avoid inadvertently admitting liability. For example, in the case of a data breach, the Liaison Officer would liaise with regulatory bodies regarding notification requirements and with communications teams to draft public statements or customer advisories that are informative yet measured, adhering to legal advice.

The strategic importance of pre-incident engagement cannot be overstated. Before any cyber crisis unfolds, the Liaison Officer should be actively involved in developing and maintaining a directory of key external contacts. This includes understanding the escalation paths within LEAs, the appropriate points of contact for specific regulatory bodies, and the mechanisms for engaging with industry-specific threat intelligence sharing groups. This proactive preparation involves understanding the reporting requirements for different types of incidents, the types of information that are typically requested by law enforcement or regulators, and the legal frameworks that govern information sharing. Building these relationships is not a task that can be effectively undertaken in the heat of an incident; it requires sustained effort and investment in professional networking and relationship management. This groundwork ensures that when an incident occurs, the pathways for communication and collaboration are already established, significantly shortening response times and improving overall effectiveness.

Furthermore, the Liaison Officer must be a keen observer of the evolving threat landscape and the corresponding regulatory environment. Changes in data protection laws, new international agreements on cybercrime, or shifts in the modus operandi of threat actors all have implications for how an organization must engage with external entities. The Liaison Officer stays abreast of these developments, providing critical intelligence to the incident response team and to senior leadership. This foresight allows the organization to adapt its response strategies and communication plans proactively, ensuring continued compliance and effective collaboration. For instance, the introduction of a new data privacy regulation in a key market would require the Liaison Officer to engage with relevant authorities in that jurisdiction to understand the implications for incident reporting and data handling, and to ensure the organization's response protocols are updated accordingly.

The Liaison Officer also acts as an internal champion for external collaboration, educating internal teams on the importance of engaging with external agencies and the procedures involved. Incident response team members may be focused on the technical aspects of containment and eradication and might not fully appreciate the legal or procedural requirements of external interactions. The Liaison Officer clarifies these requirements, provides guidance on what information can be shared, and helps to navigate the internal approval processes for external communications. This internal advocacy is crucial for ensuring that the organization's external engagement is consistent, compliant, and effective, preventing ad-hoc or unauthorized disclosures that could compromise the response effort or create legal liabilities.

In the context of a national security incident, the Liaison Officer's role can escalate significantly. For incidents involving nation-state actors, critical infrastructure compromise, or widespread impact on public services, the engagement with national cybersecurity agencies, intelligence services, and potentially military cyber commands becomes paramount. The Liaison Officer navigates the protocols and security clearances required for such high-level interactions, ensuring that classified or sensitive information is shared appropriately and that the organization's actions are coordinated with national response efforts. This level of engagement requires a deep understanding of government structures, inter-agency cooperation frameworks, and the specific legal authorities that govern national cybersecurity operations. The Liaison Officer's ability to operate effectively in this complex governmental arena is crucial for protecting national interests and ensuring a coordinated, robust defense against sophisticated threats.

The concept of Information Sharing and Analysis Centers (ISACs) and similar industry forums is also a key area of the Liaison Officer's responsibility. These organizations serve as vital hubs for threat intelligence exchange within specific sectors, such as finance, healthcare, or energy. The Liaison Officer ensures that the organization actively participates in its relevant ISAC, contributing relevant threat indicators and receiving valuable intelligence that can aid in proactive defense and incident response. During an incident, the ISAC can be an invaluable resource for understanding if other organizations in the sector are experiencing similar attacks, identifying common tactics, techniques, and procedures (TTPs) used by the adversary, and sharing effective mitigation strategies. The Liaison Officer manages the organization's membership, facilitates the sharing of information, and ensures that intelligence gained from these forums is integrated into the organization's security posture.

Finally, the Liaison Officer's role embodies the principle that cybersecurity is a collective endeavor. No single organization, however well-resourced, can effectively combat the ever-evolving landscape of cyber threats in isolation. By building and nurturing robust relationships with external agencies, industry partners, and regulatory bodies, the Liaison Officer ensures that the organization is not only prepared to respond to incidents but is also an integral part of a broader, collaborative defense ecosystem. This interconnectedness amplifies the effectiveness of individual response efforts, fosters a shared understanding of threats, and ultimately contributes to a more secure digital environment for all. The Liaison Officer's diligent work in forging these external connections is, therefore, a critical component of an organization's overall cyber resilience strategy.

Proactive and vigilant incident detection forms the bedrock of any effective cybersecurity defense strategy. Without robust mechanisms to identify malicious activities or policy violations as they occur, or shortly thereafter, an organization remains vulnerable to significant damage, data loss, and reputational harm. The goal of incident detection is to achieve the shortest possible time between the initiation of a malicious act and its discovery, thereby minimizing the potential impact. This requires a multi-layered approach, leveraging a combination of automated tools, human observation, and external intelligence.

One of the most fundamental automated detection mechanisms is the Intrusion Detection System (IDS). IDSs are designed to monitor network traffic or system activities for suspicious patterns that indicate a potential security breach. These systems can operate in various modes. Network-based IDSs (NIDS) analyze traffic passing through a specific network segment, looking for known attack signatures or deviations from normal traffic patterns. For example, a NIDS might flag an unusual surge in outbound traffic from a server that typically has low network activity, potentially indicating data exfiltration. Conversely, Host-based IDSs (HIDS) are installed on individual systems (servers, workstations) and monitor system logs, file integrity, and process activity for signs of compromise. A HIDS might detect unauthorized modifications to critical system files or the execution of suspicious processes, alerting administrators to a potential local intrusion. The effectiveness of IDS relies heavily on its configuration and the quality of its signature databases or anomaly detection models. Regular updates to signature files are crucial to detect the latest known threats, while well-tuned anomaly detection algorithms can identify novel or zero-day attacks that lack pre-defined signatures. However, both signature-based and anomaly-based detection can generate false positives (flagging legitimate activity as malicious) or false negatives (failing to detect actual malicious activity), underscoring the need for human oversight and correlation with other detection sources.

Complementing the capabilities of IDSs are Security Information and Event Management (SIEM) systems. SIEMs are powerful aggregation and correlation engines that collect log data from a vast array of sources across the entire IT infrastructure. This includes logs from network devices (firewalls, routers, switches), servers (operating systems, applications), endpoints (workstations, mobile devices), security tools (IDPS, antivirus), and even cloud services. By centralizing and normalizing these diverse log streams, SIEMs enable security analysts to gain a holistic view of security events. The real power of a SIEM lies in its correlation capabilities. It can link seemingly isolated events from different sources to identify sophisticated, multi-stage attacks that individual tools might miss. For instance, a SIEM could correlate an alert from a firewall about an unauthorized port scan, followed by a login attempt from an unexpected IP address on a sensitive server, and then a spike in CPU usage on that server. This pattern, when viewed together, strongly suggests a targeted attack. SIEMs also play a critical role in compliance and forensics by providing a centralized, searchable repository of audit logs. Effective SIEM deployment requires careful planning, including defining what logs to collect, establishing appropriate retention policies, and developing sophisticated correlation rules and alerts that are relevant to the organization's specific threat landscape and risk profile. Regularly reviewing and refining these rules is essential to reduce alert fatigue and ensure that critical events are not overlooked amidst a deluge of notifications.

Beyond automated systems, human observation and reporting remain a vital component of incident detection. Employees, as the first line of defense, often encounter unusual or suspicious activities that may not trigger automated alerts. This could range from receiving a phishing email and recognizing its deceptive nature, to noticing a colleague's computer behaving erratically, or observing unauthorized physical access to sensitive areas. Establishing clear, accessible, and non-punitive channels for employees to report such suspicions is paramount. This might involve a dedicated email address, a ticketing system, or a specific contact within the IT or security department. Training employees on common cyber threats, such as phishing, social engineering, and malware, empowers them to become active participants in the detection process. When an employee reports a suspicious activity, it is crucial that this report is taken seriously and followed up promptly. A well-defined process for handling user-reported incidents ensures that these valuable insights are not lost and can potentially lead to the early detection of a developing incident.

Threat intelligence feeds provide an external perspective that can significantly enhance an organization's detection capabilities. These feeds, sourced from various vendors, government agencies, and security communities, offer information about emerging threats, known malicious IP addresses and domains, indicators of compromise (IOCs) such as file hashes or registry keys associated with malware, and details about attacker tactics, techniques, and procedures (TTPs). Integrating these feeds into security tools, such as SIEMs, firewalls, and endpoint detection and response (EDR) solutions, allows for proactive identification of threats. For example, if a threat intelligence feed indicates that a particular IP address is being used by a known command-and-control (C2) server for a specific malware strain, a firewall configured to block traffic to or from that IP can prevent an infection before it even begins. Similarly, EDR solutions can use IOCs to scan endpoints for any signs of compromise. The value of threat intelligence is maximized when it is contextualized to the organization's specific industry, technology stack, and threat landscape. Organizations often subscribe to curated feeds that are tailored to their environment, or they may participate in information-sharing groups to receive more relevant intelligence.

Once a potential incident is detected, either through automated systems, user reports, or threat intelligence, the next critical step is accurate and timely reporting. A well-defined incident reporting mechanism ensures that suspected incidents are escalated efficiently to the appropriate personnel for assessment. This reporting process should be standardized to ensure consistency and completeness. A typical incident report form might include fields such as: the date and time of detection, the source of the detection (e.g., IDS alert, user report, SIEM correlation), a description of the suspected incident, the systems or data potentially affected, the impact of the incident to date, and the actions already taken. This standardized approach ensures that all necessary information is captured upfront, facilitating a faster and more informed initial assessment.

The reporting mechanism should clearly outline the escalation path. For instance, an alert from an IDS might automatically generate a ticket in a security operations center (SOC) platform, which is then triaged by an analyst. If the analyst confirms a high-confidence incident, it would be escalated to a senior security engineer or incident response team lead. Similarly, a user reporting a suspicious email might be directed to submit a ticket through an internal IT service desk, which then routes it to the security team if the content suggests a security-related issue. The reporting procedure must also specify the urgency and severity levels associated with different types of potential incidents. For example, a suspected ransomware infection would be treated with the highest urgency, requiring immediate escalation, while a report of a single suspicious login attempt might be handled with lower priority, allowing for further investigation before triggering a full incident response.

The reporting channels should be readily accessible and clearly communicated to all relevant personnel. This includes not only IT and security staff but also potentially department heads, legal counsel, and executive leadership, depending on the severity and nature of the suspected incident. For example, reports of potential data breaches involving customer information would likely need to be communicated to the legal and compliance departments very quickly. Establishing clear communication protocols and contact lists for incident escalation is a crucial part of the preparedness phase. This ensures that when an incident occurs, there is no confusion or delay in alerting the right individuals.

Moreover, the reporting mechanism should facilitate the capture of not only the initial detection but also any subsequent findings or developments during the initial assessment phase. This creates a historical record of the event, which is invaluable for post-incident analysis, lessons learned, and tuning future detection and reporting processes. Some organizations utilize specialized incident response platforms or ticketing systems that are specifically designed to manage the lifecycle of an incident, from detection and reporting through investigation, containment, eradication, and recovery. These platforms can automate aspects of the reporting and escalation process, enforce workflows, and provide a centralized repository of all incident-related information.

The integration of threat intelligence into the reporting and detection process is also vital. When an alert is generated or a suspicious activity is reported, the system or analyst should be able to cross-reference it against known IOCs from threat intelligence feeds. If a match is found, this can significantly increase the confidence in the detection and inform the initial assessment of the incident's severity and scope. For example, if an IDS flags an outbound connection to an IP address that is listed on a reputable threat intelligence feed as a known C2 server, this strongly indicates a compromised system actively communicating with an attacker. This intelligence should be automatically included in the incident report or alert that is presented to the incident response team.

It is also important to consider the human element in reporting. Fear of reprisal or a lack of understanding of the reporting process can lead employees to hesitate in reporting potential incidents. Therefore, fostering a security-aware culture where reporting is encouraged and seen as a positive contribution is essential. This involves clear communication about the importance of reporting, providing easy-to-use reporting tools, and demonstrating that reports are handled professionally and without undue blame. Regular security awareness training should reinforce these messages and provide practical guidance on what constitutes a reportable event and how to report it.

In essence, the incident detection and reporting mechanisms work in concert to ensure that potential security threats are identified swiftly and brought to the attention of the incident response team. This involves a layered defense approach, utilizing automated tools like IDSs and SIEMs, leveraging external threat intelligence, and empowering human observers through clear reporting channels and security awareness training. The establishment of standardized reporting procedures ensures that when a potential incident is detected, it is accurately documented and promptly escalated, setting the stage for an effective and organized incident response. This proactive approach to detection and reporting is fundamental to minimizing the potential damage caused by cyberattacks and maintaining the overall security posture of the organization.

To further elaborate on the nuances of these mechanisms, let's consider the evolving landscape of threat detection. Traditional signature-based IDS systems, while still relevant, are increasingly challenged by the rise of polymorphic malware and sophisticated attack techniques that constantly change their TTPs to evade detection. This necessitates a greater reliance on behavioral analysis and machine learning-based anomaly detection. Modern SIEM systems are incorporating advanced analytics and AI to identify subtle deviations from normal network and user behavior that might indicate a compromise. For instance, a user who typically logs in from a specific geographic location and at a particular time of day suddenly logs in from an entirely different continent at an unusual hour, and then begins accessing sensitive data they have never accessed before, would trigger an anomaly detection alert. This kind of advanced analysis requires significant computational resources and sophisticated algorithms, but it offers a powerful way to detect novel and evasive threats.

The role of endpoint detection and response (EDR) solutions has also grown significantly in the detection phase. Unlike traditional antivirus software that primarily relies on known malware signatures, EDR systems continuously monitor endpoint activities, collecting rich telemetry data about processes, network connections, file system changes, and registry modifications. This data is then analyzed, often using behavioral analytics and machine learning, to identify malicious activity. When a suspected threat is detected, EDR solutions can provide incident response teams with deep visibility into the affected endpoint, enabling them to understand the attack chain, isolate the endpoint to prevent lateral movement, and remediate the threat. This detailed, endpoint-centric view is invaluable for both detection and subsequent investigation.

The integration of threat intelligence needs to move beyond simply blocking known bad IPs or domains. Advanced threat intelligence platforms allow for the ingestion of structured data (like STIX/TAXII feeds) and unstructured data (from security blogs, news articles, dark web forums) to build a more comprehensive picture of threats relevant to the organization. This intelligence can then be used to proactively hunt for threats within the network, rather than just passively waiting for alerts. Threat hunting involves proactively searching for evidence of compromise that may have evaded automated defenses. This requires skilled analysts who can ask the right questions, analyze log data, and utilize threat intelligence to guide their investigations.

Regarding user reporting, organizations can implement gamification techniques or reward systems to incentivize employees to report suspicious activities. For example, a monthly "security champion" award could be given to the employee who submits the most valuable security leads. This not only encourages reporting but also fosters a positive security culture. Furthermore, making the reporting process as simple as a single click from an email client or a dedicated mobile app can significantly lower the barrier to entry for employees.

When it comes to standardized reporting procedures, organizations should consider adopting frameworks like the MITRE ATT&CK® framework to describe attacker tactics and techniques observed during the detection and initial investigation phases. This provides a common language and structured way to categorize and report on threats, facilitating better analysis and communication. For instance, a report might state that an initial detection indicated "T1059.001: PowerShell Command and Scripting Interpreter" as a suspected technique, which then allows for more targeted follow-up investigations and reporting.

The speed and accuracy of reporting are critical. In high-impact scenarios, such as a widespread ransomware attack or a critical data breach, delays in reporting can lead to catastrophic consequences. Organizations need to have clear escalation matrices and defined communication channels that can be activated rapidly. This might involve pre-defined communication templates for different types of incidents and scenarios, allowing for quick dissemination of information to key stakeholders, including executive management, legal, and public relations teams. The incident response plan should detail these communication flows and include contact information for all relevant parties, ensuring that critical notifications are made without delay.

Furthermore, the reporting mechanism should not be a one-way street. Feedback loops are essential to improve the detection and reporting processes. When an incident is resolved, the incident response team should provide feedback to the individuals or systems that initially reported the suspected incident, explaining the outcome and, where appropriate, the steps taken. This reinforces the value of reporting and helps to refine the accuracy of future reports. Similarly, analysis of false positives from IDS alerts or SIEM correlations should lead to adjustments in system configurations or correlation rules to reduce noise and improve detection accuracy.

The digital transformation, with its increasing adoption of cloud computing, IoT devices, and remote workforces, introduces new complexities to incident detection and reporting. Cloud environments, for example, require visibility into logs from cloud service providers, as well as robust security configurations within the cloud. IoT devices, often with limited security capabilities, can present a significant attack surface, requiring specialized monitoring and reporting mechanisms. The dispersed nature of a remote workforce necessitates effective endpoint security and reliable methods for detecting and reporting incidents from devices outside the traditional corporate network perimeter. Incident detection strategies and reporting workflows must be adapted to account for these distributed and diverse IT environments.

In summary, the comprehensive approach to incident detection and reporting involves a blend of advanced technology, informed human vigilance, and structured processes. Leveraging sophisticated tools like IDSs, HIDS, SIEMs, and EDR solutions, combined with the strategic use of threat intelligence, forms the technological backbone. Empowering employees through security awareness training and providing accessible reporting channels ensures human oversight. Crucially, standardized reporting procedures, clear escalation paths, and continuous feedback loops are essential to ensure that detected anomalies are accurately assessed, promptly escalated, and effectively managed, thereby mitigating the impact of cyber threats and bolstering the organization's overall resilience. This proactive and integrated approach to identifying and reporting potential security incidents is a non-negotiable element of a mature cybersecurity program.

Upon the confirmation of a potential security event, either through automated alerts or human observation, the ensuing moments are critical. The phase of initial assessment and triage forms the immediate gateway into the formal incident response process. This stage is not merely about acknowledging an alert; it is a dynamic, rapid evaluation designed to understand what has happened, how severe it is, and what the immediate risks are. It's about quickly distinguishing between a false alarm and a genuine threat that requires immediate, significant intervention. The goal is to gather just enough information, as swiftly as possible, to make informed decisions about the next steps, preventing wasted effort on minor issues while ensuring that major threats receive the urgent attention they demand. This initial assessment acts as the primary filter, determining the trajectory of the incident response, from its earliest stages to the full activation of dedicated incident response teams and resources.

The methodology for this initial assessment and triage hinges on a structured yet agile approach. It begins with consolidating all available information related to the suspected incident. This involves bringing together the originating alert (e.g., an IDS signature match, a SIEM correlation rule trigger, a user's detailed report), any contextual data from related systems (e.g., network flow logs, endpoint telemetry, firewall logs), and initial observations from the first responder. The objective is to paint a preliminary picture of the event. Key questions must be addressed: What specific systems or data are involved? What is the observed behavior? When did the activity start, and when was it detected? Who or what appears to be responsible? What is the potential impact on business operations, data confidentiality, integrity, and availability? The answers to these questions will shape the subsequent triage decision. It's akin to a paramedic's rapid assessment of a patient – identifying the most critical symptoms to prioritize treatment.

A cornerstone of effective triage is the ability to categorize incidents based on their severity and potential impact. This categorization is not arbitrary; it is typically guided by pre-defined criteria established in an organization's incident response plan. These criteria often consider factors such as the sensitivity of the affected assets, the potential for data exfiltration or loss, the disruption to critical business functions, and the potential legal or reputational ramifications. For example, an unauthorized access attempt to a non-critical development server might be classified as low severity, manageable through standard IT procedures. In contrast, evidence of ransomware encryption spreading across production servers would undoubtedly be classified as critical severity, demanding immediate, full-scale incident response.

The categorization process directly informs the decision-making regarding resource allocation and the activation of the incident response structure. A low-severity incident might be assigned to a general IT support team or a junior security analyst for investigation and remediation, with reporting requirements kept to a minimum. However, a high-severity incident, such as a confirmed breach of sensitive customer data or a widespread denial-of-service attack against core services, would necessitate the immediate activation of the full incident response team (IRT). This typically involves invoking a formal incident response structure, which might include a designated incident commander, technical leads for different areas (e.g., network, endpoint, forensics), communication specialists, legal counsel, and executive liaisons. The swiftness of this decision is paramount, as delays in mobilizing the appropriate resources can exacerbate the damage and prolong recovery efforts.

The triage process also involves a rapid scope assessment. This means determining, as quickly as possible, how widespread the incident is. Is it confined to a single machine, or has it spread laterally across the network? Are multiple applications or services affected? Understanding the scope helps in estimating the resources needed and in prioritizing containment efforts. For instance, if an incident appears to be confined to a single isolated workstation, containment might involve simply disconnecting that machine from the network. If it's a widespread network compromise, containment strategies become far more complex, potentially involving the segmentation of critical network zones or the disabling of certain services.

Furthermore, the initial assessment must consider the potential impact on business operations. How critical are the affected systems? What is the immediate effect on users, customers, or partners? For example, if the incident involves the compromise of a public-facing web server that handles e-commerce transactions, the impact on revenue and customer trust is immediate and substantial, demanding urgent response.

Conversely, if a development server is compromised, the impact might be limited to a temporary setback in a project timeline, allowing for a more measured response. This understanding of business impact is crucial for prioritizing response efforts and communicating with stakeholders.

The triage phase is also where the first attempt is made to understand the nature of the threat. Is it malware? Is it an insider threat? Is it a sophisticated external actor? While a full forensic analysis will come later, initial indicators can provide valuable clues. For example, the types of alerts generated, the commands being executed on an affected system, or the network traffic patterns can offer early insights into the attacker's tactics, techniques, and procedures (TTPs). This preliminary understanding helps in selecting the right tools and expertise for the subsequent investigation.

It is essential to emphasize that the initial assessment and triage are iterative processes. Information gathered during this phase may lead to a re-evaluation of the incident's severity or scope. For example, an incident initially assessed as low severity might reveal itself to be more serious as further investigation uncovers evidence of data exfiltration. Similarly, an incident that appeared to be isolated might later be found to have spread to other systems. Therefore, the triage team must remain flexible and prepared to adjust their assessment and response strategy as new information emerges.

The communication aspect of triage is often overlooked but is critical. Even at this early stage, it is important to have a defined protocol for communicating findings. This doesn't necessarily mean alerting the entire organization, but rather ensuring that key personnel within the incident response framework are informed. This might include the incident response lead, IT management, and potentially legal counsel or public relations depending on the suspected severity. Clear, concise, and timely communication during triage prevents misunderstandings and ensures that everyone is working with the same understanding of the situation.

The decision to activate the full incident response structure is a significant one. It signifies a commitment of significant resources and a shift from routine operational management to a focused, coordinated effort to contain, eradicate, and recover from a security incident. This activation should be based on clear, predefined triggers established in the incident response plan. For instance, any incident involving confirmed unauthorized access to sensitive data, significant disruption of critical business operations, or potential legal liabilities would typically trigger the full IRT activation. The incident response plan should clearly delineate who has the authority to make this decision and what the immediate steps are upon activation.

When the full incident response structure is activated, a designated incident commander takes charge. This individual is responsible for overseeing the entire incident response effort, ensuring that tasks are assigned, resources are managed effectively, and communication flows smoothly. The incident commander relies heavily on the information gathered during the initial assessment and triage phase to direct the team's efforts. For example, if triage indicated that the incident involved ransomware, the incident commander would ensure that the containment team focuses on isolating infected systems and preventing further spread, while the recovery team prepares to restore data from backups.

In scenarios where an incident is deemed to be of lower severity, it may be managed through standard operational procedures rather than a full IRT activation. This could involve a system administrator troubleshooting a performance issue that was initially flagged as suspicious, or a network engineer investigating an unusual traffic pattern that turns out to be a legitimate, albeit unusual, business activity. Even in these cases, it's crucial to document the investigation and resolution process. This documentation serves as valuable input for future threat hunting, tuning of detection systems, and refining the triage criteria. It ensures that even "minor" incidents contribute to the overall learning and improvement of the security posture.

The effectiveness of the initial assessment and triage process is directly proportional to the organization's preparedness. This preparation involves several key elements:

Firstly, a well-defined and regularly updated incident response plan is paramount. This plan should clearly outline the criteria for incident severity, the steps for initial assessment, the triggers for IRT activation, and the roles and responsibilities of various individuals and teams. Without such a plan, triage efforts can become chaotic and inconsistent, leading to suboptimal decision-making.

Secondly, robust detection and alerting mechanisms are essential. The accuracy and relevance of alerts directly impact the quality of information available during triage. An abundance of false positives can overwhelm the triage team, making it difficult to identify genuine threats. Conversely, missed detections mean that critical incidents might not even enter the triage process. Therefore, continuous tuning of security tools and vigilant monitoring are indispensable.

Thirdly, effective communication channels must be established and tested. This includes clear pathways for escalating alerts, reporting suspicions, and disseminating information within the incident response team and to relevant stakeholders. During triage, rapid and accurate communication can make the difference between a contained incident and a widespread disaster.

Fourthly, personnel involved in triage must be adequately trained and equipped. This training should cover incident categorization, risk assessment, basic investigative techniques, and the use of relevant tools. They need to understand the business context of the organization to accurately assess the impact of an incident. Furthermore, they should have access to the necessary tools and information, such as logs, network maps, and asset inventories, to perform their assessment effectively.

Finally, regular exercises and simulations are crucial for honing the triage process. Tabletop exercises, walk-throughs, and even full-scale drills allow teams to practice their assessment and decision-making skills in a controlled environment. These exercises help identify gaps in the plan, weaknesses in communication, and areas where training needs to be enhanced. They also build confidence and familiarity among the team members, ensuring a more cohesive and effective response when a real incident occurs.

The initial assessment and triage phase is, therefore, far more than a cursory glance at an alert. It is a structured, critical function that demands speed, accuracy, and informed decision-making. It is the gatekeeper of the incident response lifecycle, ensuring that organizational resources are deployed efficiently and effectively to mitigate threats. By understanding the nature, scope, and potential impact of a suspected incident, and by making rapid, data-driven decisions about escalation and resource allocation, organizations can significantly improve their ability to manage and recover from cyberattacks, thereby safeguarding their critical assets and maintaining business continuity. The process transforms a raw alert into actionable intelligence, setting the stage for a successful containment, eradication, and recovery effort. This initial diagnostic capability is a testament to an organization's maturity in managing cyber risk.

The transition from initial assessment and triage to the formal activation of the Incident Command System (ICS) is a pivotal moment in cybersecurity incident response. This activation is not a routine administrative step; it represents a deliberate decision to mobilize a structured, hierarchical command and control framework designed to manage complex and potentially high-impact events. It signifies that the incident has exceeded the scope of everyday operational handling and requires a coordinated, resource-intensive response. Defining clear triggers for this activation and establishing precise procedures for its implementation are paramount to ensuring that response efforts are timely, efficient, and effective. Without these, organizations risk delays, confusion, and ultimately, a degraded ability to mitigate damage and restore normal operations.

The decision to activate the ICS is typically driven by specific, predefined triggers outlined within the organization's Incident Response Plan (IRP). These triggers serve as objective criteria, moving the decision-making process beyond subjective interpretation and towards a standardized protocol. One of the most significant triggers is the **severity of the threat**. Incidents are often classified into categories such as low, medium, high, or critical, based on a combination of factors including the type of threat, the systems affected, the sensitivity of data involved, and the potential operational impact. A low-severity incident, such as a single instance of malware on a non-critical workstation that is quickly contained, might not warrant ICS activation. However, an incident classified as high or critical—for example, confirmed unauthorized access to a database containing personally identifiable information (PII), or a distributed denial-of-service (DDoS) attack that is successfully disrupting core business services—will almost invariably trigger the activation of the ICS. This immediate escalation ensures that the organization is prepared to deploy the necessary resources and command structure to confront a substantial threat.

Another crucial trigger relates to the **potential for widespread impact**. If initial triage suggests that an incident is not isolated to a single endpoint or system but has the potential to spread across the network, affect multiple business units, or impact a large number of users or customers, ICS activation becomes imperative. This includes scenarios like worm propagation, credential stuffing attacks that could compromise numerous accounts, or phishing campaigns that may have already enticed a significant portion of the workforce to click on malicious links. The ability of ICS to provide a scalable and flexible command structure is particularly valuable in these situations, allowing for the efficient management of multiple response teams addressing different facets of the widespread incident.

The **involvement of critical systems or data** also serves as a potent trigger for ICS activation. Critical systems are those that are essential for the organization's core operations, revenue generation, or compliance with regulatory requirements. If an incident compromises or threatens these systems – such as a payment processing gateway, an enterprise resource planning (ERP) system, a customer relationship management (CRM) database, or a critical infrastructure control system – the potential for catastrophic business disruption is high. Similarly, the compromise of highly sensitive data, such as intellectual property, trade secrets, executive communications, or classified government information, necessitates a robust and coordinated response that the ICS is designed to provide. The potential for significant financial loss, regulatory penalties, reputational damage, or even national security implications associated with such incidents mandates the immediate engagement of the ICS.

Beyond these primary triggers, other factors can also necessitate ICS activation. These may include **legal or**

regulatory implications. If an incident has the potential to lead to significant legal liabilities, such as a data breach reportable under GDPR, CCPA, or HIPAA, or if it involves potential criminal activity, the ICS activation ensures that legal counsel and relevant compliance officers are brought into the response process early and under a structured command. Similarly, incidents with a high potential for **significant reputational damage**, which could erode customer trust or investor confidence, often trigger ICS activation to ensure that communications are managed effectively by designated spokespersons and public relations professionals. The **duration and persistence of the incident** can also be a factor; if an incident cannot be resolved through standard operational procedures and persists over an extended period, it may warrant escalation to the ICS framework. Finally, the **inability of the initial response team to effectively manage the incident** due to a lack of resources, specialized skills, or authority is a clear signal that ICS activation is required.

Once the decision to activate the ICS has been made, a series of well-defined procedures must be followed to ensure a smooth and organized transition. The cornerstone of this process is the **notification of key personnel**. The IRP should clearly delineate who needs to be notified upon ICS activation. This typically includes the designated Incident Commander, the members of the core Incident Response Team (IRT), senior IT management, legal counsel, public relations, and relevant executive leadership. The notification process should be rapid and reliable, utilizing multiple communication channels if necessary (e.g., phone, secure messaging, email) to ensure that all parties receive the alert promptly. The notification should clearly state that ICS has been activated, the nature and severity of the incident, and the immediate next steps.

Following notification, the immediate priority is to **establish the initial command structure**. This involves identifying and appointing the Incident Commander, who is the overall leader responsible for managing the incident response effort. The Incident Commander may be pre-assigned in the IRP or selected based on their experience, expertise, and authority. In some organizations, the activation of ICS might automatically assign the Director of Security Operations or a Chief Information Security Officer (CISO) as the initial Incident Commander, depending on the severity. Simultaneously, other key roles within the ICS structure begin to form. This might include appointing deputy incident commanders, section chiefs (e.g., Operations, Planning, Logistics, Finance/Administration), and technical leads for specific areas such as network security, endpoint forensics, or application security. The goal is to quickly assemble the core leadership of the response effort, even if the full complement of personnel will be brought in over time.

The formalization of the command structure is often marked by the **convening of the first incident briefing**, also known as an incident kick-off meeting or an initial operational period briefing. This is a critical event where the Incident Commander brings together the key response personnel to establish a common operating picture, define objectives, and initiate action. The initial briefing typically covers:

Incident Overview: A concise summary of what is known about the incident, including its origin, observed symptoms, and initial impact assessment.

Severity and Scope: A reiteration of the incident's severity classification and the current understanding of its scope, acknowledging any uncertainties.

Objectives: Clear, measurable, achievable, relevant, and time-bound (SMART) objectives for the current operational period. These objectives might include containment of the threat, eradication of malware, preservation of evidence, or restoration of critical services.

Strategy and Tactics: The overall strategy for responding to the incident and the specific tactics that will be employed by different teams.

Roles and Responsibilities: A clear assignment of tasks and responsibilities to individual team members and sub-teams within the ICS structure. This ensures accountability and prevents duplication of effort or critical gaps.

Resource Requirements: Identification of any immediate resource needs, such as specialized personnel, equipment, software tools, or external support.

Communication Plan: Establishment of internal and external communication protocols, including who is responsible for communicating with stakeholders, what information will be shared, and the frequency of updates.

Action Items: Specific tasks assigned to individuals or teams with clear deadlines.

This initial briefing is essential for aligning the entire response team, fostering a shared understanding of the situation, and ensuring that everyone is working towards the same goals. It marks the definitive shift from ad-hoc response to a structured, managed operation under the Incident Command System. The Incident Commander will utilize this briefing to ensure that the response efforts are focused and effective, preventing the team from becoming overwhelmed or disorganized by the complexities of the incident.

The ICS framework, once activated, provides a robust and adaptable structure for managing the incident response lifecycle. It allows for scalability, meaning that as the incident evolves or requires more resources, the structure can expand to accommodate new teams and functions without compromising the overall command and control. Conversely, if the incident is contained and the response efforts can be scaled back, the structure can be streamlined accordingly. This flexibility is a key reason why ICS is the preferred model for managing significant cybersecurity incidents.

The procedures for activating and operating within the ICS must be thoroughly documented in the organization's IRP and regularly tested through tabletop exercises, simulations, and actual incident response drills. This ensures that when a real incident occurs, the activation process is not a chaotic, unplanned event but a well-rehearsed transition into a state of coordinated, effective response. The clarity of triggers and the rigor of procedures are the bedrock upon which successful incident management is built, transforming a potential crisis into a manageable, albeit challenging, operational event. The ICS activation, therefore, is not merely a procedural formality; it is a strategic decision that signals a heightened level of organizational readiness and commitment to defending its digital assets and operational integrity.

Furthermore, the transition into ICS activation necessitates a clear delineation of authority and responsibility. The Incident Commander, by definition, holds the ultimate authority for managing the incident response. However, their effectiveness hinges on the ability to delegate tasks and empower section chiefs and team leads to execute their assigned responsibilities. This collaborative approach, guided by the hierarchical structure of ICS, ensures that decision-making is both centralized at the command level and decentralized at the operational level, allowing for agility and specialized expertise to be applied efficiently. The initial briefing serves as the critical forum where this delegation and empowerment are formally established for the current operational period.

The procedures also extend to the physical or virtual "Incident Command Post" (ICP). While for many cybersecurity incidents, this ICP might be a virtual war room or a dedicated communication channel, for highly severe events, it might involve a physical location where key response personnel convene. The establishment of a designated ICP, whether physical or virtual, ensures that there is a central point of coordination and communication for the response team, minimizing confusion and maximizing efficiency. This also helps in maintaining situational awareness among all involved parties. The activation process must include protocols for setting up and operating this ICP, ensuring that it is equipped with the necessary communication tools, information displays, and collaborative platforms.

Moreover, the activation of ICS often implies a shift in operational priorities. Routine IT operations may be temporarily deprioritized or re-tasked to support incident response efforts. For example, network engineers might be redirected from routine maintenance to focus on network segmentation and traffic analysis. System administrators might pivot from patching systems to isolating potentially compromised endpoints. This shift requires clear communication and authorization from IT management and executive leadership, which is facilitated by the formal ICS activation and the accompanying briefings. The Incident Commander, in consultation with relevant stakeholders, must ensure that these operational shifts are understood and supported across the organization.

The procedural aspects of ICS activation also encompass the **logging and documentation** of all activities. From the moment of ICS activation, every decision, action, communication, and observation must be meticulously recorded. This documentation is vital for several reasons: it provides a chronological record of the response, supports post-incident analysis and lessons learned, serves as evidence for legal or forensic purposes, and helps in justifying resource allocation and expenditures. The Incident Planning Section, once formed, typically takes responsibility for maintaining this comprehensive incident log. The initial briefing should emphasize the importance of diligent record-keeping to all participants.

The reliance on pre-defined triggers and established procedures is a testament to the principle of **preparedness** in incident response. Organizations that invest time and resources in developing a robust IRP, clearly defining ICS activation criteria, and regularly training their personnel on these procedures will be far better equipped to manage a crisis when it strikes. The activation of ICS is not an end in itself, but rather the formal commencement of a structured, methodical, and resource-intensive effort to neutralize a threat, restore affected systems, and minimize damage. The success of this entire process is directly proportional to the clarity of its initiation.

In summary, the activation of the Incident Command System for a cybersecurity incident is a critical step that transforms a reactive security event into a managed response. This activation is triggered by objective criteria related to threat severity, potential impact, and the involvement of critical assets, ensuring that escalation is timely and appropriate. The subsequent procedures—notifying key personnel, establishing the command structure, and convening an initial briefing—are designed to create a clear, coordinated, and efficient operational framework. By adhering to these triggers and procedures, organizations can ensure that their response efforts are well-organized, effectively resourced, and ultimately successful in mitigating the damage caused by sophisticated cyber threats. This structured approach underscores the maturity of an organization's cybersecurity program, demonstrating its capacity to not only detect threats but also to manage them decisively and systematically.

The success of any cybersecurity incident response hinges significantly on the individual appointed as the Incident Commander (IC). This role is not merely an administrative designation; it is the lynchpin that holds the entire response effort together, particularly during the critical initial stages. From the moment of escalation and the formal activation of the Incident Command System (ICS), the Incident Commander assumes the mantle of ultimate responsibility for managing the incident. This encompasses a multifaceted set of duties that begin with gaining a comprehensive understanding of the evolving situation, establishing a clear strategic direction, and initiating immediate actions to mitigate the threat. The IC's leadership style, decisiveness, and ability to communicate effectively set the tone for the entire response, influencing the morale, focus, and efficacy of all involved personnel. Without a strong and capable Incident Commander, even the most well-defined incident response plan can falter, leading to a chaotic, inefficient, and ultimately less successful outcome.

Upon assuming command, the Incident Commander's immediate priority is to establish situational awareness. This involves actively seeking and synthesizing information from all available sources. This could include reports from the initial detection and analysis teams, alerts from security monitoring tools, input from system administrators about affected infrastructure, and intelligence gathered by threat hunters. The IC must quickly develop a high-level understanding of what has happened, what systems are involved, the potential scope of the compromise, and the nature of the threat actor, if known. This initial assessment is rarely complete; it is a dynamic process that evolves as more information becomes available.

The IC must be adept at dealing with ambiguity and incomplete data, making informed decisions based on the best available intelligence while acknowledging the inherent uncertainties. This might involve requesting immediate data dumps from security logs, initiating network traffic analysis, or tasking forensic investigators to begin preserving evidence on critical systems. The IC's role is to steer this information gathering process, ensuring that the most critical questions are being answered and that the response is moving in a logical direction.

A crucial aspect of the Incident Commander's initial responsibilities is the establishment of clear, actionable objectives. These objectives, derived from the overall incident response strategy and tailored to the current phase of the incident, provide focus and direction for the entire response team. They must be SMART: Specific, Measurable, Achievable, Relevant, and Time-bound. For instance, an initial objective might be to "Contain the lateral movement of the ransomware payload within the finance department's network segment within the next two hours," or "Identify all compromised user credentials associated with the administrative portal by the end of the current operational period." These objectives guide the selection of tactics and the allocation of resources. The IC, in collaboration with subject matter experts within the response team, crafts these objectives, ensuring they align with the organization's overarching goals, which often include protecting critical data, restoring business operations, and minimizing financial and reputational damage. The ability of the IC to articulate these objectives clearly and concisely ensures that every member of the response team understands their contribution to the overarching mission.

Following the assessment of the situation and the establishment of objectives, the Incident Commander is responsible for assigning initial response tasks. This delegation is critical for efficient resource utilization and for ensuring that critical actions are taken promptly. The IC must leverage the strengths and expertise of the individuals within the activated ICS structure. This might involve assigning specific responsibilities to Section Chiefs if they have already been appointed. For example, the Operations Section Chief might be tasked with coordinating containment efforts, while the Planning Section Chief might be directed to begin developing a detailed timeline of events and identifying resource needs. Technical leads might be directed to focus on specific areas such as malware analysis, network forensics, or endpoint isolation. The IC must ensure that these assignments are clear, that the individuals understand their roles and responsibilities, and that they have the necessary authority and resources to execute their tasks. Effective delegation empowers the team while ensuring accountability.

The Incident Commander also plays a vital role in managing communications, both internal and external. Internally, the IC is the central point of contact for the response team. They ensure that information flows effectively between different sub-teams and that a common operating picture is maintained. This involves conducting regular briefings, facilitating information sharing, and resolving any inter-team conflicts or communication breakdowns. Externally, the IC, often in conjunction with Public Relations or Legal departments, may be involved in approving or directing communications to stakeholders, including executive leadership, legal counsel, regulatory bodies, and potentially affected customers or the public. The IC must ensure that all communications are accurate, consistent, and strategically aligned with the overall response goals. Misinformation or poorly managed communications can exacerbate an incident, leading to panic, loss of trust, and increased reputational damage. Therefore, the IC's oversight of communication is paramount.

Furthermore, the Incident Commander's leadership during the initial response phase is crucial for maintaining team morale and focus. Cybersecurity incidents can be stressful, high-pressure events. The IC must project an aura of calm competence, demonstrating confidence in the team's ability to manage the situation. This involves providing encouragement, acknowledging the hard work of the response personnel, and making decisive leadership decisions, even when faced with incomplete information. The IC's ability to remain objective, avoid panic, and maintain a structured approach can significantly influence the psychological state of the response team, enabling them to perform at their best. They are the beacon of leadership in what can be a chaotic and disorienting environment.

The concept of "escalation of authority" is also inherent in the Incident Commander's role. As the incident evolves, or as new information comes to light, the IC may need to escalate certain decisions or requests to higher levels of management or even the board of directors. This could involve requesting additional resources beyond the initial budget, seeking approval for disruptive but necessary containment measures, or deciding on the strategic direction of the response when faced with significant business impact.

The IC acts as the conduit for these escalations, ensuring that the necessary information is presented clearly and persuasively to decision-makers.

In essence, the Incident Commander is the strategic architect and operational conductor of the cybersecurity incident response during its nascent stages. They are the individual who transforms raw data and reactive measures into a coherent, organized, and purposeful effort. Their ability to rapidly assess, strategize, delegate, and communicate under pressure is what differentiates a controlled, effective response from a potential catastrophe. The foundation of a successful incident response is laid by the Incident Commander's actions in those critical first hours, setting the trajectory for the entire mitigation and recovery process.

The IC's initial responsibilities extend to ensuring that the incident response process adheres to established protocols and legal requirements. This includes overseeing the preservation of digital evidence in a forensically sound manner, which is crucial for any subsequent investigation, whether internal or external. The IC must ensure that the teams tasked with evidence collection understand the criticality of chain of custody and are using appropriate tools and techniques. This proactive approach to evidence management can save significant time and resources later in the investigation and can be vital for legal proceedings or regulatory compliance. For instance, if a data breach is suspected, the IC must ensure that logs from affected servers, network devices, and security appliances are captured and stored securely before they can be overwritten or tampered with. This might involve directing the IT operations team to create forensic images of affected hard drives or to ensure that log aggregation systems are configured to retain data for an extended period.

Moreover, the Incident Commander is responsible for ensuring that the response team is operating within the legal and regulatory framework applicable to the organization and the incident. This involves close collaboration with the legal department to understand obligations related to data breach notification, reporting requirements to government agencies, and potential liabilities. The IC must factor these external constraints into their strategic planning and decision-making. For example, if the incident involves the potential compromise of personal data regulated by GDPR, the IC must ensure that the response plan includes timely notification to the relevant supervisory authority and affected individuals, as dictated by the regulation. The IC's awareness of these compliance requirements prevents missteps that could lead to significant fines and legal repercussions.

The Incident Commander also plays a critical role in managing the interface between the technical response team and the business stakeholders. Often, the severity of a cyber incident has direct implications for business operations, financial standing, and public reputation. The IC must be able to translate technical jargon into business impact statements and vice versa. They need to facilitate understanding between the IT security professionals on the ground and the executive leadership who are responsible for making high-level decisions. This communication bridge is essential for ensuring that the response efforts are aligned with business priorities and that the organization's leadership is kept informed of the situation, the potential risks, and the proposed course of action in a manner that is comprehensible and actionable. For instance, if the incident involves a ransomware attack on a critical manufacturing control system, the IC must be able to explain to the C-suite the potential downtime, the estimated cost of recovery, and the options for dealing with the threat, enabling them to make an informed decision about whether to pay a ransom or pursue alternative recovery strategies.

Furthermore, the Incident Commander often has the authority to make on-the-spot decisions regarding resource allocation. This might involve authorizing overtime for critical personnel, requisitioning specialized tools or external consulting services, or temporarily reassigning personnel from other projects to support the incident response. The ability to act swiftly in procuring necessary resources can significantly accelerate the containment and eradication phases of the incident. The IC must balance the immediate needs of the response with the potential impact on other ongoing projects or operational activities. This requires a keen understanding of the organization's resource landscape and the ability to make pragmatic trade-offs.

In many organizations, the Incident Commander may not be a single individual but rather a role that is filled by different people depending on the nature and severity of the incident. However, regardless of who fills the role, the core responsibilities remain consistent. This might involve the Chief Information Security Officer (CISO) acting as the IC for major security breaches, or a Director of IT Operations leading the response for significant infrastructure failures caused by a cyberattack. Regardless of the specific title, the individual in the IC role must possess a unique blend of technical understanding, strategic thinking, leadership acumen, and strong communication skills. They must be able to understand the technical nuances of a cyber threat while also comprehending its broader business implications.

The initial assessment conducted by the Incident Commander is also instrumental in determining the subsequent phases of the incident response. The clarity of the objectives set, the effectiveness of the initial containment strategies implemented, and the accuracy of the scope assessment will directly influence the complexity and duration of the eradication, recovery, and post-incident activities. If the IC misses a critical piece of information during the initial assessment, or if containment measures are not effectively implemented, the incident can escalate, requiring a more extensive and resource-intensive response. This underscores the immense importance of the IC's leadership in the early hours of an incident. They are not just managing the current situation; they are shaping the future course of the incident response.

Finally, the Incident Commander's role is also one of continuous learning and adaptation. Cybersecurity threats are constantly evolving, and so too must the response strategies. The IC must remain vigilant, open to new information, and willing to adjust the response plan as the incident unfolds. This includes regularly reviewing progress against objectives, re-evaluating the threat landscape, and incorporating lessons learned from previous incidents or exercises. The IC's ability to foster a culture of continuous improvement within the incident response team is vital for long-term organizational resilience against cyber threats. They are not just managing a crisis; they are helping the organization become more robust and capable of facing future challenges. The initial actions taken under the guidance of the Incident Commander lay the crucial groundwork for an organized, effective, and ultimately successful resolution of the cybersecurity incident, protecting the organization's assets, reputation, and operational integrity.

The cornerstone of an effective cybersecurity incident response, even before the formal activation of an Incident Command System (ICS) or the definitive appointment of an Incident Commander (IC), begins with the immediate and systematic capture of information. The instant a potential incident is suspected, the imperative to document should be paramount. This is not merely an administrative chore; it is the foundational activity that underpins every subsequent step of the response. This critical initial phase involves establishing a comprehensive record of observations, actions, and decisions as they occur. This proactive approach to documentation serves multiple indispensable purposes: it provides the raw material for forensic analysis, enables thorough post-incident reviews, supports any potential legal or regulatory proceedings, and ultimately ensures that a clear, accurate, and auditable account of the entire incident and the organization's response is meticulously maintained from the very outset.

The genesis of this documentation typically lies with the individuals who first detect or suspect a security event. This might be an analyst monitoring security alerts, an administrator noticing anomalous system behavior, or even a user reporting a suspicious email. Their initial observations, no matter how seemingly minor, must be recorded. This includes the precise time of observation, the source of the information (e.g., specific log file, alert ID, user report), and a detailed description of what was observed. For instance, if an alert indicates a potential brute-force login attempt on a critical server, the documentation should capture the timestamp of the alert, the source IP address, the target username, and any other associated metadata. This level of detail is not about artistic flair; it's about providing irrefutable factual data that can later be corroborated or expanded upon.

As the incident escalates and personnel are mobilized, the responsibility for this detailed record-keeping becomes more formalized. Even in the very early stages, before a full incident response team is assembled, a designated point person or the individual leading the initial investigation should be tasked with centralizing these initial notes. This ensures that information is not siloed or lost. This centralized log should ideally capture not just observations but also the immediate actions taken. For example, if the initial analyst, upon seeing the brute-force alert, decided to temporarily block the source IP address at the firewall, this action, along with the rationale for it and the timestamp, must be recorded. This prevents duplicated efforts, ensures that critical steps are not missed, and provides an immediate history of the evolving situation.

The documentation process should also meticulously track all personnel involved. For each observation, action, or decision, it is vital to record who was involved, their role (even if informal at this stage), and the time they participated or made a contribution. This creates accountability and allows for easy identification of subject matter experts or witnesses as the investigation progresses. For example, if a system administrator was consulted about the potential impact of disabling a specific service, their name, the time of consultation, and their advice should be noted. This is crucial for understanding the context behind certain decisions and for reconstructing the sequence of events.

Furthermore, the documentation must capture the observed behavior of affected systems. This goes beyond simple alerts. It involves noting any changes in system performance, unusual network traffic patterns, unexpected process execution, or file modifications. For instance, if a server starts exhibiting high CPU utilization and increased disk I/O without any apparent legitimate cause, these symptoms must be documented, along with the specific timestamps and the affected systems. This observational data is invaluable for later identifying the scope of the compromise and the modus operandi of the threat actor.

The importance of timestamps cannot be overstated. Every entry in the incident log should be time-stamped with the highest possible precision, ideally including milliseconds if the underlying systems support it. This is crucial for establishing a chronological order of events, which is fundamental for understanding causality. When dealing with complex attacks that unfold over time or involve multiple stages, an accurate timeline is the backbone of the entire investigation. Without precise timestamps, it becomes nearly impossible to determine whether an observed event was a cause, an effect, or an unrelated occurrence. This level of temporal accuracy is also vital for correlating events across different systems and security tools.

In situations where immediate containment actions are taken, such as isolating a compromised machine or resetting user credentials, the documentation must detail the specific actions performed, the rationale behind them, and the precise moment they were executed. This allows for an assessment of the effectiveness of these actions and helps in understanding whether they inadvertently disrupted evidence or triggered other unforeseen consequences. For instance, if a decision is made to shut down a suspicious server, the documentation should include the decision-maker, the time of the decision, the time of shutdown, and the justification for this drastic measure. This detail is essential for post-incident analysis and for refining future response strategies.

The initial documentation phase is also where the groundwork for forensic preservation begins. Even before specialized forensic tools are deployed, the simple act of documenting what systems are affected, their current state, and any actions taken on them can inform the forensic team about what needs to be preserved and in what order. For example, noting that a particular workstation is exhibiting unusual file activity might prompt the immediate imaging of its hard drive, with the documentation serving as the initial record of why this action was deemed necessary. This collaborative aspect between initial responders and forensic specialists, facilitated by good documentation, ensures that valuable evidence is not lost due to hasty or uninformed actions.

The nature of the documentation can vary depending on the tools available. In some organizations, this might be as basic as a shared document or spreadsheet where team members log their activities. In more mature environments, specialized incident response platforms or ticketing systems might be employed, which can automate some aspects of logging and timestamping, and can facilitate the aggregation of information from various security tools. Regardless of the medium, the principles remain the same: capture accurate, timely, and relevant information about the incident and the response.

The purpose of this initial documentation extends beyond just tracking the immediate response. It forms the primary source material for building a comprehensive incident report. This report will be crucial for understanding what happened, why it happened, how it was handled, and what lessons can be learned to prevent similar incidents in the future. Without a robust log of initial observations and actions, the accuracy and completeness of this report would be severely compromised, diminishing its value for organizational learning and improvement.

Moreover, in the event of a data breach or a significant security incident, regulatory bodies and legal entities will demand a clear account of what occurred. The initial documentation serves as the bedrock for this account. It demonstrates due diligence, shows that the organization took the incident seriously, and provides evidence of the steps taken to mitigate the damage. A well-documented response can significantly influence legal outcomes, regulatory penalties, and public perception. Conversely, poor or absent documentation can lead to assumptions of negligence, increased scrutiny, and harsher penalties.

The act of documentation also imposes a discipline on the responders. It forces them to be systematic in their thinking and deliberate in their actions. The process of articulating an observation or an action often clarifies one's own understanding of the situation. It encourages critical thinking and can help prevent impulsive decisions driven by panic or pressure. This deliberate recording of events fosters a more controlled and rational response, even in the most chaotic circumstances.

Therefore, the emphasis on initial information gathering and documentation is not merely a procedural step; it is a strategic imperative. It is the proactive measure that sets the stage for an organized, effective, and defensible incident response. It transforms a potential cascade of unmanaged events into a structured investigation and mitigation effort, providing the essential thread of continuity and accountability that guides the entire process from suspicion to resolution. Every piece of information captured, no matter how small it may seem at the time, contributes to the larger picture and is an investment in the successful outcome of the incident response.

The immediate aftermath of detecting a cybersecurity incident is characterized by a pressing need to arrest its progression. Once the initial information-gathering phase, as detailed previously, confirms a genuine threat, the focus shifts sharply to containment. This is not a phase of exhaustive eradication or in-depth forensic analysis, though those will follow. Instead, containment is about damage control – stemming the bleeding and preventing the malicious actor from gaining further access, exfiltrating more data, or wreaking havoc across the organization's digital landscape. The primary objective here is to halt the spread of the compromise. The strategies employed must be swift, decisive, and tailored to the specific nature of the incident and the organization's unique technical environment. Failure to effectively contain an incident can lead to a domino effect, where a localized breach rapidly escalates into a widespread organizational crisis, amplifying the potential financial, reputational, and operational damage.

The effectiveness of containment hinges on a deep understanding of the network architecture and the potential vectors of attack. Modern enterprises are complex ecosystems, often comprising diverse systems, cloud services, remote workers, and interconnected third-party applications. This complexity presents numerous opportunities for an adversary to move laterally once initial access is achieved. Therefore, containment strategies are not a one-size-fits-all proposition; they require careful consideration of the threat landscape, the criticality of affected assets, and the acceptable level of operational disruption. The decision-making process during this phase needs to be agile, allowing responders to adapt their approach as new information emerges or as the adversary's actions evolve.

One of the most fundamental and powerful containment strategies is **network segmentation**. This involves dividing a network into smaller, isolated zones or segments, each with its own defined security policies and controls. The underlying principle is that if one segment is compromised, the segmentation prevents the threat from easily spreading to other, potentially more critical, segments. For example, a hospital might segment its network so that the patient records database is in a highly isolated zone, separate from the general administrative network or the guest Wi-Fi. If a workstation on the administrative network is compromised by malware, the segmentation would act as a barrier, preventing that malware from directly accessing the sensitive patient data.

Implementing effective network segmentation requires careful planning and ongoing management. This can be achieved through various technologies, including firewalls, Virtual Local Area Networks (VLANs), and Software-Defined Networking (SDN). Firewalls, acting as gatekeepers between network segments, can enforce strict access control policies, allowing only approved traffic to pass. VLANs allow administrators to logically group devices and users on the same physical network, creating separate broadcast domains and effectively segmenting traffic. SDN offers a more dynamic and programmable approach, enabling granular control over network traffic flow and facilitating rapid re-configuration of network segments in response to an incident.

During an incident, network segmentation can be leveraged in several ways. If the initial compromise is detected within a specific subnet or VLAN, responders can immediately reinforce the security policies governing that segment. This might involve tightening firewall rules to allow only essential communication, or even temporarily isolating the entire segment from the rest of the network if the threat is severe and widespread within that zone. This isolation, while potentially disruptive to operations within that segment, is a critical step in preventing the compromise from spreading further. The key benefit is that it contains the incident to a defined area, allowing other parts of the organization to continue operating with reduced risk. The speed at which these network controls can be adjusted is paramount. In a well-designed segmented network, administrators can often reconfigure firewall rules or VLAN memberships quickly, sometimes within minutes, to achieve the desired isolation. This rapid response capability is what makes segmentation such a potent tool for containment.

However, it's crucial to acknowledge that segmentation is not an impenetrable shield. Sophisticated attackers can sometimes find ways to bypass segmentation controls, especially if those controls are not robustly implemented or if there are pre-existing misconfigurations. Furthermore, the effectiveness of segmentation relies on the assumption that the internal network is inherently trusted, which is a principle challenged by modern zero-trust security models. Nevertheless, for most organizations, robust network segmentation remains a foundational element of a strong defense-in-depth strategy and a vital component of incident containment. It provides a crucial first line of defense by limiting the blast radius of an initial compromise.

Beyond network-level segmentation, a critical containment strategy involves the **isolation of compromised systems**. This is often a more granular approach, targeting individual machines or endpoints that are confirmed or strongly suspected to be infected or controlled by an attacker. The goal here is to sever the connection of the compromised system from the rest of the network, preventing it from communicating with malicious command-and-control servers, spreading malware to other devices, or exfiltrating data.

The method of isolation can vary. For physical machines, this might involve physically disconnecting the network cable or disabling the network interface card (NIC). For virtual machines or cloud-based instances, isolation can be achieved by reconfiguring network security groups, modifying firewall rules to block all inbound and outbound traffic, or even suspending or shutting down the instance entirely. Endpoint detection and response (EDR) solutions have become invaluable in this regard, allowing security teams to remotely isolate infected endpoints with a few clicks, often before the full extent of the compromise is understood. These tools can automate the process of blocking network traffic to and from the endpoint, effectively quarantining it without requiring direct physical access or complex manual configuration.

The decision to isolate a system is a trade-off. While it effectively stops the spread of the threat from that specific machine, it also renders the system unavailable for legitimate use, potentially impacting business operations. Therefore, responders must carefully weigh the risk of leaving the system connected against the impact of its isolation. Factors to consider include the criticality of the compromised system, the potential for it to be a pivot point for further attacks, and the sensitivity of the data residing on it. In some cases, it might be more prudent to quickly isolate a system that exhibits even minor suspicious activity to prevent a potentially catastrophic breach, even if it means a temporary loss of functionality. Conversely, if the system is non-critical and the suspected threat appears contained or low-risk, responders might opt for less drastic measures initially. The documentation of this decision-making process, including the rationale, is paramount for post-incident review.

Another crucial aspect of containment is the **disabling of affected accounts**. If an attacker has gained unauthorized access to user credentials, service accounts, or administrative privileges, these compromised accounts can be used as a powerful tool to move laterally across the network, elevate privileges, and access sensitive resources. Therefore, promptly identifying and disabling these accounts is a vital containment measure.

This involves recognizing the tell-tale signs of account compromise, such as unusual login activity (e.g., logins from unexpected geographic locations or at unusual times), repeated failed login attempts followed by a successful login, or the modification of critical account settings. Security Information and Event Management (SIEM) systems and identity and access management (IAM) solutions play a significant role in detecting such anomalies. Once a compromised account is identified, the immediate action is to disable or lock it, preventing any further malicious activity.

In addition to disabling, resetting the passwords for affected accounts is essential. However, simply resetting a password without further investigation might not be sufficient if the attacker still possesses other means of access or if the account itself is being used for automated processes or services. Responders need to understand the scope of the account compromise and ensure that all associated access methods are secured. This might involve reviewing and revoking any associated security tokens, API keys, or authorized sessions. For service accounts, which often have elevated privileges and are used for automated tasks, their compromise can be particularly dangerous. Disabling and thoroughly investigating these accounts requires careful coordination with system administrators to minimize disruption to critical services. The principle of least privilege should be applied rigorously when re-enabling or creating new service accounts, ensuring they have only the necessary permissions to perform their intended functions.

Furthermore, containment can involve **blocking malicious IP addresses and domains**. Threat intelligence feeds and security logs often reveal communication between compromised internal systems and known malicious external IP addresses or domains used for command-and-control (C2) infrastructure. By identifying these indicators of compromise (IoCs), security teams can proactively block traffic to and from these malicious entities at their network perimeter, such as through firewalls or web proxies. This prevents compromised systems from communicating with attackers and stops further malicious payloads from being downloaded.

This strategy is particularly effective against known malware families or active attacker campaigns where C2 infrastructure is well-documented. However, it's an ongoing battle, as attackers frequently change their IP addresses and domains to evade detection. Therefore, the effectiveness of this approach relies on up-to-date threat intelligence and the ability to rapidly update security controls. It's also important to consider the potential for false positives; blocking a legitimate IP address or domain inadvertently can disrupt critical business operations. Therefore, a thorough vetting process and careful management of blocklists are crucial. Automation plays a key role here, with security tools capable of ingesting threat intelligence and automatically updating firewall rules or proxy configurations.

The speed of deployment for these blocking measures is critical. The longer a compromised system can communicate with a C2 server, the more data it can exfiltrate, the more sophisticated its commands can become, and the more entrenched the attacker can get within the network. Therefore, integrating threat intelligence directly into network defense systems allows for near real-time blocking of identified malicious IPs and domains. This proactive stance significantly reduces the attack surface and limits the attacker's ability to direct their operations.

The choice and sequencing of these containment strategies are highly dependent on the specific incident. For instance, a ransomware attack might prioritize isolating infected endpoints immediately to prevent the encryption of files. A data exfiltration attempt might focus on blocking outbound traffic to suspicious destinations and disabling compromised accounts that have access to sensitive data. A phishing campaign leading to credential compromise would necessitate immediate disabling and password resets for affected accounts, alongside network monitoring for any lateral movement.

Ultimately, containment is an iterative process. Initial containment actions might not be perfect, and the threat landscape can change rapidly. Responders must continuously monitor the environment to assess the effectiveness of their containment measures and adapt their strategies as needed. This might involve moving from broader isolation to more refined controls as the investigation progresses and a clearer picture of the compromise emerges. The overarching goal remains the same: to minimize the impact of the incident and create a secure environment for the subsequent phases of eradication and recovery. The success of the entire incident response often hinges on the speed and effectiveness of these initial containment efforts.

The successful containment of a cybersecurity incident marks a critical juncture, shifting the operational focus from damage control to complete threat removal. This phase, known as eradication, is about meticulously and permanently expunging the adversary's presence from the compromised environment. It’s not merely about sweeping away the immediate symptoms, but about systematically dismantling the attacker's footholds, patching the vulnerabilities they exploited, and ensuring that the threat cannot re-establish itself. Eradication is a precise, often intricate, process that demands a thorough understanding of the attack vectors, the attacker's methods, and the organization's infrastructure. Failure to fully eradicate can render containment efforts futile, as a lingering presence can allow for a swift resurgence of the threat, potentially leading to a more damaging and prolonged incident.

A primary objective within eradication is the complete removal of any malicious software that has infiltrated the network. This can range from simple viruses and worms to sophisticated rootkits and advanced persistent threats (APTs). The approach to malware eradication is multifaceted, often beginning with automated scanning and removal tools. Antivirus and anti-malware software are the first line of defense, designed to detect and quarantine known malicious files. However, their effectiveness is often limited against novel or highly evasive malware. Consequently, more advanced techniques are frequently required.

One of the most definitive methods for eradicating malware from individual systems is **system re-imaging or rebuilding**. This involves completely wiping the affected system's storage and reinstalling the operating system and all applications from a known good source. This process guarantees that any malware, including deeply embedded rootkits or boot sector viruses that might evade standard removal tools, is eliminated. While effective, re-imaging is a resource-intensive process. It requires significant downtime for the affected system, potential data loss if backups are not current or complete, and the time-consuming task of reinstalling software and reconfiguring settings. Therefore, it is typically reserved for systems where malware infection is confirmed and deeply entrenched, or where other removal methods have proven unsuccessful. The decision to re-image often hinges on the criticality of the system, the potential impact of lingering malware, and the availability of clean system images and restoration procedures. For many organizations, maintaining a library of pre-configured, hardened system images is a crucial component of their incident response capability, allowing for rapid restoration of essential systems.

When re-imaging is not immediately feasible due to operational constraints, or for less severe infections, **thorough manual cleanup and disinfection** becomes the chosen path. This process requires deep technical expertise and can be a painstaking endeavor. It involves identifying all malicious files, registry entries, scheduled tasks, and other artifacts left behind by the malware. This often necessitates the use of specialized forensic tools that can analyze system memory, disk images, and running processes to uncover hidden threats. For instance, identifying a rootkit might involve booting the system from a trusted external media and analyzing the file system for anomalies or using kernel-level debugging tools. Disinfecting a system in this manner requires meticulous documentation of every step taken, ensuring that no trace of the malware remains. It's a process where overlooking a single malicious entry can lead to the malware reasserting control once the system is back in full operation.

Beyond malware, eradication must also address the **elimination of unauthorized access points and backdoors**. Attackers frequently establish persistent access mechanisms to ensure they can regain entry even if their initial exploit is discovered and patched. These can include newly created user accounts, modified system services, scheduled tasks designed to launch malicious code, or the installation of legitimate-looking but malicious software. Identifying and removing these requires a comprehensive review of system configurations, user privileges, and network services.

For instance, an attacker might create a new, hidden administrator account with a seemingly innocuous name. Detecting such an account requires scrutinizing the list of all user accounts, paying attention to those with unusual UIDs, SIDs, or those that are not visible through standard user management interfaces. Similarly, attackers may hijack legitimate system services or create new ones to host their malicious code or establish covert communication channels. A thorough audit of running services, their dependencies, and their associated executable files is critical. Scheduled tasks, often overlooked, can be a common hiding place for malware that is set to execute at specific intervals or system events. Reviewing all scheduled tasks for unusual entries, particularly those set to run with high privileges, is a non-negotiable step in eradication.

Another common tactic is the exploitation of existing vulnerabilities to gain and maintain access. Therefore, a crucial part of eradication is **patching the exploited vulnerabilities**. This involves identifying the specific security flaw that the attacker leveraged to gain initial access or to escalate privileges. Once identified, the appropriate security patches, hotfixes, or configuration changes must be applied to all vulnerable systems across the organization. This is not just a reactive measure; it is a fundamental proactive security practice that should be integrated into the ongoing security posture of the organization. However, during an incident, the urgency of patching becomes paramount. It's essential to prioritize patching based on the severity of the vulnerability and its role in the current attack. This might involve applying emergency patches to critical systems before wider rollout. Furthermore, if the attacker exploited a zero-day vulnerability for which no patch exists, eradication might involve implementing compensating controls, such as stricter access controls, network segmentation, or intrusion prevention system (IPS) signatures, until a patch becomes available.

The compromise of **credentials and access tokens** presents a significant challenge during eradication. If an attacker has successfully stolen user credentials, service account credentials, or API keys, simply removing malware from a system is insufficient. These credentials could be used to authenticate into other systems, gain elevated privileges, or access sensitive data. Therefore, a comprehensive eradication strategy must include the **resetting and revocation of compromised credentials**. This means forcing a password reset for all affected user accounts, and potentially for all accounts if the scope of compromise is unclear. For service accounts, which are often used by applications to interact with other systems, their compromise can be particularly dangerous. Their credentials must be securely reset, and any associated access tokens or API keys must be revoked and reissued. This process requires careful coordination to minimize disruption to legitimate business operations, especially for automated processes that rely on service accounts.

Furthermore, the eradication of persistent threats often involves

identifying and eliminating the attacker's command-and-control (C2) infrastructure. While blocking malicious IP addresses and domains was a containment measure, eradication requires a more profound understanding and dismantling of the attacker's operational infrastructure. This might involve analyzing network traffic logs to identify persistent communication channels, dissecting malware samples to understand their C2 protocols, and correlating this information with threat intelligence to map out the attacker's network. The goal is to sever all communication lines, preventing the attacker from receiving further instructions, exfiltrating data, or maintaining control over compromised systems. This can be a complex task, especially if the attacker uses sophisticated techniques like domain generation algorithms (DGAs) or encrypted C2 channels.

The process of eradication also requires a robust **forensic analysis** of the compromised systems. While initial containment might have focused on broad strokes, eradication demands a detailed understanding of *how* the compromise occurred, *what* systems were affected, and *what* data was accessed or exfiltrated. Forensic analysis involves creating bit-for-bit copies of storage media and memory from compromised systems and analyzing these images in a secure, isolated environment. This provides an immutable record of the system's state at the time of the incident, allowing investigators to trace the attacker's movements, identify the root cause, and confirm the complete removal of all malicious elements. The findings from forensic analysis are crucial for validating the effectiveness of eradication efforts and for informing future security enhancements.

Moreover, eradication is not just about removing the immediate threat; it's also about **preventing recurrence**. This involves implementing **security enhancements** based on the lessons learned from the incident. This could include strengthening access controls, implementing multi-factor authentication

(MFA) more broadly, improving network segmentation, deploying more advanced endpoint detection and response (EDR) solutions, enhancing security awareness training for employees, or refining vulnerability management processes. If the incident revealed weaknesses in security policies or procedures, those need to be addressed and updated. For example, if an attacker exploited weak password policies, the organization might implement stronger password complexity requirements or mandating regular password changes. If the incident involved a sophisticated phishing attack, enhanced employee training on identifying and reporting phishing attempts would be a critical follow-on action.

The decision to declare an incident eradicated should not be taken lightly. It requires confidence that all malicious artifacts, unauthorized access points, and exploited vulnerabilities have been addressed. This often involves multiple layers of verification, including re-scans of systems with updated security tools, review of system logs for any residual suspicious activity, and confirmation from forensic investigators. In some cases, it might be prudent to keep affected systems under heightened monitoring for a period after eradication to ensure the threat does not resurface. The process also demands meticulous documentation of all eradication steps, findings, and decisions made. This documentation is vital for post-incident reviews, legal and regulatory compliance, and for building a knowledge base that can inform future incident response efforts.

Ultimately, eradication is a methodical and often iterative process. It's about leaving no stone unturned in the effort to cleanse the environment of the adversary. It requires a combination of automated tools, expert manual intervention, and a deep understanding of the organization's digital ecosystem. The success of eradication directly impacts the subsequent phases of recovery and the overall resilience of the organization. A thorough eradication ensures that the organization can confidently move forward, knowing that the threat has been neutralized and that the integrity of its systems and data has been restored.

The successful eradication of a cybersecurity threat marks a pivotal transition in the incident response lifecycle. Having meticulously purged the digital environment of the adversary's presence and patched the exploited vulnerabilities, the organization now stands at the threshold of restoration. This phase, known as recovery, is not merely about returning systems to their pre-incident state; it is a strategic endeavor to reinstate operational normalcy while ensuring that the resilience gained through the incident response process is maintained and even enhanced. It's a complex interplay of technical restoration, business continuity, and the re-establishment of trust in the integrity of the organization's digital assets. The meticulous work done during containment and eradication provides the foundation for a confident and secure recovery, minimizing the lingering shadows of the incident and paving the way for uninterrupted business operations. Without a well-defined and effectively executed recovery plan, even the most successful eradication can lead to prolonged disruption, financial losses, and a damaged reputation.

The cornerstone of effective recovery is a robust and well-rehearsed **recovery plan**. This plan should not be an afterthought, but rather an integral component of the organization's overall incident response strategy, developed proactively and refined based on lessons learned from previous incidents or tabletop exercises. A comprehensive recovery plan serves as a roadmap, detailing the steps, procedures, and responsibilities required to restore systems and business functions to an operational state. It begins with a clear definition of what constitutes "normal" operational status for each critical system and business process. This involves documenting baseline configurations, essential services, and interdependencies between different IT components.

Developing this plan requires a deep understanding of the organization's critical assets and their associated business functions. A crucial initial step is to conduct a **business impact analysis (BIA)** if one has not been performed or updated recently. The BIA helps to identify critical business functions, assess the potential impact of their disruption (including financial, reputational, and legal consequences), and determine the maximum tolerable downtime for each function. This analysis forms the bedrock for **prioritizing systems for restoration**. Not all systems are created equal in terms of their criticality to business operations. Following an incident, it is imperative to bring the most essential services back online first to mitigate the most significant business impacts. This prioritization might be based on factors such as:

Revenue generation: Systems directly involved in sales, order processing, or service delivery typically take precedence.

Customer interaction: Systems that facilitate direct customer engagement, such as websites, customer portals, or communication platforms, are often high priorities.

Regulatory compliance: Systems essential for meeting legal or regulatory obligations, such as financial reporting or data privacy controls, must be restored quickly.

Core business operations: Systems that underpin fundamental day-to-day activities of the organization.

Interdependencies: Systems that are required for other critical systems to function.

The recovery plan must clearly delineate the order in which systems will be restored, often grouped into tiers of criticality. For example, Tier 1 systems might include core infrastructure like domain controllers, essential network services, and primary production databases. Tier 2 systems could encompass applications that support critical but not immediate revenue-generating functions, while Tier 3 systems might include less critical internal applications or development environments. This tiered approach allows for a phased restoration, ensuring that resources are focused on the most impactful areas first and that dependencies are managed effectively.

Central to any recovery plan are **backup and restore procedures**. The effectiveness of these procedures hinges on the quality, frequency, and security of the backups themselves. Organizations must ensure that they have regular, verified backups of all critical data and system configurations. These backups should be stored securely, preferably offsite or in a separate, isolated environment, to prevent them from being compromised by the same incident that affected the primary systems. The recovery plan must detail:

Backup schedule and retention policies: How often backups are taken and for how long they are retained.

Backup verification processes: Regular testing of backups to ensure they are complete, uncorrupted, and restorable. This is a critical step that is often overlooked. A backup that cannot be restored is effectively no backup at all. This includes testing the restoration process itself, not just the integrity of the backup files.

Restore procedures: Step-by-step instructions for restoring data and systems from backups, including the necessary tools, permissions, and personnel.

Point-in-time restoration: The ability to restore systems to a specific point in time, which is crucial for ensuring that restored systems are free from any residual malware or unauthorized modifications introduced before the backup was made, but after the incident began.

During the recovery phase, the team will leverage these procedures to bring systems back online. This typically involves restoring data from the most recent, known-good backup. For systems that were completely rebuilt or reimaged during the eradication phase, the process involves reinstalling the operating system and applications from trusted sources, followed by the restoration of data from backups. The recovery plan should also account for situations where recent backups may be compromised or unavailable, outlining alternative strategies such as manual data reconstruction or leveraging older, less granular backups, while clearly communicating the increased risk and potential data loss associated with such scenarios.

Beyond simply restoring data, the recovery process must also focus on **safely bringing systems back online**. This is not a passive act of pushing a button, but an active and deliberate process that requires careful execution to avoid reintroducing threats or creating new vulnerabilities. The recovery plan should mandate that:

Restored systems are isolated initially: Before reconnecting a restored system to the wider production network, it should be placed in a quarantined or isolated environment. This allows for a final round of security scans and integrity checks without the risk of it impacting other production systems.

Security configurations are re-applied: During the restoration process, it's essential to ensure that all security configurations, including firewalls, access controls, and intrusion detection/prevention systems, are correctly re-applied and hardened. This is an opportunity to implement any new security measures identified during the incident response.

Systems are scanned for residual threats: Even after meticulous eradication, a final scan of restored systems using up-to-date security tools is a critical step. This scan should look for any anomalies or indicators of compromise that might have been missed or that could indicate a subtle re-emergence of the threat.

Monitoring is enhanced: For a period after restoration, affected systems should be placed under heightened monitoring. This involves closely observing logs, network traffic, and system performance for any unusual activity that might suggest the threat has not been fully neutralized or that the attacker is attempting to regain access.

Validating the integrity of restored systems is paramount. This validation goes beyond automated scans. It involves functional testing to ensure that restored applications and services are operating as expected and that data is consistent and accurate. This often requires collaboration with business units to confirm that their critical functions are working correctly and that all data is present and usable. For example, a financial system might require reconciliation of transaction data, or an e-commerce platform would need its product catalog and order processing flows verified. The recovery plan should outline specific validation procedures, including who is responsible for performing these checks and what criteria define successful validation.

The ultimate goal of the recovery phase is to **ensure that normal business operations can resume without compromising security**. This means not only bringing systems back online but doing so in a manner that instills confidence in their security and stability. This often involves a gradual reintroduction of systems into the production environment, starting with the most critical and progressing through the tiers of prioritization. Each step should be carefully documented and monitored.

Furthermore, the recovery phase is an opportune moment to implement **security enhancements identified during the incident response**. The lessons learned from containment and eradication should directly inform the security posture moving forward. This could include:

Strengthening authentication: Implementing multi-factor authentication (MFA) more broadly, especially for remote access and privileged accounts.

Improving access controls: Adopting a principle of least privilege more rigorously, ensuring users and systems only have the access they absolutely need.

Enhancing network segmentation: Further dividing the network into smaller, isolated zones to limit the lateral movement of threats.

Deploying advanced endpoint solutions: Implementing or upgrading Endpoint Detection and Response (EDR) or Extended Detection and Response (XDR) solutions for more comprehensive threat visibility and response capabilities.

Updating security awareness training: Incorporating lessons learned from phishing attacks, social engineering attempts, or insider threats into employee training programs.

Refining vulnerability management: Adjusting the cadence or focus of vulnerability scanning and patching based on the types of vulnerabilities exploited.

Improving logging and monitoring: Ensuring that sufficient logging is enabled across critical systems and that security information and event management

(SIEM) systems are configured to detect relevant threats.

The decision to declare a system or the entire environment as "recovered" should be a deliberate one, made by the incident response team in consultation with relevant stakeholders. It signifies a return to a stable, secure, and operational state, where the risk of residual impact from the incident is deemed minimal. This declaration should be supported by evidence, including successful validation checks, absence of suspicious activity in logs, and confirmation from business units.

A critical aspect of recovery, often intertwined with technical restoration, is the **communication and stakeholder management**. Keeping relevant parties informed throughout the recovery process is vital. This includes:

Internal stakeholders: Informing employees about the status of systems, expected timelines for restoration, and any necessary actions they need to take.

External stakeholders: Communicating with customers, partners, and potentially the public about the incident, the steps being taken, and the expected resolution. Transparency can help maintain trust and manage expectations.

Regulatory bodies: If the incident has reporting obligations, ensuring timely and accurate communication with relevant regulatory authorities.

The **minimization of downtime and associated**

business impact is the overarching objective of the recovery phase. Every decision, every step taken, should be weighed against its potential to accelerate this process or, conversely, to prolong disruption. This requires efficient execution of the recovery plan, swift decision-making, and effective coordination among various teams, including IT operations, security, and business unit representatives. The ability to execute recovery procedures smoothly is a direct reflection of the preparedness and maturity of the organization's incident response capabilities.

In instances where the incident involved significant data loss or corruption that cannot be fully restored from backups, the recovery plan may need to include provisions for **data reconstruction or manual remediation**. This could involve engaging with business users to re-enter data, utilizing alternative data sources, or performing manual integrity checks and corrections. Such scenarios underscore the importance of comprehensive data backup strategies and disaster recovery planning.

The **post-recovery validation and ongoing monitoring** are not just checkboxes but a continuous process. Even after systems are deemed "recovered," vigilance is key. The incident response team should continue to monitor the environment closely for a defined period, looking for any subtle signs of lingering compromise or attempts by the adversary to re-establish a foothold. This heightened monitoring period allows for the early detection of any latent threats that may have evaded initial recovery efforts.

Finally, the conclusion of the recovery phase doesn't signify the end of the incident response process. It seamlessly transitions into the **post-incident review and lessons learned** phase, where the entire incident lifecycle, including the recovery efforts, is analyzed. This review will identify what worked well, what could have been improved, and what new policies, procedures, or technologies need to be implemented to enhance future resilience. The recovery plan itself should be updated based on these findings, ensuring that it remains a living document that reflects the evolving threat landscape and the organization's operational realities. Effective recovery is thus a testament to an organization's ability to not only withstand a cyberattack but to emerge from it stronger and more secure, ready to face future challenges with renewed confidence. The meticulous planning, prioritized execution, and rigorous validation inherent in a well-managed recovery process are critical for safeguarding business continuity and restoring stakeholder trust.

The conclusion of the recovery phase marks a critical juncture in the cybersecurity incident response lifecycle. While the immediate threat has been neutralized and systems are being brought back online, the organization's journey is far from over. The true measure of effective incident response lies not just in the swiftness of restoration, but in the organization's ability to learn from the experience and proactively enhance its defenses. This necessitates a dedicated focus on two paramount activities: conducting a comprehensive "lessons learned" review and producing a detailed incident report. These two interwoven processes are the bedrock upon which future resilience is built, transforming a disruptive event into a catalyst for organizational improvement. Neglecting these final, yet crucial, steps leaves an organization vulnerable to repeating past mistakes and susceptible to new threats exploiting the same, or similar, vulnerabilities. Therefore, dedicating adequate resources, time, and intellectual capital to these post-incident activities is not merely good practice; it is a strategic imperative for long-term cybersecurity health.

The "lessons learned" session is a cornerstone of this post-incident activity. It is a structured and often collaborative debriefing designed to critically examine every facet of the incident response process, from initial detection and reporting through containment, eradication, recovery, and finally, the activities that led to the incident itself. The primary objective is to foster an environment of open and honest feedback, encouraging all participants, regardless of their role or seniority, to share their observations, insights, and concerns without fear of reprisal. This session is not about assigning blame; it is about collective learning and identifying actionable improvements.

To facilitate a productive "lessons learned" session, it is vital to establish a clear agenda and invite a diverse group of stakeholders. This typically includes members of the incident response team, IT operations personnel, security analysts, relevant business unit representatives, legal counsel, and even communications teams if the incident had public-facing implications. The session should begin with a concise overview of the incident timeline, followed by a systematic review of each phase. Key questions to guide the discussion might include:

What were the initial indicators of compromise, and how effectively were they detected? Was the detection mechanism adequate, or did it rely on manual observation rather than automated alerting? What were the strengths and weaknesses of the initial triage and assessment process? Did the incident response plan provide clear guidance for the initial stages of the incident?

During the containment phase, critical questions arise: How effective were the chosen containment strategies in preventing the spread of the threat? Were there any delays or challenges in implementing containment measures, and if so, what were the root causes? Did the containment actions inadvertently cause disruption to legitimate business operations, and could this have been mitigated? Were the tools and techniques used for containment readily available and effective against the specific threat actor's tactics?

The eradication phase also warrants deep scrutiny: How thoroughly was the threat removed from the environment? Were there any indications of persistence that were missed or difficult to uncover? What were the challenges associated with removing malware, backdoors, or other malicious artifacts? Were the restoration of systems from clean backups or the rebuilding of compromised systems executed efficiently and without introducing new vulnerabilities?

The recovery phase, which has just concluded, is equally important to dissect: Was the recovery plan sufficiently detailed and well-rehearsed? Were the prioritization of systems for restoration appropriate and aligned with business needs? Did the validation procedures for restored systems provide sufficient confidence in their integrity and security? Were there any unexpected dependencies or interdependencies that complicated the recovery process?

Beyond the technical execution, the "lessons learned" session must also address broader organizational aspects. This includes evaluating the effectiveness of communication channels, both internal and external, throughout the incident. Were stakeholders kept informed in a timely and accurate manner? Was the leadership team provided with the necessary information to make informed decisions? Furthermore, the session should assess the availability and usability of incident response tools and resources. Were all necessary personnel and technologies readily accessible? Were there any gaps in the available toolset that hindered the response effort?

A crucial element of the "lessons learned" session is the identification of the root cause(s) of the incident. This often requires delving beyond the immediate technical exploit to understand the underlying systemic weaknesses that allowed the incident to occur in the first place. Was it a failure in patching, a lapse in access control, a successful social engineering campaign, or a combination of factors? Understanding these root causes is paramount for developing effective preventative measures.

The output of the "lessons learned" session is typically a formal document that outlines the key findings, both positive and negative, and provides specific, actionable recommendations for improvement. These recommendations should be categorized and prioritized, assigning ownership and target completion dates to ensure accountability. For example, a recommendation might be to implement multi-factor authentication for all remote access by a specific date, or to revise the incident response plan to include more detailed procedures for handling ransomware attacks within the next quarter. These recommendations should span various aspects of the organization's security program, including technology, processes, and people. This might involve recommending new security tools, updating existing policies and procedures, enhancing employee training programs, or reallocating resources to strengthen specific areas of defense. The iterative nature of cybersecurity means that these lessons learned sessions should not be a one-off event but a recurring activity, ideally conducted after every significant incident and at regular intervals even in the absence of major events, to ensure continuous improvement.

Complementary to the "lessons learned" session, the creation of a comprehensive incident report is the second critical post-incident activity. This report serves as a formal, detailed, and authoritative record of the entire incident. It is a vital document for several reasons: it provides a historical account for future reference, supports post-incident reviews, aids in legal or regulatory investigations, and serves as a basis for updating security policies and procedures. Unlike the often more free-flowing "lessons learned" discussion, the incident report must be meticulously structured, objective, and fact-based.

A well-crafted incident report typically begins with an executive summary that provides a high-level overview of the incident, its impact, the response taken, and the key outcomes. This is followed by a detailed chronological timeline of events, beginning from the initial detection or reporting of the incident and extending through all phases of the response and recovery, up to the point where the incident is officially closed. Each entry in the timeline should include the date, time, a description of the event, and the individuals or teams involved.

A significant portion of the report should be dedicated to describing the nature of the incident. This includes detailing the type of attack (e.g., malware, phishing, denial-of-service, advanced persistent threat), the affected systems and data, the scope of the compromise, and the estimated impact on business operations, finances, and reputation. Technical details, such as the specific vulnerabilities exploited, the attack vectors used, and the tactics, techniques, and procedures (TTPs) employed by the adversary, are crucial for understanding how the incident occurred and for developing effective countermeasures. This section may include technical artifacts such as logs, forensic analysis findings, and malware samples, often appended or referenced.

The report must also meticulously document the incident response activities undertaken. This section details the steps taken during containment, eradication, and recovery, including the tools and methodologies employed. It should explain the rationale behind the decisions made by the incident response team and highlight any challenges encountered and how they were overcome. This provides valuable insight into the practical application of the incident response plan and identifies areas where the plan may need refinement.

The impact assessment is another vital component of the incident report. This section quantifies the damage caused by the incident, including financial losses, operational disruptions, data breaches, reputational damage, and any legal or regulatory consequences. Where exact figures are not yet available, estimations should be provided with clear assumptions. This assessment helps to justify the resources invested in incident response and informs future risk management strategies.

Furthermore, the report should include a detailed account of the communication efforts throughout the incident. This involves outlining who was informed, when they were informed, and what information was shared. It should also assess the effectiveness of these communication channels and identify any areas for improvement in future incident response scenarios. This ensures that internal and external stakeholders are kept abreast of critical situations and that regulatory obligations are met.

Crucially, the incident report must incorporate the findings from the "lessons learned" session. This means translating the identified weaknesses and opportunities for improvement into concrete, actionable recommendations. These recommendations should be specific, measurable, achievable, relevant, and time-bound (SMART), and they should address both immediate remediation needs and long-term strategic enhancements to the organization's cybersecurity posture. This section acts as a bridge between the reactive response to a past incident and the proactive strengthening of defenses against future threats. It might include recommendations for enhancing security awareness training, implementing new security technologies, revising access control policies, or improving incident response plan testing and drills.

The report should conclude with a summary of the incident's resolution and the current status of affected systems. It may also include appendices with supporting documentation, such as raw log data, forensic reports, or evidence of system restoration. The distribution of the incident report should be carefully controlled, ensuring it reaches the appropriate individuals and departments within the organization, while also considering any legal or regulatory requirements for data protection.

The process of generating these post-incident artifacts, the "lessons learned" review and the incident report, is not merely a bureaucratic exercise. It is an integral part of a mature cybersecurity program. It demonstrates accountability, fosters a culture of continuous improvement, and ultimately strengthens the organization's ability to detect, respond to, and recover from future cyber threats. The insights gained from meticulously dissecting past events are invaluable for anticipating and mitigating emerging risks, ensuring that the organization does not remain static in its defense but evolves alongside the ever-changing threat landscape. By committing to these post-incident activities, organizations transform the negative experience of a cyberattack into a powerful learning opportunity, paving the way for enhanced security, improved operational resilience, and greater stakeholder confidence in the face of digital adversity. The investment in these final stages of the incident response lifecycle yields dividends far beyond the immediate cost savings of a averted breach; it builds a more robust and adaptive security posture for the future.

The thoroughness and efficacy of the "lessons learned" process are directly proportional to the honesty and openness of the participants. To cultivate such an environment, it is often beneficial for the facilitator of the session to be an individual who was not directly involved in the day-to-day operational response, or perhaps an external consultant. This can help to depersonalize the feedback and reduce any perceived pressure to conform or avoid admitting mistakes. The facilitator's role is to guide the discussion, ensure all voices are heard, and meticulously capture the key takeaways. Techniques such as anonymized feedback forms or pre-session surveys can also be employed to gather initial thoughts and concerns, which can then be discussed in a more structured group setting. The aim is to create a psychologically safe space where individuals feel empowered to share candid observations about what worked well, what didn't, and why. This includes discussing the efficacy of pre-defined playbooks, the responsiveness of critical personnel, the adequacy of communication protocols, and the availability of necessary technical resources. For instance, if a critical piece of monitoring software failed during the incident, the "lessons learned" session is the opportune moment to discuss why it failed, whether it was properly maintained, and what steps are needed to ensure its reliability in the future. Similarly, if a particular containment strategy proved unexpectedly difficult to implement due to network configuration issues, this feedback loop is essential for refining operational procedures and network architectures.

The "lessons learned" report, therefore, should not just be a passive document gathering dust on a shelf. It needs to be a living document that drives tangible change. Mechanisms for tracking the implementation of recommendations are essential. This could involve establishing a formal action item registry, assigning owners to each recommendation, and setting regular review cadences to monitor progress. Failure to act upon the insights gleaned from a difficult incident is, in essence, a failure to learn, rendering the entire response effort less impactful in the long run. The cybersecurity team should actively work with relevant departments and leadership to advocate for the necessary resources and policy changes to address the identified shortcomings. This might involve requesting budget for new security tools, proposing updates to HR policies regarding security awareness, or collaborating with engineering teams to implement more secure coding practices. The continuous improvement cycle, a hallmark of effective cybersecurity management, is powered by the consistent application of lessons learned.

The incident report, while detailed and factual, also serves a critical educational purpose within the organization. By clearly articulating the threat landscape, the attack methodologies, and the consequences of compromise, it raises the overall security awareness of employees and management. It can be used as a basis for targeted training programs, illustrating real-world scenarios and reinforcing the importance of security best practices. For example, if a phishing attack was the initial entry point, the incident report can detail the deceptive tactics used, helping employees to better recognize and report similar attempts in the future. When detailing the technical aspects of the compromise, the report should aim for clarity and accessibility, avoiding overly technical jargon where possible or providing clear explanations, so that stakeholders with varying technical backgrounds can understand the core issues and their implications.

The process of writing the incident report itself can also reveal gaps in documentation or understanding. It forces the incident response team to consolidate information, verify facts, and ensure a consistent narrative. This can highlight areas where better logging, more comprehensive monitoring, or improved incident documentation procedures are needed. For instance, if reconstructing the timeline proves difficult due to insufficient log data from a particular system, this becomes a direct recommendation for enhancing logging configurations. The report should also clearly delineate between confirmed facts, hypotheses that were investigated but not proven, and areas where further investigation might be beneficial.

Finally, the formal closure of an incident, as documented in the report and often formalized by a declaration from incident response leadership, is a critical administrative step. This signifies that the immediate crisis has been managed, recovery efforts have concluded, and the organization is transitioning back to normal operations, albeit with enhanced vigilance and improved defenses.

However, the closure of the incident does not mean the end of the security team's work. The ongoing monitoring for residual threats, the implementation of long-term recommendations, and the periodic review of the incident report and lessons learned document are all part of the extended post-incident lifecycle. This diligent approach ensures that the lessons learned are internalized and that the organization emerges from each incident stronger, more resilient, and better prepared to face the dynamic challenges of the cybersecurity domain. The commitment to this thorough post-incident activity is a testament to an organization's maturity and its dedication to safeguarding its digital assets and its stakeholders' trust.

The imperative to meticulously preserve digital evidence cannot be overstated in the context of cybersecurity incident response. When an incident occurs, the data within affected systems, network traffic logs, and system event logs become invaluable artifacts. These pieces of information are not merely technical details; they are the digital breadcrumbs that can illuminate the path of an attacker, reveal the extent of a compromise, and ultimately provide the factual basis for an investigation, remediation efforts, and any subsequent legal proceedings. Without proper evidence preservation, the ability to understand what happened, how it happened, and who was responsible can be severely hampered, rendering remediation efforts less effective and potentially undermining any attempts to seek recourse or prosecute offenders.

Throughout the entire incident response lifecycle, a consistent and rigorous approach to evidence preservation must be maintained. This begins at the very earliest stages, even before an incident is definitively confirmed. The initial detection and reporting phases, while focused on understanding the immediate threat, must also incorporate considerations for preserving the state of the systems involved. This might involve taking immediate snapshots or memory dumps of critical systems exhibiting anomalous behavior. The goal is to capture a "point-in-time" representation of the compromised environment before any actions taken to contain or eradicate the threat inadvertently alter or destroy crucial evidence. This requires a proactive mindset, where the possibility of an incident is always a consideration, and preparatory steps are taken to facilitate evidence collection.

During the containment phase, where the primary objective is to limit the scope and impact of an incident, careful consideration must be given to how containment actions might affect evidence. For instance, isolating a compromised system from the network, while necessary for containment, can also prevent further log data from being generated or transmitted. If remote access is used to contain a system, the logs generated by that remote access tool itself can become critical evidence. Therefore, containment strategies must be designed not only to stop the bleeding but also to do so in a manner that minimizes the destruction or alteration of existing evidence. This might involve carefully documenting all actions taken, including the specific commands executed and the timing of these actions. Whenever possible, containment should involve creating forensically sound copies of affected systems before taking actions that might alter their state.

The eradication phase, which aims to remove the threat from the environment, presents similar challenges. When removing malware, for example, the malware itself, its associated files, and any registry modifications it made are vital pieces of evidence.

Simply deleting a malicious file without proper forensically sound procedures can destroy valuable information about the malware's characteristics, its origin, or its operational methods. Ideally, eradication involves identifying and removing all traces of the threat while preserving copies of malicious artifacts for later analysis. This might necessitate working with forensic specialists to ensure that the removal process is conducted in a way that allows for the extraction and preservation of evidence. Rebuilding systems from known good backups is a common eradication technique, but it's crucial to preserve the original compromised system or its forensically sound image before the rebuild occurs.

Even the recovery phase, which focuses on restoring systems and services to normal operation, can have implications for evidence. If recovery involves restoring data from backups, it is important to ensure that the integrity of the evidence from the compromised state is not lost. Furthermore, the act of restoring systems can overwrite logs or alter file timestamps, potentially obscuring the timeline of the incident. Therefore, the recovery process must be coordinated with evidence preservation efforts, ensuring that any necessary forensic images or copies are made before restoration activities commence.

To effectively preserve evidence, organizations must establish clear policies and procedures for evidence handling. These procedures should outline how digital evidence is identified, collected, documented, transported, and stored. The principle of chain of custody is fundamental here. Every individual who handles a piece of evidence must be documented, along with the date, time, and purpose of their interaction with it. This ensures that the integrity of the evidence can be maintained and validated throughout its lifecycle, which is crucial for its admissibility in legal proceedings. Forensically sound collection methods are paramount. This means using tools and techniques that ensure the evidence is not altered during the collection process. For example, creating a bit-for-bit copy (an image) of a hard drive rather than simply copying files is essential. Tools like `dd` on Linux or specialized forensic imaging software are used to create these exact replicas, preserving every bit of data, including deleted files and unallocated space.

When collecting volatile data, such as information held in system memory or network connections, time is of the essence. This data is lost when a system is powered off or rebooted. Therefore, specific procedures for capturing volatile evidence, often using specialized tools and scripts, must be in place. The documentation of these volatile data collection efforts must be equally rigorous, noting the exact state of the system at the time of capture.

The storage of digital evidence also requires careful consideration. Evidence must be stored in a secure location, with access strictly controlled. This prevents unauthorized access, tampering, or accidental alteration. Digital evidence should ideally be stored on write-once media or in secure, access-controlled repositories that maintain an audit trail of all access. Physical security of storage media is also important.

Beyond the technical aspects of evidence preservation, personnel training is a critical component of forensic readiness. Incident response team members, IT staff, and any other personnel who might be involved in handling digital evidence must be adequately trained in evidence handling procedures, the importance of chain of custody, and the use of forensic tools and techniques. This training should be part of their onboarding process and reinforced through regular refreshers and drills. Understanding the legal and regulatory requirements related to digital evidence is also crucial for all involved personnel.

Forensic readiness is not a reactive measure but a proactive strategy. It involves preparing an organization to be able to conduct digital forensic investigations effectively when an incident occurs. This readiness encompasses several key areas:

Firstly, it involves ensuring that systems are configured to capture relevant data. This means having robust logging enabled on critical systems, servers, network devices, and applications. Logs should capture detailed information about user activity, system events, network connections, authentication attempts, and changes to system configurations. However, it's not just about enabling logging; it's about *effective* logging. Logs need to be configured to capture the *right* information, with sufficient detail and in a standardized format. For example, a firewall log should record source and destination IP addresses, ports, protocols, timestamps, and the action taken (allow/deny). Web server logs should record the requested URL, the client IP address, the user agent, and the HTTP status code. Application logs should record specific user actions, transaction details, and any errors encountered.

Secondly, log management is a critical component of forensic readiness. Simply generating logs is insufficient if they are not properly managed. This involves centralizing logs from various sources into a Security Information and Event Management (SIEM) system or a dedicated log aggregation platform. Centralization allows for easier correlation of events across different systems and provides a unified view of security-relevant activities. It also facilitates efficient searching and analysis during an investigation. Furthermore, logs must be retained for a sufficient period, in compliance with legal and regulatory requirements, and protected from tampering. This often involves storing logs in immutable storage or using secure, append-only mechanisms. Log rotation and archiving policies should be clearly defined and implemented.

Thirdly, forensic readiness includes having the necessary tools and technologies in place. This can range from disk imaging and memory analysis tools to network traffic analysis platforms and malware analysis sandboxes. Having these tools readily available and ensuring that the relevant personnel are trained in their use significantly reduces the time it takes to initiate and conduct a forensic investigation. This also extends to having access to necessary hardware, such as forensic workstations and secure evidence storage devices.

Fourthly, it involves establishing clear roles and responsibilities for incident response and digital forensics. This ensures that when an incident occurs, there is a clear understanding of who is responsible for evidence preservation, collection, and analysis. This may involve designating specific individuals or teams as forensic investigators, defining their authority, and outlining their interaction with other stakeholders, such as legal counsel and law enforcement. The incident response plan should explicitly detail the procedures for invoking forensic capabilities.

Fifthly, regular testing and exercises are crucial for maintaining forensic readiness. This can include simulated incident response scenarios that require the collection and analysis of digital evidence. These exercises help to identify gaps in procedures, tools, or training and provide an opportunity to refine the organization's forensic capabilities in a controlled environment. These drills can also help to build muscle memory for the team, ensuring they can react effectively under the pressure of a real incident.

A key aspect of forensic readiness is understanding what data is available on which systems and how to access it. This often requires maintaining an accurate inventory of all IT assets, including servers, endpoints, network devices, and cloud resources, along with their operating systems, installed software, and key configurations. Knowing where sensitive data resides – for example, customer Personally Identifiable Information (PII), financial records, or intellectual property – is also critical, as these systems will be of particular interest during an investigation. This asset management, coupled with an understanding of data flows within the organization, forms the foundation for targeted evidence collection.

The concept of "forensically aware" system design and deployment is also gaining traction. This involves building security and logging capabilities into systems from the ground up, rather than trying to retroactively implement them. This can include hardening systems to minimize attack surface, configuring audit trails to capture security-relevant events, and designing applications with robust logging mechanisms. For cloud environments, this means leveraging the logging and monitoring services provided by cloud providers and ensuring that these services are configured to capture the necessary telemetry data.

Moreover, organizations must be prepared for the possibility of legal or regulatory scrutiny. This means understanding the specific data retention policies required by laws such as GDPR, CCPA, HIPAA, or industry-specific regulations. These regulations often dictate the types of data that must be collected, the duration for which it must be retained, and the security measures that must be in place to protect it. Forensic readiness must align with these compliance obligations, as failure to do so can result in significant penalties.

The chain of custody for digital evidence is a formal process that documents the handling of evidence from the time it is collected until it is presented in court or otherwise disposed of. Each transfer of custody must be recorded, noting who transferred the evidence, to whom it was transferred, the date and time of the transfer, and the reason for the transfer. This unbroken chain is vital for demonstrating that the evidence has not been tampered with or altered. Any break in the chain can render the evidence inadmissible. This includes ensuring that evidence is transported securely, whether physically or digitally, and that any digital transfers are encrypted and logged.

When evidence is collected, it is often necessary to create multiple copies for different purposes. A working copy might be used for initial analysis, while a pristine, original forensic image is kept secure and used only when absolutely necessary for verification or in court. This principle of preserving the original evidence is a cornerstone of sound forensic practice. All analysis should ideally be performed on copies of the original evidence, ensuring that the original remains untouched and its integrity is preserved.

The documentation associated with digital evidence is as critical as the evidence itself. This includes detailed notes on how the evidence was collected, the tools and software used, the settings employed, and any observations made during the collection process. Similarly, all analysis performed on the evidence must be meticulously documented, including the steps taken, the commands executed, and the results obtained. This detailed documentation allows for the reproducibility of the analysis, which is often a requirement in legal proceedings. It also serves as a reference for future investigations.

Furthermore, organizations should consider the need for specialized expertise. While internal IT and security teams may possess significant skills, complex digital forensic investigations may require the engagement of external forensic specialists. Establishing relationships with reputable forensic consulting firms *before* an incident occurs can significantly expedite the response and ensure that the organization has access to the highest level of expertise when needed. This includes having pre-negotiated contracts or service level agreements that outline response times and costs.

The evolving nature of threats means that forensic readiness must be a continuous process of evaluation and adaptation. As new technologies emerge and attack techniques become more sophisticated, an organization's forensic capabilities must evolve in tandem. This requires staying abreast of the latest developments in digital forensics, investing in ongoing training for personnel, and regularly reviewing and updating policies, procedures, and tools. The ability to forensically investigate an incident is not a one-time setup but an ongoing commitment to maintaining a high level of preparedness in the face of a dynamic threat landscape. The investment in robust evidence preservation and forensic readiness is an investment in the organization's ability to understand, respond to, and recover from cyber incidents, while also ensuring accountability and legal defensibility.

The development of a cybersecurity framework for Industrial Control Systems (ICS) is not a one-size-fits-all endeavor. While generic models provide a valuable blueprint, their true efficacy hinges on meticulous adaptation to an organization's specific context. This subsection delves into the practical methodologies and strategic considerations for tailoring a generic ICS cybersecurity framework to align with the unique operational realities, threat landscapes, risk appetites, and resource constraints of a particular entity. The overarching goal is to forge a robust, yet flexible, system that can adeptly manage incidents of diverse scales and complexities, ensuring the framework possesses the inherent capability to expand or contract its operational scope as the organization's needs and challenges evolve.

The initial and perhaps most crucial step in customizing a generic ICS cybersecurity framework involves a comprehensive assessment of the organization's existing operational technology (OT) environment. This deep dive must go beyond a superficial inventory and extend to understanding the intricate interdependencies between various ICS components, the criticality of each system to the overall production or service delivery, and the specific protocols and communication methods employed. For instance, a power utility's framework will necessarily differ from that of a manufacturing plant or a water treatment facility. The former might prioritize the resilience of Supervisory Control and Data Acquisition (SCADA) systems that manage grid stability and distribution, while the latter might focus on the integrity of Programmable Logic Controllers (PLCs) governing assembly lines or chemical processes. Understanding the unique vulnerabilities inherent in these specific technologies and their operational contexts is paramount. This requires close collaboration between cybersecurity professionals and OT engineers, who possess the in-depth knowledge of how these systems function, their typical failure modes, and their susceptibility to cyber-physical attacks.

Following the environmental assessment, the next phase is to define the organization's specific threat landscape. A generic framework might broadly categorize threats, but a tailored approach necessitates identifying the most probable and impactful threats relevant to the organization's industry, geographic location, and geopolitical standing. For a chemical plant, the threat of targeted attacks aimed at disrupting processes to cause physical damage or environmental harm would be a high priority. For a financial institution's operational technology managing critical infrastructure, the threats might lean towards ransomware or data exfiltration that could cripple operations or compromise sensitive information. This involves analyzing historical incident data, intelligence reports from industry-specific information sharing and analysis centers (ISACs), and considering the motivations and capabilities of potential adversaries. A tailored framework will allocate resources and define response protocols that directly address these identified threats, rather than spreading them thinly across a wide, often irrelevant, range of potential attacks.

Resource availability is another critical determinant in framework customization. Organizations operate with varying levels of budget, skilled personnel, and technological infrastructure. A comprehensive, enterprise-grade solution that is feasible for a large corporation may be prohibitively expensive or complex for a small to medium-sized enterprise (SME). Therefore, the framework must be adapted to fit the organization's practical limitations. This might involve prioritizing investments in technologies that offer the greatest return on security investment, leveraging existing infrastructure where possible, and developing internal expertise through targeted training rather than relying solely on external consultants. For instance, an organization with limited budget might focus on robust network segmentation and secure remote access solutions, which are often more cost-effective than deploying advanced, real-time intrusion detection systems across an entire OT network. Similarly, a shortage of skilled OT cybersecurity personnel might necessitate a framework that emphasizes automation and simplified response procedures, reducing the reliance on highly specialized expertise for routine tasks.

The structure of the framework itself needs to be molded to the organization's unique operational structure. This involves defining clear roles and responsibilities that align with existing organizational charts and reporting lines. In a highly centralized organization, a single, dedicated ICS cybersecurity team might be appropriate. Conversely, a decentralized organization might benefit from a federated model, where cybersecurity responsibilities are distributed among different business units, with a central oversight committee ensuring consistency and adherence to overall policy. The incident response plan, a core component of any framework, must be designed to reflect how decisions are made and communicated within the organization. This means identifying the key stakeholders who need to be involved in different types of incidents, establishing clear escalation paths, and defining the communication channels that will be used during a crisis. For example, in an incident that could impact public safety, the framework must clearly delineate the roles of regulatory bodies, emergency services, and public relations teams alongside the technical response teams.

Adaptability and scalability are not mere buzzwords; they are fundamental requirements for a successful ICS cybersecurity framework. The operational landscape of an organization is rarely static. New technologies are adopted, production processes are modified, and the threat landscape is in perpetual flux. A rigid framework will quickly become obsolete and ineffective. Therefore, the customization process must embed mechanisms for continuous review and adaptation. This includes establishing regular review cycles for policies and procedures, incorporating lessons learned from both internal incidents and external events, and ensuring that the framework can accommodate growth or contraction in the organization's operational footprint. For example, if an organization acquires a new plant or expands its service offerings, the framework must be able to seamlessly integrate the new assets and operational areas into its security umbrella. Similarly, if the organization downsizes or divests certain operations, the framework should be adaptable enough to scale back its coverage without compromising the security of the remaining assets.

The process of tailoring a generic framework often involves a phased implementation approach. Rather than attempting a complete overhaul in one go, organizations can prioritize the most critical areas and implement changes incrementally. This might start with foundational elements such as asset inventory and network segmentation, followed by the implementation of more advanced security controls and incident response capabilities. This phased approach allows for learning and adjustments along the way, reducing the risk of disruption to ongoing operations and enabling the organization to demonstrate tangible progress and build momentum. Each phase of implementation should be accompanied by appropriate training and awareness programs for personnel at all levels, ensuring that everyone understands their role in maintaining the security posture of the ICS environment.

A critical aspect of customization is the selection of appropriate security technologies and tools that align with the organization's specific needs and existing infrastructure. Generic frameworks might recommend a broad suite of tools, but a tailored approach requires careful evaluation of which technologies will provide the most significant security benefits within the organization's budget and technical capabilities. This could involve selecting specific ICS-aware intrusion detection systems (IDS), network security monitoring (NSM) solutions, secure remote access gateways, or data diode technologies that are best suited for the organization's particular operational environment and threat profile. The integration of these tools into the existing IT and OT ecosystems is also a vital consideration, ensuring interoperability and avoiding the creation of new security gaps. For instance, an organization with a highly distributed network of remote substations might prioritize mobile security solutions and secure connectivity options over a centralized monitoring system that would be difficult to implement and maintain in such an environment.

Furthermore, the customization process must explicitly consider the organization's regulatory and compliance obligations. Different industries and regions are subject to varying legal and regulatory requirements concerning the security of ICS. A tailored framework must incorporate these requirements, ensuring that all security controls, policies, and procedures are designed to meet or exceed the mandated standards. This includes establishing robust audit trails, defining data retention policies for security logs, and ensuring that incident reporting mechanisms align with regulatory timelines and protocols. For example, a company operating in a sector governed by strict critical infrastructure protection mandates will need a framework that is meticulously designed to address those specific regulations, potentially involving more stringent security controls, more frequent audits, and more comprehensive documentation than an organization in a less regulated industry.

The human element cannot be overstated in framework customization. Even the most sophisticated technological solutions are only as effective as the people who operate and manage them. Therefore, tailoring the framework must involve developing robust training and awareness programs that are specific to the organization's ICS environment and threat landscape. This includes educating personnel on the unique risks associated with OT systems, the importance of following security protocols, and their specific roles and responsibilities during an incident. For a manufacturing plant, training might focus on the risks of unauthorized USB device usage or phishing attacks targeting OT personnel. For an energy utility, it might emphasize the importance of secure remote access procedures for field technicians. The goal is to foster a security-conscious culture where every individual understands their contribution to the overall cybersecurity posture of the ICS.

Ultimately, developing a scalable ICS cybersecurity framework is an ongoing journey, not a destination. The customization process should lay the groundwork for continuous improvement and adaptation. This involves establishing clear metrics for evaluating the framework's effectiveness, regularly assessing the organization's security posture against evolving threats, and making necessary adjustments to policies, procedures, and technologies. A framework that is meticulously tailored to an organization's specific needs, that is flexible enough to adapt to changing circumstances, and that is continuously reviewed and improved, will provide the most effective defense against the increasingly sophisticated threats targeting critical industrial control systems. This dedication to refinement ensures that the framework remains relevant and robust, capable of protecting the organization's operations, assets, and reputation in the long term. The ability to scale up response capabilities during a major incident or scale down monitoring efforts during periods of reduced operational activity without compromising security is a hallmark of a well-customized and adaptable framework. This ensures that resources are always optimally allocated to meet the prevailing risk and operational demands.

Defining Incident Severity Levels and Activation Thresholds

A cornerstone of any effective incident response capability, particularly within the complex and often unforgiving environment of Industrial Control Systems (ICS), is the clear and unambiguous categorization of security incidents by their severity. Without a well-defined system for classifying incidents, organizations risk a chaotic and inefficient response, leading to the misallocation of valuable resources, prolonged system downtime, and potentially catastrophic consequences for operations, safety, and the environment. Establishing distinct severity levels allows for a tiered approach to response, ensuring that the appropriate level of attention, expertise, and resources are mobilized based on the actual or potential impact of an incident. This subsection will elaborate on the process of developing these severity levels and the corresponding activation thresholds that trigger specific response actions.

The classification of incident severity should be a structured process, driven by predefined criteria that are consistently applied across the organization. These criteria typically revolve around several key dimensions: the potential or actual impact on operational availability, the scope of the affected systems, the criticality of the compromised assets, the sensitivity of the data involved, and the nature of the threat. For ICS environments, the impact on operational availability is often paramount, as disruptions can have immediate and far-reaching consequences.

For example, an incident that halts production lines in a manufacturing plant or disrupts the control of critical infrastructure like a power grid would be considered high severity due to its immediate and substantial impact on output and public services.

Beyond operational impact, the scope of an incident is a critical factor. An attack that is confined to a single, non-critical workstation will naturally be classified differently from one that has propagated across multiple segments of the ICS network, potentially affecting supervisory control systems or safety instrumented systems (SIS). The criticality of the compromised assets also plays a significant role. If the incident involves unauthorized access to or manipulation of Programmable Logic Controllers (PLCs) responsible for core process control, or Supervisory Control and Data Acquisition (SCADA) systems that provide centralized monitoring and command, its severity is inherently higher than an incident affecting a less critical historian server or an office workstation connected to the OT network. Data sensitivity, while often more associated with IT security, can also be relevant in ICS contexts, particularly if sensitive process parameters, proprietary algorithms, or personally identifiable information (PII) handled by the ICS are compromised. Finally, the nature of the threat itself can inform severity. For instance, an incident involving known nation-state actors with a history of disruptive attacks might be treated with a higher degree of urgency than an opportunistic malware infection.

To operationalize these criteria, organizations typically define a tiered severity matrix, often using numerical scales (e.g., 1 to 5) or descriptive labels (e.g., Critical,

High, Medium, Low, Informational). Let's consider a common framework for defining these levels, focusing on the impact and scope within an ICS context:

Critical (Severity Level 1): This level represents incidents that pose an immediate and severe threat to human life, environmental safety, or the continuous operation of critical infrastructure. These incidents typically involve:

Widespread loss of control or visibility of critical processes.

Confirmed malicious manipulation of safety instrumented systems (SIS) or critical control loops.

Significant environmental release or immediate risk of one.

Inability to operate essential functions of the industrial process, leading to immediate cessation of operations and potential unrecoverable damage.

Confirmed compromise of systems that directly impact public safety or national security.

Widespread system outage across multiple critical processes or plant-wide.

High (Severity Level 2): Incidents at this level present a significant risk to operational availability, safety, or security, but do not necessarily pose an immediate, catastrophic threat. They typically involve:

Partial loss of control or visibility of critical processes.

Unauthorized access to or modification of critical control parameters that could lead to process degradation or safety violations if not addressed promptly.

Significant disruption to production or service delivery, leading to substantial financial losses or reputational damage.

Compromise of systems that, while not directly safety-related, are crucial for operational efficiency and integrity.

Widespread impact affecting a significant portion of a single process or multiple non-critical processes.

Malware or unauthorized access that is actively spreading but has not yet reached critical control systems.

Medium (Severity Level 3): These incidents have a noticeable impact on operations or security but do not immediately threaten safety or critical infrastructure. They typically involve:

Degradation of operational performance or efficiency.

Unauthorized access to non-critical systems or data.

Disruption to specific functions or components that can be bypassed or managed with workarounds.

Potential for an incident to escalate to a higher severity level if not contained.

Localized impact affecting a limited number of assets or a single non-critical function.

Suspicious activity that warrants investigation but has not yet confirmed malicious intent or impact.

Low (Severity Level 4): Incidents at this level have a minimal or negligible impact on operations, safety, or security. They are often minor policy violations or routine security events that require documentation and awareness. Examples include:

Failed login attempts that do not indicate a broader compromise.

Minor policy violations that have no discernible operational impact.

Alerts from security tools that are likely false positives but require verification.

Unsuccessful attempts at unauthorized access that are quickly detected and blocked.

Informational (Severity Level 5): These are events that do not constitute a security incident but are logged for monitoring, auditing, or potential future analysis. They include:

Routine system events.

Performance monitoring alerts that are not security-related.

System updates or configuration changes.

Crucially, the definition of each severity level must be supported by clear, objective criteria. For example, "widespread loss of control" should be further elaborated. Does it mean loss of control over 50% of critical actuators? Does it mean loss of SCADA visibility to more than three operational areas? Providing these granular details ensures consistency in classification. Furthermore, the process for escalating or de-escalating an incident's severity must be clearly defined. An incident initially classified as "Medium" due to limited scope might be reclassified as "High" if it is discovered to be actively spreading towards critical systems.

Once these severity levels are defined, the next critical step is to establish specific **activation thresholds**. These thresholds are the triggers that determine when and how the incident response framework is invoked, and which resources are allocated to manage the incident. They bridge the gap between detection and action, ensuring that the response is commensurate with the threat.

Activation thresholds should be directly linked to the defined severity levels. For instance:

Critical (Severity Level 1) Activation Threshold: Any incident classified as Critical warrants immediate, full-scale activation of the incident response team (IRT) and potentially external support (e.g., law enforcement, specialized forensic teams, regulatory bodies). This includes:

Immediate notification of all senior management and executive leadership.

24/7 availability of the core IRT.

Deployment of advanced forensic tools and expertise.

Initiation of business continuity and disaster recovery plans if operations are severely impacted.

Potential activation of emergency response services if safety or environmental risks are present.

Formal communication protocols with relevant regulatory agencies and potentially the public.

This threshold might be triggered by alerts indicating safety system bypass, critical process parameters exceeding safe operating limits due to suspected malicious activity, or widespread SCADA unavailability.

High (Severity Level 2) Activation Threshold: Incidents classified as High require the prompt engagement of the full IRT and potentially specialized support, with a focus on containment and eradication. This involves:

Notification of relevant operational managers and IT/OT security leads.

Full engagement of the primary IRT members within a defined timeframe (e.g., 1 hour).

Initiation of detailed investigation and analysis.

Implementation of containment strategies (e.g., network segmentation, system isolation).

Preparation for potential escalation to Critical severity.

This threshold could be activated by confirmed unauthorized access to critical control servers, malware detected on multiple operator workstations impacting production visibility, or evidence of tampering with non-safety critical process setpoints.

Medium (Severity Level 3) Activation Threshold: Incidents classified as Medium require investigation and containment by a subset of the IRT or designated security personnel. The response is more measured but still proactive. This includes:

Notification of IT/OT security leads and immediate supervisors.

Assignment of an incident lead within a defined timeframe (e.g., 4 hours).

Initiation of investigation to determine the scope and nature of the incident.

Application of containment measures as appropriate, without significantly impacting operations.

Monitoring for potential escalation.

This threshold might be triggered by a single workstation exhibiting unusual behavior, suspicious network traffic patterns detected by monitoring tools, or a security alert related to a system with moderate operational importance.

Low (Severity Level 4) Activation Threshold: Incidents classified as Low are typically handled by routine IT/OT operations or security support teams. The primary action is documentation and follow-up. This involves:

Logging of the event for review.

Investigation by the relevant support team to confirm the nature of the event and ensure no underlying issue exists.

Resolution and closure of the ticket.

No IRT activation is typically required.

Examples include a surge in failed login attempts on a non-critical server that quickly subsides, or a single instance of unauthorized software installation that is immediately quarantined by endpoint protection.

Informational (Severity Level 5) Activation Threshold: No specific activation is required beyond normal operational logging and monitoring procedures. These events are reviewed periodically as part of system health checks or security posture assessments.

The establishment of these thresholds is not a static exercise. They must be regularly reviewed and updated to reflect changes in the organization's operational environment, its risk appetite, the evolving threat landscape, and lessons learned from past incidents. For instance, if the organization adopts new technologies that increase the interconnectedness of its ICS, previously 'Low' severity events might now warrant a higher level of scrutiny and a more proactive response due to the increased potential for lateral movement. Similarly, as new threats emerge that are known to be particularly damaging or difficult to contain, the thresholds for invoking specific response actions might need to be lowered.

A critical aspect of effective activation thresholds is ensuring they are tied to actionable intelligence and predefined playbooks. For example, if a threshold is met for a 'Critical' incident involving suspected ransomware on a critical server, the activation should immediately trigger a specific playbook designed for ransomware response, detailing containment steps, communication plans, and recovery procedures. The clarity and measurability of these thresholds are vital. Vague language like "significant disruption" should be replaced with quantifiable metrics. For instance, a "significant disruption" could be defined as "more than 30 minutes of unscheduled downtime affecting a primary production line" or "loss of communication with more than 10 remote terminal units (RTUs) for longer than 15 minutes."

Furthermore, the activation thresholds must consider the reporting and escalation pathways within the organization. Who is responsible for making the final decision to classify an incident at a certain severity level and thus activate the corresponding response? This responsibility often lies with a designated incident commander or a cybersecurity lead. The decision-making process should be clear and documented, ensuring that critical incidents are not downplayed and that resources are mobilized swiftly and appropriately. The process of classifying an incident and triggering an activation should also involve feedback loops. As an incident evolves, its severity classification and the corresponding response level must be re-evaluated. A rapid re-classification and adjustment of the response are essential when new information emerges that changes the perceived impact or scope of the incident.

The success of defining severity levels and activation thresholds hinges on clear communication and training. All personnel involved in the ICS environment, from operators and engineers to IT staff and management, must understand these definitions and the implications of different severity levels. Regular training exercises, including tabletop simulations and drills, should incorporate scenarios that test the correct classification of incidents and the adherence to activation thresholds. This ensures that when a real incident occurs, there is no confusion or hesitation in initiating the appropriate response. Without this foundational clarity, even the most sophisticated incident response plan will falter at the critical moment of detection and initial reaction. The careful crafting and consistent application of these elements are therefore not merely administrative tasks, but fundamental enablers of a resilient and effective cybersecurity posture for any industrial control system.

In the intricate landscape of industrial control systems (ICS) cybersecurity, a significant hurdle often lies not in the technical detection of threats, but in the organizational integration of response roles. When an incident unfolds within an ICS environment, the established cybersecurity teams, typically structured around Information Technology (IT) principles, must seamlessly collaborate with Operational Technology (OT) personnel and specialized ICS incident responders. A critical step in achieving this seamless integration is the clear mapping of defined ICS incident response roles to existing positions and teams within the broader cybersecurity and IT organization. This process demystifies reporting lines, clarifies responsibilities during an active incident, and ensures that the necessary expertise, regardless of its departmental origin, is efficiently mobilized.

The necessity for such mapping stems from the inherent differences in operational paradigms between IT and OT. IT cybersecurity teams are accustomed to dealing with data breaches, network intrusions, and system downtime that, while disruptive, often do not carry the immediate, life-or-death implications found in ICS environments. Conversely, ICS personnel, including operators and engineers, are focused on process uptime, safety, and efficiency, with cybersecurity often being a secondary, albeit increasingly critical, concern. When an incident strikes an ICS, it requires a coordinated effort that bridges these two worlds. Without a pre-defined mapping, confusion can arise regarding who is in charge, who is responsible for specific actions, and how communication flows should be managed, leading to delays, missteps, and potentially exacerbating the incident's impact.

Let us consider the archetypal ICS Incident Response Team (IRT) structure and how its key roles can be aligned with established cybersecurity positions. The **Incident Commander (IC)**, often the central figure orchestrating the entire response, needs a counterpart within the existing organizational structure. In many mature cybersecurity departments, this role could be filled by the **Chief Information Security Officer (CISO)**, the **Director of Security Operations**, or a **Senior Security Manager**. The IC's mandate is to make strategic decisions, manage resources, and ensure the overall success of the response effort. The CISO, with their broad organizational purview and ultimate accountability for security, is a natural fit. Alternatively, the Director of Security Operations, who typically oversees the Security Operations Center (SOC) and the day-to-day management of security incidents, possesses the operational command experience necessary to step into the IC role, particularly for IT-centric aspects of a hybrid IT/OT incident. For organizations where the CISO role is more strategic and less hands-on, a dedicated **Incident Response Manager** or **Lead Incident Handler**, if such a position exists, would be an excellent mapping for the Incident Commander. This individual is already trained in incident management methodologies and often leads the IRT.

Following the Incident Commander, the **Operations Chief** plays a pivotal role in managing the operational aspects of the response, focusing on containment, eradication, and recovery of the affected systems. This role is crucial in bridging the gap between technical cybersecurity actions and the physical processes of the ICS. In a traditional IT cybersecurity structure, the **Manager of Security Operations Center (SOC) Operations** or a **Senior Security Analyst** responsible for threat hunting and incident containment would be a strong candidate. These individuals understand the mechanics of network segmentation, system isolation, and malware removal – actions that directly impact operational systems. Furthermore, if the organization has a dedicated **IT Operations Manager** or **Infrastructure Manager**, they can also serve as key points of contact and potentially embody aspects of the Operations Chief role, especially when the incident has significant implications for core IT infrastructure that supports the OT environment. The key is that this role requires a deep understanding of system functionality and the ability to implement technical countermeasures that align with operational constraints.

The **Technical Lead** is another critical role, responsible for deep technical analysis, forensics, and guiding the technical execution of response actions. This position is often well-represented within existing cybersecurity teams. The **Senior Security Engineer**, **Forensic Analyst**, or a **Senior Threat Intelligence Analyst** are prime candidates. These individuals possess the specialized skills required to analyze malware, dissect network traffic, perform digital forensics on compromised systems, and understand the intricacies of attack vectors. In organizations with advanced capabilities, a dedicated **OT Security Specialist** who reports into the cybersecurity function could also be designated as the Technical Lead, bringing a crucial understanding of the specific ICS technologies involved. The mapping here emphasizes deep technical expertise and problem-solving capabilities.

The **Communications Chief** is responsible for managing internal and external communications, ensuring all stakeholders are informed appropriately, and maintaining situational awareness. This role is vital for managing the broader impact of an incident. Within an IT department, this function can be integrated with existing **IT Communications Specialists**, **Public Relations Liaisons**, or even a **Business Continuity Manager**. If a dedicated **Corporate Communications** department exists, they would be the primary partners. The challenge here is ensuring that the Communications Chief understands the technical nuances of an ICS incident sufficiently to convey accurate information without causing undue alarm or revealing sensitive operational details. Therefore, the individual mapped to this role must be adept at translating technical jargon into accessible language and managing diverse stakeholder expectations.

For ICS incidents, the **Safety Officer** role is paramount, ensuring that response actions do not introduce new safety hazards or compromise the physical integrity of the plant or facility. This role often requires a specific skill set and a deep understanding of industrial processes and safety protocols. The most effective mapping for this role is typically an individual from the **Operations or Engineering department** who holds a specific safety designation or has extensive experience with the physical processes. While not strictly a cybersecurity position, their integration into the IRT is non-negotiable. The cybersecurity team's responsibility is to ensure this critical role is identified, informed, and empowered within the incident response structure, even if they do not directly report to the CISO. This highlights a key difference in mapping ICS roles – some vital functions will inherently reside outside the traditional cybersecurity org chart and require strong interdepartmental collaboration protocols.

The **Logistics Chief** ensures that the IRT has the necessary resources, tools, and personnel available to conduct the response effectively. This role can be aligned with existing **IT Procurement Specialists**, **IT Asset Managers**, or individuals within **Facilities Management** who manage physical resources. In a cybersecurity context, a **Senior SOC Analyst** or **Incident Response Coordinator** who is responsible for managing the lifecycle of incidents and ensuring the team has the necessary tools (e.g., forensic software licenses, secure communication channels) can also embody parts of this role. This mapping ensures that the practical needs of the response team, from software access to secure workspaces, are met promptly.

Beyond these core roles, it is beneficial to map specific supporting functions. For instance, **legal counsel** and **risk management** representatives, who are typically part of the broader corporate structure, need to be clearly identified as key stakeholders and potentially activated as part of the response. Similarly, **human resources** will need to be integrated for any personnel-related issues that may arise.

The process of mapping these roles should not be a one-time exercise but a living document, regularly reviewed and updated. This review should coincide with organizational changes, shifts in the threat landscape, and lessons learned from exercises or actual incidents. When mapping, consider the following:

1. **Identify Core ICS IRT Roles:** Clearly define the essential functions required for an effective ICS incident response, as outlined in established frameworks like NIST SP 800-61 or ISA/IEC 62443. This includes roles like Incident Commander, Operations Chief, Technical Lead, Communications Chief, and Safety Officer.

2. **Inventory Existing Cybersecurity and IT Roles:** Conduct a thorough audit of current positions within the cybersecurity department, SOC, IT operations, and potentially other relevant departments (e.g., engineering, facilities). Document their primary responsibilities, skill sets, and reporting structures.

3. **Perform a Gap Analysis:** Compare the required ICS IRT roles against the existing roles. Identify which existing positions can directly fulfill an ICS role, which can fulfill it with additional training or authority, and where there are significant gaps.

4. **Define the Mapping:** For each ICS IRT role, clearly

articulate which existing position(s) will be responsible for fulfilling that role during an incident. Document the specific responsibilities and authority granted to the mapped individual for the duration of the incident. For example:

ICS Role: Incident Commander

Mapped Existing Role: CISO or Director of Security Operations

Key Responsibilities during Incident: Strategic decision-making, resource allocation, ultimate accountability for the response effort, liaison with executive leadership.

5. **Establish Authority and Reporting Lines:** Crucially, define the reporting structure and lines of authority during an activated incident. An ICS Incident Commander, even if their day-to-day title is CISO, must have clear authority over the entire IRT, including personnel from other departments, for the duration of the incident. This might require pre-approved executive mandates or documented agreements that temporarily supersede standard reporting lines. Similarly, the Operations Chief needs clear authority over technical containment and eradication actions within the OT environment, in coordination with OT personnel.

6. **Develop Activation Protocols:** Specify how and when individuals mapped to ICS roles are notified and activated. This ties directly into the severity levels and activation thresholds previously discussed. For instance, a 'Critical' severity incident might trigger the

immediate activation of the full mapped ICS IRT structure, while a 'Medium' incident might activate only a subset of these roles.

7. **Address Cross-Functional Training Needs:** The mapping process will invariably reveal training needs. Cybersecurity personnel mapped to ICS roles will require training in OT systems, industrial processes, and ICS-specific risks. Conversely, OT personnel participating in the response may need training in incident handling methodologies and cybersecurity best practices. The mapping should inform the development of a comprehensive training program. For example, a Senior SOC Analyst mapped to the Operations Chief role would benefit from understanding the specific control logic of the plant they are protecting, the implications of shutting down certain processes, and the safety interlocks.

8. **Document and Communicate:** The finalized mapping, activation protocols, and updated reporting structures must be thoroughly documented and communicated across all relevant departments. This documentation should be readily accessible to all personnel involved in incident response. Regular tabletop exercises and simulations are essential for validating the mapping and ensuring that individuals understand their assigned roles and responsibilities.

Consider a scenario where a ransomware attack impacts both the IT network and the ICS. The CISO, mapped as the Incident Commander, would lead the overall response. The Director of IT Operations, potentially mapped as the Operations Chief, would focus on containing the spread within the IT environment and coordinating with OT teams. A Senior Forensic Analyst, mapped as the Technical Lead, would analyze the ransomware, guide eradication efforts, and advise on forensic evidence collection from both IT and OT systems. Simultaneously, the plant's Safety Manager, acting as the Safety Officer, would provide critical input on the safety implications of any isolation or shutdown procedures. The Corporate Communications department, guided by the Communications Chief (perhaps the Senior IT Security Manager), would manage external messaging. This layered approach, enabled by clear mapping, ensures that all critical aspects of the incident are addressed by the right people at the right time, even when those people come from different organizational silos.

The integration of ICS incident response roles into existing cybersecurity structures is not merely an administrative formality; it is a strategic imperative. It bridges the cultural and technical divides between IT and OT, fostering a unified approach to security. By meticulously mapping roles, defining responsibilities, and establishing clear lines of authority and communication, organizations can build a resilient incident response capability that effectively protects their critical industrial assets from an increasingly complex threat landscape. This mapping effort is foundational to ensuring that when an incident occurs, the response is swift, coordinated, and ultimately successful in mitigating damage and restoring operations securely.

In the crucible of a cybersecurity incident, particularly within the sensitive realm of Industrial Control Systems (ICS), time is not merely a metric; it is a critical determinant of success or failure. When systems falter, processes halt, and potentially, safety is compromised, the ability to pivot from detection to decisive action with speed and precision becomes paramount. This is where the strategic deployment of standardized Incident Action Plans (IAPs) for cyber events transforms a chaotic response into a structured, efficient, and effective operation. Moving beyond the foundational understanding of role mapping, the next logical progression in bolstering an organization's cyber resilience involves codifying response procedures into actionable, repeatable plans. This subsection delves into the creation and utilization of these standardized cyber IAPs, emphasizing their role in accelerating response, ensuring comprehensiveness, and facilitating systematic documentation during high-stakes situations.

The rationale behind developing standardized IAPs for cyber events is multi-faceted, primarily rooted in the need to overcome the inherent pressures and cognitive load experienced during an active incident. In the immediate aftermath of detecting a compromise, team members are often inundated with information, facing complex technical challenges, and grappling with a rapidly evolving situation. In such an environment, the cognitive burden of devising an entire response strategy from scratch can lead to critical oversights, missed steps, and delayed actions. Standardized IAPs act as pre-built frameworks, providing a clear roadmap that responders can rapidly populate with incident-specific details. This template-driven approach ensures that fundamental elements of incident response are never forgotten, irrespective of the incident's nature or the specific individuals leading the charge. It brings an element of predictability to an otherwise unpredictable scenario, allowing responders to focus their cognitive energy on the unique aspects of the current threat rather than reinventing the wheel of incident management.

A well-structured cyber IAP serves as a crucial communication and coordination tool, a single source of truth that synchronizes the efforts of diverse teams. It articulates the overarching goals, defines the specific tasks and assignments, identifies the resources required, and establishes the communication channels to be used. This clarity is especially vital in ICS environments where cybersecurity, operations, and engineering teams must collaborate closely. An IAP bridges potential communication gaps by providing a common language and a shared understanding of objectives and responsibilities. For example, a standardized IAP for a ransomware incident affecting a critical production network would clearly outline objectives such as isolating infected segments, preventing lateral movement, preserving forensic evidence, and ultimately restoring operations safely. It would then break down these objectives into tactical assignments, detailing who is responsible for network segmentation, who will perform forensic imaging, who will manage communication with leadership, and who will liaise with external cybersecurity firms, if necessary.

The development of these standardized IAPs requires a systematic approach, beginning with an analysis of the most probable and impactful cyber threats that an organization faces. Organizations often categorize common cyber incidents into types, such as malware infections (including ransomware), unauthorized access, denial-of-service (DoS) or distributed denial-of-service (DDoS) attacks, advanced persistent threats (APTs), insider threats, and supply chain compromises. For each of these categories, a corresponding template IAP can be drafted. These templates should be built upon established incident response frameworks, such as those provided by NIST (National Institute of Standards and Technology), SANS Institute, or ISA/IEC 62443, ensuring that best practices are embedded within the planning process.

Let us consider the essential components that constitute a robust cyber IAP template. At the apex of the plan, a section dedicated to

Incident Objectives provides a clear, concise statement of what the response aims to achieve. These objectives should be SMART – Specific, Measurable, Achievable, Relevant, and Time-bound, where feasible. For instance, in a phishing-driven malware outbreak, objectives might include: "Contain the spread of the 'XYZ' malware to all critical ICS network segments within 4 hours," "Eradicate malware from all affected workstations and servers within 24 hours," and "Restore critical ICS functionality with verified integrity by [specific time/date]." The clarity of these objectives ensures that all responders are aligned and working towards a common, well-defined outcome, preventing a diffusion of effort.

Following the objectives, the **Tactical Assignments** section forms the operational backbone of the IAP. This is where the broad objectives are translated into granular, actionable tasks. Each task should be assigned to a specific role or individual, along with a deadline and any specific instructions or dependencies. This section is critical for ensuring accountability and facilitating progress tracking. For a DDoS attack, tactical assignments might involve: "Identify and block malicious IP ranges at the network perimeter (Network Operations Team) - ongoing," "Analyze traffic patterns to identify attack vectors (SOC Analysts) - within 1 hour," "Implement rate limiting on external facing services (Network Engineers) - within 2 hours," and "Communicate with Internet Service Provider regarding attack mitigation (Communications Lead) - within 30 minutes." The level of detail here is paramount; it should be sufficient to guide action without being overly prescriptive, allowing for flexibility based on the evolving nature of the incident.

The **Resource Needs** component of the IAP is equally vital. This section proactively identifies the personnel, tools, equipment, and information required to execute the tactical assignments. By anticipating these needs in advance, organizations can minimize delays associated with procurement, access, or activation. For a complex forensic investigation following an unauthorized access incident, resource needs might include: "Access to secure forensic workstations with specialized imaging software (e.g., FTK, EnCase)," "Chain-of-custody forms and evidence bagging supplies," "Secure storage for collected media," "Personnel with certified forensic analysis expertise," and "Access to historical network logs and authentication records." Pre-identifying these resources allows the Logistics Chief, or their mapped equivalent, to begin mobilizing them proactively as soon as an incident is confirmed, significantly streamlining the response.

Communication Protocols represent another cornerstone of the standardized IAP. This section dictates how information will flow within the response team, to executive leadership, to affected business units, and potentially to external stakeholders like regulatory bodies or law enforcement. It specifies preferred communication channels (e.g., secure chat, dedicated conference bridges, email distribution lists), frequency of updates, escalation paths, and designated points of contact for different stakeholder groups. For an ICS-specific incident with potential safety implications, communication protocols might emphasize direct, rapid communication between the Safety Officer and the Incident Commander, and a clear escalation path to plant management and emergency services if safety thresholds are breached. The Communications Chief, in collaboration with the IAP's technical leads, will ensure that technical details are translated into understandable language for non-technical audiences. This section also typically includes pre-approved messaging templates for common scenarios, further accelerating the communication process during a crisis.

A critical aspect of tactical assignments within ICS environments, and thus within IAPs, is the nuanced consideration of **operational impact**. Unlike IT incidents where system isolation might be a straightforward decision, in ICS, shutting down or segmenting a process can have direct consequences on production, safety, and environmental compliance. Therefore, every tactical assignment within an ICS IAP must be reviewed for its potential operational impact. This often involves cross-referencing with operational runbooks or process-specific safety procedures. For example, an assignment to isolate a compromised Programmable Logic Controller (PLC) might require specific steps to safely ramp down the associated physical process, ensuring that valves are closed, pressures are relieved, and emergency shutdown procedures are followed. The IAP template should include a mandatory checkpoint for operational impact assessment before implementing any containment or eradication measure directly affecting control systems.

Furthermore, the concept of **documentation within the IAP** itself needs emphasis. The IAP is not just a static plan; it is a dynamic document that is updated as the incident progresses. Standardized templates should include fields for "Date/Time Implemented," "Status (e.g., In Progress, Complete, On Hold)," "Notes/Observations," and "Assigned To." This ensures that a real-time log of actions taken, decisions made, and challenges encountered is maintained. This detailed record is invaluable for post-incident analysis, lessons learned, and potentially for legal or regulatory purposes. It transforms the IAP from a preparatory document into a living chronicle of the incident response itself.

To facilitate the effective use of these standardized IAPs, organizations must invest in comprehensive **training and exercises**. Simply having templates is insufficient; personnel must be trained on how to use them, how to populate them under pressure, and how to adapt them to specific situations. Regular tabletop exercises, simulations, and functional drills that involve activating and using these IAPs are crucial. These exercises help to identify gaps in the templates, reveal areas where responders struggle, and build muscle memory for executing the plans. For instance, a tabletop exercise simulating a cyber-physical attack that manipulates sensor data might require the team to walk through an IAP template, assigning specific roles for data validation, system re-calibration, and safety checks, thereby revealing any ambiguities in the plan or deficiencies in team coordination.

The application of standardized IAPs is particularly beneficial when dealing with **novel or zero-day threats**. While the specifics of the attack vector may be unknown, the fundamental objectives of containment, eradication, and recovery remain consistent. A standardized IAP for "Unauthorized Access - Novel Threat" would still outline procedures for initial triage, evidence preservation, communication, and escalation, even if the exact tools or methods of the attacker are yet to be determined. This provides a crucial baseline, allowing responders to act decisively on known principles while simultaneously gathering intelligence to tailor more specific countermeasures.

Consider the scenario of a sophisticated **supply chain compromise** affecting a critical software component used within the ICS. A standardized IAP for this scenario would prompt immediate questions about the scope of deployment, the criticality of the affected systems, and the potential for the compromise to propagate. Tactical assignments might focus on identifying all systems using the compromised component, assessing the integrity of vendor-provided updates, and potentially initiating a rollback to a known-good version. Resource needs would likely include access to vendor support, dedicated security analysis teams to vet the component, and operational personnel to manage system downtime.
Communication protocols would need to involve the vendor, potentially regulatory bodies, and internal stakeholders about the potential operational impacts. Without a pre-defined template, the initial response might devolve into chaotic information gathering

rather than structured mitigation. The template ensures that the right questions are asked and the necessary initial steps are taken, regardless of the attack's origin.

The creation and maintenance of these standardized IAPs are not static activities. They must be a continuous process. As the threat landscape evolves, new attack vectors emerge, and organizational infrastructure changes, the IAP templates must be reviewed and updated. This review process should be a scheduled activity, perhaps annually, and should also be triggered by lessons learned from exercises, actual incidents, or significant changes in the IT or OT environments. A post-incident review, for example, might reveal that a particular tactical assignment in the ransomware IAP was consistently delayed due to insufficient access permissions for the assigned analyst. This feedback loop is essential for refining the templates and ensuring their continued relevance and effectiveness.

Furthermore, the integration of **legal and regulatory considerations** into standardized IAPs is crucial, especially in regulated industries. Depending on the nature of the incident and the jurisdiction, there may be strict notification requirements for data breaches, system compromises, or safety incidents. The IAP template should include sections that prompt the Communications Chief or Incident Commander to consult with legal counsel regarding reporting obligations and to ensure that all communications and actions taken are consistent with legal and regulatory frameworks. This proactive integration prevents costly compliance failures that can arise from reactive legal engagement during a crisis.

In essence, standardized Incident Action Plans for cyber events are more than just documents; they are a manifestation of an organization's commitment to preparedness and resilience. They embody a proactive approach to cybersecurity, transforming the reactive scramble of an incident into a measured, systematic, and efficient response. By providing pre-defined structures for objectives, tactics, resources, and communication, these templates empower incident response teams to act swiftly, decisively, and comprehensively, minimizing damage, restoring operations, and safeguarding the integrity of critical industrial processes. The ongoing development, training, and refinement of these plans are not optional; they are fundamental pillars of robust ICS cybersecurity.

Effective resource management stands as a cornerstone of any robust cybersecurity incident response capability. It transcends the mere identification of potential threats; it delves into the practical, tangible assets that an organization can mobilize when its defenses are breached. The ability to quickly and efficiently deploy the right resources – whether they are technical tools, specialized expertise, or pre-negotiated services – can be the decisive factor between a contained incident and a widespread crisis. This section focuses on the critical steps involved in identifying, cataloging, and, crucially, pre-authorizing these essential response assets, thereby ensuring that the organization is not caught flat-footed when an incident inevitably occurs. By proactively understanding and preparing for resource needs, organizations can significantly shorten response times, enhance the effectiveness of their actions, and ultimately mitigate the potential damage to their operations and reputation.

The initial phase of resource management for cybersecurity incident response involves a comprehensive inventory of what constitutes a "response asset." This is a broad category that encompasses a wide spectrum of items, from the readily available to the require significant lead time for acquisition or activation. At the most basic level, this includes the technical infrastructure that supports the incident response function itself. This can range from dedicated, hardened forensic workstations equipped with specialized imaging and analysis software to secure network segments isolated from production environments, designed for the safe analysis of malware samples or compromised data. It also extends to communication tools, such as secure, out-of-band communication channels that can be used if primary network infrastructure becomes unavailable or is compromised. The availability of up-to-date network diagrams, asset inventories, and configuration management databases is also paramount, as these provide the essential context for understanding the scope and impact of an incident. Without this foundational knowledge of the environment, even the most skilled responders can struggle to make informed decisions.

Beyond the immediate technical infrastructure, the cataloging process must also extend to software and licensing. Many advanced security tools, such as Security Information and Event Management (SIEM) systems, Endpoint Detection and Response (EDR) solutions, intrusion detection/prevention systems (IDPS), and digital forensics suites, often come with specific licensing requirements. During an incident, there might be a need to scale up the usage of these tools, to deploy additional agents to endpoints, or to access specialized modules that are not in regular use. Therefore, maintaining an accurate record of all relevant software licenses, their expiry dates, and the process for acquiring additional licenses or temporary use permits is crucial. This proactive approach prevents frustrating delays caused by licensing issues when every minute counts. For instance, if a ransomware attack demands the rapid deployment of EDR agents across thousands of endpoints, ensuring that the organization has sufficient licenses and the ability to quickly deploy them can be the difference between a successful containment and a widespread encryption event.

Personnel are, arguably, the most critical resource in any incident response scenario. Identifying the required skill sets and understanding who possesses them within the organization is a fundamental step. This involves not just the core cybersecurity team but also individuals with specialized knowledge in networking, system administration for various operating systems (Windows, Linux, macOS), database administration, cloud security, and, in ICS environments, operational technology (OT) and control systems engineering. Moreover, specific incident types may require niche expertise. For example, responding to a sophisticated state-sponsored APT might necessitate deep knowledge of reverse engineering, memory forensics, and threat intelligence analysis, skills that may not be part of the daily duties of the typical security analyst. Cataloging these skills, identifying the individuals who possess them, and understanding their availability (considering vacation schedules, other project commitments, etc.) is a vital component of resource management. This also extends to identifying internal "champions" or subject matter experts within business units who can provide critical context about specific applications or processes.

In many instances, internal resources alone may not be sufficient to manage a complex or large-scale cybersecurity incident. This is where the pre-identification and pre-authorization of external consulting services become indispensable. Many organizations establish retainer agreements with specialized cybersecurity firms that can provide on-demand support for a variety of needs, including digital forensics, incident response coordination, malware analysis, threat intelligence, legal counsel specializing in cyber law, and public relations crisis management. Cataloging these services involves maintaining an up-to-date list of approved vendors, their contact information, the scope of services covered under their contracts, and pre-negotiated rates or service level agreements (SLAs). Crucially, the procurement process for these services should be streamlined. During an active incident, the time spent on vendor selection, contract negotiation, and obtaining purchase orders can be prohibitively long. Therefore, having pre-approved vendors and clear authorization procedures in place allows the incident commander to quickly engage external expertise without bureaucratic hurdles. This pre-authorization is key; it means that the decision-maker has already vetted the vendor and committed to engaging them under specific circumstances, reducing the friction of engagement.

The pre-authorization aspect cannot be overstressed. It involves establishing clear lines of authority and pre-approved budgets or spending limits for incident response activities. When an incident occurs, particularly one that is rapidly escalating or requires immediate external support, the incident commander or designated lead needs the authority to commit resources without delay. This might involve authorizing overtime for internal staff, purchasing emergency hardware or software, or engaging external consultants. Without pre-authorized spending limits, response efforts can be severely hampered by internal financial approval processes. For example, if a critical server needs to be immediately sent to an external lab for forensic analysis, the ability to authorize that shipment and associated costs without waiting for multiple levels of financial sign-off is paramount. This requires clear policies and documented delegation of authority from senior leadership. These policies should outline the thresholds for requiring higher-level approval and the specific individuals or roles empowered to make immediate financial commitments for incident response.

For Industrial Control Systems (ICS) environments, resource management takes on an added layer of complexity due to the criticality of operational continuity and safety. Identifying and cataloging response assets in this domain requires careful consideration of the unique hardware and software components involved. This includes ensuring access to spare parts for critical equipment, the availability of vendor-specific diagnostic tools, and specialized software for analyzing the behavior of Programmable Logic Controllers (PLCs), Distributed Control Systems (DCS), and Supervisory Control and Data Acquisition

(SCADA) systems. Furthermore, personnel with deep knowledge of the specific industrial processes and their associated control systems are invaluable. This might include process engineers, control room operators, and maintenance technicians who understand the normal operating parameters and the implications of any deviations. Cataloging these individuals and ensuring their availability during a cyber incident is as important as cataloging IT assets. Moreover, safety procedures related to system shutdown, isolation, or restart must be readily available and integrated into the resource planning. The "resource" here might not just be a piece of equipment but also a documented, pre-approved safety procedure that must be followed before certain actions can be taken.

The cataloging process should not be a one-time event but rather a continuous cycle of identification, documentation, validation, and refinement. As the organization's infrastructure evolves, as new technologies are adopted, and as the threat landscape shifts, the inventory of response assets must be updated accordingly. This necessitates regular reviews, perhaps quarterly or semi-annually, of the resource catalog. During these reviews, it's essential to validate the availability and functionality of tools, the currency of software licenses, the contact information for external vendors, and the current roles and responsibilities of internal personnel. Exercises and simulations are invaluable in this validation process. By actively using the documented resources during drills, organizations can identify any discrepancies or shortcomings in their cataloging efforts. For instance, a tabletop exercise might reveal that the contact person listed for a critical software vendor is no longer with the company, or that a particular diagnostic tool has been decommissioned without updating the resource list.

Another critical aspect of resource management is ensuring the accessibility and maintainability of these assets. Simply having a list of tools or services is insufficient if those tools are outdated, if licenses have expired, or if access credentials are lost or forgotten. Regular maintenance schedules for incident response tools, such as keeping forensic software up-to-date, ensuring that backup power supplies for critical response equipment are functional, and periodically testing communication channels, are essential. For external services, this means ensuring that contracts are renewed well in advance of their expiration and that key personnel in the organization maintain regular contact with their vendor counterparts. For personnel, it involves providing ongoing training and professional development to keep their skills sharp and up-to-date with the latest threats and response techniques. The "resource" is not just the tool or the person, but their readiness and capability to perform when called upon.

The concept of "playbooks" – detailed, step-by-step guides for responding to specific types of incidents – is intrinsically linked to resource management. A well-developed playbook will explicitly identify the tools, personnel, and external services required for each phase of the response. By integrating resource requirements directly into these playbooks, organizations create a natural mechanism for their identification and cataloging. For example, a playbook for a distributed denial-of-service (DDoS) attack might list the need for access to the organization's border gateway protocol (BGP) routing information, the contact details for the upstream internet service provider (ISP), and the specific traffic scrubbing services that have been pre-contracted. Similarly, a playbook for a data exfiltration incident might call for specific database querying tools, anonymization software, and the engagement of legal counsel to advise on notification requirements. This playbook-centric approach ensures that resource planning is context-specific and directly supports the execution of established response procedures.

Moreover, the effective management of response assets extends to the physical security and disposition of sensitive materials collected during an investigation. This includes the secure storage of digital media, physical evidence, and forensic images. The cataloging process should extend to documenting the chain of custody for all collected evidence, specifying where it is stored, who has access to it, and the procedures for its handling and eventual destruction or return. This meticulous record-keeping is vital for maintaining the integrity of the investigation and ensuring that any findings are admissible in legal or disciplinary proceedings. The "resource" here encompasses not just the act of collection but also the secure and compliant management of what is collected.

Finally, the success of resource management hinges on a culture of preparedness and continuous improvement. It requires buy-in from all levels of the organization, from executive leadership who must authorize the necessary investments in tools and services, to operational staff who understand the critical systems and processes. Regular communication about the importance of incident response readiness, including the role of well-managed resources, helps to foster this culture. Post-incident reviews and post-exercise analyses should always include an assessment of resource availability and effectiveness. Were the right tools present and functional? Was the necessary expertise available? Were external services engaged efficiently? The answers to these questions provide valuable feedback for refining the resource management strategy and ensuring that the organization is continually strengthening its ability to respond to cyber incidents. This iterative process of identification, cataloging, pre-authorization, validation, and refinement ensures that the organization's response arsenal remains robust, relevant, and ready for deployment when the need arises.

The transition from identifying and managing response resources to actively employing them in a simulated environment underscores the critical need for robust, realistic cybersecurity incident scenarios. Simply having the tools, personnel, and pre-approved services is insufficient if the team does not know how to deploy them effectively under pressure. Developing pertinent scenarios is the linchpin that bridges preparedness and practical execution, transforming theoretical readiness into tangible incident response capability. This subsection delves into the methodologies and importance of crafting these scenarios, ensuring that the training and exercises an organization undertakes are not only engaging but also directly applicable to the threats it is most likely to face and the operational impacts it needs to mitigate.

At its core, scenario planning for cybersecurity incident response is about creating plausible narratives that mimic real-world attacks. These narratives must be more than just a generic description of a threat; they need to be tailored to the specific context of the organization. This involves a deep understanding of the organization's unique threat landscape, its technological architecture, its critical business processes, and its regulatory obligations. A multinational corporation operating in the financial sector, for instance, will face a different set of probable threats and potential impacts than a small manufacturing firm or a government agency. Therefore, the development process must be grounded in thorough analysis.

One of the foundational steps in developing realistic scenarios is to conduct a comprehensive threat modeling exercise. This exercise aims to identify the most likely adversaries targeting the organization, their motivations, their typical tactics, techniques, and procedures (TTPs), and the specific assets they would likely target. For example, a company that holds sensitive personal health information (PHI) might be a prime target for financially motivated cybercriminals seeking to exploit that data on the dark web, or for sophisticated nation-state actors seeking intelligence. Understanding these potential attackers and their objectives helps shape the nature of the simulated attack. A scenario involving the theft of customer PII will look very different from one focused on disrupting a manufacturing process.

Equally important is understanding the organization's technological footprint. This includes not only the IT infrastructure but also any operational technology (OT) or industrial control systems (ICS) that are critical to business operations. The complexity and interconnectedness of modern systems mean that an attack can propagate in unexpected ways. A scenario should therefore consider the interdependencies between different systems and how a compromise in one area might cascade to others. For instance, a scenario involving a compromise of a cloud-based customer relationship management (CRM) system might also need to consider its potential impact on sales operations, marketing campaigns, and even customer support channels, if those are integrated.

Furthermore, the business impact of a cyber incident is a crucial element that must be woven into the fabric of any realistic scenario. What are the critical business functions that, if disrupted, would cause significant financial loss, reputational damage, or regulatory penalties? Scenarios should be designed to stress-test the organization's ability to maintain continuity for these functions. For a retail organization, a scenario might focus on the inability to process online orders or manage inventory due to a ransomware attack on its e-commerce platform. For a healthcare provider, a scenario could simulate a disruption of electronic health record (EHR) systems, impacting patient care and potentially leading to life-threatening delays. The "injects" within a scenario – the events that unfold during the exercise – should reflect these business consequences, forcing responders to prioritize actions based on their impact on the organization's core mission.

The development of specific, actionable scenarios requires a structured approach. Several methodologies can be employed. One common and effective method is to start with broad incident categories and then refine them into specific, detailed situations. Typical categories include:

Malware Infections: This can range from widespread ransomware attacks that encrypt critical data to targeted malware designed for espionage or system disruption.

Phishing and Social Engineering Attacks: These often serve as the initial entry vector for more sophisticated attacks, leading to credential compromise, malware deployment, or financial fraud.

Denial-of-Service (DoS) and Distributed Denial-of-Service (DDoS) Attacks: These aim to overwhelm network resources and make services unavailable, directly impacting business operations.

Data Breaches and Exfiltration: These involve unauthorized access to and/or theft of sensitive information.

Insider Threats: These scenarios involve malicious or accidental actions by employees or trusted individuals.

Advanced Persistent Threats (APTs): These are highly sophisticated, often state-sponsored attacks characterized by stealth and persistence.

Supply Chain Attacks: These target vulnerabilities in third-party vendors or software used by the organization.

Physical Security Breaches with Cyber Implications: For example, unauthorized access to a server room.

Once these categories are identified, they can be fleshed out into detailed scenarios. For instance, under the "Malware Infections" category, a specific scenario could be:

Scenario Title: Ransomware Encrypts Financial Records and Claims Department Systems

Scenario Description: At approximately 09:00 AM on a Monday morning, users in the Finance and Claims departments begin reporting that their critical applications and data files are inaccessible, displaying an alert message demanding a ransom payment in cryptocurrency for decryption. Analysis confirms a ransomware infection has spread rapidly across the financial servers and associated workstations, impacting core accounting, payroll, and claims processing systems. The organization's business continuity plan for financial operations is immediately put to the test.

This detailed description provides the foundation for an exercise. It specifies the type of attack (ransomware), the affected systems (financial records and claims department systems), the impact (inaccessibility and ransom demand), and the immediate business consequence (disruption of core financial operations). From this, specific injects can be planned, such as the discovery of the malware's propagation vector, confirmation of data exfiltration prior to encryption, communication from the attackers, or the discovery that a critical backup system was also impacted.

Another example, under the "Phishing and Social Engineering Attacks" category:

Scenario Title: Credential Harvesting via Spear-Phishing Leads to Cloud Service Compromise

Scenario Description: Over the course of a week, several employees in the Marketing and Human Resources departments receive highly personalized spear-phishing emails impersonating a senior executive, requesting them to "verify their account access" by clicking a link and logging in to a seemingly legitimate portal. Unbeknownst to them, this portal is a credential harvesting site. Consequently, multiple user accounts are compromised, leading to unauthorized access to the organization's cloud-based productivity suite and a customer database. The incident response team must identify the compromised accounts, contain the unauthorized access, and assess the extent of data exposure.

This scenario highlights the subtlety of modern phishing attacks and their progression to broader system compromise. Injects could include: identifying the phishing emails and their characteristics, tracing the source of the attack, determining which cloud services were accessed and what data was viewed or downloaded, and coordinating with cloud service providers to revoke compromised credentials and secure the environment.

For organizations with ICS or OT environments, scenarios must reflect the unique risks. Consider this example:

Scenario Title: Malicious Command Injection Disrupts Water Treatment Plant Operations

Scenario Description: An unexpected surge in turbidity levels at a municipal water treatment facility is detected by the SCADA system. Simultaneously, operators notice anomalous changes in the setpoints of critical process control logic for the chemical dosing pumps. Initial investigations suggest that unauthorized commands have been injected into the control network, potentially leading to incorrect chemical concentrations and compromising water quality. The incident response team, comprising both IT security personnel and OT engineers, must rapidly identify the source of the injection, revert to safe operating parameters, and secure the control network without causing further disruption to essential services.

This scenario emphasizes the direct link between cyber actions and physical world consequences. Injects could include: detecting unusual network traffic on the ICS network, analyzing PLC logs for unauthorized commands, performing a controlled shutdown or bypass of affected systems, and verifying that safe operational parameters are restored and maintained. The involvement of both IT and OT personnel is crucial here, as is the consideration of safety protocols and regulatory compliance related to public utilities.

When crafting these scenarios, it's essential to incorporate a range of complexity. Some exercises might be designed to test specific, contained aspects of the response plan, such as the initial detection and containment of a malware outbreak. Others might be more comprehensive, simulating a multi-stage attack that unfolds over several days and involves multiple teams and external agencies. The frequency and type of exercises should align with the organization's risk appetite and its overall incident response maturity.

Moreover, the development of realistic scenarios is an iterative process. After each exercise or real-world incident, the team should debrief, analyze what went well, and identify areas for improvement. This feedback loop is critical for refining existing scenarios and developing new ones that reflect the evolving threat landscape and the organization's changing environment. For instance, if an exercise reveals that the team struggled with the legal notification requirements following a data breach, future scenarios involving data exfiltration should specifically include this aspect, perhaps with an inject from the legal department or a regulatory body.

Another key aspect of scenario development is the identification of "injects." These are discrete pieces of information or events that are introduced to the exercise participants at specific times to simulate the unfolding of an incident. Injects can take many forms: alerts from security monitoring tools, emails from attackers, phone calls from concerned stakeholders, news reports about related breaches, or even the discovery of new technical indicators of compromise. Effective injects are designed to:

Mimic real-world information flow: They should represent how responders would typically receive information during an actual incident.

Challenge decision-making: They should force participants to analyze information, make critical decisions, and prioritize actions.

Drive the scenario forward: They should introduce new developments, escalate the situation, or require specific response actions.

Test specific capabilities: They should be aligned with the objectives of the exercise, focusing on particular skills or procedures.

For example, in the ransomware scenario described earlier, injects might include:

Inject 1 (09:05 AM): IT Helpdesk receives multiple calls reporting inaccessible files and a ransomware message on workstations in the Finance department.

Inject 2 (09:30 AM): Security Operations Center (SOC) alerts on unusual network traffic originating from a server in the Finance department, consistent with ransomware propagation.

Inject 3 (10:00 AM): An email arrives at the CISO's inbox, purportedly from the attackers, demanding $500,000 in Bitcoin within 48 hours.

Inject 4 (11:00 AM): The Head of Finance reports that payroll processing cannot commence, impacting employee payments scheduled for the end of the day.

Inject 5 (1:00 PM): A forensic analysis confirms that sensitive financial data was exfiltrated before encryption.

These injects create a dynamic environment that requires the incident response team to react and adapt. The pacing of the injects is also important; too rapid can overwhelm participants, while too slow can lead to stagnation.

The development of realistic scenarios also necessitates a clear understanding of the exercise's objectives. What specific capabilities or processes are being tested? Are we focusing on technical detection and eradication, communication and coordination, decision-making under pressure, or the effective engagement of external resources? Clearly defined objectives help tailor the scenario and its injects to achieve the desired learning outcomes. For instance, if the objective is to test the team's ability to manage public relations during a breach, injects related to media inquiries or social media reactions will be paramount.

Furthermore, it is beneficial to categorize scenarios based on their complexity and the type of exercise they are designed for. A simple tabletop exercise might focus on a single aspect of a scenario, such as initial notification and escalation, with participants discussing their roles and actions. A more complex functional exercise might involve simulated actions within a controlled environment, such as isolating a compromised segment of the network. A full-scale simulation or live-fire exercise would replicate a real incident as closely as possible, involving all relevant personnel and systems. The choice of scenario should align with the intended exercise format and the maturity of the incident response program. A nascent program might start with simpler tabletop exercises based on common threats, gradually progressing to more complex functional and full-scale exercises as their capabilities mature.

A critical, yet often overlooked, aspect of scenario development is ensuring they are relevant to the organization's specific industry and regulatory environment. For example, a financial institution must consider scenarios that involve compliance with regulations like SOX, PCI DSS, or GDPR, and the potential for regulatory fines or reporting obligations. A healthcare organization must consider HIPAA compliance, patient privacy, and the potential impact on patient safety. Scenarios should reflect these specific pressures and requirements, making the training more impactful and ensuring that responders are prepared for the unique challenges of their sector. This means incorporating elements like data breach notification timelines, specific reporting requirements to regulatory bodies, or the need to preserve evidence for potential legal proceedings related to compliance violations.

The creation of realistic scenarios is not a task to be undertaken lightly. It requires collaboration between cybersecurity professionals, IT operations, legal counsel, public relations, business unit leaders, and potentially even external subject matter experts. This cross-functional input ensures that the scenarios accurately reflect the technical realities, business impacts, and legal/regulatory considerations that an organization would face during a genuine cyber crisis. The effort invested in developing these realistic scenarios pays dividends by fostering a prepared, confident, and effective incident response capability that can withstand the pressures of a real-world attack. It is through these carefully constructed simulations that organizations can identify weaknesses, refine their strategies, and ultimately protect themselves against the ever-evolving landscape of cyber threats.

Tabletop exercises serve as a vital stepping stone in the journey toward a robust incident response capability. They offer a practical, yet controlled, environment for evaluating an organization's preparedness without the significant resource commitment and operational risks associated with full-scale simulations. By focusing on specific incident scenarios, particularly those involving the activation and coordinated response within an Industrial Control Systems (ICS) environment, these exercises bring theoretical plans to life. This subsection will explore the methodology for designing and conducting effective tabletop exercises, emphasizing the critical aspects of ICS activation, cross-functional team coordination, and the identification of actionable improvements.

The fundamental purpose of a tabletop exercise is to stimulate critical thinking and problem-solving among the incident response team and key stakeholders. Unlike live-fire drills or functional exercises, tabletop sessions are primarily discussion-based. Participants, gathered around a table (hence the name), are presented with a simulated incident scenario and are guided through a series of events and decisions. The facilitator's role is paramount in steering these discussions, ensuring they remain focused, productive, and aligned with the exercise objectives. This approach allows for the exploration of complex decision trees, communication pathways, and interdependencies that might be difficult or impossible to replicate in a less interactive format. For organizations with significant ICS or Operational Technology (OT) footprints, tabletop exercises are particularly valuable for bridging the often-significant divide between IT security teams and OT engineering or operations personnel. These exercises can uncover misunderstandings about system criticality, operational tolerances, and the unique safety protocols that govern ICS environments, which are fundamentally different from typical IT infrastructure.

Designing an effective tabletop exercise begins with a clear definition of its objectives. What specific aspects of the ICS incident response plan are being tested? Is the focus on the initial detection and alerting mechanisms? The process for isolating compromised ICS components? The communication protocols between IT, OT, and executive leadership? Or perhaps the coordination with external regulatory bodies and emergency services? For instance, a primary objective might be to assess the team's ability to collectively identify a cyber threat targeting the ICS, understand its potential impact on physical processes, and initiate the correct isolation and containment procedures without jeopardizing safety or essential services. Another objective could be to evaluate the effectiveness of the pre-defined communication tree and the clarity of information shared between different operational units during a critical event.

Once objectives are set, a realistic and relevant scenario must be developed. For ICS environments, these scenarios should reflect the unique threat vectors and potential impacts associated with industrial operations. Common themes include:

Ransomware affecting ICS network segments: This could involve the encryption of Programmable Logic Controllers (PLCs), Human-Machine Interfaces (HMIs), or supervisory control and data acquisition (SCADA) servers, leading to the shutdown or erratic behavior of industrial processes. The exercise would explore the decision-making process for identifying the scope of the attack, determining whether to pay a ransom (often not an option for critical infrastructure), and the procedures for restoring operations from backups, which are frequently air-gapped or on separate operational networks.

Denial-of-Service (DoS) or Distributed Denial-of-Service (DDoS) attacks targeting ICS communication infrastructure: This could disrupt the flow of data between sensors, controllers, and operators, rendering the system unresponsive or prone to unsafe states. The exercise would focus on the detection of communication loss, the diagnostic steps to determine the cause, and the activation of manual or backup control mechanisms.

Malicious code injection into PLCs or other control devices: This scenario might involve the alteration of control logic, leading to incorrect process parameters, equipment damage, or safety hazards. The exercise would test the ability to detect anomalous process behavior, correlate it with potential network intrusions, and perform forensic analysis on control devices to identify the injected malicious code.

Compromise of remote access points to the ICS: This could involve attackers gaining unauthorized access through VPNs, third-party vendor connections, or legacy remote management tools. The exercise would scrutinize the authentication and authorization procedures, the monitoring of remote access sessions, and the incident response steps to revoke compromised credentials and secure the access pathways.

Insider threats, both malicious and accidental, within the OT environment: This could range from an engineer inadvertently introducing malware via a USB drive to a disgruntled employee intentionally manipulating control parameters. The exercise would test access controls, activity logging, and the internal investigation procedures.

When developing an ICS-specific scenario for a tabletop exercise, it is crucial to include detailed "injects" that mimic the progression of a real incident. These injects serve as the narrative drivers, presenting new information or challenges to the participants at predetermined intervals. For an ICS scenario, these injects should be technically specific and operationally relevant. For instance, an inject might read: "At 09:15, SCADA alarms indicate a deviation from normal pressure setpoints in Reactor 3. Simultaneously, the HMI for this unit becomes unresponsive. The OT historian shows a significant increase in error rates for communication with PLC *R3*01 over the last 15 minutes." This inject immediately presents a dual problem: a process anomaly and a communication failure, prompting the team to consider both physical and cyber causes.

Another type of inject could focus on communication challenges: "At 10:00 AM, a call comes in from the Operations Manager stating that the plant supervisor has ordered a controlled shutdown of the affected process line due to safety concerns. The incident response team has not yet confirmed the root cause or initiated containment. Discuss how you will coordinate your actions with the operations team and manage this conflicting priority." Such an inject forces participants to grapple with real-world operational pressures and the need for clear, timely communication between different departments, especially when safety is paramount.

Facilitating an effective tabletop exercise requires more than just presenting a scenario. The facilitator acts as the narrator, the referee, and, at times, the devil's advocate. They must guide the participants through the exercise, posing questions that probe their understanding of the plan and their decision-making processes. Key questions include:

"Who is notified first, and why?" This probes the escalation matrix and the understanding of roles and responsibilities.

"What information do you need to make a decision about isolating this segment?" This assesses the team's understanding of diagnostic requirements and their confidence in identifying the true impact.

"What are the potential consequences of taking action X versus action Y on the physical process?" This highlights the critical IT vs. OT decision-making trade-offs.

"How is communication managed with external stakeholders, such as regulatory bodies or the public?" This tests the crisis communication plan and the designation of spokespersons.

"What evidence needs to be preserved, and how will it be secured?" This focuses on the forensic aspects and the chain of custody for digital evidence.

During the exercise, it is also beneficial to have a dedicated scribe to meticulously record the discussions, decisions made, challenges encountered, and any identified gaps. This documentation is invaluable for the post-exercise debrief and for generating the final report. The scribe should capture not only what was said but also the rationale behind decisions, the questions raised, and any emergent issues.

A critical component of ICS tabletop exercises is the inclusion of personnel from both IT security and OT engineering/operations. These individuals often speak different technical languages and have distinct priorities. IT security professionals are primarily concerned with data integrity, system availability, and threat containment from a network perspective. OT engineers, on the other hand, are focused on process stability, safety, efficiency, and uptime for the physical operations. A well-facilitated exercise can create a common ground for these teams to collaborate, understand each other's perspectives, and develop a unified response strategy. For example, an inject might highlight a situation where IT wants to immediately disconnect an affected server from the network, while OT explains that doing so would lead to an uncontrolled shutdown of a critical manufacturing process, posing a safety risk. The discussion that ensues would explore alternative containment strategies that satisfy both IT security requirements and OT operational constraints.

The discussion around ICS activation is particularly important in tabletop exercises. This involves more than just turning on a switch; it's about the sequence of events, the identification of the responsible parties, and the establishment of the command structure for managing the incident. The exercise should prompt participants to discuss:

Triggering events: What specific indicators or alarms would lead to the formal activation of the ICS incident response plan? Is it a single high-priority alarm, or a combination of events?

Notification and reporting: Who needs to be informed immediately when the plan is activated? What is the established communication channel? How are notifications cascaded up to executive leadership and down to operational teams?

Establishment of the Incident Command Post (ICP): Where will the ICP be located? Who will lead it? What are the roles and responsibilities of each member of the core incident response team? This is especially crucial for ICS incidents where both IT and OT leadership must be present and integrated.

Resource allocation: What personnel, tools, and external support are immediately required? This includes ensuring that specialized OT personnel with knowledge of specific control systems are available.

Activation of specialized sub-teams: Are there specific sub-teams for forensics, communications, legal, or external liaison that need to be activated based on the incident type and severity?

For instance, a scenario might involve a suspected compromise of a Distributed Control System (DCS) managing a chemical plant. The exercise would prompt discussions about the trigger for activating the ICS IR plan: "If an operator observes anomalous temperature readings in the primary distillation column that deviate by more than 15% from the expected range, and the DCS logs indicate intermittent communication failures with the PLC controlling the heating elements, does this constitute an activation trigger for the ICS IR plan?" Following this, participants would discuss who is responsible for making that activation decision and to whom they report it. They would then be asked to outline the immediate steps for establishing the ICP, designating an incident commander (who might be a senior OT manager with overall responsibility, supported by an IT security lead for technical response), and mobilizing the necessary technical teams for assessment and containment.

A key benefit of tabletop exercises is their ability to uncover gaps in existing procedures, documentation, and training. During the discussions, participants may realize that:

Roles and responsibilities are unclear: Different individuals might believe they are responsible for the same task, or critical tasks might fall through the cracks because no one assumes ownership.

Communication channels are inadequate: The established communication methods might be inefficient, or key stakeholders might not be included in the communication tree.

Technical understanding is lacking: IT personnel may not fully grasp the implications of their actions on physical processes, or OT personnel may not understand the nuances of network security.

Documentation is incomplete or outdated: Response plans might not reflect current system architectures, or contact lists may be out of date.

Tools and resources are insufficient: The exercise might reveal that the team lacks the necessary diagnostic tools for ICS networks or that required external support contacts are not readily available.

These identified gaps become the focus of the post-exercise debrief and subsequent action items. For example, if the exercise highlights a lack of understanding regarding the specific network protocols used by a particular PLC vendor, the action item might be to develop a supplementary guide for the IT security team on how to monitor and troubleshoot that specific protocol, or to schedule cross-training sessions between IT and OT teams.

Following the exercise, a thorough debriefing session is essential. This is where the real learning takes place. The facilitator, with input from the scribe and all participants, guides a discussion to:

Review the exercise objectives: Were the objectives met?

Identify successes: What went well? What procedures or actions were effective?

Identify challenges and areas for improvement: What were the major obstacles encountered? Where did the team struggle? What decisions were difficult?

Discuss lessons learned: What new insights were gained about the incident response process, the ICS environment, or team coordination?

Develop actionable recommendations: What specific steps will be taken to address the identified gaps and improve future readiness? These recommendations should be concrete, assigned owners, and given deadlines.

The output of the debriefing session should be a formal report that summarizes the exercise, its outcomes, and the agreed-upon action plan. This report should be shared with relevant stakeholders, including senior management, to ensure buy-in and support for the necessary improvements.

For ICS environments, the debriefing often involves a more in-depth discussion of the interdependencies between IT and OT. For instance, a key lesson learned might be the critical need for IT security to understand the concept of "fail-safe states" in OT, meaning that in the event of an incident, the system must revert to a known safe operating condition, even if that means temporarily halting production. Conversely, OT personnel might learn about the importance of detailed logging of all operational changes, which is crucial for forensic investigation and attribution.

Furthermore, tabletop exercises, when conducted periodically, foster a culture of preparedness and continuous improvement. They are not a one-time event but an integral part of an ongoing incident response program. The frequency of these exercises should be determined by the organization's risk profile, the complexity of its ICS environment, and regulatory requirements. For critical infrastructure organizations, annual or even semi-annual tabletop exercises focusing on various ICS-related scenarios are highly recommended. The scenarios themselves should evolve over time, becoming more complex and realistic as the organization's response capabilities mature and as new threats emerge. For example, an organization that successfully conducted an exercise on ransomware might then progress to a more complex scenario involving a coordinated attack that combines ransomware with a physical manipulation of control parameters, requiring a more integrated and sophisticated response.

Finally, the insights gained from tabletop exercises can inform other aspects of incident response planning and execution. They can highlight the need for additional training for specific teams, the procurement of new security tools or technologies, the refinement of communication protocols, or even the revision of the overall incident response policy. By diligently designing, facilitating, and debriefing tabletop exercises, organizations can significantly enhance their ability to effectively activate and coordinate ICS incident response, thereby protecting their critical operations and ensuring business continuity in the face of evolving cyber threats. This iterative process of simulation, discussion, and improvement is fundamental to building a resilient and effective defense posture for any organization that relies on industrial control systems.

Functional exercises represent a critical evolution from the discussion-based nature of tabletop exercises, shifting the focus to the practical execution of specific incident response capabilities within an Industrial Control Systems (ICS) environment. While tabletop exercises excel at testing decision-making, communication flows, and the overall understanding of procedures, functional exercises dive deeper by demanding active performance of tasks. These drills are designed to validate that teams can not only *talk* about responding but can actually *do* it, under simulated conditions that mimic operational stress and technical complexity. By isolating and testing discrete functions, organizations can pinpoint specific areas of weakness and refine their operational readiness with a tangible, hands-on approach. This subsection will explore the methodology for designing, conducting, and evaluating functional exercises that target critical ICS incident response capabilities.

The fundamental principle behind a functional exercise is to move beyond theoretical discussion and into the realm of practical application. Unlike tabletop exercises, which rely on verbal responses and hypothetical actions, functional exercises require participants to actively perform predefined tasks. This could involve anything from establishing a secure communication link with a remote diagnostic team to executing the steps for isolating a compromised ICS network segment, or even simulating the recovery of a critical controller from a backup. The scope of a functional exercise is deliberately narrowed to focus on a specific capability or a tightly integrated set of capabilities, allowing for in-depth validation and refinement.

Designing an effective functional exercise begins with a clear definition of the specific capability or function to be tested. For ICS environments, these capabilities often revolve around the unique technical and operational requirements of industrial systems. Some common examples of specific capabilities that can be tested through functional exercises include:

Communication Protocol Validation: Testing the ability to establish and maintain secure, reliable communication channels between different response teams (e.g., IT security, OT engineering, control room operators) and between these teams and external entities (e.g., critical vendors, regulatory bodies). This could involve setting up ad-hoc communication links, verifying encryption protocols, or testing backup communication systems when primary channels are disrupted. For instance, an exercise might simulate the loss of primary network connectivity to a remote substation and require the team to establish a secure cellular or satellite link for remote monitoring and control.

Containment Procedure Execution: Practicing the precise steps involved in isolating compromised ICS components or network segments without causing undue disruption to essential physical processes. This is a highly sensitive area in ICS response, as improper isolation can lead to safety hazards or uncontrolled shutdowns. A functional exercise might involve simulating a malware outbreak on an HMI and requiring the team to follow a predefined playbook for disconnecting that specific device or segment from the rest of the ICS network, while ensuring that critical safety systems remain operational.

Forensic Data Acquisition and Preservation: Testing the ability to collect relevant digital evidence from ICS devices (e.g., PLCs, HMIs, SCADA servers) in a forensically sound manner. This includes understanding the unique challenges of ICS data, such as proprietary file formats, limited storage on embedded devices, and the potential impact of data collection on system operation. An exercise could involve tasking a forensic team with imaging a specific PLC's memory or collecting log files from a SCADA historian, while adhering to chain-of-custody protocols.

System Restoration and Recovery: Practicing the procedures for restoring critical ICS functions or components from backups after an incident. This might involve restoring configuration files, firmware, or operational data, and verifying the integrity and functionality of the restored systems. For example, an exercise could simulate the failure of a critical controller due to a logic error or corruption and require the team to restore it from a validated backup, then perform functional tests to ensure it operates within safe parameters.

Incident Triage and Analysis: Simulating the arrival of multiple alerts and alarms from different ICS monitoring systems and testing the team's ability to quickly triage, prioritize, and analyze them to identify potential security incidents. This could involve using security information and event management (SIEM) tools, specialized ICS anomaly detection systems, and collaborative analysis platforms.

Vendor and Third-Party Coordination: Testing the procedures for engaging and coordinating with external vendors or third-party support for specific ICS components or systems. This is crucial, as many critical ICS operations rely on specialized knowledge held by external experts. An exercise could involve simulating a situation where a specific vendor's support is required to diagnose or resolve an issue on a unique piece of control equipment, and assessing the team's ability to effectively brief the vendor and guide their actions.

Failover and Redundancy Testing: For systems that employ redundancy, a functional exercise can specifically test the automatic or manual failover mechanisms designed to maintain operational continuity during an outage or failure. This could involve deliberately taking a primary component offline and verifying that the backup component seamlessly takes over without impacting the physical process.

The design of functional exercises requires careful planning to ensure realism without introducing unacceptable risks. Unlike tabletop exercises, which can be conducted in a conference room, functional exercises often require access to a controlled test environment or a subset of the production environment that can be temporarily isolated or placed in a safe mode. The "scenario" in a functional exercise is less about a narrative and more about the specific task or set of tasks to be performed and the conditions under which they must be executed.

For instance, if the objective is to test containment procedures, the exercise might involve a simulated malware injection into a non-critical but representative ICS network segment. Participants would then be tasked with executing the documented steps to firewall off this segment, reconfigure network devices, and verify the absence of lateral movement. The success of the exercise would be measured by how efficiently and accurately these steps are performed, and whether the physical process remains unaffected.

A crucial element of functional exercises is the selection of the appropriate environment and the precise definition of the "injects" or triggers that initiate the task. Injects for functional exercises are not narrative events, but rather specific conditions or prompts that require a defined action. For example, an inject might be: "System alert: PLC

*X shows a pattern of irregular command execution consistent with malicious injection. Task: Initiate isolation of PLC*X and its associated network segment according to Procedure 7.3. Verify network separation using ping tests to adjacent network devices." This inject is a direct command to perform a specific task, referencing a documented procedure.

Facilitation of functional exercises takes on a different character compared to tabletop sessions. The facilitator's role shifts from guiding discussion to observing performance, providing clear instructions for the task, and ensuring that participants adhere to safety protocols and documented procedures. The facilitator also acts as the "inject manager," introducing the specific tasks and monitoring progress. In many cases, a "white cell" or a separate team of technical experts might be involved to simulate system responses, provide simulated data, or even act as adversaries if the exercise is designed to test defensive capabilities directly.

Key questions posed during functional exercises are action-oriented and focused on execution:

"Are you following the steps outlined in Procedure X?" This probes adherence to documentation.

"What is the expected outcome of this action on the physical process?" This checks for understanding of operational impact.

"What safety checks do you need to perform before executing this command?" This emphasizes safety protocols.

"Can you confirm the successful completion of this containment step?" This requires validation of task completion.

"Who needs to be notified upon successful isolation of the compromised segment?" This tests the immediate follow-on communication.

The "scribe" in a functional exercise is critical for documenting not just decisions, but the precise actions taken, the time taken for each step, any deviations from procedure, and the outcomes observed. This detailed log forms the basis for evaluating the efficiency and effectiveness of the tested capability. For example, if a containment procedure is documented to take 15 minutes but the team took 45 minutes to complete it, the scribe's notes will highlight the specific delays and potential reasons, such as lack of familiarity with the tools or inadequate access permissions.

The integration of IT and OT personnel is equally, if not more, critical in functional exercises. These drills often highlight the practical challenges of collaboration when IT security actions have direct physical consequences, and vice versa. For instance, when testing network segmentation, an IT security team might perform actions that impact network traffic flow. An OT engineer needs to be present to confirm that these actions do not disrupt critical control loops or safety interlocks. Conversely, if an OT operator needs to manually adjust a process parameter as part of a recovery step, an IT security analyst needs to understand the implications of that adjustment from a security monitoring perspective. Functional exercises provide a live environment to work through these interdependencies, identify misalignments in understanding, and refine cross-functional operating procedures.

A particularly valuable aspect of functional exercises in ICS environments is the testing of specialized communication and activation protocols. Beyond the initial activation of an incident response plan, functional exercises can test the readiness to establish dedicated incident communication channels, activate emergency operations centers (EOCs) or incident command posts (ICPs) with specific ICS response teams, and confirm the availability and functionality of specialized communication equipment. For instance, an exercise might require the activation of a redundant communication system that relies on a different network infrastructure than the primary ICS network, ensuring that critical communication can be maintained even if the main network is compromised.

The identification of gaps and areas for improvement is a primary outcome of functional exercises. These exercises are designed to expose deficiencies that might not be apparent in tabletop discussions. These gaps can be technical, procedural, or human-factor related:

Technical Deficiencies: This could include discovering that diagnostic tools are not compatible with certain ICS protocols, that remote access capabilities are insufficient for effective troubleshooting, or that backup systems are not properly configured for rapid restoration. For example, an exercise might reveal that the IT team's standard tools for network analysis cannot interpret the proprietary data packets from a specific PLC vendor, necessitating the acquisition of new tools or specialized training.

Procedural Weaknesses: Participants may find that documented procedures are unclear, incomplete, or simply impractical to execute under pressure. This could lead to delays, incorrect actions, or safety risks. For instance, a containment procedure might be too complex, requiring multiple authorization steps that significantly slow down the isolation of a compromised system, or it might fail to account for the specific shutdown sequence required for a particular industrial process.

Skill and Training Gaps: Functional exercises often highlight where personnel lack the necessary skills or training to perform critical tasks. This might involve a lack of familiarity with specific ICS hardware, software, or diagnostic interfaces. For example, an exercise testing forensic data acquisition from a specific SCADA server might reveal that the designated forensic analyst has never worked with that particular server operating system or its unique logging mechanisms.

Resource Shortages: The execution of tasks might reveal a shortage of necessary equipment, tools, or personnel. This could include a lack of available laptops with specialized software, insufficient spare parts for critical components, or an insufficient number of trained personnel to manage multiple concurrent tasks.

Communication Breakdowns: Even with clear communication plans, functional exercises can reveal practical failures in communication. This might involve issues with clarity of technical jargon between IT and OT, failure to pass critical information in a timely manner, or the inability to reach key personnel. For example, during a simulated system restoration, the OT team might fail to adequately inform the IT security team about specific diagnostic tests being performed, leading to security alerts that are misinterpreted as a new incident.

The post-exercise debriefing is where the practical lessons learned from functional exercises are consolidated and translated into actionable improvements. This debriefing should involve all participants, the facilitators, the scribes, and potentially observers or subject matter experts. The discussion should focus on:

Task Performance Analysis: Detailed review of how each task was performed, including the time taken, the accuracy, adherence to procedures, and any deviations.

Root Cause Analysis of Failures: For tasks that were not completed successfully or were completed inefficiently, a thorough analysis of why the failure occurred is essential. Was it a problem with the procedure, the tools, the training, or the team dynamics?

Effectiveness of Tools and Technologies: Evaluation of whether the tools and technologies used were adequate and effective for the task.

Clarity and Usability of Procedures: Assessment of whether the documented procedures were clear, concise, and actionable under the simulated conditions.

Interpersonal and Interdepartmental Dynamics: Discussion of how well the different teams collaborated, communicated, and supported each other during the exercise.

The output of the debriefing is a set of concrete, measurable, achievable, relevant, and time-bound (SMART) recommendations. These recommendations should be prioritized and assigned owners. For example, if a functional exercise revealed that the team lacked the necessary scripts to automate a routine diagnostic check on a specific type of PLC, the recommendation might be: "Develop and validate automated diagnostic scripts for [Specific PLC Type] by [Date], assigned to [IT/OT Team Lead]." Or, if a procedure for isolating a network segment was found to be overly complex, the recommendation might be: "Revise Procedure 7.3 for network isolation to incorporate [Specific Simplification] and reduce execution time by 20%, by [Date], assigned to [Procedure Owner]."

Functional exercises are not meant to be a one-off event. They should be conducted regularly and should evolve in complexity and scope as the organization's incident response capabilities mature. The frequency of these exercises should be informed by the organization's risk assessment, regulatory requirements, and the rate of change in its ICS environment. For organizations with critical infrastructure, a regular cadence of functional exercises, perhaps quarterly or semi-annually, focusing on different sets of capabilities, is highly recommended. This iterative process of testing, identifying weaknesses, and implementing improvements is fundamental to building a truly resilient and effective ICS incident response capability.

Furthermore, the insights gained from functional exercises can directly inform the development and refinement of training programs. If an exercise repeatedly exposes a lack of proficiency in a particular area, it indicates a need for targeted training for the relevant personnel. This might involve hands-on workshops, simulations using the actual tools and systems in a lab environment, or cross-training initiatives between IT and OT teams to build a shared understanding of operational and security imperatives. For instance, if a functional exercise simulating a ransomware attack on an HMI reveals that the control room operators are hesitant to initiate a manual override due to a lack of confidence in the procedure or potential consequences, this would directly translate into a need for enhanced operator training on manual control procedures during cyber incidents.

The value of functional exercises lies in their ability to translate theoretical preparedness into demonstrable competence. By actively engaging teams in performing critical tasks under simulated pressure, organizations can identify and rectify deficiencies before a real incident occurs. This hands-on approach, when meticulously planned, executed, and debriefed, is indispensable for safeguarding the integrity, availability, and safety of industrial control systems in an increasingly complex threat landscape. It bridges the gap between knowing what to do and being able to do it effectively, efficiently, and safely when it matters most.

The culmination of rigorous incident response preparation in the Industrial Control Systems (ICS) domain is the full-scale simulation, often referred to as integrated response drills. Moving beyond the focused, single-capability validation of functional exercises, these simulations are designed to test the interconnectedness and holistic effectiveness of an organization's entire incident response framework. They are characterized by their ambition to replicate the multifaceted nature of a real-time cyber incident, demanding simultaneous engagement from multiple departments, testing communication channels under extreme duress, and evaluating the overarching resilience of the ICS structure in a dynamic, high-fidelity environment. The ultimate aim is to foster confidence in the established protocols and systems, while simultaneously revealing critical areas that necessitate further refinement before a genuine threat materializes.

Planning a full-scale simulation is an undertaking of significant complexity, requiring meticulous coordination across diverse organizational silos. Unlike tabletop exercises that can be conducted with minimal logistical demands or functional exercises that might focus on a specific technical function, a full-scale simulation necessitates the active participation of virtually all stakeholders involved in incident response. This includes, but is not limited to, IT security operations, OT engineering and operations, control room personnel, physical security, legal counsel, corporate communications, executive leadership, and potentially external partners such as regulatory bodies or key vendors. The sheer scale of coordination involved in bringing these disparate groups together, aligning their understanding of the simulated scenario, and ensuring their availability for the duration of the drill is a formidable challenge in itself. It demands a dedicated planning team with a deep understanding of both the operational technology (OT) environment and the incident response lifecycle, capable of weaving together a believable and challenging narrative that stresses all facets of the response.

The core of a full-scale simulation lies in its fidelity to a real-world event. This is achieved through the development of a comprehensive scenario that mimics the progression of a sophisticated cyber-attack against an ICS environment. Such scenarios are often designed to be multi-vector, meaning they involve an initial intrusion that then escalates to impact various layers of the ICS, potentially affecting data integrity, system availability, and even physical processes. For instance, a simulation might commence with a phishing attack that compromises an IT workstation, leading to the deployment of malware that subsequently breaches the network segmentation and begins to impact operational HMIs or PLCs. The simulation must account for the cascading effects of such an attack, mirroring the unpredictable nature of real incidents where an initial compromise can quickly evolve into a broader crisis. This requires a scenario development process that considers not just the technical attack vectors but also the human element, the communication breakdowns that can occur under stress, and the decision-making pressures faced by leaders.

A critical aspect of these integrated drills is the rigorous testing of inter-departmental communication under simulated crisis conditions. In a real incident, the effectiveness of the response hinges on the seamless flow of information between IT and OT teams, whose priorities and technical languages can often differ. Full-scale simulations deliberately create communication bottlenecks and stresses to identify weaknesses. This might involve simulating the loss of primary communication channels, forcing teams to rely on secondary or ad-hoc methods, or introducing conflicting information that teams must resolve. The simulation scenario will often include "injects" that specifically require cross-functional communication and decision-making. For example, an inject might state: "Alert: Uncommanded changes detected in the control logic of Turbine 3 HMI. OT engineering is observing abnormal sensor readings from the associated turbine. IT security has identified a potential malware signature on the HMI. Task: Establish a conference call between IT Security Lead, OT Operations Manager, and Control Room Supervisor to assess the threat and determine immediate containment actions, ensuring no disruption to critical safety systems." The success of this inject is not just in the action taken, but in how efficiently and effectively the teams communicate, share information, and collaboratively decide on a course of action. This highlights the need for pre-defined communication protocols, clear escalation paths, and potentially the use of dedicated incident command structures.

The evaluation of an organization's overall ICS incident response structure is a primary objective of full-scale simulations. This involves assessing not just the technical capabilities but also the procedural adherence, the decision-making processes, and the command and control mechanisms. A detailed observation framework is essential, with trained evaluators meticulously documenting participant actions, communication patterns, decision points, and adherence to documented procedures. These evaluators, often referred to as the "white cell" or "observer-controller team," play a crucial role in injecting realism into the simulation. They might act as external entities, such as regulators demanding information, or as unforeseen technical challenges that arise during the exercise, forcing the response team to adapt. The white cell also monitors the overall tempo of the exercise, ensuring that it remains challenging and realistic without becoming overwhelming or leading to a complete breakdown of the simulated response. Their observations are the foundation for the post-exercise analysis and the subsequent improvement of the response plan.

Success in these high-fidelity simulations translates directly into enhanced organizational confidence. When teams successfully navigate a complex, multi-stage simulated cyber-attack, it validates their training, their procedures, and their collective ability to respond effectively. This confidence is invaluable, as it reduces the uncertainty and hesitation that can plague an organization during a genuine incident. It allows response personnel to act with a greater degree of certainty, knowing that their actions have been tested and proven under simulated pressure. Moreover, the debriefing process following a successful simulation reinforces positive behaviors and strengthens the collective understanding of what constitutes effective incident response within the specific context of the organization's ICS environment. This builds a culture of preparedness and resilience.

However, the true power of full-scale simulations lies not just in their successes, but in their ability to uncover latent weaknesses and areas requiring refinement. These drills are designed to stress test the system to its breaking point, revealing gaps that might go unnoticed in less comprehensive exercises. For example, a simulation might reveal that the incident response plan, while comprehensive on paper, is overly complex to execute under time constraints, leading to delays in critical containment actions. It might expose a lack of clear roles and responsibilities during the escalation of an incident, resulting in confusion and duplicated efforts. Technical deficiencies can also be exposed, such as the inability to rapidly acquire forensic data from a specific type of ICS device or the failure of redundant communication systems to activate as expected. These findings, no matter how uncomfortable, are invaluable. They provide concrete, actionable intelligence that can be used to revise procedures, update training, procure necessary tools, or restructure response teams to address identified shortcomings.

The integration of IT and OT personnel in full-scale simulations is paramount. These exercises serve as a crucible for the often-challenging collaboration between these two critical domains. By placing them in a high-pressure scenario together, simulations highlight the practical implications of IT security actions on OT operations and vice versa. For instance, the IT security team might be tasked with isolating a segment of the network to contain a simulated malware spread. During the full-scale simulation, this action requires real-time coordination with OT engineers to ensure that the isolation does not inadvertently disrupt critical processes, compromise safety systems, or cause an uncontrolled shutdown. Conversely, OT operators might need to perform manual overrides or adjust process parameters as part of a recovery effort, and the IT security team needs to be in a position to monitor these actions from a security perspective and advise on potential risks. Full-scale simulations provide a tangible environment to work through these interdependencies, identify misunderstandings, and refine cross-functional operating procedures. They foster a shared understanding of the unique challenges and priorities faced by each domain, building a stronger, more cohesive incident response capability.

The complexity of coordinating diverse departments in a full-scale simulation cannot be overstated. It requires a robust logistical framework that includes a designated incident command post (ICP) or emergency operations center (EOC) where key decision-makers can convene. This physical or virtual space needs to be equipped with reliable communication systems, access to relevant documentation, and the ability to visualize the evolving situation, whether through dashboards displaying system status, network maps, or status reports from different teams. The simulation often involves pre-scripted injects, but also allows for dynamic unfolding of events based on the decisions made by the response team. For example, if the response team successfully contains the initial malware, the white cell might introduce a secondary attack vector or a simulated physical consequence of the initial compromise, such as a sensor failure. This dynamic element makes the simulation more realistic and tests the adaptability of the response team. The simulation must also account for the potential impact on business operations and public perception, requiring the involvement of corporate communications and executive leadership to practice crisis communication strategies.

Evaluating the effectiveness of communication channels under stress is a hallmark of these drills. This goes beyond simply testing whether phones or radios work. It involves assessing the clarity, accuracy, and timeliness of information exchange. Are IT and OT teams using a common lexicon when discussing threats and impacts? Are status updates concise and actionable? Are critical decisions being effectively communicated down the chain of command? The simulation might introduce scenarios where communication lines are degraded or deliberately jammed, forcing participants to adapt and find alternative means of relaying vital information. This practical experience in overcoming communication hurdles is invaluable, as it prepares individuals and teams for the realities of high-stress environments where clear and concise communication is paramount for successful resolution. The debriefing phase critically analyzes these communication exchanges, identifying patterns of miscommunication, information overload, or insufficient situational awareness.

The ultimate success of a full-scale simulation is measured by its contribution to tangible improvements in the organization's incident response posture. It is not merely an exercise in validating existing capabilities, but a strategic tool for identifying vulnerabilities and driving change. The actionable insights derived from these drills inform the revision of incident response plans, the development of targeted training programs, the enhancement of security technologies, and the refinement of cross-functional collaboration strategies. Organizations that regularly engage in these high-fidelity simulations are better positioned to withstand the inevitable cyber threats that target their critical ICS infrastructure, ensuring operational continuity, safety, and the integrity of their industrial processes in an increasingly complex and dangerous digital landscape. The commitment to conducting these comprehensive drills demonstrates a mature understanding of the evolving threat environment and a proactive approach to safeguarding vital industrial assets.

The conclusion of any incident response exercise, whether a simple tabletop discussion or a complex full-scale simulation, is merely the commencement of the truly transformative phase: post exercise evaluation and the subsequent implementation of improvement cycles. This is where the real value of preparedness investment is realized, transforming observed performance into tangible enhancements that fortify an organization's defenses against future cyber threats targeting its Industrial Control Systems (ICS). Without a structured and diligent approach to reviewing what transpired during an exercise, the exercise itself risks becoming a perfunctory event, consuming valuable resources with little lasting impact.

The cornerstone of this post-exercise phase is the debriefing. This is not merely a casual conversation among participants but a formal, structured session designed to elicit candid feedback, identify successes, and critically, uncover shortcomings. The debriefing should ideally involve all participants who actively engaged in the exercise, along with the evaluators or the "white cell" team. It is crucial to establish an environment of psychological safety where individuals feel comfortable discussing their experiences, challenges, and perceived failures without fear of reprisal. The facilitator of the debriefing plays a pivotal role in guiding the discussion, ensuring it remains focused on the exercise objectives and observable behaviors, rather than devolving into personal critiques. A common and effective technique is to begin by asking participants to recount their perspective on how the exercise unfolded, starting from the initial inject or scenario trigger through to the simulated conclusion. This allows for a chronological reconstruction of events from multiple vantage points, revealing divergences in perception and understanding.

During the debriefing, several key areas must be thoroughly explored. Firstly, the alignment of exercise actions with the pre-defined objectives is paramount. Were the goals of the exercise met? Were the specific capabilities or procedures intended to be tested effectively evaluated? This requires a clear understanding of what the exercise set out to achieve, which should have been communicated to participants prior to the drill. Secondly, the effectiveness of communication channels and protocols needs rigorous scrutiny. How did information flow between teams, especially between IT and OT personnel? Were there instances of miscommunication, information overload, or delays in relaying critical intelligence? The debriefing should delve into the specifics of these exchanges, analyzing not just the content but also the medium and the timeliness. For example, a debrief might reveal that while an urgent alert was sent, it was buried in a generic email chain, or that technical jargon used by IT security was not readily understood by operational staff, leading to delayed action.

Thirdly, the decision-making processes come under the spotlight. Were decisions made in a timely and informed manner? Were the correct individuals involved in key decision points? The debriefing can uncover instances where decisions were delayed due to ambiguity in roles, lack of access to crucial information, or an over-reliance on a single individual. It is also an opportunity to assess the adherence to established incident response plans and playbooks. Were the documented procedures followed? If deviations occurred, were they justified, and were they documented? The debriefing should also encourage participants to highlight what worked well. Acknowledging and reinforcing effective practices is just as important as identifying areas for improvement. This might include praising the swift action of a particular team, the clarity of a communication, or the successful application of a specific technical tool.

Following the initial debriefing, a more detailed analysis phase commences. This involves synthesizing the collective feedback from participants and the observations meticulously recorded by the white cell or evaluators during the exercise. The objective here is to move beyond anecdotal evidence and establish a clear, objective assessment of performance against the exercise's stated goals. This analytical process often leads to the creation of a comprehensive After-Action Report (AAR). The AAR is a critical document that serves as the formal record of the exercise and its outcomes. It typically includes a summary of the exercise objectives, a description of the scenario, an overview of the participating teams, a detailed analysis of performance, and, most importantly, a list of identified strengths and weaknesses, along with actionable recommendations for improvement.

When analyzing performance, it is crucial to adopt a systematic approach. For full-scale simulations in an ICS environment, this might involve evaluating specific aspects such as:

Containment Effectiveness: How quickly and effectively were the simulated threats contained? Were containment measures disruptive to critical operations, and if so, was this disruption managed appropriately?

Eradication and Recovery Efficiency: How efficiently were the threats eradicated, and how seamless was the transition to recovery and restoration of normal operations? This includes assessing the accuracy and completeness of system backups and the effectiveness of restoration procedures.

Detection and Analysis Accuracy: How rapidly and accurately were the simulated intrusions detected? Was the initial analysis of the threat sufficient to inform an effective response?

Communication and Coordination: Beyond mere functionality, was communication clear, concise, and effective across all involved parties, especially between

IT and OT domains? Was there a shared understanding of the situation and the response strategy?

Decision-Making Quality: Were decisions logical, timely, and based on the best available information? Were escalation paths clear and followed?

Adherence to Procedures: How well did teams follow established incident response plans, playbooks, and standard operating procedures?

The analytical phase is also where the invaluable lessons learned are distilled. These lessons are not merely observations; they are insights that point towards specific areas where organizational capabilities can be strengthened. For instance, a lesson learned might be that the process for requesting and obtaining external forensic support for a specific type of ICS component is too lengthy and bureaucratic. Or, it might be that the current network segmentation strategy, while theoretically sound, creates significant operational hurdles during incident containment, requiring complex workarounds.

The most critical output of the post-exercise evaluation is the identification of actionable improvements. These recommendations must be specific, measurable, achievable, relevant, and time-bound (SMART). They should directly address the weaknesses identified during the analysis and provide a clear path forward. The recommendations typically fall into several categories:

Incident Response Plan and Playbook Revisions: This is perhaps the most direct application of lessons learned. If the exercise revealed ambiguities, gaps, or outdated information in the existing plans, these must be corrected. This could involve clarifying roles and responsibilities, updating contact lists, revising procedural steps, or incorporating new threat intelligence and response strategies. For example, if a simulation highlighted a failure to adequately account for the security implications of physical access during an incident, the plan might be updated to include specific protocols for securing access points and verifying personnel identity.

Training and Awareness Enhancement: Exercises often expose deficiencies in individual or team knowledge and skills. Recommendations might include developing new training modules on specific topics (e.g., ICS forensics, secure remote access for OT, crisis communication), conducting more frequent refresher training, or enhancing awareness programs for all personnel about cyber threats to ICS. If a debrief revealed that control room operators were hesitant to report suspicious anomalies due to a lack of confidence in the reporting process, the recommendation might be to implement targeted training on anomaly detection and establish a more robust, supportive reporting mechanism.

Technology and Tooling Upgrades/Acquisitions: Exercises can reveal limitations in the existing security technology stack or the absence of critical tools. This could lead to recommendations for acquiring new security monitoring solutions, enhancing existing ones, or procuring specialized tools for ICS forensics, incident response, or secure communication. For instance, a simulation might demonstrate the need for a specialized network intrusion detection system (NIDS) tailored for ICS protocols, or the inability to rapidly acquire memory dumps from a particular brand of PLC, prompting the acquisition of appropriate tools and methodologies.

Process Improvement and Workflow Optimization: Beyond formal plans and technology, exercises can highlight inefficiencies in workflows or communication patterns. Recommendations might involve streamlining approval processes, establishing clearer escalation pathways, or improving inter-departmental collaboration mechanisms. If the simulation showed that the handoff of information between the initial IT detection team and the subsequent OT response team was a bottleneck, a recommendation might be to establish a dedicated liaison role or a more formalized transition process.

Organizational Structure and Resource Allocation: In some cases, exercises may reveal that the current organizational structure or resource allocation is not conducive to effective incident response. This could lead to recommendations for establishing dedicated incident response teams, reassigning responsibilities, or advocating for increased budget allocation for security personnel and tools.

The concept of continuous improvement is intrinsically linked to the post-exercise evaluation and improvement cycle. It is not a one-off event but a recurring process. The AAR and its recommendations should not be filed away and forgotten. Instead, they form the basis for action planning. An assigned individual or team is typically tasked with developing a concrete plan to address each recommendation, including timelines, responsible parties, and success metrics. Progress on these action plans should be tracked and reported regularly, perhaps at management review meetings or as part of ongoing operational assessments.

The insights gained from a full-scale simulation, when meticulously evaluated and translated into concrete actions, significantly elevate an organization's incident response posture. This iterative process, characterized by conducting exercises, rigorously evaluating their outcomes, and systematically implementing improvements, creates a robust feedback loop. This loop ensures that as the threat landscape evolves and the organization's operational technology environment changes, its incident response capabilities remain current, effective, and resilient. It moves the organization from a static state of preparedness to a dynamic, adaptive posture, where learning and improvement are embedded into the very fabric of its security operations.

Furthermore, the documentation generated throughout this process—from the exercise plan and scenario to the AAR and action plans—serves as an invaluable repository of organizational knowledge. This documentation is crucial for onboarding new personnel, for validating future training needs, and for demonstrating due diligence to regulators or auditors. It provides a traceable history of the organization's commitment to enhancing its ICS cybersecurity resilience.

The success of this improvement cycle also hinges on leadership commitment. Without active support from executive management, recommendations, especially those requiring significant investment in time, resources, or organizational change, may languish. Leaders must champion the process, ensuring that the findings from exercises are taken seriously and that the necessary resources are allocated to implement the recommended improvements. This demonstrates a genuine commitment to protecting the critical infrastructure that these systems manage.

In essence, the post-exercise evaluation and improvement cycle is the engine of resilience for ICS cybersecurity. It transforms the theoretical knowledge of incident response into practical, tested, and continuously refined capabilities. By embracing this cyclical approach—simulate, evaluate, improve, repeat—organizations can proactively adapt to the ever-present and evolving cyber threats, ensuring the continued safe, secure, and reliable operation of their vital industrial processes. This commitment to iterative enhancement is not merely a best practice; it is a fundamental requirement for maintaining operational integrity in today's interconnected and vulnerable world. The insights gleaned from a well-executed simulation, rigorously analyzed, are the seeds from which a truly robust and adaptive incident response capability grows. The diligent pursuit of these improvements fosters a culture of continuous learning and adaptation, ensuring that the organization is not just prepared for the next incident, but is actively becoming more resilient with every exercise conducted.

The aftermath of a cyber incident extends far beyond the technical remediation and restoration of systems. A critical, and often complex, dimension of incident response involves navigating the intricate web of legal and regulatory considerations that govern such events. Organizations operating in today's interconnected landscape are subject to a growing array of statutes, directives, and contractual obligations that dictate how they must respond to and report data breaches and other cyber-related incidents. A failure to understand and adhere to these legal frameworks can lead to severe penalties, including substantial fines, reputational damage, and protracted legal battles. Therefore, integrating legal and regulatory awareness into the core of any incident response strategy is not merely advisable; it is an absolute necessity for robust cybersecurity resilience.

The sheer volume and diversity of applicable regulations underscore the complexity of this domain. For organizations handling personal data of individuals within the European Union, the General Data Protection Regulation (GDPR) is a paramount concern. The GDPR imposes strict requirements on the processing of personal data and mandates specific actions in the event of a data breach. Article 33, for instance, requires organizations to notify the relevant supervisory authority "without undue delay and, where feasible, not later than 72 hours after having become aware of it," unless the breach is unlikely to result in a risk to the rights and freedoms of natural persons. Furthermore, if the breach is likely to result in a high risk to those rights and freedoms, individuals must also be notified "without undue delay" (Article

34). This notification obligation requires detailed information about the nature of the breach, the categories and approximate number of data subjects concerned, the likely consequences, and the measures taken or proposed to be taken by the controller. The definition of "personal data" under GDPR is broad, encompassing any information relating to an identified or identifiable natural person, making its scope far-reaching for many businesses.

In the United States, the legal landscape is more fragmented, with a patchwork of federal and state laws. The Health Insurance Portability and Accountability Act (HIPAA) is a cornerstone for entities involved in the healthcare sector. HIPAA's Breach Notification Rule (45 CFR §§ 164.400-414) requires covered entities and their business associates to provide notification following a breach of unsecured protected health information (PHI). Similar to GDPR, notifications must be made "without unreasonable delay and in no case later than 60 calendar days after discovery of the breach." The rule specifies notification requirements for individuals, the Secretary of Health and Human Services, and, in cases of breaches affecting 500 or more residents of a state or jurisdiction, prominent media outlets. The definition of "unsecured PHI" and the circumstances under which a breach is considered to have occurred are critical considerations for healthcare organizations.

Beyond HIPAA, numerous state-specific data breach notification laws exist. California's Consumer Privacy Act (CCPA), as amended by the California Privacy Rights Act (CPRA), grants California consumers significant rights regarding their personal information. While the CCPA does not mandate notification to a state authority in the same way as GDPR or HIPAA, it does impose obligations on businesses and provides a private right of action for certain data breaches, allowing consumers to recover statutory damages. This private right of action introduces a significant layer of potential liability that incident response plans must account for. Other states have enacted their own laws, often differing in definitions of reportable data, notification timelines, and the specific entities and types of data covered. For organizations operating across multiple states, the challenge lies in harmonizing their response to meet the most stringent requirements, a task that can be complex and resource-intensive.

The implications of these regulations extend directly to the incident response process. During an incident, the clock often begins ticking from the moment of "discovery" or "awareness" of a breach. This necessitates robust internal processes for identifying and categorizing potential security incidents swiftly. Organizations must have clear protocols for escalating suspected breaches to a designated incident response team, which should include legal counsel. Early involvement of legal experts is crucial for several reasons. Firstly, they can advise on attorney-client privilege, ensuring that internal investigations and communications remain confidential and protected from disclosure to third parties, including regulatory bodies and potential litigants. Secondly, legal counsel can guide the incident response team in gathering information that is essential for fulfilling notification requirements while mitigating the risk of admitting fault or liability prematurely.

The determination of whether a "breach" has actually occurred is a complex legal and technical question. Regulations often define a breach as an acquisition, access, use, or disclosure of protected information that compromises the security or privacy of the personal information. However, if the organization can demonstrate, through a risk assessment, that the compromised information has been secured and rendered unusable, unintelligible, or indecipherable (e.g., through strong encryption), then a breach may not have occurred, and notification may not be required. This risk assessment must be thorough, well-documented, and defensible. It typically involves evaluating the nature and extent of the unauthorized access or disclosure, the type of information involved, the identity of the unauthorized person (if known), whether the information was actually acquired or viewed, and the extent to which the risk of harm has been mitigated. Again, legal counsel should be involved in framing and conducting this assessment to ensure its legal validity.

Beyond data protection regulations, other legal and industry-specific frameworks impose obligations. For example, the Payment Card Industry Data Security Standard (PCI DSS) is a set of security standards designed to ensure that all companies that accept, process, store, or transmit credit card information maintain a secure environment. While not a law in the traditional sense, compliance with PCI DSS is a contractual requirement for merchants and service providers that handle payment card data. A breach of cardholder data can lead to significant fines, loss of the ability to process credit card payments, and increased scrutiny from card brands and acquirers. PCI DSS includes requirements for incident response, such as having a documented plan, conducting regular testing, and implementing processes for incident detection, containment, eradication, and recovery.

Furthermore, companies may face obligations under specific sectoral regulations, such as those governing critical infrastructure or financial services. The Network and Information Security (NIS) Directive in the European Union, for example, imposes security and incident reporting obligations on operators of essential services and digital service providers. Similarly, financial regulators in various jurisdictions have specific requirements for cybersecurity incident reporting and risk management. Understanding which of these various regulatory regimes apply to an organization is a critical first step in developing a compliant incident response strategy. This often requires a detailed mapping of the organization's operations, data flows, and the types of data it handles against the requirements of all relevant legal and regulatory frameworks.

The potential for litigation arising from a cyber incident is another significant legal consideration. Customers, partners, employees, and shareholders may all have grounds to sue if they suffer losses due to a data breach. As mentioned, CCPA/CPRA in California provides a private right of action for consumers. Class action lawsuits are a common consequence of large-scale data breaches, seeking damages for identity theft, financial losses, or emotional distress. Organizations must consider how their incident response actions, communications, and documentation might be used as evidence in such lawsuits. This reinforces the importance of careful communication, accurate record-keeping, and adherence to legal advice throughout the incident response lifecycle.

The investigation phase of incident response is particularly susceptible to legal scrutiny. Forensic investigations, while crucial for understanding the scope and impact of an attack, must be conducted in a manner that preserves evidence integrity and respects legal privileges. The use of external forensic experts can be beneficial, but it is essential to establish clear contractual agreements that define the scope of work, data handling procedures, and reporting protocols. These agreements should also address ownership of the collected data and the expert's duty of confidentiality. Documenting the chain of custody for all evidence collected is paramount for its admissibility in legal proceedings.

Communication during and after an incident is another area fraught with legal peril. Public statements, press releases, and notifications to affected individuals must be carefully crafted and reviewed by legal counsel. Misleading or inaccurate statements can lead to further liability and regulatory action. The content of breach notifications, as mandated by various regulations, must be precise and informative, covering specific details about the breach and the steps being taken. Simultaneously, organizations must be mindful of their obligations to stakeholders, including investors, partners, and employees, ensuring transparent communication without compromising ongoing investigations or admitting liability.

The legal and regulatory considerations are not static; they are constantly evolving. New laws are enacted, existing ones are updated, and regulatory interpretations can change. This dynamic environment necessitates a proactive and adaptive approach to incident response planning. Organizations must establish mechanisms for regularly monitoring the legal and regulatory landscape relevant to their operations and geographies. This might involve subscribing to legal alerts, participating in industry working groups, and engaging with external legal counsel specializing in cybersecurity and data privacy.

Furthermore, the incident response plan itself should explicitly address legal and regulatory requirements. This includes identifying the internal and external legal resources that will be engaged during an incident, outlining the procedures for legal review of communications and notifications, and detailing the process for conducting legally privileged investigations. The plan should also specify the roles and responsibilities of legal personnel within the incident response team, ensuring their timely involvement from the outset of any significant security event.

Contractual obligations also play a significant role. Service agreements with vendors, clients, and partners often contain clauses related to data security, breach notification, and liability. Organizations must review these contracts to understand their specific notification requirements and indemnification provisions in the event of a breach. A breach affecting a third-party vendor, for instance, could trigger notification obligations under contracts with clients. Similarly, contractual terms might specify the standard of care expected in protecting data, which can become a benchmark in legal disputes.

The concept of "due diligence" is central to many legal and regulatory frameworks. Regulators and courts often assess whether an organization acted reasonably and took appropriate steps to protect data and respond to incidents. This involves demonstrating that the organization had implemented adequate security measures, maintained up-to-date policies and procedures, provided appropriate training to employees, and conducted regular risk assessments. A well-documented and effectively executed incident response plan, coupled with evidence of its regular testing and refinement, serves as a powerful demonstration of due diligence. Conversely, a poorly managed or absent incident response plan can be interpreted as a failure to exercise due diligence, exacerbating legal and financial consequences.

The global nature of business today means that organizations often face a complex interplay of different legal systems. A data breach originating from an attack on a U.S.-based company that affects the personal data of EU citizens, for instance, would likely trigger obligations under both U.S. state laws and GDPR. Navigating these cross-border legal requirements demands specialized expertise and careful coordination. International legal counsel may be necessary to ensure compliance with the diverse legal obligations across different jurisdictions.

In conclusion, legal and regulatory considerations are an indispensable component of any comprehensive cyber incident response strategy. They are not an afterthought, but a foundational element that must be integrated into every stage of preparedness, response, and recovery. Proactive understanding of applicable laws, meticulous documentation, early and consistent involvement of legal counsel, careful communication, and a commitment to continuous monitoring of the evolving legal landscape are all critical to mitigating risks, avoiding penalties, and ultimately protecting the organization's interests in the challenging environment of cyber incidents. Organizations that fail to prioritize these legal dimensions do so at their own considerable peril.

The obligation to inform affected parties following a data breach is a cornerstone of modern data protection and privacy legislation. While the technical and investigative aspects of incident response focus on containing and remediating the breach, the communication element is paramount for rebuilding trust, managing reputational damage, and fulfilling legal mandates. The specific requirements for these notifications vary significantly across jurisdictions, often differing in terms of who must be notified, what information must be disclosed, and the timeframe within which these notifications must be made. Understanding these nuances is crucial for any organization operating globally or handling data from individuals in multiple regions.

In the European Union, the General Data Protection Regulation (GDPR) sets a high bar for breach notifications. As previously touched upon, Article 33 mandates that controllers notify the relevant supervisory authority of a personal data breach "without undue delay and, where feasible, not later than 72 hours after having become aware of it." This stringent timeline underscores the importance of rapid detection and internal reporting mechanisms. The notification to the supervisory authority must include, at a minimum: the nature of the personal data breach, including, where possible, the categories and approximate number of data subjects concerned and the categories and approximate number of personal data records concerned; the name and contact details of the data protection officer or other contact point; the likely consequences of the personal data breach; and the measures taken or proposed to be taken by the controller to address the personal data breach, including, where appropriate, measures to mitigate its possible adverse effects.

Beyond the regulatory notification, Article 34 of the GDPR imposes an obligation to communicate a personal data breach to the data subject when the breach is likely to result in a "high risk to the rights and freedoms of natural persons." This communication to individuals must describe the nature of the personal data breach in clear and plain language, including the name and contact details of the data protection officer or other contact point, the likely consequences of the personal data breach, and the measures taken or proposed to be taken by the controller. This dual notification requirement—to the authority and, in high-risk scenarios, to the individuals—creates a significant communication challenge. The definition of "high risk" is critical here, and its interpretation often hinges on factors such as the sensitivity of the data compromised, the volume of data, the potential for discrimination, financial loss, reputational damage, or identity theft. Organizations must be prepared to conduct a rapid, yet thorough, risk assessment to determine if individual notifications are necessary.

In the United States, the landscape is more complex due to the absence of a single federal data breach notification law that covers all types of personal information. Instead, a state-by-state approach prevails, with each state enacting its own statutes. However, many of these state laws share common principles. For instance, virtually all states require notification to affected individuals when their "personally identifiable information" (PII) or "personal information" is compromised. The definition of what constitutes such information, and what constitutes a "breach" requiring notification, can differ. Generally, a breach occurs when there is an unauthorized acquisition or access of sensitive data, and the data is not rendered indecipherable or unusable.

Common elements found across these state laws include the requirement to notify individuals "without unreasonable delay" or within a specified timeframe, often ranging from 30 to 60 days after discovery. Similar to the GDPR's high-risk threshold, many state laws allow for an exception from individual notification if the compromised information has been secured or rendered unusable through encryption or other methods, provided a risk assessment supports this conclusion. This assessment must document why the risk of harm is low. The content of the notification to individuals also typically mirrors that required by the GDPR, demanding specifics about the incident, the types of data affected, the potential consequences, and recommended steps individuals can take to protect themselves, such as monitoring credit reports or changing passwords.

Some state laws also include requirements for notifying state attorneys general or other regulatory bodies, especially when a significant number of residents are affected. For example, New York's data breach notification law requires notification to the

Attorney General, the Consumer Protection Board, and the Division of State Police if the breach impacts more than 500 residents. Massachusetts law requires notification to the Attorney General, the Secretary of the Commonwealth, and all affected consumers. These additional reporting requirements add layers of complexity, necessitating a clear understanding of the specific mandates in each state where the organization operates or has customers.

Federal laws also play a role, particularly in specific sectors. The Health Insurance Portability and Accountability Act (HIPAA), as mentioned, has its own Breach Notification Rule for protected health information (PHI). This rule requires covered entities and their business associates to notify individuals without unreasonable delay and no later than 60 calendar days after discovery. It also mandates notification to the Secretary of Health and Human Services, and for breaches affecting 500 or more individuals, it requires notification to prominent media outlets serving the affected state or jurisdiction. The definition of a "breach" under HIPAA is particularly nuanced, focusing on impermissible use or disclosure of PHI, with specific exceptions and safe harbors that organizations must carefully assess.

Another significant federal law with breach notification implications is the Children's Online Privacy Protection Act (COPPA). COPPA imposes specific requirements on operators of websites or online services directed to children under 13 years of age, and on operators of other websites or online services that have actual knowledge they are collecting personal information from children under 13. While COPPA does not have a general data breach notification requirement like HIPAA or GDPR, if an operator has a reasonable belief that a COPPA-covered child's personal information has been accessed by an unauthorized person, they must notify the parents or guardians. This notification must be clear and concise, providing information about the type of information collected, the company's COPPA policy, and steps parents can take.

Beyond direct legal mandates, contractual obligations often dictate breach notification procedures. Many service agreements, partnership agreements, and client contracts contain specific clauses related to data security and breach reporting. These clauses might stipve stricter notification timelines than legally required, specify the content of notifications, or outline procedures for joint communications. For instance, a company that suffers a breach impacting data belonging to its clients will likely have contractual obligations to notify those clients promptly, regardless of whether the law in their jurisdiction explicitly mandates such notification. Failure to adhere to these contractual terms can lead to breach of contract claims, indemnification liabilities, and loss of business.

Effectively managing the communication process during and after a data breach is paramount to maintaining stakeholder trust and mitigating reputational harm. This involves more than just ticking boxes on a compliance checklist; it requires a strategic, empathetic, and transparent approach. A well-defined incident response plan should include a robust communication strategy, outlining who is responsible for drafting, approving, and disseminating communications, and to whom. This often involves a cross-functional team including legal, communications, IT security, and senior management.

Key considerations for managing breach communications include:

First, **Timeliness and Accuracy**: While speed is essential to meet legal deadlines and demonstrate responsiveness, it is equally important that communications are accurate and based on verified facts. Rushing to communicate incomplete or incorrect information can lead to further confusion, erode trust, and potentially create new liabilities. The incident response team must establish clear fact-gathering protocols to ensure that all statements are well-supported.

Second, **Clarity and Transparency**: Communications should be written in clear, plain language, avoiding overly technical jargon that may confuse or alienate recipients. Transparency about what happened, what data was affected, and what steps are being taken to address the situation is crucial. While it may be tempting to downplay the severity of an incident, stakeholders are often more understanding of organizations that are upfront and honest, even about difficult news.

Third, **Empathy and Reassurance**: Affected individuals are likely to be concerned, anxious, or even angry. Communications should convey empathy for their situation and reassure them that the organization is taking the matter seriously and is committed to protecting their interests. Offering concrete steps individuals can take to protect themselves, such as providing credit monitoring services or identity theft protection, can be invaluable.

Fourth, **Consistency Across Channels**: Information should be consistent across all communication channels, whether it's direct notifications to individuals, public statements, press releases, or internal communications to employees. Any discrepancies can lead to suspicion and further damage credibility.

Fifth, **Legal Review**: All external communications, especially breach notifications, must undergo rigorous legal review. This is to ensure compliance with all applicable laws and regulations, avoid admissions of liability where inappropriate, and protect the organization from potential legal repercussions.

Sixth, **Stakeholder Segmentation**: Different stakeholders will require different types of information and may have different concerns. For instance, notifications to regulatory bodies will be highly technical and legalistic, while communications to affected individuals need to be clear and actionable. Communications to investors may focus on the financial and operational impact, while internal communications to employees will address their role and responsibilities. A communication plan should identify these different audiences and tailor messages accordingly.

Seventh, **Post-Breach Follow-up**: The communication process does not end with the initial notification. Organizations should maintain channels for follow-up questions, provide ongoing updates on remediation efforts, and be prepared to address evolving concerns from stakeholders. Demonstrating a commitment to remediation and learning from the incident can help rebuild confidence over time.

Managing the complex web of data breach notification laws and procedures requires a proactive and well-prepared approach. It necessitates continuous monitoring of evolving legal and regulatory landscapes across all relevant jurisdictions. Organizations must invest in developing and regularly testing comprehensive incident response plans that explicitly address these notification obligations. This includes identifying the specific legal and regulatory frameworks that apply to their operations, data processing activities, and the locations of their data subjects. Crucially, it means establishing clear internal protocols for timely incident detection, assessment, and escalation, ensuring that legal counsel and communication teams are engaged from the earliest stages of a potential breach. By integrating legal compliance, transparent communication, and a genuine commitment to protecting individuals' data into the fabric of their incident response strategy, organizations can navigate the challenging aftermath of a data breach more effectively, minimizing damage and fostering long-term trust.

The effective handling of a cyber incident extends beyond internal containment and remediation efforts; it critically involves engagement with external entities, most notably law enforcement and various government agencies. These relationships, when cultivated and managed proactively, can become invaluable assets during a crisis, facilitating faster resolution, providing crucial expertise, and ensuring legal compliance. A well-defined protocol for engaging these bodies is not merely a reactive measure but a strategic component of a robust cybersecurity posture, especially for incidents that possess a significant impact, involve potential criminal activity, or cross jurisdictional boundaries.

Establishing a clear chain of command and predefined points of contact within your organization for interacting with external agencies is the foundational step. This designation ensures that communication is centralized, consistent, and managed by individuals who understand the sensitive nature of the information being shared and the legal ramifications involved. Ideally, this role would fall to senior members of the legal or compliance department, or a designated incident response lead with significant experience in handling sensitive investigations. This individual or team should be intimately familiar with the organization's cybersecurity incident response plan, including specific protocols for law enforcement engagement.

When an incident occurs that warrants external notification or assistance, the decision-making process should be swift and guided by pre-established criteria. Factors such as the nature and severity of the incident, the potential for criminal activity (e.g., ransomware attacks, data theft for financial gain, nation-state sponsored attacks), the volume and sensitivity of compromised data, and regulatory or legal mandates will dictate when and which agencies should be contacted. For instance, an incident involving the exfiltration of intellectual property might trigger engagement with the FBI's cyber division, while a critical infrastructure attack could necessitate involving agencies like the Cybersecurity and

Infrastructure Security Agency (CISA) in the United States, or equivalent national cybersecurity centers in other countries.

The nature of the information shared with law enforcement and government agencies is a delicate balance. On one hand, transparency and the provision of timely, accurate data are essential for effective investigation and assistance. On the other hand, organizations must be mindful of protecting their own legal interests, proprietary information, and the privacy of their customers or employees. This is where the designated points of contact and their legal counsel play a critical role. They must be equipped to understand what information is legally permissible and advisable to share, what constitutes evidence, and how to document all interactions.

One of the primary benefits of engaging law enforcement early is their capacity to initiate investigative actions that may be beyond the scope or resources of the organization. This can include tracing the origin of an attack, identifying perpetrators, and potentially recovering stolen data or assets. Law enforcement agencies possess specialized tools, intelligence networks, and legal authority to pursue these objectives. For example, if a ransomware attack involves encrypted data that the organization cannot decrypt, law enforcement might be able to leverage their resources or intelligence to identify the ransomware group and potentially obtain decryption keys or disrupt their operations.

When requesting assistance, the organization should be prepared to provide a clear and concise summary of the incident, including timelines, known impacts, the types of systems or data affected, and any initial findings from the internal investigation. This includes technical details such as IP addresses, malware signatures, attack vectors, and logs, which can be crucial for law enforcement's analysis. It is also important to articulate precisely what kind of assistance is being sought. Are you looking for help identifying the perpetrators? Do you need assistance in understanding the scope of data exfiltration? Or is the primary goal to understand how to prevent further attacks of a similar nature?

Cooperation with investigations involves a commitment to providing access to relevant systems, data, and personnel. This may require establishing secure channels for evidence transfer, granting remote or physical access to compromised systems (under controlled conditions), and making subject matter experts available for interviews. Organizations should have a clear understanding of their rights and obligations in such situations, particularly concerning the preservation of evidence and potential legal implications of providing or withholding information. The involvement of legal counsel is paramount throughout this process to ensure that cooperation does not inadvertently waive legal protections or create undue liabilities.

Furthermore, many government agencies offer proactive resources and support that can be leveraged even before an incident occurs. Organizations are encouraged to register with relevant agencies, subscribe to their threat intelligence feeds, and familiarize themselves with their reporting mechanisms and best practices. For instance, CISA in the United States provides a wealth of resources, including alerts, advisories, and a 24/7 operations center that can be contacted for assistance during a cyber event. Building a relationship with these agencies during routine operations can significantly streamline communication and build trust when a crisis strikes.

In international contexts, the engagement of law enforcement and government agencies becomes even more complex due to differing legal frameworks, jurisdictions, and cooperation agreements. Incidents that span multiple countries may require coordinating with multiple national law enforcement bodies and potentially international organizations like Europol or Interpol. This necessitates a thorough understanding of mutual legal assistance treaties (MLATs) and other international cooperation mechanisms. The incident response plan should outline procedures for identifying relevant international agencies and initiating contact through appropriate diplomatic or legal channels.

Beyond direct law enforcement investigations, government agencies often play a crucial role in providing broader cybersecurity support and guidance. Agencies responsible for critical infrastructure protection, for example, may offer specialized threat intelligence, vulnerability assessments, and technical assistance to help organizations bolster their defenses and recover from attacks. Participating in sector-specific information sharing and analysis centers (ISACs) or similar forums, often facilitated or supported by government entities, can provide invaluable insights into emerging threats and effective mitigation strategies.

The documentation of all interactions with law enforcement and government agencies is a critical, yet often overlooked, aspect of incident response. This includes maintaining a detailed log of all communications, the information shared, the assistance provided, and any formal requests or directives received. Such documentation serves multiple purposes: it provides a clear record of the organization's efforts to address the incident, supports compliance with legal and regulatory requirements, can be used in legal proceedings or insurance claims, and aids in post-incident review and improvement of the incident response plan.

It is also vital to manage expectations when engaging with external agencies. While their assistance can be invaluable, it is not always immediate, nor is success guaranteed. Law enforcement agencies are often dealing with numerous ongoing investigations, and the prioritization of resources can affect response times. Organizations should maintain their own independent incident response capabilities and not solely rely on external assistance for critical functions like containment and eradication. The role of external agencies is typically to augment and support, rather than replace, the organization's internal response efforts.

Moreover, the relationship with government agencies can extend to regulatory compliance and reporting. As discussed in previous sections, many data breach notification laws and cybersecurity regulations mandate reporting to specific government bodies. Proactive engagement with these agencies, even outside of a breach scenario, can foster a more collaborative and understanding relationship, which can be beneficial when a significant incident does occur. Understanding the specific reporting requirements for different agencies well in advance is crucial. For example, in the United States, reporting requirements vary significantly based on the type of data compromised (e.g., health information under HIPAA, financial data under GLBA) and the sector in which the organization operates.

The decision to involve law enforcement should also consider the potential for public disclosure. While cooperating with an investigation is often a prudent step, it can sometimes lead to information becoming public through legal proceedings or official statements. Organizations must weigh this potential disclosure against the benefits of law enforcement assistance, with guidance from their legal counsel. In some cases, law enforcement may advise on strategies to minimize public exposure during the initial stages of an investigation.

A key element in fostering effective relationships with law enforcement and government agencies is demonstrating a commitment to cybersecurity best practices and a willingness to learn from incidents. Organizations that can show they have robust security controls in place, a well-tested incident response plan, and a culture of continuous improvement are more likely to receive favorable consideration and support. This includes conducting regular security audits, penetration tests, and tabletop exercises that simulate various cyber attack scenarios, including those that would involve external agency engagement.

In summary, the engagement with law enforcement and government agencies during a cyber incident is a critical dimension of a comprehensive incident response strategy. It requires proactive planning, clear communication protocols, a deep understanding of legal and jurisdictional nuances, and a commitment to cooperation. By building these relationships in advance, designating clear points of contact, and understanding the scope and limitations of external assistance, organizations can significantly enhance their ability to navigate complex cyber threats, mitigate damage, and contribute to the broader cybersecurity ecosystem. The effective liaison with these entities transforms a potential crisis into an opportunity for coordinated defense and recovery, reinforcing the organization's resilience and its role as a responsible stakeholder in the digital landscape.

The landscape of cybersecurity incident response is often fraught with legal complexities, and understanding the doctrines of privilege is paramount to safeguarding sensitive information. When a cyber incident strikes, the instinct to investigate and understand the full scope of the breach is immediate. However, this investigation, particularly when it involves the collection of evidence, analysis of vulnerabilities, and formulation of strategic responses, can generate documentation and communications that may later become subject to legal scrutiny. To navigate this treacherous terrain, organizations must be acutely aware of two fundamental legal protections: the attorney-client privilege and the work-product doctrine. These doctrines are not merely abstract legal concepts; they are practical tools that, when properly understood and applied, can shield critical findings and deliberations from disclosure to opposing parties in litigation or regulatory investigations.

The attorney-client privilege is a cornerstone of legal representation, designed to foster open and honest communication between clients and their attorneys. Its core purpose is to encourage individuals and organizations to seek legal advice without fear that their communications will be later revealed. For this privilege to apply, several conditions must be met. First, there must be a communication. This can be oral, written, or electronic. Second, the communication must be between a client and an attorney. In the corporate context, the "client" encompasses not only the entity itself but also its employees who are acting on behalf of the company in seeking or providing legal advice. Third, the communication must be made in confidence, meaning it was not intended to be disclosed to third parties. Finally, and crucially for our purposes, the communication must be made for the primary purpose of obtaining or providing legal advice.

When a cybersecurity incident occurs, legal counsel may be brought in to advise the organization on its legal obligations, potential liabilities, and strategic responses. This engagement can trigger the attorney-client privilege. For example, if an organization's general counsel or external cybersecurity legal counsel is involved in directing or participating in the investigation, communications between the legal team and the incident response team, or between employees and legal counsel, regarding the incident may be privileged. The key here is the *purpose* of the communication. If an employee is reporting a technical anomaly to the IT department for the purpose of fixing a system malfunction, that communication is likely not privileged. However, if that same employee is reporting the anomaly to legal counsel, or to an IT expert working under the direction of legal counsel, for the purpose of seeking legal advice on how to respond to a potential data breach, then that communication may well be protected.

The definition of "attorney" for the purposes of this privilege typically includes both in-house counsel and external legal counsel. However, special care must be taken when relying on in-house counsel, especially in larger organizations. If an in-house attorney wears multiple hats (e.g., legal advisor, business operations manager, compliance officer), it is essential to clearly delineate their role as legal advisor when seeking to invoke the privilege. Communications where the attorney is acting primarily in a business or operational capacity are not privileged. Therefore, it is often advisable to have an external law firm, or at least a designated internal legal team with clear legal responsibilities, lead or oversee privileged investigations. This ensures a clearer separation of roles and strengthens the assertion of privilege.

Furthermore, the privilege protects the communication itself, not the underlying facts. This is a critical distinction. If an employee witnesses a fire, the privilege does not protect the fact that a fire occurred. However, it can protect the employee's confidential communication with their attorney about the fire, if that communication is for the purpose of seeking legal advice. In the context of a cyber incident, this means that while the fact of a data breach cannot be hidden by privilege, the details of the internal investigation into how the breach occurred, the legal analysis of the company's liabilities, and the strategies for responding to regulatory demands or litigation can be protected.

The work-product doctrine, established in the landmark U.S. Supreme Court case *Hickman v. Taylor*, offers a complementary layer of protection. It shields materials prepared by or for an attorney in anticipation of litigation. Unlike the attorney-client privilege, which protects confidential communications, the work-product doctrine protects tangible and intangible materials that an attorney or their agents create to prepare for litigation. This doctrine is broader in scope than the attorney-client privilege and can protect documents generated by investigators, consultants, or even employees when they are acting under the direction of an attorney and in anticipation of litigation.

There are generally two types of work product: ordinary work product and opinion work product. Ordinary work product encompasses factual information gathered and assembled by an attorney or their agents. Opinion work product, which includes an attorney's mental impressions, conclusions, opinions, and legal theories, receives a higher level of protection and is rarely discoverable. This distinction is vital because while ordinary work product may sometimes be discoverable if the opposing party demonstrates a substantial need for the information and an inability to obtain it by other means without undue hardship, opinion work product is virtually immune from discovery.

In the context of a cybersecurity incident, the work-product doctrine can protect a wide range of materials. This includes reports prepared by forensic investigators, notes taken during interviews of employees about the incident, analyses of malware, timelines of events, and even draft legal documents or strategies. For these materials to be considered work product, they must be prepared "in anticipation of litigation." This does not mean that litigation must be imminent; it means that a reasonable person in the position of the attorney would anticipate litigation. Following a significant cyber incident, particularly one involving potential data loss, regulatory fines, or civil liability, it is almost always reasonable to anticipate litigation.

To effectively leverage the work-product doctrine, organizations should ensure that any external investigators or consultants are retained by legal counsel, rather than by the IT department or business unit directly. This helps to establish that their work is being performed under the direction of counsel in anticipation of litigation. Documentation of this relationship, such as engagement letters clearly stating the purpose of the engagement is for legal counsel's use in anticipation of litigation, is crucial. Similarly, internal investigations should be supervised by legal counsel, and communications within the investigation team should clearly indicate their purpose.

A critical consideration for both attorney-client privilege and work-product protection is the prevention of waiver. Waiver can occur through inadvertent disclosure or intentional sharing of privileged information with third parties. For example, if a company shares a privileged investigation report with an insurance company without a specific agreement to protect confidentiality, that privilege may be waived. Similarly, if a company voluntarily discloses privileged information to a government agency without proper safeguards, it may be deemed waived. Organizations must have strict protocols in place for managing and disseminating information related to an incident investigation.

When interacting with law enforcement or regulatory bodies, it is imperative to understand the implications for privilege. While cooperation is often beneficial, as discussed previously, it can also lead to unintended disclosures. If law enforcement requests access to investigation reports that are protected by attorney-client privilege or the work-product doctrine, the organization has the right to object. However, this requires careful navigation and often involves negotiation with the investigating authorities. Legal counsel should be involved in all communications with external agencies regarding access to investigation materials. In some cases, counsel may agree to provide certain factual information without waiving privilege, or may offer to provide summaries or carefully redacted versions of reports.

The "joint defense" or "common interest" privilege is another relevant concept that can arise when multiple parties with a shared legal interest cooperate in their defense. For example, if an organization and its key executives are all facing potential liability arising from the same cyber incident, they might enter into a joint defense agreement. This agreement allows them to share information and coordinate their legal strategies without waiving attorney-client privilege or work-product protection. However, these agreements must be carefully drafted and adhered to, as the scope of protection can be limited if not properly managed.

To maximize privilege protection during a cyber incident investigation, organizations should consider the following best practices:

1. **Involve Legal Counsel Early and Continuously:** Engage legal counsel (both internal and external, as appropriate) from the outset of the incident response. Ensure that counsel is directing or overseeing the investigative efforts.

2. **Clearly Define Roles:** When using external consultants (e.g., forensic investigators), have them retained by legal counsel, not by the IT or business units. Their engagement should be explicitly for the purpose of assisting legal counsel in anticipation of litigation.

3. **Label and Segregate Privileged Communications:** All documents, emails, and other communications that are intended to be privileged should be clearly marked as "Privileged and Confidential," "Attorney-Client Communication," or "Attorney Work Product." Maintain these documents in separate, secure locations, distinct from non-privileged operational records.

4. **Limit Distribution:** Restrict access to privileged information to those individuals who have a "need to know" for the purpose of obtaining or providing legal advice or preparing for litigation. Avoid broad internal dissemination.

5. **Educate the Incident Response Team:** Ensure that all members of the incident response team understand the importance of privilege and the protocols for handling privileged information. Train them on what types of communications and documents are likely to be protected.

6. **Be Cautious with Third-Party Disclosures:** Exercise extreme care when sharing information with

third parties, including vendors, business partners, insurance carriers, and government agencies. Obtain confidentiality agreements and ensure that any disclosure does not inadvertently waive privilege.

7. **Carefully Consider Communications with Law Enforcement:** When interacting with law enforcement, always have legal counsel present. Clearly articulate the basis for any assertion of privilege and be prepared to negotiate the scope of information sharing.

8. **Document the "Anticipation of Litigation" Rationale:** While often self-evident, it can be beneficial to maintain internal records that articulate why litigation was anticipated at the time materials were prepared. This can strengthen the work-product claim if challenged.

The interplay between attorney-client privilege and the work-product doctrine is complex and fact-specific. Both are essential tools for organizations navigating the aftermath of a cyber incident. By proactively structuring investigations, carefully managing communications, and diligently adhering to protocols designed to preserve these protections, companies can ensure that their critical legal advice and investigative findings remain confidential, thereby strengthening their position in any subsequent legal or regulatory proceedings. The investment in understanding and applying these principles from the outset of an incident response is not merely a legal formality; it is a strategic imperative for robust risk management and the protection of organizational interests.

The escalating frequency and sophistication of cyber threats have made robust incident response capabilities an absolute necessity for modern organizations. Beyond the internal preparations and legal safeguards previously discussed, two critical external components significantly shape an organization's ability to manage and recover from a cyber incident: cyber insurance and the management of third-party vendors. These elements, often interconnected, represent vital layers of defense and recovery that demand careful consideration and strategic implementation.

Cyber insurance has evolved from a niche product to an indispensable tool for financial and operational resilience in the face of cyber risks. The primary function of a cyber insurance policy is to provide financial coverage for a range of expenses and liabilities arising from a cyber incident. These can be extensive, often exceeding the immediate technical remediation costs. For instance, a policy might cover the expenses associated with forensic investigation – crucial for understanding the scope and nature of a breach, as detailed in earlier discussions on evidence preservation and privilege. Beyond the technical, it can also cover the significant costs of notification to affected individuals if their personal data has been compromised, a legal and regulatory imperative in many jurisdictions. This includes the expenses for setting up call centers, forensic analysis to determine precisely what data was accessed, and potentially credit monitoring services for affected parties.

Furthermore, cyber insurance policies often extend to cover legal defense costs and settlements or judgments arising from lawsuits filed by individuals, businesses, or regulatory bodies alleging damages due to a data breach or system disruption. The potential for class-action lawsuits following a significant data breach is a very real and substantial financial exposure that cyber insurance is designed to mitigate. Business interruption coverage is another crucial component, compensating the organization for lost profits and ongoing operating expenses when its business operations are halted or significantly impaired by a cyber event. This can be a lifeline for small to medium-sized businesses that might not survive a prolonged operational shutdown. Reputational damage, while harder to quantify, can also be indirectly addressed through coverage for public relations efforts aimed at restoring trust and mitigating the long-term impact on brand value.

However, navigating the landscape of cyber insurance requires a proactive and diligent approach. Simply purchasing a policy is insufficient. Organizations must thoroughly understand the terms, conditions, and exclusions within their chosen policy. What constitutes a "covered event"? What are the policy limits? What are the deductibles, and how do they apply? Critically, most cyber insurance policies require policyholders to adhere to certain security standards and incident response protocols. Failure to meet these requirements, or to properly document compliance, can lead to denied claims. This underscores the importance of aligning internal cybersecurity practices and incident response plans with the expectations outlined in the insurance policy. It is often advisable to involve legal counsel and cybersecurity risk advisors in the review and negotiation of cyber insurance policies to ensure adequate coverage and understanding of obligations.

The process of filing a claim also necessitates a close working relationship with the insurer, often involving designated breach coaches or legal counsel appointed or approved by the insurer. These professionals play a key role in managing the incident response process in a way that aligns with the policy's requirements and facilitates a smoother claims process. This can create a dynamic where the insurer's representatives, alongside the organization's own legal counsel, are involved in the critical early stages of incident management. As discussed previously, the involvement of legal counsel is paramount for maintaining privilege. Therefore, when engaging with cyber insurance providers and their appointed experts, organizations must be mindful of how these interactions might impact attorney-client privilege and the work-product doctrine. Clear communication protocols, including ensuring that all critical communications are channeled through legal counsel and appropriately marked as privileged, are essential.

The management of third-party vendors represents another significant frontier in cyber risk management, particularly concerning incident response. In today's interconnected business environment, organizations rely heavily on a diverse ecosystem of external service providers. These can range from cloud service providers (CSPs) and software-as-a-service (SaaS) vendors to managed service providers (MSPs), payment processors, and business process outsourcing (BPO) firms. The critical issue is that a security incident originating within a third-party vendor's environment can directly impact the organization's own systems, data, and operations. For example, if a vendor handling sensitive customer data suffers a breach, that data, which includes information about the organization's clients, is compromised. Similarly, if an MSP experiences a ransomware attack that locks down the systems it manages for multiple clients, those clients will suffer operational disruptions.

Consequently, the incident response capabilities of third-party vendors are not merely their concern; they are a direct concern for the organizations that rely on them. This necessitates a rigorous vendor risk management program that specifically assesses and addresses vendor incident response preparedness. A fundamental step in this process is conducting thorough due diligence before engaging any vendor that will have access to sensitive data or critical systems. This due diligence should include an evaluation of the vendor's security posture, their incident response plan, their data protection policies, and their compliance certifications (e.g., ISO 27001, SOC 2). Asking vendors to provide documentation of their incident response capabilities, including their own business continuity and disaster recovery plans, is a standard practice.

Beyond initial due diligence, ongoing monitoring and contractual agreements are essential. Contracts with third-party vendors must clearly define roles, responsibilities, and expectations regarding cybersecurity and incident response. This includes explicit clauses that address:

Notification Requirements: The vendor must be contractually obligated to notify the organization of any security incident affecting the organization's data or systems within a specified, often very short, timeframe. This notification period is critical for enabling the organization to initiate its own incident response and mitigation efforts promptly. The definition of a "security incident" requiring notification should be broad enough to cover various potential events, including unauthorized access, data exfiltration, malware infections, and denial-of-service attacks.

Cooperation in Investigations: The contract should stipulate that the vendor will cooperate fully with the organization's incident response efforts, including providing access to relevant logs, systems, and personnel. This cooperation is vital for understanding the root cause, scope, and impact of a breach that originates with the vendor.

Remediation Obligations: The vendor should be contractually bound to remediate any security vulnerabilities that contributed to an incident and to implement measures to prevent recurrence.

Liability and Indemnification: Clear provisions regarding liability for damages resulting from a vendor-caused incident are crucial. This may include indemnification clauses where the vendor agrees to cover the organization's losses.

Audit Rights: The contract might grant the organization the right to audit the vendor's security controls and incident response processes periodically to ensure ongoing compliance.

Subcontractor Management: If the vendor uses subcontractors, the contract should require them to impose similar cybersecurity and incident response obligations on their own subcontractors, ensuring a consistent level of protection across the entire supply chain.

When a cyber incident does occur that involves a third-party vendor, the organization's incident response plan needs to seamlessly integrate with the vendor's response. This requires pre-established communication channels and a clear understanding of who is responsible for what actions. For instance, if a breach is confirmed to have originated with a vendor, the organization must be prepared to trigger its vendor-specific response protocols, which might include engaging the vendor's security team, legal counsel, and potentially its cyber insurer.

The complexity of managing third-party vendor risk is amplified by the fact that many organizations utilize cloud services, which inherently involve a complex web of interconnected third parties. Understanding the shared responsibility model with cloud providers is paramount. While CSPs are responsible for the security *of* the cloud (e.g., infrastructure, hardware), the customer organization remains responsible for security *in* the cloud (e.g., data, applications, access controls). This means that even if the underlying cloud infrastructure is secure, misconfigurations, weak access controls, or compromised user credentials within the customer's cloud environment can lead to a breach. Therefore, the incident response plan must account for the specific security responsibilities within the cloud environment and how to engage with the CSP if an incident impacts the infrastructure layer.

In summary, while internal preparedness is the first line of defense, cyber insurance and robust third-party vendor management form essential pillars of a comprehensive incident response strategy. Cyber insurance provides a critical financial safety net, covering a wide array of costs and liabilities that can arise from an incident. However, its effectiveness hinges on understanding policy details and adhering to stipulated security and response requirements. Similarly, managing the cyber risks posed by third-party vendors is not an option but a necessity. Through thorough due diligence, clear contractual obligations, and ongoing monitoring, organizations can mitigate the downstream impact of vendor-related incidents and ensure that their own incident response capabilities are not compromised by the vulnerabilities of their supply chain. The integration of these external elements into an organization's overarching resilience strategy is a hallmark of mature cybersecurity and risk management practices.

The aftermath of a significant cybersecurity incident can be as challenging, if not more so, than the technical remediation itself. While internal technical teams work tirelessly to contain the breach, restore systems, and analyze the attack vectors, a parallel and equally crucial effort must be underway: managing public perception and communication. This is where the discipline of public relations, specifically tailored for crisis situations, becomes paramount. Effectively communicating with the public, media, stakeholders, and regulatory bodies can significantly influence the long-term impact of an incident on an organization's reputation, trust, and operational viability. The goal is not merely to inform but to reassure, demonstrate accountability, and foster understanding during a period of heightened uncertainty and potential distress.

Developing a robust crisis communication strategy is a proactive undertaking that should be integrated into an organization's overall incident response plan. This strategy needs to anticipate potential scenarios and pre-define communication protocols. Key to this is the establishment of clear, consistent, and timely messaging. In the chaos of a cyberattack, misinformation can spread like wildfire, fueled by speculation and the inherent public anxiety surrounding data breaches and system disruptions. Therefore, having a dedicated team, or at least designated individuals, responsible for crafting and disseminating official statements is critical. These statements must be factually accurate, avoiding hyperbole or premature conclusions. They should also be delivered through established and trusted channels to ensure they reach the intended audiences effectively.

A core tenet of crisis communication is transparency, balanced with the need for discretion and legal compliance. Organizations must resist the urge to go silent or issue vague platitudes. Instead, they should aim for a communication approach that acknowledges the situation, outlines the steps being taken to address it, and provides an estimated timeline for further updates, even if that timeline is simply to say "we will update you as soon as we have more confirmed information." This demonstrates a commitment to keeping affected parties informed and builds credibility. The language used in these communications is vital. It should be clear, concise, and devoid of technical jargon that may alienate or confuse the general public or non-technical stakeholders. Empathy is also a critical component; acknowledging the potential impact on individuals whose data may have been compromised, or businesses that rely on the affected services, is essential for fostering goodwill.

Within the structured framework of an incident response, particularly when leveraging models like the Incident Command System (ICS), the role of the Public Information Officer (PIO) is indispensable. The PIO serves as the central point of contact for all external communications regarding the incident. This individual or team is responsible for coordinating the dissemination of information to the media, the public, affected individuals, and other relevant parties. The PIO acts as a bridge between the technical response team and the outside world, translating complex technical details into understandable and actionable information. Crucially, the PIO works closely with legal counsel to ensure that all public statements adhere to legal and regulatory requirements, such as data breach notification laws, and do not inadvertently compromise any ongoing investigations or legal proceedings.

The establishment of a Public Information Center (PIC) or a dedicated communication hub is a common practice in large-scale incident management. This PIC can be a physical location or a virtual team responsible for managing incoming media inquiries, developing press releases, updating website information, and monitoring social media for public sentiment and misinformation. The PIO's team will be trained to handle a wide range of questions, from the technical specifics of the breach to its potential implications for customers and partners. They must be prepared to provide consistent answers and to escalate complex or sensitive queries to the appropriate internal experts, always through established protocols to maintain message discipline.

A critical aspect of crisis communication is managing the narrative. Without proactive and strategic communication, the narrative can be shaped by external actors, be it the media, malicious entities, or simply rumor mills. The organization has a vested interest in ensuring that the public understands the scope of the incident, the measures being taken, and the commitment to recovery and future prevention. This involves not just responding to inquiries but also actively disseminating information. This might include publishing FAQs on the company website, issuing regular updates via email newsletters, or leveraging social media platforms to directly address concerns and correct inaccuracies.

The nature and scale of a cybersecurity incident will dictate the complexity of the communication strategy. A minor internal system issue might only require an internal memo, while a major data breach affecting millions of customers will necessitate a comprehensive public relations campaign. For instance, if a financial institution experiences a breach of customer account information, the communication strategy would need to be highly detailed and carefully coordinated with regulatory bodies, law enforcement, and legal counsel. This would involve not only notifying affected individuals as legally required but also proactively communicating with the broader customer base to reassure them about the security of their funds and the steps being taken to prevent future incidents. This might include offering credit monitoring services, enhancing security protocols, and clearly communicating these changes to the public.

In scenarios involving sensitive data, such as personal health information (PHI) or personally identifiable information (PII), the communication strategy must be particularly sensitive and aligned with regulations like GDPR, HIPAA, or CCPA. These regulations often mandate specific timelines and content for breach notifications, including details about the type of data compromised, the potential risks, and the measures individuals can take to protect themselves. The PIO, working in tandem with legal and compliance teams, ensures that all notifications meet these stringent requirements, thereby avoiding legal penalties and demonstrating a commitment to privacy.

The media, both traditional and social, plays a pivotal role in shaping public perception during a crisis. A well-executed media relations strategy involves building rapport with journalists, providing them with accurate and timely information, and being available for interviews. The PIO will often designate spokespersons who are trained to communicate effectively on behalf of the organization. These spokespersons must be knowledgeable about the incident, calm under pressure, and capable of conveying the organization's message clearly and empathetically. It's often beneficial to have pre-approved talking points and Q&A documents to ensure consistency across all interviews and statements.

Social media presents a dual-edged sword during a crisis. On one hand, it offers a direct channel to reach a large audience quickly and to monitor public sentiment. On the other hand, it can be a breeding ground for misinformation and can amplify negative reactions. A comprehensive crisis communication strategy must include a robust social media monitoring and engagement plan. This involves actively listening to what people are saying online, responding to inquiries and concerns promptly, correcting false information, and using the platforms to disseminate official updates. The tone of social media communication should be consistent with the overall organizational voice – empathetic, professional, and reassuring.

Beyond immediate communication during the incident, a crucial part of the strategy involves post-incident communication. Once the immediate crisis has subsided and technical remediation is complete, the organization needs to communicate the lessons learned, the improvements made, and the ongoing commitment to security. This can involve publishing post-incident reports (though these need to be carefully managed to avoid revealing vulnerabilities), updating security policies and procedures, and actively communicating these enhancements to customers and stakeholders. This demonstrates accountability and a commitment to continuous improvement, which can help to rebuild trust and confidence.

The financial implications of poor crisis communication are significant. A mishandled communication strategy can lead to a severe decline in stock value, loss of customer loyalty, and increased regulatory scrutiny. Conversely, effective and transparent communication can mitigate these financial risks, foster goodwill, and even strengthen customer relationships by demonstrating resilience and a commitment to ethical practices. This underscores the strategic importance of investing in crisis communication preparedness.

In summary, managing public perception and communication during and after a cybersecurity incident is not an afterthought but a core component of the incident response lifecycle. It requires a proactive strategy, clear messaging, dedicated resources, and a deep understanding of legal and regulatory obligations. The Public Information Officer, operating within frameworks like ICS, plays a central role in ensuring that communications are accurate, empathetic, and effective in mitigating reputational damage and maintaining stakeholder trust. By prioritizing clear, consistent, and timely communication, organizations can navigate the turbulent waters of a cyber crisis and emerge with their reputation intact, or even enhanced, by demonstrating their commitment to security and transparency. This strategic approach to communication is a hallmark of resilient and responsible organizations in the digital age.

The critical importance of internal communication during and after a cybersecurity incident cannot be overstated. While external stakeholders often receive the most visible attention, the organization's own employees are on the front lines, directly impacted by system disruptions, operational changes, and the emotional toll of an attack. Neglecting their need for information and support can lead to a cascade of negative consequences, including decreased productivity, heightened anxiety, the spread of rumors, and even a weakened security posture due to misinformed actions. Therefore, crafting a deliberate and comprehensive internal communication strategy is not merely a supplementary task; it is an integral component of a successful incident response and recovery effort, essential for maintaining organizational cohesion and resilience.

The initial phase of internal communication post-incident must prioritize clarity and timeliness. As soon as an incident is confirmed and its potential impact is understood, employees need to be informed. This initial communication should acknowledge the situation, providing a high-level overview of what has occurred without overwhelming them with technical jargon or speculative details. The message should convey that leadership is aware of the situation and is actively managing it. For instance, following the detection of an unauthorized access attempt that might have compromised internal credentials, an immediate internal memo or email could state: "We are currently investigating a potential security incident affecting a subset of our internal systems. Our IT security team is working diligently to assess the situation and ensure the integrity of our network. We will provide further updates as soon as confirmed information is available. In the meantime, please remain vigilant and report any unusual system behavior." This approach demonstrates transparency and reassures employees that the organization is taking the matter seriously.

Beyond the initial announcement, a crucial element of internal communication is providing actionable guidance to employees. Depending on the nature of the incident, specific instructions may be necessary to bolster security and mitigate further risks. For example, if the incident involved a phishing campaign that successfully compromised some user accounts, a follow-up communication would be essential to guide employees through necessary security measures. This might include mandatory password resets for all users, instructions on how to enable multi-factor authentication (MFA) if it wasn't already universally applied, and a reminder about recognizing and reporting suspicious emails. Such guidance should be presented in a clear, step-by-step format, accompanied by links to resources or support channels. An example of this guidance could be: "As part of our ongoing security enhancement efforts following the recent phishing incident, we require all employees to reset their network passwords by [Date]. Please visit [Link to password reset portal] and follow the on-screen instructions. Ensure your new password meets our complexity requirements. Additionally, please review our updated guidelines on identifying phishing attempts at [Link to training material]. Your cooperation is vital to safeguarding our organization."

The communication must also address the emotional and psychological impact of a cybersecurity incident on employees. Working in an environment where sensitive data might be at risk, or where systems are unreliable due to an attack, can be stressful. Internal communications should acknowledge these potential concerns and offer support. This can involve highlighting available employee assistance programs (EAPs), providing contact information for HR representatives who can address individual concerns, or simply fostering an environment where employees feel comfortable discussing their anxieties. Managers play a pivotal role here, and providing them with talking points and resources to support their teams is essential. Acknowledging the human element demonstrates empathy and reinforces the organization's commitment to its people, which is crucial for maintaining morale.

One of the most significant challenges in managing internal communications during a crisis is preventing the spread of rumors and misinformation. In the absence of official updates, employees will naturally seek information from colleagues, informal channels, or even speculate. This can lead to confusion, panic, and potentially harmful actions. To counteract this, internal communications must be consistent, frequent, and comprehensive. Establishing a single, authoritative source for information – such as a dedicated section on the company intranet, a specific email alias, or regular all-hands meetings led by the incident response leadership – is paramount. When an incident unfolds, the organization should commit to regular updates, even if the update is simply to reiterate that the situation is ongoing and no new actionable information is available. This consistent flow of information helps to manage expectations and reduces the vacuum that misinformation can fill.

For instance, if a data breach has occurred that might affect employee personal information, the internal communication strategy must be particularly sensitive. Employees will be concerned about their own data and potential identity theft. The communication should clearly outline what happened, what data may have been compromised, and what steps the organization is taking to protect them. This might include offering identity theft protection services or credit monitoring. An internal message could read: "We understand that the recent data breach may cause concern regarding your personal information. We are committed to transparency and providing you with the support you need. The compromised data may include [Specific data types]. To help protect you, we are offering [Service name] identity protection services free of charge for [Duration]. You will receive a separate email with instructions on how to enroll. We are also implementing enhanced security measures to prevent future incidents." This proactive and supportive approach helps to mitigate fear and demonstrates accountability.

Furthermore, the incident response itself can necessitate changes in daily workflows and protocols, and employees need to be informed about these adjustments. If certain systems are offline, if access is restricted, or if new procedures are in place, clear communication about these operational changes is vital for maintaining productivity and preventing errors. For example, if a ransomware attack has encrypted critical servers, employees might need to revert to manual processes or use alternative systems.

The communication should detail these temporary measures, explain their purpose, and provide training or support for their implementation. "Due to the ongoing ransomware incident, access to the main server is temporarily unavailable. All new client requests must be processed using the 'Manual Intake Form' located on the shared drive. Please refer to the 'Temporary Workflow Guide' for detailed instructions. We appreciate your patience and adaptability as we work to restore full system functionality." This type of directive minimizes confusion and ensures business continuity.

The process of informing employees should be integrated into the organization's broader incident response plan. This means that roles and responsibilities for internal communications should be clearly defined. Who is responsible for drafting the messages? Who approves them? What channels will be used? Who will monitor employee feedback and questions? Establishing these protocols in advance ensures a coordinated and efficient response when an incident occurs. This might involve designating a specific individual or team to handle internal communications, working in conjunction with the Public Information Officer (PIO) who manages external communications, to ensure message consistency across all audiences.

Post-incident, internal communication plays a crucial role in reinforcing lessons learned and fostering a culture of security awareness. Once the immediate crisis is over and systems are restored, it's important to debrief employees, share insights from the incident, and highlight how their actions contributed to the resolution or could help prevent future incidents. This might involve follow-up training sessions, updated security policies, or an internal review of the incident response process. Communicating these improvements internally demonstrates a commitment to continuous learning and strengthens the organization's overall security posture. For instance, a post-incident communication could announce: "Following our recent security event, we have implemented a number of enhancements to our network defenses and security protocols. These include [List of improvements]. We will be rolling out mandatory refresher training on phishing awareness and secure data handling next month. Your ongoing vigilance and adherence to these updated policies are essential to our collective security."

Moreover, involving employees in the recovery and rebuilding process can be empowering. When employees feel that they are part of the solution, their engagement and commitment to security increase. This could involve soliciting feedback on new security tools, involving them in pilot programs for new technologies, or creating employee-led security champions networks. These initiatives not only improve security but also boost morale and foster a sense of shared responsibility for the organization's well-being.

The frequency and depth of internal communication should be tailored to the severity and duration of the incident. A minor internal system glitch might only require a brief notification, while a major, protracted cyberattack impacting operations and potentially employee data will necessitate sustained and detailed communication over an extended period. The key is to maintain an appropriate level of transparency and support throughout the incident lifecycle, from initial detection through to long-term recovery and improvement. This dedication to clear, consistent, and empathetic internal communication is fundamental to building trust, maintaining productivity, and ensuring that employees are informed, engaged, and resilient participants in the face of cybersecurity challenges. It transforms them from passive recipients of news into active contributors to the organization's security and recovery.

The immediate aftermath of a cybersecurity incident often presents a dual challenge: managing the technical response and navigating the public relations fallout. While internal stakeholders require clear, reassuring communication, external stakeholders, particularly the media, will be clamoring for information. The media's role is powerful; they are the primary conduit through which the public, customers, partners, and investors will form their understanding of the incident and, by extension, the organization itself. Mishandling media inquiries can exacerbate a crisis, leading to reputational damage that can far outlast the technical remediation efforts. Conversely, a well-managed media response can demonstrate competence, transparency, and accountability, fostering trust and mitigating long-term harm.

A cornerstone of effective media management during a cyber incident is the principle of designated spokespersons. In times of crisis, it is imperative to centralize information dissemination. Allowing multiple individuals, especially those without proper media training or a clear understanding of the incident's nuances, to speak with the press can lead to inconsistent messaging, factual errors, and the inadvertent disclosure of sensitive or proprietary information. Therefore, the organization must identify and train a select few individuals to serve as official spokespersons. These individuals should possess strong communication skills, a deep understanding of the incident (or access to those who do), and the authority to speak on behalf of the organization. Typically, this role falls to senior leadership, such as the CEO, CISO, or a dedicated communications executive. However, the key is not just the title but the preparation. Spokespersons must undergo media training that covers how to handle difficult questions, remain calm under pressure, and articulate complex information clearly and concisely. They should be equipped with pre-approved talking points and understand the organization's overall communication strategy. This centralized approach ensures a unified voice, reinforcing the organization's official stance and preventing the spread of conflicting or speculative information that can confuse the public and damage credibility.

Developing key messages is another critical component of maintaining narrative control. Before any media interaction occurs, the organization must formulate clear, concise, and consistent messages that accurately reflect the situation while aligning with its values and strategic objectives. These messages should address the fundamental questions: what happened, what is being done about it, and what is the impact on stakeholders. For instance, if a data breach has occurred, a key message might be: "We recently identified a cybersecurity incident that may have accessed certain customer information. Our top priority is the security and privacy of our customers. We are working diligently with leading cybersecurity experts to investigate the extent of the incident, strengthen our defenses, and provide support to those affected. We are committed to transparency and will share further information as it becomes available." These messages should be crafted with input from legal, technical, and communications teams to ensure accuracy and legal compliance. They should be adaptable enough to address specific inquiries but firm enough to provide a stable foundation for all communications. Regularly reiterating these core messages across all platforms helps to shape the media narrative and prevent external actors from defining the story.

Proactive engagement, where feasible and appropriate, can be a powerful tool in managing the media spotlight. While the immediate reaction to a cyber incident might be to go into a defensive crouch, organizations should consider opportunities to control the narrative from the outset. This might involve issuing a press release or a statement before media outlets begin reporting based on speculation or leaked information. A proactive statement allows the organization to frame the situation, provide factual information, and convey its commitment to resolving the issue. For example, if the organization has detected a sophisticated phishing campaign targeting its employees and customers, it might proactively issue a consumer alert detailing the nature of the threat and advising individuals on how to protect themselves. This demonstrates a commitment to stakeholder safety and positions the organization as a helpful resource rather than a victim. However, proactive engagement requires careful consideration. It should only be undertaken when there is sufficient information to provide a credible and accurate account, and when the potential benefits of controlling the narrative outweigh the risks of premature disclosure. The timing and content of proactive statements must be meticulously planned to avoid appearing to downplay the severity of an incident or to prematurely release unverified details.

When responding to accusations or negative reporting, a calm, evidence-based approach is crucial. The media landscape can be unforgiving, and organizations may face scrutiny and even direct accusations of negligence or wrongdoing. In such instances, it is vital to avoid emotional responses or defensive posturing. Instead, spokespersons should focus on presenting facts and outlining the actions being taken. If a report contains inaccuracies, the organization should politely but firmly correct them, providing evidence where possible. For example, if a news outlet claims the organization failed to implement basic security measures, the spokesperson might respond by stating, "We take these allegations very seriously and are conducting a thorough review. However, our incident response protocols include a multi-layered security approach, and our logs indicate that [specific security control] was operational at the time of the incident. We are cooperating fully with all investigations to ascertain the full facts." It is also important to acknowledge valid concerns without necessarily admitting fault prematurely, especially when legal investigations are ongoing. Phrases like, "We understand the concern this incident has raised, and we are committed to a full and transparent investigation to determine the root cause and prevent recurrence," can be effective.

Demonstrating accountability is paramount to rebuilding and maintaining trust, both with the media and the broader public. This involves more than just acknowledging an incident; it means showing a genuine commitment to learning from it and improving security. Communications should highlight the steps the organization is taking not only to resolve the current incident but also to prevent similar events from happening in the future. This could include investments in new technologies, enhancements to security policies and procedures, and expanded employee training. For instance, following a ransomware attack that disrupted operations, the organization might announce: "In response to the recent ransomware incident, we have accelerated our deployment of advanced endpoint detection and response (EDR) solutions across our network and have implemented mandatory annual security awareness training for all employees, with a focus on recognizing and reporting advanced phishing techniques. We are also conducting a comprehensive review of our data backup and recovery strategies to ensure business continuity in the face of future threats." Such disclosures signal a proactive and responsible approach, reassuring stakeholders that the organization is not only addressing the immediate crisis but is also investing in its long-term resilience.

Furthermore, the organization's response to media inquiries should be guided by a comprehensive incident response plan that includes a dedicated crisis communications strategy. This strategy should outline roles and responsibilities for media management, including who is authorized to speak, what information can be shared, and the process for approving communications. It should also establish protocols for monitoring media coverage, identifying potential misinformation, and responding quickly and effectively. For example, the plan might stipulate that all media inquiries are to be directed to the communications department, which will then consult with the legal and technical teams before providing a response. This ensures that all official statements are vetted and consistent. Having such a plan in place *before* an incident occurs is crucial, as it allows the organization to act decisively and coherently when under pressure, rather than scrambling to establish communication channels and protocols in the midst of a crisis. The plan should also account for different types of media, from traditional news outlets to social media, and outline strategies for engaging with each. Social media, in particular, can be a double-edged sword during a crisis. While it offers a direct channel for communication, it also provides a platform for rapid dissemination of rumors and unverified information. Therefore, social media monitoring and engagement strategies must be robust and integrated into the overall crisis communications plan.

The process of engaging with the media during a cybersecurity incident is not a one-time event; it is an ongoing effort that continues throughout the resolution and recovery phases. As the incident evolves, so too will the information available, and the organization must commit to providing regular updates to the media. These updates should be timely, accurate, and transparent, reinforcing the key messages and demonstrating progress in resolving the incident and strengthening defenses. Even when there is no significant new information to report, a brief statement acknowledging that the situation is still being managed can be beneficial in preventing media speculation and maintaining stakeholder confidence. For example, if an investigation into a complex breach is taking longer than initially anticipated, the organization might issue an update stating: "Our investigation into the cybersecurity incident is ongoing, and our teams are meticulously analyzing the available data. While this process requires time to ensure accuracy, we remain committed to providing a comprehensive understanding of the event and the steps we are taking to enhance our security. We will provide further significant updates as they become available." This consistent communication signals that the organization is actively engaged and not trying to hide information, which is crucial for preserving credibility.

The ultimate goal of managing media inquiries and maintaining narrative control during a cybersecurity incident is to protect the organization's reputation and ensure the continued trust of its stakeholders. By designating trained spokespersons, developing clear key messages, engaging proactively when appropriate, responding to accusations with evidence, demonstrating accountability, and adhering to a well-defined crisis communications plan, organizations can navigate the media spotlight effectively. This strategic approach transforms potential reputational damage into an opportunity to showcase resilience, transparency, and a steadfast commitment to security and stakeholder well-being. It requires careful planning, disciplined execution, and a deep understanding of how media dynamics can shape public perception in the wake of a digital threat.

When navigating the aftermath of a cybersecurity incident, the organization's responsibilities extend far beyond managing public perception through the media. A critical, often more sensitive, aspect involves direct communication with key stakeholder groups whose trust and continued engagement are vital for the organization's survival and future success. These groups – investors, business partners, and customers – have unique interests and require tailored communication strategies that address their specific concerns, demonstrate accountability, and reinforce confidence in the organization's ability to manage risks and protect their investments, operations, and data. Neglecting these crucial relationships during a crisis can lead to significant financial repercussions, operational disruptions, and a severe erosion of brand loyalty, potentially causing more long-term damage than the incident itself. Therefore, a deliberate and strategic approach to engaging these core stakeholders is not merely a best practice; it is an essential component of a robust incident response and recovery framework.

For investors, the primary concern often revolves around the financial implications of a cybersecurity incident. This can encompass direct costs associated with remediation, legal fees, regulatory fines, and potential compensation to affected parties. Furthermore, investors will be keenly interested in the potential impact on future revenue streams, market share, and the overall valuation of the company. Therefore, communication with investors must be transparent, timely, and provide a clear assessment of the financial risks and mitigation strategies. This often involves providing detailed briefings that outline the nature of the incident, the estimated financial impact, and the steps being taken to prevent recurrence. For publicly traded companies, adherence to regulatory reporting requirements is paramount. Announcements regarding material events, which a significant cybersecurity incident often represents, must be made in accordance with securities laws to ensure all shareholders receive timely and accurate information. Beyond formal disclosures, maintaining an open dialogue with major investors and financial analysts is crucial. This can involve conference calls, one-on-one meetings, and dedicated reports that offer deeper insights into the incident's impact and the organization's resilience. The emphasis should be on demonstrating proactive risk management, strong governance, and a clear plan to restore and enhance security measures. This reassures investors that the organization is not only capable of weathering the crisis but is also committed to strengthening its security posture to safeguard future value. It's about demonstrating that the investment is protected and that the leadership team possesses the foresight and capability to navigate such challenges effectively. This might include detailing investments in advanced security technologies, enhancements to cybersecurity talent, and rigorous testing of incident response capabilities. The goal is to shift the narrative from one of vulnerability to one of resilience and strategic foresight.

Business partners, including suppliers, distributors, and strategic allies, are another vital stakeholder group whose operational continuity and trust are directly impacted by a cybersecurity incident. If the incident affects shared systems, data, or supply chains, it can disrupt their own operations, leading to financial losses and reputational damage for them. Communication with business partners needs to be collaborative and focused on ensuring minimal disruption to their activities. This requires clear articulation of the incident's scope, particularly as it pertains to any shared data or systems, and a detailed plan for remediation and recovery. For instance, if a supplier experiences an incident due to a vulnerability within the organization's systems, the primary organization must swiftly inform them, provide assistance if possible, and outline the corrective actions being taken to prevent future cross-contamination. Similarly, if a partner's services are impacted by an incident within the organization, prompt notification and a clear recovery timeline are essential. Building trust with business partners also involves demonstrating a commitment to their security and the integrity of the shared ecosystem. This might involve inviting partners to participate in joint security assessments, sharing best practices, and collaborating on incident response drills. The communication should highlight the organization's dedication to maintaining the security and reliability of the entire value chain. For critical infrastructure or sensitive data sharing relationships, this might even necessitate providing assurances regarding data segregation, encryption protocols, and audit trails. The objective is to reinforce the understanding that the organization views these partnerships as long-term strategic assets and is committed to safeguarding them through robust security measures and transparent communication. This can lead to stronger, more resilient partnerships that are better equipped to handle future disruptions, both cybersecurity-related and otherwise.

Customers, as the end-users of products and services, are often the most directly impacted by cybersecurity incidents, especially those involving personal data breaches or service disruptions. Their trust is the bedrock of any successful business, and its erosion can lead to significant customer churn, negative reviews, and long-term brand damage. The communication strategy for customers must prioritize transparency, empathy, and clear guidance on how they can protect themselves and what support the organization will provide. When a data breach occurs, for example, it is imperative to notify affected customers promptly and directly, clearly stating what types of data were compromised, the potential risks, and the steps the organization is taking to address the situation. Offering services such as credit monitoring or identity theft protection can demonstrate a commitment to mitigating harm and rebuilding trust. The language used in customer communications should be accessible, avoiding overly technical jargon, and should convey a sense of genuine concern for their well-being. It's also important to provide clear instructions on how customers can report suspicious activity or seek further assistance. This might involve establishing dedicated helplines, FAQs, or secure online portals. Beyond direct notification, ongoing communication is crucial. Customers need to feel assured that the organization is actively working to enhance its security and prevent future incidents. This can be achieved through general security awareness campaigns, updates on security enhancements, and reaffirmations of the organization's commitment to protecting their data and privacy. For service disruptions, clear and frequent updates on the estimated time to resolution and the nature of the problem are essential to manage expectations and minimize frustration. In essence, customer communication during a cyber incident is about demonstrating that the organization values their trust, takes their security seriously, and is committed to rectifying the situation and earning back their confidence. This often involves going beyond the minimum legal requirements to provide a level of support and reassurance that fosters loyalty even in the face of adversity. It's about transforming a moment of crisis into an opportunity to solidify the customer relationship by showcasing genuine care and a steadfast commitment to their protection and satisfaction. The organization must be prepared to handle a high volume of inquiries with empathy and efficiency, ensuring that every customer feels heard and supported.

The interconnected nature of these stakeholder groups means that communication strategies must be coordinated. A consistent message, adapted for the specific concerns of each audience, is essential. For instance, the core facts of an incident communicated to investors should align with the details provided to business partners and customers, even if the emphasis and level of detail differ. Inconsistency can breed confusion and distrust across all groups. The incident response plan, therefore, must incorporate a robust stakeholder communication matrix that maps out communication channels, key messages, and responsible parties for each group. This ensures a cohesive and strategic approach that addresses the diverse needs and expectations of investors, partners, and customers, ultimately reinforcing the organization's resilience and commitment to security and trust. This proactive planning is the foundation upon which effective stakeholder engagement is built, turning potential crises into opportunities for strengthening vital relationships. It requires ongoing assessment and adaptation, as the landscape of threats and stakeholder expectations is constantly evolving. The aim is not just to survive the incident, but to emerge stronger, with more secure relationships and a fortified reputation for reliability and integrity.

The immediate aftermath of a cybersecurity incident is a period of intense scrutiny. However, the work doesn't end when the systems are restored and the initial wave of public relations management has passed. True recovery and resilience are built on a foundation of sustained effort in reputation management and brand rebuilding. This phase is about actively demonstrating that the organization has not only learned from the incident but has fundamentally transformed its approach to security and operational integrity. It's a long-term commitment that requires a strategic, multifaceted approach, moving beyond damage control to proactively cultivate trust and reinforce the brand's core values.

A cornerstone of post-incident reputation management is the demonstrable improvement of security measures. Simply stating that security has been enhanced is insufficient; organizations must show tangible evidence of these improvements. This involves not just the implementation of new technologies, such as advanced threat detection systems, enhanced encryption, or robust multi-factor authentication, but also a rigorous review and upgrade of existing policies and procedures. This could include implementing a more comprehensive vulnerability management program, conducting more frequent and thorough penetration testing, and establishing a dedicated security operations center (SOC) if one was not previously in place. Furthermore, the human element of security cannot be overstated. Investing in continuous security awareness training for all employees, from the executive suite to entry-level staff, is crucial. This training should go beyond basic phishing awareness to cover topics like secure coding practices, data handling protocols, and incident reporting procedures. The goal is to foster a culture where security is an ingrained responsibility for everyone. Evidence of these investments can be communicated through various channels, demonstrating a concrete commitment to preventing future breaches. This might involve publishing annual security reports that detail the specific enhancements made, the metrics used to measure their effectiveness, and the ongoing investments in security. These reports can serve as a valuable tool for rebuilding confidence with investors, partners, and customers alike, providing a transparent view into the organization's enhanced defenses.

Transparency in ongoing security efforts is another critical component of rebuilding trust. This involves communicating not just what has been done, but also the continuous journey of security improvement. Organizations should proactively share updates on their security initiatives, highlighting key milestones and achievements. This could take the form of blog posts detailing new security features, webinars explaining the organization's security philosophy, or regular newsletters providing insights into the evolving threat landscape and how the organization is adapting. It's about demystifying cybersecurity and making it accessible to all stakeholders. For instance, a company that experienced a breach affecting customer data might launch a dedicated section on its website that details its ongoing commitment to data privacy, explains the technologies and processes in place to protect personal information, and offers resources for customers to manage their own digital security. This consistent, open communication helps to normalize the conversation around security and positions the organization as a responsible steward of its customers' data. Moreover, this transparency can extend to the disclosure of security certifications and compliance with industry standards, such as ISO 27001 or SOC 2. Achieving and maintaining these certifications provides an independent validation of the organization's security practices, offering a credible assurance to stakeholders. Communicating these achievements, and the rigorous processes involved in obtaining them, further solidifies the brand's reputation for reliability and security. It's about showing that security is not a one-time fix but an ongoing, evolving discipline that is deeply embedded in the organization's operations.

Engaging with the broader community, both online and offline, can also play a significant role in reputation and brand rebuilding. This can involve participating in industry forums, contributing to open-source security projects, or sponsoring cybersecurity awareness events. By actively contributing to the collective knowledge and defense against cyber threats, organizations can demonstrate their commitment to the wider digital ecosystem. For example, a company that develops advanced threat intelligence might share anonymized, aggregated data with security researchers or participate in threat-sharing initiatives. This not only helps to improve overall cybersecurity but also positions the organization as a thought leader and a responsible corporate citizen. Publicly sharing insights and expertise through articles, presentations, or white papers can further enhance the brand's credibility. This might involve dissecting emerging threat vectors, offering best practices for particular industries, or contributing to public discourse on cybersecurity policy. Such activities, when undertaken with sincerity and a genuine desire to contribute, can significantly shift public perception from one of vulnerability to one of leadership and proactive engagement.

Furthermore, actively seeking and responding to feedback from customers and partners is vital. This can involve implementing customer satisfaction surveys specifically focused on security perceptions, establishing dedicated channels for security-related feedback, and actively monitoring social media for mentions of the organization's security posture. When constructive criticism is received, it should be addressed promptly and transparently, demonstrating a willingness to adapt and improve. This could involve acknowledging a valid concern, explaining the steps being taken to address it, or even apologizing if shortcomings are identified. This open dialogue reinforces the idea that the organization is listening and is committed to meeting the evolving expectations of its stakeholders. The goal is to create a feedback loop that informs and refines the organization's security strategy and communication efforts.

Beyond direct communication about security, rebuilding the brand involves reinforcing the organization's core mission and values. While security incidents can shake confidence, they also present an opportunity to reaffirm what the brand stands for and why customers and partners should continue to engage with it. This means highlighting the positive aspects of the organization's products, services, and customer relationships. It involves telling compelling stories about innovation, customer success, and the positive impact the organization has on its stakeholders and the wider community. The narrative should shift from focusing solely on the incident to showcasing the organization's resilience, adaptability, and unwavering commitment to its customers. This can be achieved through a variety of marketing and communications initiatives, such as customer testimonials, case studies, and feature stories that emphasize the company's strengths and its forward-looking vision. The aim is to remind stakeholders of the intrinsic value the organization provides, beyond its security assurances.

In the long term, a proactive and resilient approach to cybersecurity becomes an integral part of the brand's identity. Organizations that successfully navigate a cybersecurity incident and emerge stronger often do so by embedding security into their strategic planning and decision-making processes. This means treating cybersecurity not as a technical IT issue, but as a fundamental business imperative that underpins all operations and stakeholder relationships. The lessons learned from an incident should inform future investments, product development, and strategic partnerships. This holistic integration of security ensures that the brand is not only perceived as secure but is, in fact, fundamentally more secure and reliable. This forward-looking perspective is key to moving beyond the shadow of past incidents and establishing a brand that is synonymous with trust, integrity, and enduring value in an increasingly complex digital world. The consistent demonstration of vigilance, transparency, and a commitment to continuous improvement will ultimately solidify the organization's reputation and foster long-term loyalty among its stakeholders.

The preceding discussion has elaborated on the crucial post-incident activities of reputation management and brand rebuilding. This involves a concerted effort to demonstrate enhanced security, foster transparency, engage with the community, and reinforce core organizational values. However, to truly move from a reactive stance to a proactive and resilient posture against cyber threats, organizations must embrace the power of threat intelligence. Understanding and effectively leveraging this intelligence is not merely an IT function; it is a strategic imperative that underpins robust cybersecurity defenses and informs critical business decisions. This section delves into the fundamental concept of threat intelligence and its inherent lifecycle, illustrating how it transforms raw data into actionable insights that can anticipate and neutralize threats before they materialize.

At its core, threat intelligence is information about existing or emerging threats that an organization can use to make better decisions about defending against them. It's about understanding not just *that* an attack might happen, but *how*, *why*, *who* might be behind it, and *what* their likely targets and motivations are. This goes far beyond simply knowing that vulnerabilities exist or that malware is circulating. It involves a systematic approach to gathering, processing, analyzing, and disseminating information that provides context, relevance, and actionable insights into the threat landscape. Without a structured framework for managing this information, even the most valuable data can remain inert and ineffective. This is where the concept of the threat intelligence lifecycle becomes paramount. It provides a methodical pathway for transforming disparate pieces of information into a cohesive and strategic understanding of potential adversaries and their methodologies.

The threat intelligence lifecycle is typically understood as a cyclical process comprising several key stages. While variations exist in how these stages are defined and segmented, the fundamental flow remains consistent: requirements gathering, collection, processing, analysis, dissemination, and feedback. Each stage is critical and interconnected; a breakdown in one can compromise the effectiveness of the entire process.

The initial and often overlooked stage is **requirements gathering**. This is the foundation upon which all subsequent intelligence activities are built. It involves understanding what the organization *needs* to know to make informed decisions. This isn't about simply collecting every piece of data available; it's about strategic alignment. What are the organization's critical assets? What are its most significant business risks? Who are the likely threat actors that would target it, and why? What are the organization's current defensive capabilities, and where are the potential gaps? By answering these questions, security leaders and intelligence analysts can define clear intelligence requirements (IRs) or priority intelligence requirements (PIRs). These requirements act as a compass, guiding the collection efforts and ensuring that the intelligence produced is relevant and actionable. For instance, a financial institution might have a PIR focused on understanding emerging ransomware strains that target banking infrastructure and the typical tactics, techniques, and procedures

(TTPs) used by threat groups specializing in financial cybercrime. A retail company, on the other hand, might prioritize intelligence on card-skimming operations and the actors involved in stealing and monetizing payment card data. Without clearly defined requirements, collection efforts can become unfocused, leading to an overwhelming volume of irrelevant data and a significant waste of resources. The leadership of the organization, including business executives, legal counsel, and IT security personnel, must collaborate to establish these requirements, ensuring that the intelligence produced directly supports business objectives and risk mitigation strategies.

Following the definition of intelligence requirements, the next stage is **collection**. This is where raw data is gathered from a multitude of sources. These sources can be broadly categorized as open-source intelligence (OSINT) and closed-source intelligence (CINT). OSINT encompasses publicly available information, which can be surprisingly rich and valuable. This includes news articles, academic papers, security blogs, social media platforms, public forums, dark web marketplaces (though access and interpretation require specialized skills and caution), government reports, and even publicly available code repositories. For example, a security team might monitor specific Twitter accounts of known hacktivist groups or track discussions on cybersecurity forums for early indicators of new exploit kits or compromised credentials. OSINT can also involve observing global trends in malware adoption, tracking the geopolitical motivations behind state-sponsored attacks, or monitoring the public statements of threat actors.

Closed-source intelligence, in contrast, involves data obtained from sources that are not publicly accessible. This can include proprietary threat feeds from commercial vendors, information shared through industry-specific threat-sharing groups (e.g., Information Sharing and Analysis Centers or ISACs), internal security logs and telemetry from the organization's own systems (such as intrusion detection systems, firewalls, and endpoint detection and response solutions), and information obtained through human intelligence (HUMINT) or technical intelligence gathering operations. For example, a threat intelligence platform might ingest indicators of compromise (IoCs) – such as IP addresses, domain names, or file hashes – from a commercial vendor that specializes in tracking advanced persistent threats (APTs). Internally, correlating network traffic anomalies with alerts from endpoint security software can provide critical CINT about an ongoing attack. The effectiveness of collection hinges on the diversity and reliability of the sources used. A robust threat intelligence program will leverage a mix of OSINT and CINT to gain a comprehensive view of the threat landscape, avoiding over-reliance on any single source. The quality of the data collected is as important as the quantity; inaccurate or outdated information can lead to flawed conclusions.

Once data is collected, it must be **processed** to make it ready for analysis. This stage involves organizing, filtering, and enriching the raw data. Processing can include tasks such as deduplication, normalization of data formats, correlation of related pieces of information, and enrichment with contextual data. For instance, a raw IP address collected from a suspicious log file might be enriched by querying public databases to determine its geographical location, the associated domain name, and whether it has been flagged in known malicious IP lists. Similarly, a malware hash might be processed to retrieve information about its known family, its typical behavior, and the operating systems it targets. This stage often involves the use of automated tools and platforms that can ingest vast amounts of data from various sources and prepare it in a structured format. Data cleansing is a critical aspect of processing; irrelevant, erroneous, or duplicated data must be identified and removed to prevent it from skewing the analysis. The goal of processing is to transform the collected raw data into a usable dataset that can be effectively analyzed to extract meaningful insights. This might involve converting unstructured text from news articles into structured data points that can be queried, or aggregating logs from different security tools into a unified format for easier review.

The heart of the threat intelligence lifecycle is **analysis**. This is where raw, processed data is transformed into actionable intelligence. Analysts examine the processed data, looking for patterns, trends, and anomalies that can indicate a threat. This involves applying critical thinking, domain expertise, and various analytical methodologies to understand the implications of the gathered information. Different types of analysis can be performed, including technical analysis, which focuses on malware characteristics, exploit techniques, and infrastructure; strategic analysis, which looks at the broader geopolitical and economic motivations behind threat actors and their long-term objectives; and operational analysis, which examines the TTPs used in specific attack campaigns.

For example, an analyst might correlate a series of seemingly unrelated phishing attempts targeting specific departments within an organization with chatter observed on a dark web forum discussing potential access to that organization's internal network. By analyzing the TTPs used in the phishing emails, the malware payloads delivered, and the nature of the forum discussions, the analyst can deduce that a targeted attack campaign is likely underway. This analysis would involve understanding the sophistication of the threat actor, their likely capabilities, and their potential objectives. Furthermore, analysis often involves attributing attacks to specific threat groups or nation-states, which can provide valuable insights into their motives and potential future actions. This attribution, however, is often challenging and requires a high degree of confidence and supporting evidence. Analysts must be adept at identifying false positives and distinguishing between opportunistic attacks and deliberate, targeted campaigns. They also need to assess the confidence level of their findings, understanding that intelligence is rarely 100% certain. The output of the analysis stage is not just raw findings, but a synthesized understanding of the threat, its potential impact, and recommended courses of action.

Once intelligence has been analyzed and validated, it must be **disseminated** to the appropriate stakeholders in a timely and understandable manner. The format and content of the dissemination will vary depending on the intended audience. For technical teams, this might involve providing detailed IoCs, TTPs, and recommended blocking rules for security tools. For security operations center (SOC) analysts, it could be alerts on active threats or proactive indicators that can be used for hunting. For executive leadership, it might be a high-level summary of significant risks and their potential business impact, along with strategic recommendations.

Effective dissemination ensures that the intelligence is not just produced, but is actually used to inform decisions and improve defenses. This often involves leveraging threat intelligence platforms (TIPs) that can automate the distribution of intelligence to various security tools and personnel. For example, IoCs identified by the intelligence team can be automatically pushed to firewalls and endpoint detection systems to block known malicious activity. Strategic intelligence summaries might be delivered via reports or presentations to management. The timeliness of dissemination is critical, especially for tactical intelligence. An alert about an imminent phishing campaign, for instance, needs to reach the relevant teams immediately to allow for proactive defense measures, such as updating email filters or warning employees. Misunderstandings can arise if the intelligence is presented in a format that is not tailored to the audience's technical expertise or operational needs. Therefore, analysts must be skilled communicators, capable of translating complex technical findings into clear, concise, and actionable information for diverse stakeholders.

Finally, the lifecycle concludes with the **feedback** loop. This stage is crucial for refining the entire process and ensuring its ongoing relevance and effectiveness. Stakeholders who receive the intelligence provide feedback on its accuracy, timeliness, and usefulness. This feedback helps intelligence producers understand what is working well and where improvements are needed. Did the disseminated intelligence enable the SOC to effectively detect and respond to a threat? Was the strategic brief clear enough for the executive team to make an informed decision? This feedback directly informs the requirements gathering stage for the next cycle, helping to refine intelligence requirements and collection priorities.

For example, if a SOC team consistently finds that a particular type of intelligence feed is generating too many false positives, that feedback can be used to adjust collection sources or analytical methodologies. Conversely, if executive leadership finds strategic intelligence reports to be particularly insightful, that reinforces the value of those types of analyses. This continuous feedback mechanism ensures that the threat intelligence program remains dynamic and responsive to the evolving needs of the organization and the ever-changing threat landscape. It transforms threat intelligence from a static report into a living, breathing process that continuously adapts and improves. Without this feedback mechanism, a threat intelligence program can quickly become stale and ineffective, producing information that is no longer relevant or actionable. The commitment to fostering this feedback loop demonstrates a mature and adaptive approach to cybersecurity, recognizing that threat intelligence is not a destination, but an ongoing journey of learning and improvement.

The strategic value of understanding and implementing the threat intelligence lifecycle cannot be overstated. In today's complex and interconnected digital environment, organizations face a constant barrage of sophisticated threats. Relying solely on reactive security measures, such as incident response, is akin to closing the barn door after the horses have bolted. Threat intelligence provides the foresight needed to anticipate attacks, understand the motivations and capabilities of adversaries, and proactively strengthen defenses. It moves an organization from a defensive posture to a more offensive, predictive one, allowing it to prioritize its security investments and allocate resources effectively. By understanding the TTPs of common threat actors, organizations can tune their security controls to detect and block those specific techniques. For example, if intelligence indicates that a particular APT group commonly uses PowerShell for lateral movement, the security team can implement specific detection rules and policies to identify and alert on such activities within their environment. This proactive adaptation significantly reduces the attack surface and increases the likelihood of early detection, minimizing the potential damage of a successful breach.

Moreover, threat intelligence informs risk management decisions. By understanding the likelihood and potential impact of various threats, organizations can make more informed decisions about where to invest their security budget. For instance, if intelligence suggests a heightened risk of a specific type of ransomware attack that could cripple operations, the organization might prioritize investments in endpoint detection and response (EDR) solutions, robust backup and recovery systems, and user awareness training focused on phishing and social engineering. This data-driven approach ensures that security spending is aligned with the most pressing risks. The insights gained from threat intelligence can also guide strategic business decisions, such as market entry into regions with higher cyber threats or the adoption of new technologies that might introduce new vulnerabilities.

The effective implementation of a threat intelligence lifecycle also fosters collaboration and knowledge sharing, both internally and externally. Internally, it breaks down silos between different security teams (e.g., SOC, incident response, vulnerability management) and even between IT and business units, fostering a unified approach to security. Externally, participation in threat-sharing communities allows organizations to benefit from the collective intelligence of their peers, gaining insights into threats that might not be visible through their own internal monitoring alone. This collaborative approach is essential in combating sophisticated, widespread threats that often target multiple organizations simultaneously. The ability to rapidly share and ingest relevant threat data can mean the difference between a minor security incident and a catastrophic breach.

In conclusion, the threat intelligence lifecycle is a fundamental framework for any organization serious about establishing a robust and proactive cybersecurity posture. From defining clear requirements to collecting, processing, analyzing, disseminating, and continuously refining intelligence through feedback, each stage plays a vital role. By embracing this cyclical process, organizations can transform raw data into actionable insights, enabling them to anticipate threats, understand adversaries, make informed risk management decisions, and ultimately, strengthen their defenses against the ever-evolving landscape of cyber threats. It is a continuous journey that requires dedication, resources, and a commitment to staying ahead of the curve in the ongoing battle for digital security.

Integrating threat intelligence into the fabric of an organization's security monitoring operations is not merely an enhancement; it is a fundamental shift from a passive, reactive stance to an active, predictive posture. The preceding discussion laid the groundwork for understanding the threat intelligence lifecycle, illustrating how raw data is transformed into actionable insights. Now, we pivot to the practical application of these insights within the critical domain of incident detection. The objective is to imbue existing security infrastructure and processes with the foresight and contextual understanding that only high-quality threat intelligence can provide, thereby enabling the identification of malicious activities with unprecedented speed and accuracy. Early detection is the cornerstone of effective incident response, drastically reducing the potential blast radius of an attack, minimizing financial and reputational damage, and allowing security teams to reassert control over the environment before irreversible harm is done.

At the forefront of leveraging threat intelligence for enhanced detection are Indicators of Compromise (IoCs). IoCs are observable artifacts that provide a high degree of confidence that a malicious activity has occurred or is ongoing on a system or network. These can manifest in various forms, including specific IP addresses or domain names associated with command-and-control (C2) servers, unique file hashes of known malware, unusual registry keys, suspicious network traffic patterns, or even specific patterns within log files that deviate from established baselines. The power of IoCs lies in their specificity. When an organization proactively ingests and correlates IoCs from trusted threat intelligence feeds with its own telemetry data, it creates a potent detection mechanism. For instance, if a threat intelligence provider identifies a new botnet infrastructure and shares the associated IP addresses, and these IPs are subsequently observed attempting to communicate with an organization's internal servers, this constitutes a high-fidelity alert. Without the threat intelligence, such communication might be lost in the noise of legitimate network traffic, or its significance might only be realized much later, after significant damage has been inflicted.

The integration process for IoCs typically involves several key steps. First, selecting reliable and relevant threat intelligence sources is paramount. Not all IoC feeds are created equal; some may be outdated, prone to false positives, or lack the necessary context. Organizations often subscribe to commercial threat intelligence feeds, participate in industry-specific information sharing groups (such as ISACs), or leverage open-source intelligence (OSINT) communities that curate and disseminate IoCs. Second, these IoCs must be ingested into security tools capable of real-time or near-real-time correlation. This commonly includes Security Information and Event Management (SIEM) systems, Security Orchestration, Automation, and Response (SOAR) platforms, Network Intrusion Detection Systems (NIDS), and Endpoint Detection and Response (EDR) solutions. For example, a SIEM can be configured to continuously scan incoming log data, comparing it against a constantly updated list of malicious IPs and domains provided by a threat intelligence feed. Upon a match, the SIEM can trigger an alert, flagging the suspicious activity for immediate investigation by security analysts.

Beyond static IoCs, a more sophisticated approach involves the use of threat actor profiles. These profiles provide a deeper understanding of the adversary, moving beyond specific indicators to encompass their motivations, objectives, preferred attack vectors, and typical operational methodologies. By understanding *who* is likely to attack and *why*, security teams can better anticipate their actions and tailor their detection strategies. For example, an organization operating in the defense sector might be a prime target for state-sponsored espionage groups. Threat intelligence may reveal that a particular state actor group frequently employs spear-phishing campaigns to gain initial access, followed by the use of specific custom malware to exfiltrate sensitive data, and then attempts to cover their tracks through sophisticated log manipulation. Armed with this profile, the security team can focus their detection efforts on these specific TTPs. This includes implementing more stringent email filtering for highly targeted phishing attempts, deploying advanced malware detection capabilities tuned to identify the signatures and behaviors of the known custom malware, and enhancing log monitoring to detect anomalies indicative of log tampering.

Threat actor profiles are invaluable for proactive hunting and defensive planning. They allow security teams to answer critical questions: "What are the most likely threats we face?", "How would these threats likely target us?", and "What are our most vulnerable points?" This understanding enables a shift from simply reacting to alerts to actively seeking out threats that might have evaded automated defenses. For instance, if intelligence suggests that a financially motivated cybercrime syndicate is actively targeting companies in a specific industry through ransomware attacks, the security team can proactively hunt for evidence of reconnaissance activities, the deployment of initial access tools, or the presence of ransomware staging files within their environment. This proactive stance significantly increases the probability of detecting an attack in its nascent stages, before encryption begins and critical business operations are disrupted. Building and maintaining these threat actor profiles requires ongoing analysis and correlation of various intelligence streams, including technical indicators, geopolitical analysis, and reports from incident response engagements.

Crucially, the integration of threat intelligence into incident detection hinges on understanding and mapping Tactics, Techniques, and Procedures (TTPs). The MITRE ATT&CK® framework has become a de facto standard for categorizing and describing adversary behaviors. TTPs are the specific methods adversaries use to achieve their objectives at various stages of an attack lifecycle, from initial reconnaissance and execution to lateral movement and data exfiltration. By mapping these TTPs to an organization's defensive capabilities and telemetry, security teams can identify gaps and develop more effective detection rules. For example, an organization might learn through threat intelligence that a particular ransomware group commonly uses the "Valid Accounts" technique (T1078) to gain access to systems by leveraging compromised credentials. They might also discover that this group employs "PowerShell" (T1059.001) for execution and "Remote Service" (T1021) for lateral movement.

Leveraging this TTP-based intelligence allows for the creation of more robust and context-aware detection mechanisms. Instead of solely relying on known malicious file hashes or IP addresses (which can change rapidly), detection rules can be designed to identify the *behaviors* associated with these TTPs. For instance, a detection rule could be configured to alert on unusual patterns of PowerShell execution originating from unexpected user accounts, or to flag multiple failed login attempts followed by a successful login to a remote service from an internal workstation. EDR solutions are particularly well-suited for this type of behavioral detection, as they can monitor process execution, file system activity, and network connections in real-time. By correlating these events and looking for sequences that match known adversary TTPs, EDR systems can provide highly accurate alerts on malicious activities, even if the specific malware or infrastructure involved is new and has not been previously identified.

The practical implementation of TTP-based detection involves several steps. First, organizations need to map their existing telemetry and security controls against common TTPs, often using frameworks like MITRE ATT&CK. This helps to identify where visibility is lacking. Second, they need to develop detection logic for high-priority TTPs that are relevant to their threat landscape. This can involve writing custom detection rules for SIEMs, configuring advanced threat hunting queries in EDR platforms, or deploying specialized security tools designed to detect specific types of adversary behavior. For example, a rule might be created to detect the use of "Mimikatz" (a credential dumping tool), which falls under the "Credential Dumping" technique (T1003). The rule would look for specific process names, command-line arguments, or memory access patterns associated with Mimikatz.

Furthermore, threat intelligence can be used to prioritize vulnerability management efforts. By understanding which vulnerabilities are actively being exploited in the wild, and by which threat actors, organizations can more effectively allocate resources to patch critical systems. If threat intelligence indicates that a specific zero-day vulnerability is being used in targeted attacks against companies in a particular sector, that vulnerability should be patched with the highest priority. This proactive approach to vulnerability management, informed by real-world threat data, is far more effective than a purely risk-based approach that might not fully account for the immediate, active threat landscape. It ensures that the most exploitable and dangerous weaknesses are addressed first, thereby reducing the attack surface for the most probable and impactful threats.

The successful integration of threat intelligence into incident detection is not a one-time project but an ongoing process. The threat landscape is dynamic, with adversaries constantly evolving their TTPs and developing new malware. Therefore, the threat intelligence feeds must be continuously updated, and detection mechanisms must be regularly reviewed and refined. This requires a dedicated team of threat intelligence analysts and security operations personnel who are skilled in interpreting intelligence, developing detection logic, and responding to alerts. The feedback loop, as discussed in the previous context, is absolutely critical here. Feedback from the security operations center (SOC) on the effectiveness of alerts, the rate of false positives, and the timeliness of intelligence can be used to refine collection requirements, improve analytical methodologies, and tune detection rules.

Automating the ingestion and operationalization of threat intelligence is key to achieving scalability and speed. Manual correlation of IoCs or TTPs is often impractical given the sheer volume of data. SOAR platforms play a significant role in this by automating the execution of playbooks that can ingest threat intelligence, enrich alerts with contextual information, and even initiate automated response actions such as blocking an IP address or isolating an endpoint. For instance, when a SIEM generates an alert related to a suspicious IP address, a SOAR platform can automatically query multiple threat intelligence sources to gather more information about that IP, check if it's associated with known malicious campaigns, and then, based on predefined playbooks, either present this enriched alert to an analyst for review or automatically implement a blocking rule on the firewall. This level of automation dramatically reduces the time it takes to detect and respond to threats, a critical factor in minimizing incident impact.

Moreover, intelligence on emerging attack trends and methodologies can inform the development of new detection capabilities. For example, if threat intelligence reports indicate an increase in attacks utilizing living-off-the-land binaries (LOLBins) – legitimate system tools like PowerShell, PsExec, or WMI that are co-opted by attackers – security teams can focus on developing specific detection rules and behavioral analytics to identify the misuse of these tools. This might involve monitoring for unusual command-line arguments, process parent-child relationships, or network connections associated with these binaries. The intelligence helps to focus these efforts on the most pertinent threats rather than trying to detect every conceivable misuse of every system tool.

The effectiveness of threat intelligence in incident detection also depends on the organization's ability to contextualize that intelligence. An IoC might be highly malicious in isolation, but its relevance to a specific organization depends on its environment and business context. For example, an IP address flagged as malicious might be an internal server that is legitimately communicating with an external research partner that uses a shared IP range. Without proper context and enrichment, such an alert could lead to a false positive, wasting valuable analyst time and potentially disrupting legitimate business operations. Therefore, threat intelligence must be integrated with internal asset inventories, network topology information, and user role data to provide a complete picture. This allows for more accurate prioritization of alerts and a better understanding of the potential impact of a detected threat.

In summary, the strategic integration of threat intelligence into incident detection transforms an organization's security posture from reactive to proactive. By leveraging Indicators of Compromise, understanding threat actor profiles, and mapping adversary Tactics, Techniques, and Procedures, security teams can significantly enhance their ability to identify malicious activities early. This requires robust data collection, sophisticated correlation engines, effective automation, and skilled personnel who can interpret and operationalize intelligence. The ongoing refinement of these processes, driven by feedback and a continuous understanding of the evolving threat landscape, is crucial for maintaining an effective defense against ever-more sophisticated cyber adversaries. The ultimate goal is to make the organization a harder target, to detect threats before they cause significant damage, and to respond with speed and precision when an incident does occur.

The preceding discussions have firmly established the critical role of threat intelligence in bolstering incident detection capabilities, moving organizations from a purely reactive stance to a more predictive and proactive security posture. We have explored how Indicators of Compromise (IoCs), detailed threat actor profiles, and a deep understanding of adversary Tactics, Techniques, and Procedures (TTPs) can significantly enhance the early identification of malicious activities. Now, our focus shifts to the subsequent, and equally vital, phase of cybersecurity operations: incident response. While effective detection is paramount, a well-defined and intelligence-driven incident response plan is the mechanism through which an organization effectively mitigates the impact of an inevitable breach. Simply detecting a threat is insufficient; the ability to swiftly and precisely contain, eradicate, and recover from an incident directly correlates with the organization's preparedness, a preparedness that can be substantially fortified by the insights gleaned from threat intelligence.

Incorporating intelligence into the incident response plan involves a fundamental reimagining of traditional response frameworks. Instead of generic, one-size-fits-all playbooks, an intelligence-informed approach allows for the development of tailored strategies that anticipate and address the most probable threats an organization is likely to face. This begins with a nuanced understanding of the adversary's motivations, capabilities, and likely objectives. For instance, if threat intelligence indicates a heightened risk of state-sponsored espionage targeting intellectual property within a specific industry, the incident response plan should be meticulously crafted to address the unique challenges posed by such adversaries. This might include enhanced protocols for data exfiltration detection, specialized forensic analysis techniques to uncover sophisticated stealthy techniques, and communication strategies that account for the potential for prolonged engagement and the sensitive nature of the data at risk. The goal is not to prepare for every conceivable threat, but to build resilience against the threats that pose the greatest and most immediate risk, as identified through continuous intelligence gathering and analysis.

One of the most significant contributions of threat intelligence to incident response planning lies in its ability to inform and prioritize response efforts. Not all incidents are created equal, and the resources available for response are finite. Intelligence provides the crucial context needed to make informed decisions about where to focus attention and allocate limited personnel and technological assets. For example, if intelligence suggests that a particular ransomware strain is being actively deployed by a financially motivated cybercrime group known for its rapid encryption and aggressive negotiation tactics, the incident response plan should include pre-defined, rapid-response playbooks specifically for ransomware. These playbooks would likely prioritize immediate network segmentation to prevent lateral movement, swift identification of affected systems, and immediate engagement with cyber-resilience or recovery specialists, potentially even pre-vetting negotiations with specialized firms if the threat actor is known for certain demands. Conversely, an alert related to a lower-tier threat actor employing less sophisticated techniques might trigger a less urgent, but still thorough, response. This intelligent prioritization ensures that the most critical and potentially damaging incidents receive the most immediate and comprehensive attention, thereby minimizing the potential blast radius and overall impact.

The refinement of containment strategies is a prime example of how intelligence can directly influence incident response planning. Containment aims to limit the spread and damage of an incident. Without intelligence, containment might involve broad, potentially disruptive, measures such as shutting down entire network segments. However, with detailed intelligence about an adversary's preferred lateral movement techniques, their typical exfiltration methods, or their specific command-and-control (C2) infrastructure, containment can become far more precise and less disruptive. For instance, if threat intelligence reveals that a particular group relies on specific C2 domains or IP addresses for communication and coordination, the incident response plan can include pre-approved firewall rules or proxy configurations to block these specific indicators immediately upon their identification. Similarly, if intelligence indicates that an attacker is exploiting a specific vulnerability to move within the network, a response action might involve isolating systems with that vulnerability or applying emergency patches, rather than a wholesale network shutdown. This level of precision, driven by actionable intelligence, is critical for preserving business operations while effectively neutralizing the threat.

Similarly, eradication efforts can be significantly improved through the application of threat intelligence. Eradication focuses on removing the threat from the environment. This often involves removing malware, closing backdoors, and remediating compromised systems. Intelligence can guide the identification of the full scope of the adversary's presence and their persistence mechanisms. For example, if intelligence indicates that a sophisticated APT group uses rootkits or advanced fileless malware techniques to maintain persistence, the eradication playbook needs to incorporate specialized tools and forensic procedures designed to detect and remove such deeply embedded threats. This might involve using boot-time scanning tools, memory forensics, or advanced endpoint detection and response (EDR) capabilities that are specifically tuned to identify these advanced techniques. Knowing *what* to look for and *how* the adversary operates allows responders to ensure that the threat is truly eliminated and not just temporarily suppressed, preventing costly re-infections.

Recovery, the final stage of incident response, also benefits immensely from an intelligence-driven approach. Recovery aims to restore systems and services to normal operations. Threat intelligence can inform the prioritization of recovery efforts based on business criticality and the nature of the threat. If intelligence suggests that an attacker's primary goal was data theft, recovery might focus on verifying the integrity of sensitive data and re-establishing secure access channels. If the threat was a destructive attack, recovery would prioritize restoring critical systems from known good backups and ensuring that no lingering malicious code could compromise the restored environment. Furthermore, intelligence about the adversary's modus operandi can help inform security hardening measures implemented during the recovery phase. For example, if the initial compromise was facilitated by compromised credentials obtained through a phishing attack, the recovery plan would include enhanced multi-factor authentication (MFA) enforcement, user security awareness training, and robust credential management practices. This proactive hardening, informed by the root cause of the incident, is crucial for preventing recurrence.

The development of specialized incident response playbooks is a tangible outcome of integrating threat intelligence. Instead of a generic "malware outbreak" playbook, an organization can develop specific playbooks for:

Ransomware Attacks: Detailing immediate isolation procedures, identification of ransomware variants through intelligence feeds, communication protocols with law enforcement and potentially negotiators, and specialized data recovery strategies.

Data Exfiltration Incidents: Outlining steps to trace data movement, identify compromised data sets, contain data transfer channels, and manage potential regulatory and reputational fallout, informed by intelligence on typical exfiltration methods and target data types.

Insider Threats: Defining procedures for investigating user activity, preserving digital evidence in a forensically sound manner, and collaborating with HR and legal departments, potentially informed by intelligence on insider threat motivations and common techniques.

Distributed Denial-of-Service (DDoS) Attacks: Specifying methods for traffic analysis, engagement with upstream providers or DDoS mitigation services, and prioritization of critical services to remain accessible, often based on intelligence about common attack vectors and botnet infrastructures.

Advanced Persistent Threats (APTs): Developing detailed procedures for deep forensic investigation, long-term monitoring for stealthy persistence, threat hunting for specific TTPs associated with known APT groups, and secure communication protocols for sensitive incident handling.

Each of these playbooks would be populated with specific, actionable steps derived from threat intelligence about the adversaries most likely to conduct such attacks against the organization. This includes identifying the types of systems or data they are likely to target, their preferred initial access vectors, their typical lateral movement techniques, and their ultimate objectives. This intelligence directly shapes the sequence of actions, the tools to be deployed, and the expertise required for effective response.

Moreover, threat intelligence can significantly enhance the allocation of resources within the incident response team. By understanding the most prevalent threats and attack vectors targeting the organization or its industry, leadership can justify investments in specific skill sets, technologies, and training programs.

For instance, if intelligence consistently highlights the growing threat of supply chain attacks, the organization might invest in dedicated personnel or specialized tools for supply chain risk assessment and incident response. This proactive resource allocation, guided by intelligence, ensures that the incident response capability is aligned with the actual threats faced, rather than being based on outdated assumptions or generic risk assessments. It allows for the development of a more efficient and effective response force, capable of handling the challenges that are most likely to materialize.

The intelligence gathered during an incident itself is also crucial for refining future response plans. This concept of "threat intelligence feedback" is a critical loop that continuously improves the organization's security posture. After an incident is resolved, a thorough post-incident review should incorporate an analysis of the threat intelligence available *during* the incident, as well as an assessment of *new* intelligence that emerged from the event. Were there indicators that were missed? Were the response playbooks effective? What new TTPs or IoCs were observed that should be incorporated into future planning and detection efforts? This post-incident intelligence analysis can reveal gaps in current intelligence sources, highlight the need for new data feeds, or underscore the importance of developing more sophisticated detection rules based on observed adversary behaviors. By systematically feeding lessons learned back into the intelligence cycle and the incident response planning process, organizations build a more adaptive and resilient defense over time.

Consider an organization that experiences a significant data breach. Through forensic analysis and external intelligence gathering, it is determined that the compromise was facilitated by an exploited vulnerability in a third-party software component. The initial incident response plan may have focused on isolating the affected servers and rebuilding them. However, the post-incident intelligence review reveals that the threat actor group responsible for this attack is known to persistently target organizations through their supply chains, employing social engineering to gain initial access and then exploiting vulnerabilities in commonly used enterprise software. This intelligence would prompt a revision of the incident response plan to include:

Enhanced Supply Chain Due Diligence: Pre-incident intelligence gathering on the security posture of critical vendors and software providers.

Proactive Vulnerability Scanning for Third-Party Software: Specific focus on known exploitable vulnerabilities in software used by the organization.

Improved Detection of Initial Access Techniques: Tuning security controls to better identify phishing attempts or other social engineering tactics targeting employees who interact with third-party systems.

Broader Network Segmentation: Implementing stricter network segmentation to limit the lateral movement potential of attackers who gain a foothold through a compromised vendor.

This iterative process, where intelligence informs response planning, and the outcomes of response refine future intelligence requirements, creates a powerful synergy. The incident response plan transforms from a static document into a dynamic, living blueprint that evolves in lockstep with the changing threat landscape. This adaptive capability is what distinguishes leading security organizations and allows them to effectively navigate the persistent and evolving challenges posed by cyber adversaries. Without this continuous infusion of intelligence, incident response plans risk becoming obsolete, leaving organizations vulnerable to attacks they were technically "prepared" for, but not against the specific methods and motives of the current adversaries.

Furthermore, the effectiveness of intelligence in incident response planning is intrinsically linked to the organization's ability to operationalize that intelligence. Raw intelligence, no matter how valuable, is useless if it cannot be translated into actionable steps within the incident response framework. This requires clear communication channels between intelligence analysts, security operations center (SOC) analysts, and incident response teams. It necessitates the development of standardized methods for integrating intelligence findings into incident response playbooks, threat hunting queries, and detection rules. For example, a newly identified TTP used by a prevalent threat actor should not just be documented; it should trigger the creation of specific detection alerts, inform the development of new forensic procedures for responders, and be incorporated into training exercises for the incident response team.

The human element is also critical. Incident responders need to be trained to interpret and utilize threat intelligence effectively. This includes understanding the confidence levels associated with different intelligence sources, recognizing the context of the information, and knowing how to apply it to real-time incident scenarios. Ongoing training and simulations that incorporate intelligence-driven attack scenarios are invaluable. These exercises allow responders to practice applying intelligence to make critical decisions under pressure, refining their skills and ensuring that the intelligence-informed playbooks are not just theoretical but practically executable.

In conclusion, integrating threat intelligence into incident response planning is not an optional add-on; it is a strategic imperative for building robust cyber resilience. By leveraging intelligence to understand the most probable threats, anticipate adversary behavior, and prioritize response actions, organizations can move beyond generic, reactive measures to develop tailored, effective strategies for containment, eradication, and recovery. This proactive approach ensures that limited resources are deployed judiciously against the most significant risks, minimizing damage and accelerating the return to normal operations. The continuous feedback loop, where incident outcomes inform future intelligence requirements and response strategies, creates a dynamic and adaptive defense mechanism that is essential for navigating the ever-evolving landscape of cyber threats. An intelligence-driven incident response plan is, therefore, a cornerstone of a mature and effective cybersecurity program, enabling organizations to not just detect threats, but to effectively and decisively neutralize them.

The critical juncture where the strategic insights derived from threat intelligence are translated into tangible actions within an Industrial Control System

(ICS) environment demands meticulous attention. This transition from abstract understanding to concrete application is paramount for ensuring the resilience and operational integrity of systems that underpin vital infrastructure and industrial processes. It's not enough to merely possess intelligence; its effective operationalization within the unique context of ICS is the true measure of its value. This involves a deliberate integration into the planning and execution phases of security operations, ensuring that every level of the response mechanism is informed and empowered by the latest threat landscape understanding.

Within the overarching framework of an ICS incident response, threat intelligence plays a pivotal role in bolstering the Planning Section. This section, responsible for synthesizing information and charting the course of action, becomes significantly more effective when imbued with intelligence-driven insights. Situational awareness is dramatically enhanced when the Planning Section can access, analyze, and leverage intelligence regarding the specific threat actors most likely to target the organization's ICS environment. This includes understanding their motivations, their preferred entry points into industrial networks, the specific vulnerabilities they are known to exploit within ICS components (such as legacy protocols, unpatched firmware, or human-machine interface weaknesses), and their ultimate objectives—whether it be disruption, sabotage, data theft, or espionage. For instance, intelligence highlighting an increase in nation-state-sponsored activity targeting energy sector ICS with the intent to disrupt power grids would immediately elevate the prioritization of certain response strategies and resource allocation within the

Planning Section. This granular understanding allows for a proactive posture, enabling the planning team to anticipate the potential scope and nature of an attack, rather than reacting to it in a vacuum.

Furthermore, threat intelligence informs strategic decision-making by providing context on the potential impact of various attack scenarios. If intelligence indicates that a particular ransomware variant actively targets ICS environments and includes functionalities designed to specifically impact operational technology (OT) processes—such as disabling safety instrumented systems (SIS) or manipulating control parameters—the Planning Section can develop contingency plans that account for these specific operational disruptions. This might involve pre-identifying manual override procedures, establishing communication channels with critical equipment vendors for expedited support, or even preparing alternative operational modes for affected processes. The intelligence provides the "why" and "how" behind potential threats, allowing the Planning Section to move beyond generic incident response playbooks and develop situationally aware strategies tailored to the specific threats facing the ICS. The confidence and accuracy of these plans are directly proportional to the quality and relevance of the threat intelligence fed into them. This intelligence might originate from various sources, including government agencies, industry-specific information sharing and analysis centers (ISACs), commercial threat intelligence providers specializing in OT security, or even internal threat hunting operations that identify early warning signs. The crucial aspect is the systematic ingestion and contextualization of this data for planning purposes.

Beyond the strategic level of the Planning Section, the operationalization of threat intelligence is equally, if not more, critical for the tactical execution carried out by operational teams. These teams, often comprising system administrators, network engineers, security analysts, and field technicians, are on the front lines of defending and responding to incidents within the ICS environment. Threat intelligence provides them with the actionable data needed to perform their duties effectively and efficiently. This can manifest in several ways, from enhancing detection capabilities to guiding immediate containment and eradication efforts.

For example, if threat intelligence identifies specific Indicators of Compromise (IoCs) associated with a campaign targeting ICS, such as particular IP addresses of command-and-control (C2) servers, unique malware hashes, or specific network traffic patterns indicative of reconnaissance or lateral movement within OT networks, these IoCs can be directly integrated into the operational teams' detection and monitoring tools. Security Information and Event Management (SIEM) systems, Intrusion Detection/Prevention Systems (IDS/IPS), and Endpoint Detection and Response (EDR) solutions deployed within the ICS environment can be configured to alert operational teams when these IoCs are observed. This transforms passive monitoring into active threat hunting, enabling operational teams to identify potential intrusions at their earliest stages. The intelligence acts as a set of breadcrumbs, guiding the operational teams' attention to areas of the network or specific system behaviors that warrant closer scrutiny. This is particularly important in ICS where the attack surface can be vast and the operational complexity can obscure malicious activity.

Moreover, threat intelligence provides vital context to the alerts generated by these security tools. A generic alert indicating suspicious network traffic might be flagged by operational teams as low-priority. However, if that same alert is correlated with threat intelligence indicating that the originating IP address is known to be associated with a particular threat actor group actively targeting critical infrastructure, the operational team's response priority and methodology would immediately shift. They would understand that this is not a routine anomaly but a potentially targeted attack, and their investigation would be guided by the known TTPs of that specific threat actor. This intelligence-driven context allows operational teams to differentiate between benign system behavior and sophisticated malicious activity, thereby optimizing their time and resources and ensuring that critical threats receive immediate and appropriate attention. This is a significant departure from traditional security operations where a plethora of alerts can lead to alert fatigue and missed critical events.

The operationalization of intelligence also directly influences the development and execution of tactical containment and eradication procedures. When a threat is identified within an ICS environment, the speed and precision of the response are paramount to minimize disruption to critical operations and prevent escalation. Threat intelligence can provide operational teams with crucial information to guide these actions. For instance, if intelligence indicates that a specific malware is designed to disable safety interlocks on a particular type of industrial equipment, the operational team can be prepared to implement specific, pre-defined mitigation steps for that equipment to prevent it from entering an unsafe state, even before the malware is fully eradicated. This might involve manually engaging certain safety systems or isolating the affected control loops. The intelligence informs the "what to do" and "how to do it" at a granular level, allowing for a more targeted and less disruptive response than broad, sweeping network shutdowns that could have severe operational consequences.

Consider a scenario where threat intelligence reveals that a prevalent advanced persistent threat (APT) group is using a specific zero-day vulnerability in a widely deployed ICS protocol to gain initial access and then leverages known vulnerabilities in associated Human-Machine Interface (HMI) software for lateral movement. When an incident occurs, the operational team, armed with this intelligence, can immediately focus their containment efforts on systems running the vulnerable HMI software and ensure that any detected exploitation attempts targeting that specific protocol are treated with the highest urgency. They can deploy specific blocking rules on network segments known to be susceptible to this type of lateral movement, or initiate targeted scans for the known persistence mechanisms employed by that APT group. Without this intelligence, the operational team might be left scrambling, attempting to identify the scope of the compromise through general network monitoring and vulnerability assessments, thereby losing valuable time and potentially allowing the attacker to achieve their objectives. The intelligence provides a "head start" and a roadmap for effective tactical response.

Furthermore, the ability of operational teams to perform effective threat hunting is significantly enhanced by operationalized threat intelligence.

Threat hunting involves proactively searching for threats that have evaded existing security controls. When intelligence provides insights into the TTPs of adversaries targeting ICS, operational teams can formulate specific hypotheses and queries to search for evidence of these TTPs within their network traffic, system logs, and endpoint data. For example, if intelligence highlights that a particular threat actor consistently uses obscure PowerShell commands to establish persistence on Windows-based ICS servers, threat hunting queries can be specifically crafted to detect such unusual command-line activities. This proactive approach allows organizations to uncover and neutralize threats before they can cause significant damage, demonstrating a mature and intelligence-driven security posture. The effectiveness of threat hunting is directly correlated to the actionable intelligence available to guide the search.

The integration of threat intelligence into the day-to-day operations of ICS security teams also necessitates robust processes for intelligence dissemination and assimilation. This is not a one-time activity but a continuous cycle. Raw intelligence feeds need to be processed, contextualized for the ICS environment, and translated into actionable intelligence products. This could involve creating concise threat briefs for operational teams, developing new detection rules based on observed adversary behaviors, or updating incident response playbooks with specific tactical steps derived from intelligence. Effective communication channels between intelligence analysts and operational teams are crucial to ensure that the right information reaches the right people at the right time. This might involve regular intelligence briefings, dedicated collaboration platforms, or integrated workflows within security orchestration, automation, and response (SOAR) platforms.

The "operationalization" aspect is key. It signifies that the intelligence is not just passively consumed but actively *used* to shape security operations. For an ICS environment, this can be particularly challenging due to the unique constraints and sensitivities of OT. For instance, implementing new detection rules or modifying network configurations might require extensive testing and approval processes to avoid disrupting critical industrial processes. Therefore, the operationalization of threat intelligence in ICS security must be a collaborative effort involving not only the cybersecurity team but also operations personnel, engineering, and management to ensure that security measures are both effective and compatible with operational requirements.

A practical example of operationalizing threat intelligence within an ICS context could involve intelligence that identifies a new phishing campaign targeting employees with access to the OT network, using spear-phishing emails that impersonate legitimate IT support personnel and contain malicious attachments designed to deliver a specific ICS-targeting trojan. The operational response, guided by this intelligence, would involve several proactive steps:

1. **Information Dissemination:** The intelligence team would immediately disseminate a warning to all relevant personnel, including IT, cybersecurity, and key OT operators, detailing the nature of the phishing campaign, the likely indicators of compromise (e.g., specific sender email addresses, subject lines, attachment names), and the expected payload.

2. **Technical Countermeasures:** The SOC operational team would implement email filtering rules to block known phishing indicators and deploy updated signatures for antivirus and endpoint detection solutions to specifically identify the trojan. They might also create specific network monitoring rules to detect any outbound communication from internal systems attempting to connect to known C2 servers associated with this campaign.

3. **User Awareness Augmentation:** Security awareness training platforms would be updated with specific modules or alerts about this current phishing threat, reinforcing best practices for identifying and reporting suspicious emails.

4. **Threat Hunting:** Operational teams would proactively hunt for any signs of the trojan or associated malicious activity on endpoints and servers, particularly those with elevated privileges or direct access to ICS components. This would involve executing specific queries based on the intelligence's description of the trojan's behavior and persistence mechanisms.

5. **Incident Response Preparedness:** If the intelligence suggests the trojan has specific disruptive capabilities within the ICS, the incident response plan would be reviewed, and relevant playbooks, such as those for malware containment and system recovery, would be pre-staged and personnel briefed on potential immediate actions required for critical OT assets.

This multi-faceted approach, directly driven by actionable threat intelligence, ensures that the operational teams are not merely reacting to an attack but are actively anticipating and mitigating it. The intelligence is not just a report; it is a directive that shapes the security posture and operational tempo. The ultimate goal is to create a feedback loop where the effectiveness of these operationalized intelligence actions is constantly evaluated, leading to further refinements in intelligence collection, analysis, and dissemination. This continuous improvement cycle is what transforms a static security program into a dynamic and resilient defense mechanism, particularly crucial in the high-stakes world of Industrial Control Systems. The careful weaving of threat intelligence into the fabric of ICS operations transforms defensive capabilities from being merely reactive to becoming truly predictive and pre-emptive.

The efficacy of any threat intelligence program, particularly within the specialized domain of Industrial Control Systems (ICS), hinges on two fundamental pillars: the reliability and relevance of its sources, and the efficiency and appropriateness of its dissemination. Without a robust understanding of where to acquire high-quality intelligence and how to effectively channel it to those who need it most, even the most sophisticated analytical capabilities will falter. This section delves into the diverse origins of threat intelligence relevant to ICS environments and explores the critical strategies for ensuring this vital information permeates the organization, empowering proactive defense and swift response.

The landscape of threat intelligence sources is multifaceted, ranging from highly curated commercial offerings to the vast, often unstructured, realm of open-source information. For organizations operating ICS, identifying and vetting these sources is a crucial first step. Commercial threat intelligence feeds represent a significant segment of the market, offering subscription-based services that aggregate, analyze, and package threat data from a variety of proprietary and public sources. These providers often specialize in specific industries or threat types, which can be particularly beneficial for ICS operators seeking intelligence tailored to their unique operational technology (OT) environment. Such feeds might include curated lists of Indicators of Compromise (IoCs) such as malicious IP addresses, domain names, file hashes, and malware signatures, alongside information on emerging attack techniques, targeted vulnerabilities, and adversary group profiles. For instance, a commercial feed might highlight an increase in activity from a known nation-state actor group that has historically targeted critical infrastructure, providing details on their current campaigns, preferred tools, and potential targets within a specific sector like energy or water treatment. The advantage of commercial feeds lies in their often professional curation, timeliness, and the provision of context that helps translate raw data into actionable insights. However, the cost can be a significant barrier, and it is essential for organizations to rigorously evaluate the quality, relevance, and applicability of the intelligence provided to their specific ICS infrastructure, ensuring it goes beyond generic IT threats to address OT-specific attack vectors.

Complementing commercial offerings, government agencies and national cybersecurity bodies serve as invaluable sources of threat intelligence. These entities, often possessing a broad national security mandate, collect and analyze threat data related to nation-state activity, cyber espionage, and critical infrastructure protection. For example, agencies like the Cybersecurity and Infrastructure Security Agency (CISA) in the United States, or similar organizations in other countries, regularly publish alerts, advisories, and reports detailing threats that pose a risk to vital sectors. These government-generated intelligence products often carry significant weight due to the authoritative nature of the issuing body and their deep insights into sophisticated threats. They may provide detailed analyses of nation-state actor tactics, techniques, and procedures (TTPs), highlight newly discovered vulnerabilities in widely used ICS components, or issue specific warnings about ongoing campaigns targeting national critical infrastructure. The intelligence from these sources can be particularly crucial for understanding the geopolitical motivations behind certain attacks and anticipating nation-state-level threats that might be beyond the scope or resources of commercial providers. Moreover, many government agencies offer programs for direct sharing of threat information with trusted partners, fostering a collaborative defense environment.

Industry-specific Information Sharing and Analysis Centers (ISACs) and similar organizations play a vital role in fostering collaboration and intelligence sharing within particular sectors. For ICS environments, there are ISACs dedicated to sectors such as electricity (E-ISAC), oil and gas (O-ISAC), water and wastewater (WaterISAC), and manufacturing (MANU-ISAC). These organizations act as conduits for threat intelligence relevant to their respective industries, allowing member organizations to anonymously share threat information and receive aggregated intelligence tailored to their specific operational contexts. The benefit here is the highly specialized nature of the intelligence. An E-ISAC, for instance, might share alerts about emerging threats targeting Supervisory Control and Data Acquisition (SCADA) systems used in power grids, specific vulnerabilities found in substation automation equipment, or the common TTPs observed in attacks against energy infrastructure. This sector-specific focus ensures that the intelligence is more likely to be relevant and actionable than generic threat feeds. The collaborative aspect is also a significant advantage, as it allows organizations to learn from the experiences of their peers, identify common vulnerabilities, and collectively develop more effective defense strategies. Participation in an ISAC often requires a commitment to share threat information, fostering a community of trust and mutual defense.

Beyond these structured sources, Open-Source Intelligence (OSINT) offers a vast and ever-expanding reservoir of threat-related information. This encompasses a broad spectrum of publicly available data, including security blogs, research papers, news articles, social media discussions, technical forums, and code repositories. While OSINT can be rich in detail and provide early indicators of emerging threats, it also presents challenges in terms of veracity, volume, and relevance. For ICS security professionals, effectively leveraging OSINT involves a disciplined approach to identify, filter, and validate information. For example, researchers might publish detailed analyses of a new malware family discovered targeting ICS protocols, including its technical characteristics, command-and-control infrastructure, and potential impact. Security news outlets might report on successful cyberattacks against industrial facilities, providing details on the attack vectors and consequences. Technical forums could host discussions among security practitioners about observed malicious activities or novel exploitation techniques. The challenge with OSINT lies in sifting through the noise to find high-fidelity intelligence. This often requires skilled analysts with deep domain knowledge to discern credible information from speculation or misinformation. Tools and techniques for automated OSINT collection and analysis can be employed, but human judgment remains indispensable for contextualizing and validating the findings, especially when dealing with the sensitive nature of ICS environments where misinterpretation can have severe consequences.

A critical aspect of OSINT for ICS is understanding the adversaries' online presence and discourse. Threat actors, especially those involved in sophisticated operations, may inadvertently reveal information through their use of specific online platforms, communication channels, or even public code repositories. Monitoring these avenues can provide insights into their capabilities, intentions, and evolving methodologies. For instance, a threat actor group might publicly release tools or exploit code on platforms like GitHub, which, while malicious, can also serve as an intelligence source for defenders to understand the tools being developed and used. Similarly, discussions on underground forums, even if not directly accessible, can be indirectly monitored through publicly reported intelligence or by analysts who specialize in threat actor profiling. The key is to have a strategy for identifying and analyzing OSINT that is directly relevant to the ICS threat landscape, focusing on threat actors known to target critical infrastructure or specific industrial sectors.

Furthermore, internal threat intelligence generation through threat hunting, incident response, and security monitoring within the organization itself represents a crucial, albeit often overlooked, source. While external feeds provide a broad view of the threat landscape, internal intelligence offers highly specific insights into how those threats manifest within the organization's unique ICS environment. When security teams actively hunt for threats that may have bypassed existing defenses, analyze the TTPs of successful attacks during incident response, or meticulously scrutinize security logs and network traffic for anomalies, they generate invaluable, context-rich intelligence. This internal intelligence can highlight unique vulnerabilities in the ICS architecture, peculiar configurations that attackers might exploit, or the specific impact of certain malware on operational processes. For example, if an incident response team discovers that a particular phishing email, originating from a known external threat actor, successfully bypassed the organization's email filters and led to the deployment of a specific payload on an HMI workstation, this information becomes a critical piece of internal intelligence. It validates the external threat information, provides specific details on the compromise path within the ICS, and informs immediate defensive actions. Similarly, threat hunting activities might uncover subtle signs of reconnaissance or lateral movement that are unique to the organization's network topology and operational protocols. This internally generated intelligence is often the most actionable because it directly relates to the organization's own environment, its specific assets, and its operational risks. It can also serve as a crucial feedback loop to validate or refine the consumption of external intelligence feeds.

The challenge with so many diverse sources is managing the sheer volume of data and ensuring that only relevant, high-fidelity intelligence is actioned. Organizations must develop robust processes for intelligence vetting, correlation, and enrichment. This involves establishing criteria for evaluating the credibility and relevance of each source, correlating data points from multiple sources to increase confidence, and enriching raw data with contextual information about the organization's specific ICS assets, vulnerabilities, and operational dependencies. For instance, a generic IoC from an external feed might be correlated with internal network logs. If that IoC appears in traffic originating from a critical control server within the ICS, its priority and the urgency of the response would be significantly elevated. Conversely, if the IoC is observed in a segment of the network that is less critical or air-gapped, its immediate impact might be assessed differently. This meticulous process of validation and contextualization transforms raw data into actionable intelligence, ensuring that security teams are not overwhelmed by irrelevant alerts but are focused on genuine threats that pose a significant risk to the ICS.

Once intelligence has been collected, analyzed, and deemed actionable, its effective dissemination becomes paramount. This is not a one-size-fits-all process; rather, it requires a nuanced approach tailored to the different roles and responsibilities within an organization, particularly concerning ICS security. The goal is to ensure that the right intelligence reaches the right people at the right time, enabling them to make informed decisions and take appropriate actions.

For strategic decision-makers, such as C-suite executives, plant managers, and senior security leadership, intelligence needs to be presented at a high level, focusing on potential business impact, risk assessment, and resource allocation. This might involve executive summaries, threat landscape briefings, and risk-based reports that quantify the potential financial, operational, and reputational damage of specific threats. For example, intelligence indicating a significant increase in nation-state-sponsored attacks targeting the energy sector with the intent to disrupt power grids would be presented to executives with an emphasis on the potential for widespread outages, economic losses, and regulatory implications. This level of intelligence helps justify security investments, shape strategic security policies, and ensure organizational buy-in for critical security initiatives. The language used here must be business-oriented, avoiding overly technical jargon, and clearly articulating the "so what" for the organization's objectives and continuity.

At the tactical and operational levels, the intelligence dissemination needs to be much more granular and immediate. Security operations center (SOC) analysts, network engineers, system administrators, and incident response teams require specific, actionable data that they can directly use to detect, analyze, and respond to threats. This could include IoCs (IP addresses, domain names, file hashes), TTPs of known threat actors, specific vulnerability details, and recommended mitigation steps. For instance, if intelligence identifies a new command-and-control server being used by an APT group targeting ICS, this IP address should be disseminated to the SOC for immediate inclusion in firewall rules, intrusion detection systems (IDS), and SIEM correlation engines. Similarly, if intelligence reveals a novel exploitation technique for a common ICS protocol, this information should be shared with network engineers and security analysts to enable proactive monitoring for such activity and to guide defensive configurations. The format of this intelligence can vary, from structured data feeds that automatically update security tools to detailed technical advisories and playbooks.

Within the ICS structure, special considerations must be given to disseminating intelligence to personnel who may not have a traditional cybersecurity background. This includes plant operators, field technicians, and maintenance staff who have direct access to and control over critical physical processes. For these individuals, intelligence must be translated into clear, concise, and easily understandable instructions or warnings that relate directly to their operational tasks and potential risks. For example, if intelligence suggests a new malware variant is designed to manipulate safety instrumented systems (SIS), operators must be informed about the specific indicators to look for on their control system interfaces, the potential consequences of certain actions, and the emergency procedures to follow. This might involve visual aids, simplified checklists, or brief, in-person briefings. The communication channels used for these groups also need to be carefully selected to ensure reliability and accessibility within the operational environment, which might include pre-shift briefings, updated operating procedures, or dedicated communication systems.

The methodology for disseminating intelligence is as crucial as its content. Manual distribution via email can be effective for high-level summaries or urgent alerts, but it often falls short for the rapid, continuous flow of technical intelligence required by operational teams. Automated distribution mechanisms are therefore essential. This can involve:

Security Information and Event Management (SIEM) Systems: Integrating threat intelligence feeds directly into SIEM platforms allows for automated correlation of external intelligence with internal logs, generating prioritized alerts for SOC analysts.

Threat Intelligence Platforms (TIPs): TIPs serve as a central hub for ingesting, processing, and distributing threat intelligence across an organization. They can normalize data from various sources, enrich it with internal context, and push curated intelligence to downstream security tools and teams.

Security Orchestration, Automation, and Response (SOAR) Platforms: SOAR platforms can take actionable intelligence from TIPs or SIEMs and automate response workflows, such as blocking malicious IPs on firewalls, isolating infected endpoints, or triggering incident response playbooks. This significantly reduces the time between detection and response.

Dedicated Dashboards and Portals: For different stakeholder groups, customized dashboards or secure web portals can provide access to relevant intelligence, threat summaries, and risk dashboards, ensuring that information is easily accessible and tailored to their needs.

Regular Briefings and Meetings: While automation is key, human interaction remains vital. Regular threat intelligence briefings, threat hunting debriefs, and post-incident reviews facilitate knowledge sharing, discussion, and the assimilation of intelligence insights, particularly for complex or evolving threats.

Furthermore, the dissemination process must incorporate a feedback loop. It is essential to gather feedback from the recipients of the intelligence to assess its usefulness, timeliness, and clarity. This feedback can inform improvements in intelligence collection, analysis, and dissemination strategies. For instance, if operational teams consistently find that certain types of IoCs are not effective in detecting threats within their environment, this feedback should be used to refine the intelligence collection requirements or analysis methodologies. Similarly, if executive summaries are perceived as lacking in actionable insights for decision-making, they need to be revised.

In the context of ICS, ensuring the secure and reliable dissemination of intelligence is paramount. Sensitive intelligence, such as details about vulnerabilities in critical infrastructure or nation-state actor capabilities, must be protected from unauthorized access and disclosure. Encryption, access controls, and secure communication channels are essential components of the dissemination infrastructure. Additionally, the operational constraints of ICS environments must be considered. Disseminating intelligence that might trigger an automated response that could inadvertently disrupt critical operations requires careful planning, testing, and, often, human oversight. The integration of intelligence into operational workflows should never compromise the stability and safety of the ICS. This means that any automated responses triggered by intelligence must be thoroughly tested in non-production environments and accompanied by clear human-in-the-loop procedures for critical actions.

Ultimately, the success of threat intelligence within an ICS framework relies on a continuous cycle of collection, analysis, dissemination, and feedback. By diligently identifying and leveraging a diverse range of reliable intelligence sources, and by implementing a sophisticated, role-based dissemination strategy, organizations can transform raw threat data into a powerful force multiplier for defending their critical industrial systems against an ever-evolving threat landscape. The intelligence must be a living, breathing component of the security program, constantly informing and guiding the organization's defenses at every level.

A well-structured and proficient Cyber Incident Response Team (CIRT) is not merely a reactive mechanism; it is the cornerstone of an organization's resilience in the face of sophisticated cyber threats. The establishment of such a team is a strategic imperative, demanding careful consideration of its purpose, composition, and operational framework. This section delves into the critical steps and considerations involved in building an effective CIRT, ensuring it is equipped to navigate the complexities of modern cyber incidents, particularly within an Industrial Control Systems (ICS) environment.

The foundational step in building a CIRT is the meticulous definition of its mission and scope. What precisely is the team intended to achieve? The mission statement should clearly articulate the overarching goals, such as minimizing the impact of cyber incidents, restoring normal operations swiftly, protecting sensitive data, and preventing future occurrences. For an ICS environment, this mission must extend beyond traditional IT concerns to encompass the unique operational risks associated with industrial processes. This could mean a mission focused on safeguarding the availability and integrity of critical industrial processes, preventing physical damage, ensuring operator safety, and maintaining regulatory compliance. The scope dictates the boundaries of the team's authority and responsibility. Does the CIRT have the authority to disconnect compromised systems from the network? What types of incidents fall under its purview – from minor malware infections to nation-state-level advanced persistent threats (APTs) targeting operational technology (OT)? Defining these boundaries prevents confusion during high-pressure situations and ensures that the team operates within its designated capabilities and legal frameworks. A clear scope also informs the required resources, tools, and expertise, forming the basis for subsequent planning. For instance, if the scope includes responding to physical security breaches stemming from cyber intrusions, the CIRT might need to integrate with physical security teams and have access to on-site personnel. Conversely, a CIRT focused solely on detecting and remediating malware on IT networks would have a different set of requirements. The scope must also consider the organization's risk appetite and its tolerance for operational disruption versus security risks, a balance that is particularly delicate in ICS environments where operational continuity is paramount.

Once the mission and scope are established, the crucial task of defining the required skill sets and team composition begins. A successful CIRT is a multidisciplinary entity, bringing together a diverse array of expertise to address the multifaceted nature of cyber incidents. At its core, a CIRT needs strong technical acumen. This includes deep knowledge of operating systems, networking protocols (both IT and OT specific, such as Modbus, DNP3, PROFINET), malware analysis, digital forensics, vulnerability assessment, and cryptography. Team members must be adept at understanding how systems are interconnected and how a compromise in one area can cascade to others. For an ICS CIRT, this technical expertise must extend to a profound understanding of industrial control systems themselves – the PLCs, HMIs, SCADA systems, and the unique software and hardware that drive industrial processes. Understanding the physics of the processes being controlled, the safety implications of system manipulation, and the typical operational workflows is as vital as understanding network packets.

Beyond purely technical skills, analytical and investigative capabilities are indispensable. CIRT members must be able to think critically, piece together disparate pieces of evidence, and formulate hypotheses about the nature, scope, and origin of an incident. This includes skills in threat intelligence analysis, enabling them to understand adversary motivations, TTPs, and potential future actions. The ability to perform forensic investigations, trace attacker movements, and reconstruct timelines is critical for both remediation and attribution. Furthermore, strong communication and interpersonal skills are paramount, though often underestimated. During an incident, chaos can ensue. Team members must be able to communicate clearly, concisely, and calmly under pressure, both within the team and with external stakeholders. This includes writing clear incident reports, briefing executive leadership, liaising with legal counsel, and potentially interacting with law enforcement or regulatory bodies. In an ICS context, this also means being able to communicate technical details in a way that is understandable to plant managers, operators, and engineers, ensuring their cooperation and understanding of the situation.

A balanced CIRT composition typically includes roles such as:

Incident Response Manager/Lead: Oversees the entire incident response process, coordinates team activities, makes critical decisions, and serves as the primary point of contact. This role requires strong leadership, strategic thinking, and decision-making skills.

Forensic Analysts: Specialists in collecting, preserving, and analyzing digital evidence to understand the 'who, what, when, where, and how' of an incident.

Malware Analysts: Experts in reverse-engineering malicious software to understand its functionality, propagation methods, and indicators of compromise.

Network Security Analysts: Focus on network traffic analysis, intrusion detection, and understanding network-based attack vectors. In an ICS environment, this role would heavily involve analyzing OT network traffic.

System Administrators/Engineers (IT and OT): Provide in-depth knowledge of the organization's infrastructure, assist with containment and eradication efforts, and manage system recovery. Their role is crucial for understanding system dependencies and operational impacts.

Threat Intelligence Analysts: Monitor external threat landscapes, identify relevant threats, and provide context to ongoing incidents. This role is vital for anticipating adversary actions and understanding the broader threat environment impacting ICS.

Communications/Liaison Officer: Manages internal and external communications, ensuring consistent messaging and providing updates to stakeholders. This role is critical for managing public relations and stakeholder confidence.

Legal and Compliance Advisor: Provides guidance on legal obligations, regulatory requirements, and evidence handling procedures.

The ideal size of a CIRT can vary significantly based on the organization's size, industry, risk profile, and the complexity of its ICS infrastructure. A small organization might have a core team of 3-5 individuals who wear multiple hats, while a large, critical infrastructure entity might have dozens of specialists organized into functional groups. The key is to ensure that all critical skill sets are covered, either by dedicated personnel or by individuals with cross-functional expertise. Cross-training is therefore an essential component of building a robust CIRT, enabling team members to step into different roles when necessary and fostering a deeper understanding of the incident response lifecycle.

Recruiting and retaining qualified personnel for a CIRT is a significant challenge, particularly given the scarcity of individuals with specialized ICS cybersecurity experience. Organizations must adopt proactive and strategic approaches to talent acquisition. This begins with crafting compelling job descriptions that accurately reflect the role's responsibilities and the unique challenges of ICS security. Highlighting the opportunity to work with cutting-edge technology, protect critical infrastructure, and make a tangible difference can attract top talent.

Internal recruitment can be a valuable strategy. Employees with existing knowledge of the organization's ICS and IT infrastructure, coupled with a strong aptitude for cybersecurity, can be groomed for CIRT roles. This approach benefits from pre-existing institutional knowledge and loyalty. For external recruitment, leveraging specialized cybersecurity recruitment agencies can be effective. Networking within the cybersecurity community, attending industry conferences, and engaging with universities that offer cybersecurity programs are also crucial for building a talent pipeline.

The interview process should be rigorous and multi-faceted, assessing not only technical proficiency but also problem-solving abilities, teamwork, and communication skills. Practical, scenario-based questions are invaluable for evaluating how candidates would approach real-world incident response situations. For example, presenting a simulated incident scenario involving a compromise of a SCADA network and asking the candidate to outline their immediate steps, analytical process, and communication plan can reveal a great deal about their capabilities.

Once recruited, ongoing training and professional development are non-negotiable. The threat landscape is constantly evolving, and new technologies and attack vectors emerge regularly. A CIRT must commit to continuous learning. This includes:

Formal Training: Pursuing certifications in incident response, digital forensics, malware analysis, and ICS cybersecurity (e.g., GIAC GCIH, GCFA, GRID, GICSP).

Tabletop Exercises and Simulations: Regularly conducting simulated incident scenarios, ranging from tabletop discussions to full-scale drills, allows the team to practice their response plans, identify gaps, and refine their coordination. These exercises should specifically incorporate ICS scenarios to test OT-specific response procedures.

Knowledge Sharing: Fostering a culture of continuous learning through internal brown bag sessions, participation in webinars, and sharing of research findings.

Staying Current with Threat Intelligence: Ensuring team members are actively consuming and analyzing threat intelligence relevant to their sector and ICS environments.

Cross-Training: Encouraging team members to develop skills in adjacent areas to increase the team's overall flexibility and resilience. For example, a network analyst could gain basic forensic skills, or a forensic analyst could learn about OT protocols.

The retention of skilled CIRT members is as challenging as their recruitment. High-pressure environments, the constant demand to be "on call," and the emotional toll of dealing with major security breaches can lead to burnout. Organizations must invest in creating a supportive and rewarding work environment. This includes:

Competitive Compensation and Benefits: Recognizing the highly specialized and in-demand nature of these roles with appropriate salary packages.

Work-Life Balance: Implementing clear on-call rotations, providing sufficient time off, and actively managing workload to prevent chronic stress.

Career Development Opportunities: Providing clear pathways for advancement, opportunities to specialize further, or move into leadership roles.

Recognition and Appreciation: Acknowledging the critical work performed by the CIRT and celebrating successes.

Psychological Support: Recognizing the potential for emotional distress and providing access to counseling or mental health resources.

Furthermore, the CIRT's integration within the broader organizational structure is critical for its effectiveness. It should not operate in a vacuum. Establishing strong relationships with IT operations, OT engineering, legal, human resources, corporate communications, and senior management ensures seamless collaboration and support during an incident. This integration is crucial for obtaining necessary access, resources, and decision-making authority. For instance, the CIRT's ability to effectively contain a threat within the OT environment might depend on the close cooperation of plant engineers who understand the operational implications of system isolation or shutdown. Similarly, legal counsel must be involved early to ensure that evidence is collected and preserved in a legally admissible manner and to navigate regulatory reporting obligations.

The operational readiness of the CIRT is maintained through comprehensive documentation and well-defined processes. This includes developing and regularly updating an Incident Response Plan (IRP) that outlines procedures for various types of incidents, roles and responsibilities, communication protocols, escalation paths, and recovery steps. Playbooks, which are step-by-step guides for responding to specific common incidents (e.g., ransomware, phishing, denial-of-service attacks), are invaluable for ensuring consistency and speed in response. These playbooks should be regularly reviewed and updated based on lessons learned from exercises and actual incidents. The CIRT must also have access to a well-equipped incident response toolkit, which includes specialized hardware and software for forensic analysis, network monitoring, malware analysis, and secure communication. This toolkit should be readily available and regularly maintained.

In summary, building a Cyber Incident Response Team is a strategic undertaking that requires a clear vision, meticulous planning, and sustained investment. From defining a precise mission and scope that accounts for the unique challenges of ICS environments to recruiting individuals with a diverse blend of technical, analytical, and communication skills, every step is critical. The ongoing commitment to training, professional development, and fostering a supportive work environment is paramount for retaining these highly specialized professionals. By establishing robust processes, clear documentation, and strong interdepartmental relationships, an organization can ensure its CIRT is not just a team, but a resilient, dynamic force capable of defending critical assets against the ever-evolving landscape of cyber threats. This preparedness is the bedrock upon which an organization can build trust, ensure operational continuity, and protect its reputation in the digital age.

The successful integration of a Cyber Incident Response Team (CIRT) into an Industrial Control Systems (ICS) environment is not a matter of mere proximity but of deep, functional alignment. It necessitates a deliberate structuring of the CIRT's operational posture such that its members are not only aware of the ICS landscape but are actively embedded within its operational paradigms. This embedding goes beyond simply assigning individuals to an ICS security task force; it involves a strategic placement of CIRT expertise within the established functional areas and command structures that govern ICS operations. The objective is to ensure that cybersecurity considerations are not an afterthought but are intrinsically woven into the fabric of incident management, thereby enhancing the speed, efficacy, and overall resilience of the response.

A key mechanism for achieving this seamless integration is the allocation of CIRT personnel to specific ICS functional areas. In many established incident response frameworks, particularly those adapted from emergency management principles, distinct functional areas are defined to compartmentalize and manage the complexities of a crisis. These typically include Operations, Planning, Logistics, and Finance/Administration. A sophisticated CIRT integration strategy would see CIRT specialists assigned to these very same areas, albeit with a cybersecurity lens. For instance, within the Operations section, CIRT members would focus on the immediate technical containment and eradication of cyber threats impacting the control systems. They would work hand-in-hand with OT engineers and plant operators to understand the real-time impact of a cyber event on physical processes and to implement technical countermeasures that minimize disruption to operations. This could involve isolating compromised segments of the ICS network, disabling specific control functions under strict operational guidance, or verifying the integrity of control commands before they are executed.

In the Planning section, CIRT analysts would take on roles focused on understanding the scope and nature of the cyber incident. This involves gathering intelligence, analyzing attack vectors, assessing the potential impact on industrial processes and safety, and developing strategic response options. They would be responsible for generating the technical aspects of the overall incident action plan, detailing the cybersecurity objectives, strategies, and required resources. Their output here is crucial for informing decision-making by the Incident Commander and other senior leaders, ensuring that response efforts are data-driven and aligned with the broader organizational objectives. This planning function requires a deep understanding of threat intelligence, vulnerability assessment, and the specific characteristics of the ICS being defended.

The Logistics section, traditionally concerned with providing resources and support, would see CIRT members ensuring that the necessary cybersecurity tools, equipment, and personnel are readily available and deployed effectively. This might involve provisioning specialized forensic analysis hardware, ensuring secure communication channels for the response team, or coordinating the deployment of security patches and updates across critical infrastructure. In an ICS context, this also extends to managing the physical security of sensitive control system components and ensuring that any access for technical remediation is properly controlled and authorized.

Finally, the Finance and Administration section would involve CIRT personnel providing input on the cost implications of cyber incidents and response efforts, as well as assisting with documentation and reporting related to cybersecurity events. While seemingly less technical, this role is vital for demonstrating the return on investment in cybersecurity measures and for ensuring that all response activities are properly accounted for and aligned with organizational financial policies.

The successful integration of CIRT roles within these functional areas is intrinsically linked to the overarching Incident Command System (ICS) structure. The Incident Commander (IC), as the ultimate authority figure responsible for the overall management of an incident, relies heavily on the accurate and timely information provided by all functional sections, including the cybersecurity elements. When a cyber incident occurs within an ICS environment, the CIRT does not operate in a parallel, disconnected track. Instead, its expertise is channeled through the established ICS hierarchy.

The CIRT Lead or a designated senior cybersecurity representative would likely sit within the Incident Command Staff, providing direct technical and strategic advice to the Incident Commander. This ensures that cybersecurity is a primary consideration from the outset of the response, rather than a secondary concern addressed after the initial operational impact has been assessed. The CIRT members embedded within the functional sections then report up through their respective chain of command, ensuring that information flows efficiently and that coordinated actions are taken. For example, a network security analyst working in the Operations section might identify a compromised segment of the OT network. This information would be relayed to the Operations Section Chief, who would then incorporate it into the overall operational picture presented to the Incident Commander. If containment requires an operational change, such as temporarily disabling a specific process, the IC, advised by both the Operations Chief and the CIRT representative, would make the final decision.

This hierarchical alignment prevents several common pitfalls. Without such integration, a CIRT might operate in isolation, focusing solely on technical remediation without fully understanding the operational impact or receiving the necessary authority to implement critical containment measures that might affect production. Conversely, without dedicated CIRT expertise within operational planning, the broader response might underestimate the cyber threat's complexity, leading to insufficient or misdirected mitigation efforts. The ICS framework, by design, facilitates multi-agency and multi-disciplinary collaboration, and the CIRT's active participation within this framework ensures that cyber defense is treated with the same seriousness and urgency as any other critical incident, whether it be a natural disaster or a physical security breach.

Furthermore, this structured integration clarifies lines of authority and responsibility during a high-stress cyber event. The Incident Commander retains ultimate decision-making authority, but their decisions are informed by the specialized knowledge of the CIRT. CIRT members, in turn, understand their roles and reporting structures within the incident management hierarchy. This clarity is crucial for preventing confusion, avoiding duplication of effort, and ensuring that resources are deployed efficiently. For instance, if multiple teams are attempting to address the same network segment or the same compromised system, a well-integrated CIRT within the ICS structure ensures that these efforts are coordinated and not working at cross-purposes.

The assignment of CIRT members to specific ICS functional areas also necessitates a clear understanding of their unique skill sets and how they map to the demands of each section. Within the Operations section, for example, CIRT members need not only deep cybersecurity knowledge but also an understanding of the specific industrial processes, the characteristics of the control hardware (PLCs, RTUs, HMIs), and the critical interdependencies within the OT network. Their ability to quickly diagnose and remediate issues within this specialized environment is paramount. This might involve expertise in OT-specific protocols, an understanding of safety instrumented systems (SIS), and the ability to work with engineers to ensure that any response action does not compromise plant safety.

In the Planning section, the focus shifts to broader situational awareness and strategic foresight. CIRT analysts assigned here would need strong analytical skills, the ability to synthesize information from various sources (including threat intelligence feeds, forensic data, and operational status reports), and the capacity to anticipate adversary actions and their potential impact. They would be responsible for developing the cybersecurity components of the Incident Action Plan, which might include objectives like "restore integrity of safety interlock systems" or "prevent lateral movement of malware into critical control loops."

The integration also fosters mutual understanding and respect between cybersecurity professionals and their counterparts in operations, engineering, and physical security. By working side-by-side within the ICS framework, CIRT members gain a greater appreciation for the operational constraints and priorities of the industrial environment, while operations personnel become more attuned to the nuances and criticality of cybersecurity threats. This cross-pollination of knowledge is invaluable for building trust and ensuring that cybersecurity is viewed as an enabler of operational resilience rather than an impediment.

To effectively implement this integration, organizations must proactively identify the critical ICS functional areas and the corresponding cybersecurity expertise required for each. This might involve creating standardized role definitions for CIRT members within the ICS structure, ensuring that these roles are clearly documented in the organization's Incident Response Plan, and that personnel are trained not only in their specific cybersecurity disciplines but also in the principles and operational context of the ICS environment and the ICS framework itself. Regular drills and exercises that specifically test the integrated response of the CIRT within the ICS structure are essential for refining these processes, identifying gaps, and building team cohesion across disciplines. This deliberate embedding of cybersecurity expertise within the operational command and control structure of ICS ensures that the organization is not just prepared to detect and respond to cyber threats, but is equipped to manage them as an integral part of its overall incident management capabilities, thereby safeguarding critical infrastructure and maintaining operational integrity.

The dynamic nature of cyber threats, particularly within the sensitive and complex realm of Industrial Control Systems (ICS), demands a commitment to continuous learning and skill enhancement for all Cyber Incident Response Team (CIRT) members. Simply establishing a CIRT and defining its integration within the Incident Command System (ICS) is only the foundational step. To truly equip the team to face the ever-evolving threat landscape, a robust and multifaceted training and skill development program must be implemented and sustained. This program should not only focus on deepening technical expertise but also on cultivating the critical thinking, problem-solving acumen, and robust communication abilities that are paramount when responding to high-stakes incidents under immense pressure. Without this ongoing investment in human capital, even the most well-structured CIRT can become a liability, outpaced by adversary sophistication and unable to effectively protect critical industrial operations.

A cornerstone of effective CIRT training is the pursuit of relevant technical certifications and specialized courses. For individuals focusing on the operational technology (OT) side of ICS cybersecurity, certifications that validate their understanding of industrial protocols, specific vendor equipment, and the unique architecture of control systems are invaluable. Examples include certifications that cover areas like SCADA security, network segmentation for OT environments, and the secure configuration of Programmable Logic Controllers (PLCs) and Human-

Machine Interfaces (HMIs). These certifications demonstrate a baseline level of competency and provide a common language and framework for technical discussions during an incident. Beyond generic cybersecurity certifications, which are undoubtedly important, there must be a deliberate emphasis on those that bridge the gap between IT and OT security. This might involve courses that delve into the Purdue Model for control hierarchy, the IEC 62443 series of standards, or specific cybersecurity practices for sectors like power generation, water treatment, or manufacturing. Such specialized training ensures that CIRT members understand not just the "what" of a cyber threat, but the "how" and "why" it specifically impacts industrial processes, and crucially, the potential physical consequences.

Furthermore, training must extend to understanding the specific ICS environment the CIRT is tasked with protecting. This means that CIRT members should undergo familiarization with the plant's specific network architecture, the critical control loops, the safety instrumented systems (SIS), and the physical processes they govern. This could involve site visits, shadowing OT engineers and operators during routine operations, and participating in controlled walkthroughs of critical infrastructure. Understanding the function of a particular pump, valve, or generator, and how it is controlled by a specific PLC, provides context that is vital for effective incident analysis and remediation. Without this operational context, a CIRT member might, for instance, recommend an action that, while technically sound from an IT perspective, could lead to severe operational disruption or even a safety hazard in the OT environment. This deep dive into operational realities transforms a generic cybersecurity professional into an indispensable ICS security expert.

Beyond formal certifications and familiarization, a critical component of CIRT skill development lies in engaging in realistic exercises. Tabletop exercises, while often perceived as less demanding, play a crucial role in refining decision-making processes and communication protocols. These exercises typically involve a facilitator presenting a simulated incident scenario, and the CIRT, along with relevant stakeholders from operations, engineering, and management, discusses how they would respond. The focus here is on strategy, policy, and communication flow within the established ICS framework. For example, a tabletop exercise might present a scenario where malware is detected in a supervisory control system, and participants must collaboratively decide on the initial containment strategy, who needs to be informed, what operational impacts are acceptable, and how the Incident Commander will be briefed. These sessions are excellent for identifying gaps in understanding roles and responsibilities, clarifying communication channels, and practicing the articulation of complex technical issues in a way that is understandable to non-technical decision-makers. They are a low-risk, high-reward method for testing the efficacy of the CIRT's integration into the broader ICS structure and incident response plan.

Moving up the fidelity ladder, functional exercises and full-scale simulations offer a more immersive and demanding training experience. Functional exercises simulate specific aspects of an incident response, such as the isolation of a compromised network segment or the restoration of a critical control function. These exercises test the technical capabilities of the CIRT and the coordination required between different teams. They allow for hands-on practice with forensic tools, network analysis equipment, and incident response playbooks in a controlled environment. For an ICS CIRT, this could involve simulating the loss of communication with remote substations due to a cyberattack and testing the procedures for manually restoring control or safely shutting down affected processes.

Full-scale simulations are the pinnacle of incident response training, mimicking a real-world incident as closely as possible. These exercises involve multiple teams, potentially across different physical locations, operating under realistic time constraints and stress levels. They test the entire incident response lifecycle, from initial detection and analysis through containment, eradication, recovery, and post-incident review. For an ICS CIRT, a full-scale simulation might involve a coordinated cyberattack that affects both IT and OT systems, requiring seamless collaboration between the CIRT, IT operations, plant engineering, and the executive leadership. The simulation would likely involve injecting realistic "noise" such as system alerts, operational alarms, and external communications to replicate the chaos of a real event. Success in these simulations is measured not only by the technical effectiveness of the response but also by the ability of the team to maintain composure, adapt to unforeseen challenges, and make sound decisions under extreme pressure. These simulations are invaluable for building team cohesion, identifying systemic weaknesses, and ensuring that the CIRT can function effectively when the stakes are highest. Post-exercise debriefings are critical, providing a structured opportunity for lessons learned to be identified, documented, and incorporated into future training and operational procedures.

Beyond the technical and procedural aspects, the development of critical soft skills is equally, if not more, important for CIRT members operating in an ICS environment. The ability to think critically and analytically under pressure is paramount. This involves dissecting complex technical data, identifying patterns in seemingly disparate events, and formulating hypotheses about attacker motivations and methods. It also means being able to assess the potential cascading effects of a cyberattack on physical processes and safety systems, which requires a blend of technical understanding and operational intuition. CIRT members must be adept at rapid problem-solving, devising creative solutions when standard procedures are insufficient or impossible to implement due to operational constraints. This might involve finding workarounds for compromised systems, developing temporary fixes, or identifying innovative ways to isolate threats without causing significant operational downtime.

Effective communication is another critical soft skill that demands constant cultivation. CIRT members must be able to articulate technical findings clearly, concisely, and accurately to a diverse audience, ranging from fellow technical specialists to plant operators, engineers, and senior management. This requires tailoring the message to the audience's level of technical understanding and operational context. During an incident, confusion and miscommunication can have catastrophic consequences. Therefore, training should emphasize clear and unambiguous reporting, active listening, and the ability to manage expectations. Practice in delivering concise briefings to an Incident Commander, explaining the technical details of a threat and its potential impact, or negotiating with operations personnel about the feasibility of a containment measure are all vital communication skills that benefit from dedicated training and practice. The ability to remain calm and professional when delivering bad news or explaining complex technical challenges is a hallmark of an experienced CIRT member.

Furthermore, resilience and stress management are increasingly recognized as essential attributes for CIRT personnel. Responding to major cyber incidents, especially those with potential safety or environmental implications, can be incredibly taxing. Training programs should incorporate elements that help team members develop coping mechanisms for stress, maintain focus, and avoid burnout. This could involve psychological preparedness training, stress inoculation techniques, and fostering a supportive team environment where members feel comfortable discussing challenges and seeking support from one another. The psychological toll of being on the front lines of defending critical infrastructure against sophisticated adversaries cannot be underestimated, and proactive measures to support the mental well-being of CIRT members are an integral part of a comprehensive skill development strategy.

The nature of threats is constantly evolving, meaning that training must also adapt. This necessitates a commitment to ongoing learning and staying abreast of emerging technologies, attack vectors, and defensive strategies. This could involve regular threat intelligence briefings, participation in industry forums and conferences, and dedicated research time for CIRT members. A culture of continuous improvement must be fostered, where lessons learned from real incidents and exercises are systematically analyzed and integrated into training curricula and operational procedures. This feedback loop is essential for ensuring that the CIRT remains at the forefront of cybersecurity defense and is not caught flat-footed by new adversary tactics. The investment in training and skill development is not a one-time event but a sustained, strategic commitment that underpins the very effectiveness and resilience of the CIRT in safeguarding critical industrial operations. It transforms a group of individuals into a cohesive, highly capable team ready to face the complex challenges of ICS cybersecurity.

The dynamic and interconnected nature of modern industrial control systems (ICS) means that a single cyber incident, particularly one of significant scale or sophistication, can rapidly overwhelm the resources and expertise of a single organization. Recognizing this inherent vulnerability, a critical component of building a resilient CIRT capability, especially within the ICS domain, lies in fostering proactive collaboration and establishing formal mechanisms for mutual support. This moves beyond internal preparedness to embrace an ecosystem of collective defense, acknowledging that the threats faced are often too pervasive and complex to be effectively managed in isolation. Therefore, a crucial strategic imperative for any organization reliant on ICS is the establishment of robust mutual aid and information-sharing agreements with other entities.

These agreements serve as formalized pacts designed to facilitate the exchange of resources, knowledge, and personnel during times of heightened cyber threat or actual incident. They are built upon the understanding that a threat to one organization within a critical sector or geographical region can, and often will, have ripple effects impacting others. By pre-negotiating the terms and conditions of such assistance, organizations can drastically reduce the response time and improve the overall effectiveness when an incident transcends the capacity of a single CIRT. This collaborative approach leverages shared strengths, mitigates individual weaknesses, and ultimately contributes to a more resilient national or regional infrastructure. The scope of these agreements can vary significantly, from informal understandings between trusted peers to legally binding contracts with defined service level agreements and resource commitments. Regardless of the formality, the underlying principle remains the same: to create a safety net of mutual support that can be deployed when needed most.

A primary benefit of establishing mutual aid agreements is the access to specialized expertise and resources that an organization might not possess internally. Consider a scenario where a sophisticated ransomware attack cripples the operational technology network of a manufacturing plant. While their internal CIRT is adept at IT security, the incident quickly spreads to the control systems, requiring deep knowledge of specific SCADA protocols, PLC programming, and the unique operational constraints of the manufacturing process. If this plant has a mutual aid agreement with a similar manufacturing facility or a specialized cybersecurity firm focused on OT, they can swiftly call upon experts who have direct experience with such systems and the specific threat vectors impacting that industry. This external assistance can be in the form of direct technical support, forensic analysis of compromised control systems, or even the temporary deployment of skilled personnel to assist with incident containment and recovery. Such rapid access to specialized skills can be the difference between a manageable disruption and a catastrophic system failure.

Furthermore, mutual aid agreements can be instrumental in addressing incidents that impact multiple organizations simultaneously. Large-scale denial-of-service attacks, widespread malware campaigns, or sophisticated nation-state sponsored intrusions are not confined by organizational boundaries. In such scenarios, individual CIRTs might find themselves battling the same threat on multiple fronts with limited capacity. Mutual aid agreements allow for the pooling of resources, enabling a coordinated response across affected entities. This could involve sharing threat intelligence to identify common attack signatures, collectively analyzing malware samples to understand propagation methods, or even distributing the workload for incident investigation and remediation. For instance, in the energy sector, a coordinated cyberattack targeting supervisory control and data acquisition (SCADA) systems across several utility providers could be met with a unified response facilitated by pre-existing mutual aid pacts. This collective action presents a more formidable defense than individual, uncoordinated efforts.

The efficacy of these agreements hinges on the quality and scope of the information sharing that underpins them. Robust information-sharing communities are essential for fostering trust and enabling timely dissemination of threat intelligence. These communities can take various forms, including industry-specific Information Sharing and Analysis Centers (ISACs), public-private partnerships, or even ad-hoc groupings of organizations with shared interests. Within these communities, members voluntarily share threat indicators, vulnerability alerts, incident details, and best practices. This collective intelligence allows participants to proactively detect and defend against emerging threats, often before they directly impact their own systems. For ICS environments, participation in relevant ISACs, such as the Multi-State Information Sharing and Analysis Center (MS-ISAC) for state, local, tribal, and territorial governments, or sector-specific ISACs for energy, manufacturing, or water, is paramount. These platforms provide a structured and secure mechanism for exchanging sensitive information.

The act of sharing information, especially concerning cyber incidents, requires a foundation of trust. Organizations are often hesitant to reveal details about breaches due to concerns about reputational damage, regulatory scrutiny, or potential exploitation by adversaries. Therefore, the establishment of clear protocols, data anonymization techniques where appropriate, and secure communication channels are vital for building and maintaining this trust. The agreements should clearly define what information can be shared, with whom, under what circumstances, and the expected timeliness of such disclosures. Legal frameworks, such as those provided by the Cybersecurity Information Sharing Act of 2015 in the United States, offer liability protection for organizations that share cyber threat information, thereby incentivizing participation and encouraging a more open exchange.

When developing mutual aid and information-sharing agreements, several key considerations must be addressed to ensure their practicality and effectiveness. Firstly, the scope of support needs to be clearly defined. What specific types of assistance will be provided? Will it be technical expertise, personnel, equipment, or a combination thereof? What are the limitations of this support? Are there geographical constraints? Understanding these parameters beforehand prevents misunderstandings and unmet expectations during a crisis. For example, an agreement might stipulate that a partner organization will provide up to 48 hours of on-site assistance from a senior OT security analyst in the event of a Level 3 or higher incident, but not beyond a 200-mile radius.

Secondly, the trigger mechanisms for activating these agreements must be clearly delineated. Under what conditions can an organization request assistance? What are the thresholds for activating a mutual aid request? This could be based on the severity of the incident, the impact on critical operations, or the inability of the internal CIRT to contain the threat within a specified timeframe. A well-defined incident severity classification system, integrated with the organization's overall incident response plan, will be crucial here. For instance, an incident classified as a "critical system compromise" impacting more than 50% of production throughput might automatically trigger a request for mutual aid under a pre-existing agreement.

Thirdly, the logistical and financial aspects of mutual aid need to be addressed. Who bears the cost of deployed personnel, travel, accommodation, and any specialized equipment that might be required? Agreements can stipulate cost-sharing arrangements, full reimbursement, or a "lend-lease" model where resources are returned or replaced. Establishing these financial arrangements in advance prevents disputes and ensures that assistance can be provided without undue financial burden or hesitation. For instance, an agreement might state that the requesting organization will cover all direct expenses incurred by the assisting party, including a pre-agreed daily rate for personnel time.

Fourthly, the process for requesting and receiving assistance should be streamlined and unambiguous. This involves identifying designated points of contact within each organization who are authorized to make and accept mutual aid requests. Communication channels for these requests should be clearly established, ensuring that they are reliable and accessible even under adverse conditions. This might include dedicated phone lines, secure messaging platforms, or a specific email address monitored 24/7. The process should also include mechanisms for updating the requesting party on the progress of the assistance being provided.

Fifthly, regular testing and exercising of these agreements are crucial. An agreement is only as good as its demonstrated operational readiness. Conducting joint tabletop exercises, functional drills, or even full-scale simulations that involve activating mutual aid components allows organizations to validate the effectiveness of the agreements, identify any procedural gaps, and ensure that the respective teams are familiar with each other's protocols and capabilities. These exercises also serve to reinforce the collaborative culture that underpins the agreements, building stronger relationships and a greater sense of shared responsibility. For example, a joint exercise between two water utilities could simulate a ransomware attack on their SCADA systems, requiring them to activate their mutual aid agreement and jointly manage the response, testing communication, resource deployment, and coordinated remediation efforts.

Finally, the legal and compliance aspects must be thoroughly reviewed. This includes ensuring that the agreements comply with all relevant national and international laws, data privacy regulations, and industry-specific compliance mandates. Legal counsel should be involved in drafting and reviewing these agreements to ensure they are legally sound and protect the interests of all parties involved. This includes provisions for intellectual property, liability, and dispute resolution.

The establishment of formal mutual aid and information-sharing agreements is not merely a procedural formality; it represents a strategic shift towards a more resilient and collaborative cybersecurity posture for ICS. In an era where cyber threats are increasingly sophisticated, widespread, and potentially devastating to critical infrastructure, no single organization can afford to operate in a vacuum. By actively participating in information-sharing communities and establishing robust mutual aid pacts, organizations can significantly enhance their ability to detect, prevent, and respond to cyber incidents. This collective approach leverages the combined strength of multiple entities, ensuring that expertise and resources are available when needed, thereby bolstering the overall security and reliability of vital industrial operations. It transforms the concept of cybersecurity from an isolated endeavor to a shared responsibility, fostering a more secure and resilient digital ecosystem for all.

The establishment of mutual aid agreements and robust information-sharing networks, as previously discussed, forms a crucial external layer of defense for any Computer Incident Response Team (CIRT), particularly those tasked with protecting Industrial Control Systems (ICS). However, the effectiveness of these external collaborations is intrinsically linked to the internal strength and readiness of the CIRT itself. A CIRT that is not continuously maintained and improved internally will struggle to effectively leverage external support or contribute meaningfully to collective defense efforts. Therefore, maintaining a state of perpetual readiness and fostering a culture of continuous improvement are paramount to the enduring success of any CIRT.

Achieving and sustaining CIRT readiness is not a static state but rather a dynamic process that demands constant attention and proactive engagement. It requires a systematic approach to evaluating existing capabilities, identifying gaps, and implementing measures to close those gaps. This involves a multifaceted strategy encompassing regular assessments, procedural refinements, and a keen awareness of the ever-shifting threat landscape. The ultimate objective is to cultivate an environment within the CIRT where preparedness is not just a goal, but an ingrained operational philosophy, ensuring that the team remains agile, effective, and responsive in the face of an increasingly complex and volatile cyber environment. This commitment to ongoing enhancement ensures that the CIRT can not only react effectively to incidents but also proactively anticipate and mitigate emerging threats.

A cornerstone of maintaining CIRT readiness is the implementation of rigorous and regular capability assessments. These assessments serve as critical diagnostic tools, allowing the CIRT to gauge its current level of preparedness across various dimensions. This includes evaluating the proficiency of its personnel, the adequacy of its technical tools and infrastructure, the clarity and completeness of its operational procedures, and the overall effectiveness of its communication and coordination mechanisms. For an ICS-focused CIRT, these assessments must extend beyond traditional IT security metrics to encompass specialized areas such as the security of operational technology (OT) environments, knowledge of specific industrial protocols (e.g., Modbus, DNP3, IEC 61850), familiarity with programmable logic controllers (PLCs) and distributed control systems (DCS), and the understanding of unique OT vulnerabilities and attack vectors.

These capability assessments should be conducted on a defined schedule, perhaps quarterly or semi-annually, and also be triggered by significant events, such as the conclusion of a major incident or the successful completion of a large-scale exercise. The methodology for these assessments can vary, but should ideally incorporate a blend of self-evaluation, peer review, and, where feasible, external validation.

This might involve reviewing incident response logs, analyzing post-incident reports, conducting skills-based testing for team members, performing vulnerability scans and penetration tests on CIRT tools and infrastructure, and reviewing documentation for accuracy and completeness. The output of these assessments should be a detailed report that clearly identifies strengths, weaknesses, and specific areas for improvement, along with actionable recommendations. For instance, an assessment might reveal that while the CIRT possesses excellent skills in network forensics for IT environments, its capabilities in analyzing memory dumps from embedded OT devices are lacking. This would then necessitate a targeted training program or the acquisition of specialized tools to address this identified deficiency. Similarly, an assessment might highlight that the communication protocols used during a recent simulated incident were inefficient, leading to delays in information dissemination. This would prompt a review and potential revision of the CIRT's communication plan.

Furthermore, these assessments should not be viewed as punitive exercises but rather as opportunities for growth and development. A culture that encourages open and honest feedback during the assessment process is crucial. Team members should feel empowered to highlight challenges they face and suggest improvements without fear of reprisal. This collaborative approach to assessment fosters a shared sense of ownership over the CIRT's readiness and encourages proactive problem-solving.

The findings derived from these capability assessments, as well as lessons learned from actual incidents and exercises, form the bedrock for updating and refining CIRT procedures. Cyber threats are not static; they evolve in sophistication, scale, and methodology. Consequently, CIRT playbooks, standard operating procedures (SOPs), and incident response plans must be living documents, regularly revised to reflect the latest threat intelligence, emerging attack techniques, and changes in the organization's own operational landscape. This iterative process of learning and adaptation is fundamental to maintaining a high level of preparedness.

For an ICS CIRT, this procedural refinement is particularly critical. Procedures that were effective against threats from five years ago may be woefully inadequate against today's advanced persistent threats (APTs) targeting industrial infrastructure. For example, a procedure for isolating a compromised IT server might be straightforward, but isolating a compromised PLC within a live manufacturing process without causing significant operational disruption requires highly specialized knowledge and meticulously crafted procedures. These procedures must account for factors such as system dependencies, safety interlocks, the potential for physical impact, and the need to maintain essential functions.

The process of updating procedures should be systematic and documented. Each update should be traceable to a specific lesson learned, assessment finding, or new threat intelligence. This ensures that procedural changes are not arbitrary but are driven by a clear rationale. When a significant incident occurs, a thorough post-incident review is essential. This review should go beyond simply identifying the root cause of the breach; it should delve into the effectiveness of the

CIRT's response. Were the procedures followed? Were they adequate? Were there any bottlenecks in the response process? What could have been done differently or more effectively? The answers to these questions should directly inform revisions to existing procedures or the creation of new ones. For instance, if a ransomware attack exploited a previously unknown vulnerability in a common ICS component, the CIRT should update its procedures for vulnerability management and patching for similar components, and perhaps develop specific incident response playbooks for ransomware targeting OT systems.

Similarly, exercises, whether tabletop, functional, or full-scale, provide invaluable opportunities to test and refine procedures in a controlled environment. During an exercise, the CIRT can practice executing its response plans, identifying where procedures may be unclear, cumbersome, or simply ineffective. For example, a tabletop exercise simulating a supply chain attack targeting the firmware of a critical ICS component might reveal that the existing procedures for verifying the integrity of software and firmware updates are insufficient. This would then lead to the development of more robust validation protocols and potentially new procedures for dealing with compromised supply chains. The feedback loop from exercises, incidents, and ongoing assessments must be continuous, ensuring that the CIRT's operational framework remains current and effective.

The dynamic nature of the cyber threat landscape necessitates a proactive approach to adaptation. CIRTs must not only react to known threats but also anticipate and prepare for future ones. This requires a commitment to continuous learning and staying abreast of emerging trends, technologies, and attacker methodologies. For an ICS CIRT, this means paying close attention to the convergence of IT and OT, the increasing adoption of cloud technologies in industrial settings, the proliferation of IoT devices within operational environments, and the evolving tactics of nation-state actors and sophisticated cybercriminal groups.

Staying informed requires a multi-pronged strategy. This includes actively monitoring threat intelligence feeds from reputable sources, participating in industry-specific cybersecurity forums and working groups, engaging with government cybersecurity agencies, and fostering relationships with researchers and academics who are at the forefront of cybersecurity innovation. For ICS CIRTs, this also means subscribing to and actively participating in sector-specific Information Sharing and Analysis Centers (ISACs), which provide tailored threat intelligence and best practices relevant to critical infrastructure.

Beyond intelligence gathering, adaptation also involves investing in the professional development of CIRT personnel. This means providing ongoing training opportunities, encouraging certifications in relevant cybersecurity domains (both IT and OT), and supporting attendance at industry conferences and workshops. The skills required to defend ICS are specialized and constantly evolving. A CIRT that does not invest in the continuous learning of its team members will inevitably fall behind. This could involve cross-training IT security personnel in OT fundamentals, or vice versa, to foster a more integrated and comprehensive understanding of the organization's cyber-physical systems.

Moreover, CIRTs must be agile enough to adapt their strategies and tools in response to evolving threats. This might mean reallocating resources to focus on emerging threat vectors, adopting new security technologies, or modifying their incident response priorities. For example, if threat intelligence indicates a significant increase in attacks targeting the remote access capabilities of ICS, the CIRT should proactively review and strengthen its remote access security protocols, potentially implementing multi-factor authentication for all remote connections, enhancing logging and monitoring of remote sessions, and developing specific playbooks for responding to compromised remote access credentials. Similarly, the rise of AI-powered cyberattacks necessitates a forward-looking approach, requiring CIRTs to explore defensive AI technologies and develop strategies to counter AI-driven malicious activities.

Ultimately, maintaining CIRT readiness and fostering continuous improvement is about cultivating a robust organizational culture. It requires leadership commitment, adequate resourcing, and a shared understanding of the critical role the CIRT plays in protecting the organization's operations and assets. This culture should emphasize vigilance, proactivity, learning, and collaboration. It is through this relentless pursuit of improvement, driven by a deep understanding of both internal capabilities and external threats, that a CIRT can ensure its enduring effectiveness and provide a strong defense against the ever-present and evolving specter of cyberattacks. This commitment to ongoing enhancement is not an optional add-on; it is a fundamental requirement for survival and success in the contemporary cybersecurity landscape.

The landscape of cybersecurity, particularly within the realm of Industrial Control Systems (ICS), often conjures images of large corporations with dedicated, well-funded security operations centers and extensive incident response teams. However, this perspective significantly overlooks the vast majority of organizations that operate critical infrastructure and utilize ICS: Small and Medium-sized Businesses (SMBs). These entities, while often possessing smaller budgets, fewer dedicated IT and security personnel, and less complex organizational structures, are equally, if not more, vulnerable to cyber threats. The sophisticated attacks that have plagued larger enterprises can, and do, cascade down to impact SMBs, often with more devastating consequences due to their limited capacity to absorb the financial and operational fallout. Therefore, adapting the principles of robust incident response, specifically for ICS environments, to the unique context of SMBs is not merely a matter of best practice, but an urgent necessity. The challenge lies in translating the comprehensive, often resource-intensive, frameworks designed for large enterprises into practical, scalable, and affordable solutions that SMBs can realistically implement and maintain.

The fundamental hurdle for SMBs in adopting comprehensive incident response capabilities is resource constraint. Unlike their larger counterparts, SMBs typically lack the luxury of dedicated cybersecurity teams, specialized hardware and software investments, and the luxury of extensive training programs. Personnel often wear multiple hats, with IT responsibilities frequently falling to individuals who also manage networks, hardware, or even general operational tasks. This inherent limitation means that a direct transplant of a large-scale Computer Incident Response Team (CIRT) model is impractical and unsustainable. The objective, therefore, must be to distill the core principles of effective incident response and adapt them into a streamlined, pragmatic approach that is tailored to the operational realities and financial capacities of SMBs. This involves a careful re-evaluation of essential functions, a focus on prioritization, and an exploration of innovative ways to leverage shared resources and simplified structures.

One of the primary considerations for SMBs is to simplify the concept of a formal CIRT. Rather than aiming for a standalone, dedicated unit, an SMB can establish a virtual or a federated incident response capability. This could involve designating specific individuals within existing IT or operational teams to take on incident response roles during an event. For example, the network administrator might be the primary point of contact for initial triage and containment, while a senior engineer with deep knowledge of the ICS could be responsible for technical analysis and recovery within the operational environment. The key is to clearly define roles and responsibilities, even if these are part-time assignments. This requires developing a concise incident response plan that outlines these roles, the escalation procedures, and the communication channels to be used during an incident. The plan does not need to be an exhaustive tome; instead, it should be a practical guide that is easily understood and readily accessible to all designated personnel. The emphasis should be on clarity, conciseness, and actionable steps.

Furthermore, SMBs can significantly benefit from prioritizing their assets and understanding their critical dependencies. Not all systems within an SMB's ICS environment carry the same risk or impact if compromised. A thorough asset inventory, coupled with a risk assessment, can help identify the most critical components – those that, if disrupted, would cause significant operational downtime, safety issues, or financial losses. This prioritization allows SMBs to focus their limited resources on protecting these high-value targets. For instance, if a manufacturing SMB identifies its primary production line's control system as the most critical asset, then efforts to harden this system, increase its monitoring, and develop specific incident response playbooks for its compromise should take precedence over less critical systems. This pragmatic approach ensures that resources are allocated where they will have the greatest impact, rather than attempting to achieve a uniform level of security across all systems, which is often an unattainable goal for resource-constrained organizations.

The development of incident response playbooks for SMBs should also be simplified. Instead of creating separate, detailed playbooks for every conceivable threat, SMBs can focus on developing generic playbooks for common incident types, such as ransomware, denial-of-service attacks, or unauthorized access. These playbooks should outline a set of core steps that can be adapted to the specific circumstances of an incident. For example, a generic ransomware playbook might include steps for identifying the scope of infection, isolating affected systems, assessing the impact on ICS operations, determining whether backups are viable, and engaging external expertise if necessary. The playbook should clearly indicate where specific ICS knowledge is required, prompting the designated ICS personnel to step in. This layered approach allows the core IT response team to handle initial actions while ensuring that the unique aspects of an ICS incident are addressed appropriately.

The challenge of securing and responding to incidents in ICS environments is often compounded by the legacy nature of many systems. SMBs may be operating older equipment that was not designed with cybersecurity in mind and for which vendor support might be limited or nonexistent. In such cases, physical security and network segmentation become even more crucial. Implementing robust network segmentation, for example, can limit the lateral movement of an attacker within the ICS network, thereby containing the impact of a breach. This can be achieved through firewalls, VLANs, and access control lists, even in a relatively modest network infrastructure. The incident response plan should explicitly detail the segmentation strategy and the procedures for reinforcing or modifying these segments during an incident. For instance, if an incident is detected on a particular segment of the ICS network, the response playbook might include instructions to immediately disable all network traffic to and from that segment, effectively quarantining the compromised area.

Given the resource limitations, SMBs should actively explore external support mechanisms. This can take several forms. Firstly, Managed Security Service Providers (MSSPs) that specialize in ICS or OT security can provide a valuable extension of an SMB's internal capabilities. These providers can offer services such as continuous monitoring, threat detection, and even incident response retainers, allowing SMBs to access specialized expertise without the overhead of maintaining a full-time team. When selecting an MSSP, it is crucial for SMBs to vet their experience with ICS environments specifically, as the nuances of OT security differ significantly from traditional IT security. The incident response plan should clearly define the roles and responsibilities of the MSSP and establish clear communication protocols and escalation paths for incident reporting and coordination.

Secondly, participation in Information Sharing and Analysis Centers (ISACs) or similar industry-specific groups can provide SMBs with access to valuable threat intelligence and best practices that they might otherwise not be able to obtain. These organizations often provide curated information on threats targeting specific industrial sectors, allowing SMBs to proactively prepare and respond to relevant risks. While direct participation in an ISAC might require a membership fee, the collective knowledge and early warning capabilities they offer can be invaluable. The incident response plan should include a procedure for monitoring and acting upon information received from such sharing communities.

Leveraging vendor support is another critical, yet often underutilized, resource for SMBs. Many ICS vendors offer security services, remote monitoring capabilities, and even incident response assistance for their products. Establishing strong relationships with ICS vendors and understanding the security services they provide can be a cost-effective way to bolster an SMB's incident response posture. The incident response plan should detail how and when to engage with ICS vendors during an incident, including pre-established contact points and escalation procedures. For example, if a specific PLC model is suspected of being compromised, the plan might direct the response team to immediately contact the vendor for guidance on containment, forensic analysis, and potential remediation.

Simplifying the command and control structure during an incident is also essential for SMBs. In a large organization, a complex incident command system might be necessary. However, for an SMB, a streamlined approach is more effective. This could involve designating a single incident commander, who is responsible for overall coordination and decision-making. This individual might be the IT manager, a senior plant manager, or a designated security lead. This commander would then work with a small core response team, which includes representatives from IT, operations, and potentially any external service providers. The focus should be on clear lines of authority and rapid decision-making, avoiding bureaucratic delays that can be detrimental during an active incident. The incident response plan should clearly outline the incident commander's authority and the composition of the core response team.

Training and awareness are critical components of any incident response capability, even for SMBs. However, the training needs to be tailored to the available resources and the specific roles. For the designated incident response personnel, this might involve specialized training on ICS cybersecurity fundamentals, common attack vectors, and the specific tools and procedures outlined in the incident response plan. For all employees, regular cybersecurity awareness training is crucial to help them identify and report suspicious activities, which can be an early indicator of an incident. This training does not need to be elaborate; simple, regular refreshers on phishing awareness, password security, and the importance of reporting anomalies can make a significant difference. The incident response plan should include a schedule for this ongoing training and awareness program.

The recovery phase of incident response is often the most challenging for SMBs, especially when dealing with ICS. Rebuilding or restoring critical operational systems requires a deep understanding of the plant's processes and dependencies. Therefore, robust and frequently tested backup and recovery procedures are paramount. SMBs need to ensure that their ICS data, configurations, and system images are regularly backed up and that these backups are stored securely and are readily accessible. Crucially, these backups must be tested periodically to ensure their integrity and the ability to restore them within an acceptable timeframe. A detailed recovery plan, integrated into the overall incident response plan, should outline the steps for restoring critical systems, prioritizing them based on operational impact. This plan should also include procedures for validating the restored systems to ensure they are functioning correctly and securely before bringing them back online. For example, a recovery playbook for a compromised SCADA system might detail the steps for restoring the server from a clean backup, re-establishing communication with field devices, and then performing functional tests to ensure that control commands are being processed accurately and safely.

Finally, the concept of continuous improvement, while a hallmark of mature incident response programs, needs to be adapted for the SMB context. This does not necessarily mean conducting extensive post-incident reviews with large teams. Instead, it can be a more informal, yet consistent, process. After any incident, or even after a significant security event or exercise, the core response team should convene for a brief "lessons learned" session. This session should focus on identifying what worked well, what did not work well, and what specific changes can be made to the incident response plan, playbooks, or procedures to improve future responses. These lessons learned should be documented and used to update the relevant documents. This iterative process, even if performed quarterly or semi-annually, ensures that the SMB's incident response capability remains relevant and effective, adapting to new threats and organizational changes without requiring substantial resource investments. The emphasis is on making small, incremental improvements that compound over time, leading to a more resilient and effective incident response capability for the SMB.

The implementation of Industrial Control Systems (ICS) within critical infrastructure sectors presents a complex and multifaceted challenge, distinct from that faced by general industries. These sectors – encompassing energy, water and wastewater, healthcare, transportation, and others deemed vital to societal functioning – are not only attractive targets for cybercriminals seeking financial gain or operational disruption but also for state-sponsored actors aiming to destabilize national security. The inherent interconnectedness of these systems, coupled with their direct impact on public safety and well-being, elevates the stakes of cybersecurity significantly. Consequently, the adaptation of ICS security frameworks and incident response strategies within these domains requires a rigorous, sector-specific approach that addresses unique threat landscapes, stringent regulatory mandates, and the critical need for seamless inter-agency and inter-organizational coordination.

In the energy sector, for instance, the disruption of power grids, oil and gas pipelines, or nuclear facilities can have catastrophic consequences, ranging from widespread blackouts and economic paralysis to environmental disasters and loss of life. Utilities operate vast networks of physical assets, often spread across large geographical areas, with a blend of legacy and modern ICS technologies. The threat actors targeting this sector are sophisticated and well-resourced, including advanced persistent threats (APTs) linked to nation-states, as well as organized cybercriminal groups. Incident response plans in the energy sector must therefore be exceptionally robust, encompassing rapid detection of anomalies in SCADA systems, immediate isolation of compromised substations or generation plants, and swift restoration of critical power flows. This necessitates deep technical understanding of power system dynamics, grid balancing, and the specific vulnerabilities of technologies like PLCs and RTUs used in substations and control rooms. Furthermore, the regulatory environment for the energy sector, particularly in North America, is heavily influenced by standards such as NERC CIP (North American Electric Reliability Corporation Critical Infrastructure Protection), which mandates stringent security controls, compliance reporting, and specific incident reporting timelines.

These regulations often dictate the minimum security posture and incident response capabilities that utilities must maintain, making adherence a critical operational imperative.

The water and wastewater sector, while perhaps perceived as less glamorous than energy, is equally critical. Disruptions can lead to the loss of potable water supply, contamination of water sources, or the failure of wastewater treatment, posing severe public health risks. The ICS in this sector often manage pumps, valves, chemical treatment processes, and monitoring sensors. While some large municipal water systems might have dedicated IT and security teams, many smaller, rural water districts operate with limited resources, similar to SMBs discussed previously, but with the added burden of serving public health needs. This dichotomy necessitates a tiered approach to incident response, where scalable, cost-effective solutions are available for smaller entities, while larger, more complex systems are held to higher standards. Compliance in this sector is often governed by entities like the Environmental Protection Agency (EPA) and state-level public health departments, which may have their own requirements for system security and incident reporting, though perhaps less prescriptive than NERC CIP. Incident response plans must therefore be practical, adaptable to varying organizational capacities, and aligned with public health protection objectives. The ability to quickly identify and remediate threats to water quality monitoring or distribution control systems is paramount, often requiring coordination with public health officials and emergency management agencies.

The healthcare sector presents a unique set of challenges, where the compromise of ICS managing medical devices, diagnostic equipment, building automation, and patient monitoring systems can directly impact patient care and safety. Devices such as MRI machines, infusion pumps, and ventilators are increasingly connected, creating new attack vectors. Moreover, the healthcare industry is a prime target for ransomware attacks due to the sensitive nature of patient data and the high pressure to restore services quickly to avoid compromising patient well-being. In this context, ICS incident response must be integrated with broader healthcare emergency preparedness plans. A cyberattack that renders a critical medical device inoperable, or compromises the environmental controls of an operating room, requires an immediate and coordinated response involving IT security, clinical engineering, and medical staff. Regulatory oversight from bodies like the U.S. Department of Health and Human Services (HHS) and adherence to HIPAA (Health Insurance Portability and Accountability Act) privacy and security rules are critical. Incident response plans must account for the extreme urgency of restoring medical device functionality, potentially involving rapid replacement, manual overrides, or even patient transfer in severe cases. The ethical considerations surrounding patient safety during an incident are paramount and must be explicitly addressed in response protocols.

Transportation infrastructure, including air traffic control, railway signaling, and port operations, relies heavily on ICS to ensure safe and efficient movement of people and goods. A cyberattack on air traffic control systems could lead to widespread flight cancellations and potential safety hazards. Compromises in railway signaling could cause collisions or significant service disruptions. Port operations, managing automated cranes and logistics, are vital for global supply chains. The interdependencies within transportation networks mean that an incident in one sub-sector can have cascading effects across others. Incident response in transportation must therefore be highly coordinated, often involving multiple government agencies (e.g., FAA, FRA, TSA), private operators, and international partners. Compliance with specific transportation security directives and standards is essential. For example, the Federal Aviation Administration (FAA) issues regulations and guidance on cybersecurity for aviation systems. The response to a cyber incident affecting air traffic management systems, for instance, would involve not only technical remediation but also extensive communication with airlines, airports, and passengers, alongside potential air traffic rerouting or grounding measures. The speed of recovery is critical, as are the contingency plans for maintaining essential services during prolonged disruptions.

A critical overarching theme across all these sectors is the paramount importance of inter-agency and inter-organizational coordination. Critical infrastructure is not operated in silos. Energy grids are interconnected, water systems may share resources or rely on power from the grid, healthcare facilities depend on transportation for supplies and patient access, and transportation systems rely on energy. A cyberattack on one sector can rapidly spill over into others. Therefore, robust communication channels and well-defined protocols for collaboration are indispensable components of ICS incident response frameworks for critical infrastructure. This often involves participation in Information Sharing and Analysis Centers (ISACs) specific to each sector, as well as broader national-level coordination mechanisms. These platforms facilitate the sharing of threat intelligence, best practices, and lessons learned, enabling a more proactive and collective defense. During an actual incident, the ability to quickly share relevant information – such as indicators of compromise, attacker tactics, or mitigation strategies – between different entities and government bodies can significantly shorten response times and reduce the overall impact.

The development and maintenance of these specialized ICS incident response plans require a deep understanding of the specific operational technology (OT) within each sector, its unique vulnerabilities, and the regulatory landscape. This is a departure from traditional IT incident response, which often focuses on data confidentiality and availability. In OT environments, the primary concerns are safety, reliability, and operational continuity. An incident response plan must prioritize actions that mitigate immediate safety risks, followed by steps to restore essential operations, and only then focus on detailed forensic analysis or data recovery if it doesn't compromise the former. The use of specialized tools and techniques for analyzing OT network traffic, understanding industrial protocols (like Modbus, DNP3, OPC UA), and safely interacting with control systems is crucial. Many critical infrastructure organizations leverage third-party expertise, such as specialized ICS security firms or managed security service providers (MSSPs) with OT expertise, to augment their internal capabilities. These external partners can provide round-the-clock monitoring, threat hunting, and rapid-response capabilities, which are often difficult for individual organizations, particularly smaller ones, to build and maintain in-house.

Compliance obligations further shape the incident response posture in critical infrastructure. Regulatory bodies often mandate specific incident reporting requirements, including timelines for notification to authorities, content of reports, and minimum investigation procedures. Failure to comply can result in substantial fines, legal repercussions, and reputational damage. Therefore, incident response plans must integrate these reporting obligations seamlessly into the workflow. This means having designated personnel responsible for liaising with regulatory bodies, maintaining accurate incident logs, and preparing required documentation. The process of gathering the necessary information for these reports, especially in the high-pressure environment of an ongoing incident, requires pre-defined procedures and readily available templates.

Furthermore, the concept of "resilience" takes on heightened significance in critical infrastructure. It's not just about detecting and responding to an incident, but about the ability to withstand and recover from disruptions while maintaining essential services. This involves building redundancy into critical systems, developing robust backup and recovery strategies that are regularly tested, and having well-rehearsed contingency plans for operating in degraded modes or without primary control systems. For instance, a water utility might have backup power generators for pump stations, or manual override capabilities for key valves in case automated controls fail. An incident response plan should not only detail the steps to contain and eradicate a threat but also the procedures for invoking these resilience measures and transitioning back to normal operations.

The evolving threat landscape, characterized by increasingly sophisticated and persistent attacks, demands continuous adaptation and improvement of ICS incident response capabilities within critical infrastructure sectors. This includes regular vulnerability assessments, penetration testing, and tabletop exercises that simulate realistic attack scenarios. These exercises should involve not only the technical response teams but also senior management, operational staff, and external stakeholders, including emergency services and regulatory agencies, to ensure that communication and coordination protocols are effective. The lessons learned from these exercises, much like those from actual incidents, must be systematically incorporated back into the incident response plans and procedures, fostering a culture of continuous improvement. The ultimate goal is to build and maintain a resilient ICS environment that can withstand cyber threats, protect public safety, and ensure the uninterrupted delivery of essential services that underpin modern society.

Government agencies and public sector organizations represent a unique and critical domain for the application of Industrial Control Systems (ICS). Unlike private enterprises, these entities are primarily driven by public service mandates, national security imperatives, and the provision of essential services that directly impact the well-being and safety of citizens. This distinct mission necessitates an ICS incident response framework that not only addresses technical vulnerabilities but also navigates complex organizational structures, multi-jurisdictional challenges, and stringent accountability requirements. The very nature of public service often involves a broader scope of impact when incidents occur, potentially affecting a larger populace and demanding a level of transparency and public communication rarely encountered in the private sector.

The operational context of government agencies in relation to ICS is incredibly diverse. Consider the Department of Defense, which manages vast networks of control systems for military bases, weapon systems, and logistical operations, all of which are high-value targets for sophisticated adversaries. Incident response here must be meticulously planned to safeguard national security interests, with strict protocols for information classification, secure communication, and operational continuity of critical defense functions. Similarly, agencies responsible for public safety, such as emergency management agencies (e.g., FEMA in the U.S.), rely on ICS for managing communication networks, coordinating disaster response efforts, and operating critical infrastructure that supports emergency services, like public warning systems or traffic management for evacuation routes. A disruption to these systems can have immediate and severe consequences for public safety, making rapid and effective incident response paramount.

Furthermore, public sector agencies often operate within highly regulated environments, where adherence to specific governmental policies, mandates, and legal frameworks is non-negotiable. This can include strict data privacy laws, public procurement regulations, and specific cybersecurity directives issued by national authorities. For instance, agencies managing national power grids or water supplies, even if operated by quasi-governmental entities, are subject to national security directives and stringent oversight from regulatory bodies. When an ICS incident occurs within such an agency, the response must not only focus on technical containment and eradication but also on meticulous documentation, evidence preservation for potential legal proceedings, and timely reporting to oversight bodies and potentially to legislative committees. The need for accountability is amplified, requiring a comprehensive audit trail of all actions taken during an incident response.

A cornerstone of effective ICS incident response in the public sector is the challenge and necessity of **interoperability and inter-agency coordination**. Public sector entities rarely operate in isolation. A cyberattack affecting a municipal water treatment plant, for example, could necessitate a coordinated response involving the local police department for physical security, the state's environmental protection agency for regulatory guidance, and potentially national cybersecurity agencies for technical assistance and threat intelligence. The incident response plan must therefore include clearly defined roles and responsibilities for each participating agency, pre-established communication channels, and mutual aid agreements. This often involves leveraging national-level cybersecurity coordination centers or specific inter-agency task forces established for critical infrastructure protection. The complexity arises from differing organizational cultures, technical capabilities, and reporting structures across agencies. Developing a unified incident response strategy that bridges these gaps requires significant planning, joint training exercises, and a shared understanding of common objectives.

The concept of Information Sharing and Analysis Centers (ISACs) is particularly relevant here, acting as crucial platforms for collaboration between government agencies and within specific sectors of critical infrastructure that are government-managed or heavily regulated. These centers facilitate the timely dissemination of threat intelligence, vulnerability information, and best practices, enabling a more proactive and coordinated defense. For government agencies, participation in sector-specific ISACs, alongside broader government cybersecurity initiatives, is essential for staying abreast of evolving threats and understanding the attack vectors targeting public sector ICS. When an incident occurs, the ability to rapidly share relevant anonymized or classified information through these trusted channels can significantly accelerate the detection of similar attacks elsewhere and inform mitigation strategies across multiple jurisdictions.

Public communication protocols represent another significant differentiator for government agencies. In the event of an ICS incident that impacts public services – such as disruptions to traffic light systems, power outages affecting residential areas, or compromised water quality monitoring – agencies have a responsibility to inform and reassure the public. This requires a carefully orchestrated communication strategy that is transparent, timely, and accurate, while also being mindful of not revealing sensitive operational details that could be exploited by adversaries. The incident response plan must designate spokespersons, establish protocols for issuing public statements, and coordinate messaging with other relevant government bodies, such as emergency management or public health departments. This often involves utilizing multiple communication channels, including official government websites, social media, press conferences, and emergency alert systems. Managing public perception and maintaining trust are critical components of the overall incident response, alongside the technical remediation efforts.

Moreover, the development of **ICS incident response plans within government agencies** must be deeply integrated with broader public sector emergency management frameworks. These frameworks, such as the National Incident Management System (NIMS) in the United States, provide a standardized approach to incident management across all hazards and jurisdictions. An ICS-specific incident response plan should align with the principles of NIMS, ensuring that ICS-related incidents are managed in a way that is consistent with the overall emergency response structure. This integration facilitates seamless coordination with first responders, emergency medical services, and other public safety organizations that may be involved in the aftermath of an ICS-related disruption. For example, if a cyberattack on a dam's control system leads to concerns about potential flooding, the ICS incident response team must be able to quickly integrate their technical containment and remediation efforts with the broader emergency response operations managed by the local emergency management agency.

The **adaptation of ICS incident response to the unique mission and operational context of public service organizations** also involves a careful consideration of resource allocation and skill development. Government agencies often face budget constraints and may struggle to attract and retain specialized ICS cybersecurity talent, which is in high demand across all sectors. This necessitates a strategic approach to building internal capabilities, leveraging partnerships with federal agencies, and exploring shared service models or managed security services where appropriate. Incident response plans should clearly delineate the internal resources available, identify external support mechanisms, and outline the process for requesting assistance from federal cybersecurity agencies or other government entities with specialized expertise. Training and exercises are paramount, not only for the technical teams but also for managers and policymakers who need to understand the implications of ICS incidents and the decisions required during a crisis.

Furthermore, government agencies are often custodians of critical national infrastructure that spans multiple jurisdictions, and sometimes even international borders. This inherently complicates incident response. For instance, an attack on a national power grid's control systems could originate in one country, traverse through networks in another, and impact critical facilities in a third. The incident response plan must therefore account for international cooperation and information sharing protocols, potentially involving diplomatic channels and agreements with foreign governments and international organizations. The complexity of attribution and the potential for state-sponsored attacks add further layers of challenge, requiring a sophisticated understanding of geopolitical factors and advanced threat intelligence capabilities.

The concept of **legacy systems** is also particularly prevalent within government and public sector ICS. Many agencies operate older, often decades-old, control systems that were not designed with cybersecurity in mind. These systems may lack basic security features, run on unsupported operating systems, and be difficult to patch or update without risking operational disruption. Incident response plans for these environments must be tailored to address the unique challenges of securing and responding to incidents on such systems. This might involve implementing compensating controls, such as network segmentation, intrusion detection systems specifically designed for industrial protocols, and rigorous access control measures, rather than relying on traditional IT security approaches. The plan should also include strategies for eventual modernization or replacement of these legacy systems, while ensuring that ongoing operations are protected in the interim.

The accountability framework for government agencies also dictates a rigorous approach to **documentation and reporting**. Every step taken during an ICS incident response must be meticulously documented – from the initial detection and triage to containment, eradication, and recovery. This documentation serves multiple purposes: it aids in post-incident analysis and lessons learned, provides evidence for potential legal or regulatory investigations, and forms the basis for reporting to oversight bodies and potentially to the public. Government agencies must have standardized templates and procedures for incident logging, evidence collection, and report generation, ensuring consistency and completeness. The reliance on public funds and the inherent trust placed in government by citizens demand a high level of transparency and rigor in these processes.

Finally, the long-term resilience of public sector ICS depends on a continuous cycle of planning, training, and improvement. Incident response plans are not static documents; they must be living blueprints that are regularly reviewed, updated, and tested. This includes conducting regular tabletop exercises, simulations, and full-scale drills that involve all relevant agencies and stakeholders. These exercises should incorporate realistic scenarios that reflect the current threat landscape and the specific vulnerabilities of the government's ICS assets. The lessons learned from these exercises, as well as from actual incidents, must be systematically fed back into the planning process, leading to ongoing enhancements in capabilities, protocols, and inter-agency coordination. For government agencies, maintaining a robust and adaptive ICS incident response capability is not merely a technical requirement but a fundamental aspect of ensuring national security, public safety, and the continued functioning of essential public services.

The interconnected nature of modern digital infrastructure means that cyber incidents are rarely confined to a single geographic location or organizational boundary. When an Industrial Control System (ICS) incident occurs, its tendrils can quickly extend across national borders, involving multiple jurisdictions, diverse legal frameworks, and varying levels of technical expertise. This inherent global and cross-border dimension introduces a profound layer of complexity to incident response efforts, demanding a coordinated, harmonized, and often unprecedented level of international collaboration. The challenge lies not only in technically containing and eradicating a threat that may have originated in one country and impacted systems in another but also in navigating the intricate web of international law, diplomatic relations, and diverse operational capabilities.

One of the most significant hurdles in global cyber incident response is the divergence of legal and regulatory frameworks. Each nation possesses its own set of laws governing data privacy, evidence collection, cybercrime prosecution, and critical infrastructure protection. For instance, what might be considered legally permissible data access or seizure in one country could be a severe violation of privacy laws in another. This disparity can create critical delays and even prevent essential investigative steps from being taken, as incident response teams must ensure compliance with the laws of every jurisdiction involved. The principle of territoriality, a cornerstone of most legal systems, means that authorities in one nation have limited jurisdiction within another. Consequently, obtaining evidence, issuing arrest warrants, or demanding cooperation from entities located in a foreign country often requires navigating complex mutual legal assistance treaties (MLATs) and diplomatic channels, processes that can be exceedingly slow and bureaucratic, especially during a rapidly evolving cyber crisis.

Consider a hypothetical scenario where a sophisticated cyberattack targets the control systems of an international pipeline. The attack might originate from a server in Country A, propagate through a compromised network in Country B, and ultimately impact the operational technology (OT) within critical infrastructure facilities located in Country C. Incident response teams in Country C would need to quickly assess the damage and initiate containment measures. However, to fully understand the attack vector, identify the perpetrators, and prevent future occurrences, they would likely require access to logs and forensic data residing on systems in Countries A and B. The legal hurdles in obtaining this information are substantial. Country A might have strict data localization laws that prevent its citizens or companies from sharing data with foreign entities without specific legal authorization. Country B might have different rules regarding the admissibility of digital evidence in court. Without pre-established agreements or swift diplomatic intervention, the investigation could be severely hampered, allowing the threat actors to escape detection or prepare for their next offensive.

To address these challenges, robust mechanisms for international collaboration are not merely beneficial; they are indispensable. The development and adoption of standardized frameworks and protocols for cyber incident response are crucial. International organizations such as the International Telecommunication Union (ITU), INTERPOL, and Europol have been instrumental in fostering dialogue and developing guidelines for cross-border cyber investigations. These bodies often facilitate information sharing between national Computer Emergency Response Teams (CERTs) or Computer Security Incident Response Teams (CSIRTs). These national CERTs act as vital nodes in the global network of cyber defense, serving as primary points of contact for reporting and responding to cybersecurity incidents. When a cross-border incident occurs, the ability of these CERTs to communicate effectively, share threat intelligence, and coordinate response actions is paramount.

However, effective information sharing goes beyond mere communication channels. It requires a degree of trust and a shared understanding of operational and technical realities. This is where principles of international cooperation, often enshrined in formal treaties or informal agreements, become critical. Initiatives like the Budapest Convention on Cybercrime, though primarily focused on criminalizing certain cyber offenses and establishing mutual legal assistance frameworks, lay a foundation for international cooperation. Nevertheless, the rapid evolution of cyber threats, particularly those targeting ICS, often outpaces the ratification and implementation of such treaties. Therefore, proactive measures, such as joint cybersecurity exercises involving multiple nations, are essential for building relationships, testing communication protocols, and identifying potential points of friction before a real crisis erupts. These exercises can simulate realistic cross-border attack scenarios, allowing participants to practice joint investigation techniques, understand each other's capabilities and limitations, and refine their response strategies in a controlled environment.

Harmonizing communication protocols is another critical aspect of global incident response. Different countries may use different terminology, reporting structures, and threat intelligence formats. A common language, both figuratively and literally, is needed. This involves developing shared lexicons for describing cyber threats, establishing standardized reporting templates for incident details, and agreeing on secure communication platforms that can be used by multiple national entities. The Global Forum on Cyber Expertise (GFCE), for example, aims to bring together various stakeholders to build cyber capacity and foster international cooperation, including efforts to harmonize approaches to incident response. The ability to share actionable intelligence rapidly and accurately, without the need for extensive translation or reformatting, can significantly shorten the time to detection, containment, and eradication of a cyber threat.

Furthermore, time zone differences present a practical challenge in coordinating response efforts across continents. An incident detected in Asia during its business hours might require immediate attention from teams in Europe or North America who are asleep. This necessitates establishing 24/7 operational capabilities and clear hand-off procedures between teams in different time zones. Incident response plans must account for this continuous operational requirement, ensuring that critical information is passed along seamlessly and that decisions can be made promptly regardless of the hour. This might involve the use of shared incident management platforms that provide a common operational picture accessible to all involved parties, regardless of their location.

The role of international organizations and alliances in fostering this cross-border cooperation cannot be overstated. Organizations like NATO, for example, have recognized the growing threat of cyberattacks against critical infrastructure and have developed frameworks for collective defense in cyberspace, including protocols for incident response and information sharing among member states. Similarly, regional bodies like ASEAN have initiatives focused on enhancing cybersecurity cooperation within their respective regions. These multilateral efforts are vital for building a collective defense posture against threats that do not respect national boundaries. They provide platforms for sharing best practices, conducting joint training, and developing common policies that can facilitate more effective cross-border incident response.

The growing sophistication of cyber adversaries, including state-sponsored groups and organized criminal syndicates, further underscores the need for international coordination. These actors often operate with significant resources and a deep understanding of geopolitical dynamics, exploiting the seams between national jurisdictions. A fragmented or uncoordinated response from individual nations can provide these adversaries with opportunities to evade capture, continue their operations, or even escalate their attacks. Therefore, a unified front, characterized by seamless information exchange, mutual legal assistance, and joint operational planning, is essential to effectively counter such threats.

When dealing with ICS specifically, the stakes are often higher due to the potential for physical consequences. An attack on a critical power grid, a water treatment facility, or a transportation network can have immediate and devastating impacts on public safety and economic stability. This shared vulnerability creates a powerful incentive for nations to cooperate on cybersecurity matters. However, national security concerns and the desire to protect sensitive technological capabilities can sometimes act as barriers to full transparency. Finding the right balance between sharing information to facilitate a collective response and protecting national interests is a delicate diplomatic challenge.

To achieve truly effective global and cross-border ICS incident response, several key elements need to be prioritized:

Firstly, **formalizing information-sharing agreements** beyond general memorandums of understanding. These agreements should specify the types of information that can be shared, the conditions under which it can be shared, and the legal protections afforded to the entities sharing the information. This could include agreements on the sharing of threat intelligence, vulnerability data, and forensic information, with clear guidelines on anonymization and classification.

Secondly, **developing and regularly exercising common operational procedures**. This involves joint training exercises that simulate various cross-border ICS attack scenarios. These exercises should not only test technical response capabilities but also the efficacy of communication channels, decision-making processes, and legal coordination mechanisms. Lessons learned from these exercises must be systematically incorporated into national and international response plans.

Thirdly, **harmonizing legal frameworks where possible**, or at least establishing clear protocols for how differing legal requirements will be managed during an incident. This could involve creating specific inter-jurisdictional agreements for cybercrime investigations or establishing dedicated liaison officers within national CERTs who specialize in international legal cooperation.

Fourthly, **leveraging technological solutions** that facilitate secure and efficient cross-border collaboration. This includes secure communication platforms, shared threat intelligence databases, and common incident management systems that provide a unified view of an evolving incident.

Finally, **fostering a culture of trust and shared responsibility** among nations. Cybersecurity is a shared global challenge, and recognizing this interdependence is crucial. This involves moving beyond a purely nationalistic approach to security and embracing a more cooperative and collaborative model.

The global nature of cyber threats, especially concerning ICS, necessitates a paradigm shift in how incident response is conceptualized and executed. It demands that nations move beyond their individualistic approaches and embrace a unified, coordinated, and collaborative strategy. By addressing the complexities of differing legal jurisdictions, harmonizing communication protocols, and fostering genuine international trust and cooperation, the global community can build a more resilient defense against the pervasive and evolving threat of cyberattacks on critical industrial control systems. The interconnectedness of our world means that a cyber incident anywhere is a potential threat everywhere, and only through a united global effort can we hope to effectively defend our interconnected digital infrastructure.

The increasing sophistication and frequency of cyber threats targeting Industrial Control Systems (ICS) necessitate a paradigm shift from reactive incident response to proactive, integrated resilience planning. While cybersecurity incident response focuses on detecting, containing, and eradicating threats, its effectiveness is significantly amplified when nested within a comprehensive framework that includes Business Continuity (BC) and Disaster Recovery (DR) planning. This subsection delves into the critical integration of ICS cybersecurity incident response with these broader organizational resilience strategies, underscoring the necessity of a unified approach to ensure operational sustainability and swift recovery in the face of disruptive events.

The essence of Business Continuity Planning (BCP) is to ensure that an organization can continue to deliver its products or services at acceptable predefined levels following a disruptive incident. Disaster Recovery (DR) planning, on the other hand, is a subset of BCP, specifically focused on the restoration of IT infrastructure and operations after a disaster. When applied to ICS environments, these disciplines are not merely supplementary; they are fundamental to safeguarding critical infrastructure and the essential services it provides. A cyberattack on an ICS can very easily escalate from a cybersecurity incident to a business disruption, potentially leading to a full-blown disaster. Therefore, the incident response plan for ICS must be inextricably linked with the organization's BCP and DR strategies. This integration ensures that the actions taken during a cyber incident are not isolated technical maneuvers but are aligned with the overarching goal of maintaining business operations and restoring them efficiently.

Consider an organization operating a network of water treatment facilities. A successful cyberattack could compromise the supervisory control and data acquisition (SCADA) systems that manage water purification, distribution, and monitoring. The immediate cybersecurity incident response would involve identifying the intrusion, isolating affected systems, and eradicating the malware. However, the ripple effects of such an attack extend far beyond the IT or OT domain. If the purification process is halted or compromised, it directly impacts the delivery of a critical public service. This is where the integration with BCP becomes vital. The BCP would have already identified the criticality of water purification and distribution services, established acceptable downtime thresholds, and outlined alternative operational procedures or manual overrides if automated systems fail. The DR plan would detail the steps required to restore the SCADA systems, including data backups, system configurations, and hardware replacement, if necessary.

The integration process begins with a thorough risk assessment that encompasses not only cybersecurity threats but also the potential business impacts of such threats. This involves identifying critical ICS functions, understanding their dependencies, and quantifying the potential financial, operational, reputational, and safety consequences of their disruption. For instance, a disruption to a manufacturing plant's production line due to a ransomware attack on its programmable logic controllers (PLCs) could lead to significant financial losses due to production downtime, missed delivery deadlines, and potential contractual penalties. The BCP would articulate the acceptable downtime for this production line, the strategies for minimizing losses (e.g., shifting production to another facility, utilizing manual processes), and the procedures for expediting the recovery of the affected systems.

A key element in this integration is the establishment of clear communication channels and protocols between the cybersecurity incident response team, the business continuity management team, and the disaster recovery team. During a cyber incident affecting ICS, it is imperative that the technical teams (cybersecurity) can quickly and accurately communicate the nature, scope, and potential impact of the incident to the business continuity managers. This enables informed decision-making regarding the activation of BCP and DR plans. Conversely, the BCP and DR teams need to provide the cybersecurity team with information on critical business priorities, acceptable recovery time objectives (RTOs), and recovery point objectives (RPOs) for different systems. This feedback loop ensures that the incident response efforts are prioritized in a way that aligns with the organization's overall resilience objectives.

For example, if a cybersecurity incident is detected within the control systems of an electricity grid, the immediate response focuses on isolating the compromised segments and preventing further spread. The business continuity implications are immense, as a widespread outage can cripple an entire region. The BCP would dictate the load shedding procedures, communication protocols with emergency services and the public, and the escalation of response to higher authorities. The DR plan would then come into play to restore the control systems. This might involve invoking redundant systems, restoring from secure backups, and conducting rigorous testing to ensure the integrity and security of the restored systems before bringing them back online. The incident response team's actions must be synchronized with these broader plans to ensure a cohesive and effective response that minimizes public impact.

The development of playbooks that bridge cybersecurity incident response with BCP/DR is a practical way to operationalize this integration. These playbooks should outline specific scenarios, such as a ransomware attack on critical ICS components, and detail the coordinated actions required from each team. For instance, a playbook for a ransomware attack on a SCADA system might specify:

1. **Detection and Initial Triage (Cybersecurity Team):** Identify the ransomware, its type, and the affected ICS components.

2. **Impact Assessment (Cybersecurity & Business Continuity Teams):** Determine the extent of system compromise and the immediate operational impact on critical services.

3. **Decision Point (Incident Management Team):** Based on the impact assessment, decide whether to activate specific BCP/DR procedures. This decision should consider factors like the criticality of the affected service, the estimated recovery time, and the availability of workarounds.

4. **Activation of BCP (Business Continuity Team):** If deemed necessary, initiate predefined business continuity measures, such as reverting to manual operations, engaging backup power, or informing stakeholders.

5. **Containment and Eradication (Cybersecurity Team):** Isolate affected systems, prevent lateral movement, and begin the process of removing the ransomware.

6. **Recovery and Restoration (Cybersecurity & Disaster Recovery Teams):** Rebuild or restore affected ICS components from clean backups, apply necessary patches, and reconfigure systems. This phase must be carefully managed to avoid reintroducing the threat.

7. **Validation and Testing (Cybersecurity & Operations Teams):** Rigorously test the restored systems to ensure functionality, integrity, and security before reconnecting them to the operational network.

8. **Resumption of Operations (Operations & Business Continuity Teams):** Gradually bring affected services back online, closely monitoring performance and security.

9. **Post-Incident Review (All Teams):** Conduct a thorough review of the incident response, BCP activation, and DR execution to identify lessons learned and update plans and procedures.

Such playbooks are most effective when developed collaboratively by all involved parties and regularly tested through tabletop exercises and simulated drills. These exercises are invaluable for identifying gaps in coordination, clarifying roles and responsibilities, and building muscle memory for effective cross-functional response. They also provide an opportunity to test the resilience of backup systems, the effectiveness of data recovery processes, and the communication infrastructure.

Furthermore, the integration extends to the technical architecture and security controls. For example, ensuring that robust, immutable backups of ICS configurations and operational data are maintained is a cornerstone of both DR and effective incident response. These backups must be stored securely, ideally offline or in a segregated environment, to prevent them from being compromised by the same attack that affects the primary systems. Similarly, having redundant control systems or fail-safe mechanisms can facilitate a smoother transition during an incident and a faster recovery. The cybersecurity measures implemented should not impede the ability to recover critical functions. This often involves a delicate balance between security hardening and operational flexibility.

The concept of "defense in depth" is crucial here. It means implementing multiple layers of security controls, both technical and procedural. When it comes to ICS, this involves network segmentation, access control, intrusion detection and prevention systems, and robust patching strategies. However, the BCP and DR plans should also incorporate redundancy and alternative operational capabilities. If one layer of defense fails, or if a system is compromised to the point of requiring extensive recovery, the organization must have other means to maintain essential operations. This might include manual control processes, backup equipment, or even temporarily ceasing non-critical operations to focus resources on restoring core functions.

The financial implications of cyber incidents on ICS are significant, and BCP/DR planning plays a crucial role in mitigating these costs. By having well-defined recovery strategies, organizations can minimize downtime, reduce the potential for extended operational disruption, and avoid the high costs associated with emergency repairs or prolonged service outages. A proactive approach, integrating cybersecurity incident response with BCP and DR, is far more cost-effective than a reactive one. The investment in robust planning and preparedness can prevent catastrophic financial losses and ensure the long-term viability of the organization.

Consider the pharmaceutical industry, where the disruption of manufacturing processes due to a cyberattack can have severe consequences, including drug shortages and significant financial losses. A well-integrated BCP/DR and incident response plan would ensure that in the event of a cyber incident affecting manufacturing control systems, the organization can:

Quickly assess the impact on production schedules and critical drug supplies.

Activate alternative production lines or facilities if available.

Implement manual overrides for certain processes where safe and feasible.

Expedite the recovery of compromised systems using secure, tested backups.

Maintain clear communication with regulatory bodies and supply chain partners.

This coordinated approach not only minimizes the immediate damage but also ensures the continuity of supply for essential medicines, thereby protecting public health.

The human element is also a critical aspect of this integration. Incident response teams, BCP teams, and DR teams need to be well-trained and understand their roles within the broader resilience framework. Regular training and cross-training exercises help ensure that individuals are familiar with the procedures and can execute their responsibilities effectively under pressure. This also fosters a culture of shared responsibility for organizational resilience, where cybersecurity is seen not just as an IT issue but as a fundamental aspect of business operations.

The evolving threat landscape, particularly the increasing convergence of IT and OT security concerns, further emphasizes the need for this holistic approach. Cyberattacks are no longer solely aimed at data theft or financial gain; they are increasingly targeting the operational capabilities of critical infrastructure, with the potential for significant physical impact. Therefore, the incident response plans must be designed to address these potential physical consequences, and BCP/DR strategies must be robust enough to manage disruptions that could have far-reaching societal implications.

In summary, the seamless integration of ICS cybersecurity incident response with business continuity and disaster recovery planning is not an option but a necessity for organizations operating critical infrastructure or relying on complex industrial processes. This integration ensures that the organization is not only prepared to defend against cyber threats but also capable of maintaining essential functions, minimizing disruption, and achieving swift recovery in the aftermath of an incident. By fostering collaboration between technical security teams, business continuity managers, and disaster recovery specialists, and by embedding these efforts within comprehensive, tested plans and playbooks, organizations can build a truly resilient operational environment capable of withstanding the ever-growing challenges of the modern digital and industrial landscape. This unified approach moves beyond simply responding to incidents to proactively ensuring the sustained operation and long-term viability of critical services and industrial processes in an increasingly interconnected and unpredictable world.

The effectiveness of any implemented framework, including the sophisticated ICS cybersecurity and resilience strategies discussed previously, hinges on our ability to measure its performance. Without robust metrics and Key Performance Indicators (KPIs), an organization is effectively flying blind, unable to ascertain whether its investments are yielding the desired outcomes or if critical gaps remain unaddressed. Developing a comprehensive set of metrics allows for an objective assessment of preparedness, responsiveness, and recovery capabilities. This objective evaluation is not merely an academic exercise; it is a vital component of continuous improvement, enabling organizations to refine their strategies, optimize resource allocation, and ultimately enhance their overall resilience against the ever-evolving threat landscape.

A fundamental aspect of measuring ICS incident response effectiveness lies in the quantification of **response times**. This encompasses several critical stages. Firstly, **detection time** – the duration from the initial occurrence of a security event or anomaly to its formal identification by the monitoring systems or personnel. A shorter detection time is paramount, as it directly influences the window of opportunity for an adversary to cause harm. This metric should be tracked for different types of incidents, from subtle policy violations to overt malicious activity. Secondly, **alert to triage time** – the interval between an alert being generated and an initial assessment of its validity and severity being completed by the security operations center (SOC) or designated response team. Delays here can lead to alert fatigue or allow genuine threats to mature. Thirdly, **triage to containment time** – the period from the initial triage to the successful isolation of the compromised system(s) or network segment. This is a critical phase where the spread of an attack is halted. It's important to distinguish between quick, automated containment actions and more complex, manual interventions that might be required for deeply embedded threats within an ICS environment. Finally, **containment to eradication/recovery time** – the duration from achieving containment to the complete removal of the threat and the restoration of affected systems to a secure, operational state. Each of these time-based metrics provides a granular view of the incident response lifecycle and highlights potential bottlenecks. For instance, a consistently long triage to containment time might indicate a need for improved network segmentation, more effective intrusion detection signatures, or enhanced automation capabilities within the SOC. Conversely, a rapid containment but an excessively long eradication phase could point to challenges in forensic analysis within the OT environment or difficulties in safely restoring complex ICS components.

Beyond mere speed, the **success rate of containment efforts** is a crucial KPI. This can be measured by tracking the percentage of incidents where the threat was successfully confined to the initially affected systems or segments without lateral movement to other critical ICS assets or the broader enterprise IT network. A low containment success rate suggests that the organization's network architecture, security policies, or response procedures are insufficient to prevent an adversary from expanding their reach. This metric should be analyzed in conjunction with the types of threats encountered; for example, success rates might differ significantly when dealing with a network worm versus a targeted advanced persistent threat (APT). Further refinement can involve categorizing containment successes based on the method employed – fully automated containment versus requiring significant manual intervention. This can reveal the maturity of automated response playbooks and the effectiveness of pre-defined containment strategies. Moreover, assessing the **scope of compromise** at the point of containment is vital. This can be quantified by the number of affected devices, the criticality of those devices, or the volume of data potentially exfiltrated or corrupted. A reduction in these figures over time, for similar types of incidents, would indicate an improvement in containment effectiveness.

The **impact reduction** achieved through incident response is perhaps the most business-relevant metric. This requires a careful mapping of cybersecurity incidents to their potential business consequences. For ICS, this means understanding the direct correlation between a cyber event and operational disruption, safety incidents, environmental damage, or financial losses. KPIs here could include: **Reduction in downtime duration** for critical processes, measured by comparing the actual downtime against predefined acceptable recovery time objectives (RTOs). This metric directly links cybersecurity response to business continuity. For example, if a ransomware attack on a water treatment plant's SCADA system would have traditionally led to 48 hours of operational disruption, but through effective response and recovery, it was limited to 12 hours, this represents a significant positive impact reduction. Another key indicator is the **reduction in the severity of operational impacts**. This can be assessed by quantifying the number of critical functions that were affected, the degree to which they were degraded, or the number of end-users or customers impacted. For an electricity grid operator, a successful containment and rapid recovery might mean preventing a widespread blackout, limiting the impact to localized, short-term outages. **Financial impact mitigation** is also a critical measure. This involves quantifying the avoided costs associated with downtime, lost production, emergency repairs, regulatory fines, reputational damage, and legal liabilities. While challenging to calculate precisely, estimates based on historical data and business impact analyses can provide a valuable benchmark. For instance, an organization might estimate that a successful ransomware attack without effective response could cost $10 million in lost revenue and recovery efforts, but a swift and efficient response limited the actual loss to $1 million. This difference of $9 million represents the value of effective incident response.

Resource utilization during an incident response provides insights into the efficiency of the deployed teams and tools. This can be measured by: **Personnel hours dedicated to incident response**, broken down by team (e.g., SOC analysts, incident responders, OT specialists, IT support, legal counsel). An increase in hours for certain roles might indicate a need for additional staffing or specialized training. Tracking the percentage of time spent on different phases of response (detection, analysis, containment, recovery) can also highlight areas where teams are spending disproportionate amounts of time, potentially indicating inefficiencies. **Tool and technology usage**, such as the volume of data analyzed by security information and event management (SIEM) systems, the number of endpoints scanned by forensic tools, or the frequency of communication channel usage. Anomalies in tool usage – for example, very high SIEM processing loads without corresponding incident detections – might suggest tuning issues or misconfigurations. **Cost of incident response**, including overtime pay, third-party forensic services, emergency hardware/software purchases, and travel expenses. Comparing these costs against the estimated business impact avoided provides a measure of return on investment for the incident response program. A high cost of response for a minor incident could indicate inefficiencies, while a low cost for a major incident might suggest effective preparedness and automation.

Ultimately, the **overall cost-efficiency and return on investment (ROI)** of the ICS cybersecurity framework can be evaluated by synthesizing the previous metrics. This involves a holistic view of the resources invested in preparedness, detection, response, and recovery against the quantifiable benefits realized in terms of reduced operational disruption, mitigated financial losses, and preserved business reputation. A simplified ROI calculation could involve: ROI = (Quantifiable Benefits - Total Cost of Incident Response Program) / Total Cost of Incident Response Program. Quantifiable benefits would include estimated losses averted from successful prevention of breaches, minimized downtime during incidents, and reduced recovery costs due to efficient response. The total cost of the incident response program would encompass salaries, training, technology investments, and retainers for external services. While obtaining precise figures for all components can be challenging, a consistent trend of increasing ROI over time, or achieving a positive ROI, demonstrates the economic value of a well-implemented and effectively measured ICS security program. Furthermore, comparing the cost of the incident response program against the potential maximum loss from a catastrophic event can highlight the proactive value proposition. If the potential loss is $100 million, and the annual cost of a robust incident response program is $1 million, the investment is clearly justifiable from a risk management perspective.

To effectively capture and analyze these metrics, organizations must invest in appropriate tooling and establish clear processes for data collection and reporting. This includes ensuring that logging mechanisms are enabled across critical IT and OT assets, that data retention policies are adequate for forensic analysis, and that standardized incident reporting templates are utilized. Automated data collection and dashboarding capabilities are essential for providing real-time visibility into the performance of the incident response program. Furthermore, a regular cadence for reviewing these metrics – perhaps quarterly or semi-annually – is crucial. This review process should involve key stakeholders from IT, OT, cybersecurity, and business leadership to discuss performance trends, identify areas for improvement, and allocate resources accordingly. The insights derived from these metrics are not static; they should inform and drive continuous improvement initiatives, leading to a more robust, responsive, and resilient ICS environment. The journey of measuring effectiveness is an ongoing cycle of data collection, analysis, interpretation, and action, ensuring that the organization is not just reacting to threats but proactively building a sustainable defense against them.

The integration of these metrics into a formal performance management framework allows for objective tracking of progress and facilitates strategic decision-making. For example, if the average **time to detect** a specific type of advanced persistent threat (APT) remains consistently high despite multiple efforts to improve endpoint detection and response (EDR) capabilities, it signals a need to re-evaluate the detection strategy. This might involve exploring new threat intelligence feeds, investing in more sophisticated analytics, or enhancing the training of SOC analysts in recognizing subtle indicators of compromise within the OT environment. Similarly, if the **containment success rate** for ransomware attacks is declining, it could indicate that threat actors are evolving their techniques to bypass existing controls, necessitating an update to containment playbooks and potentially the deployment of new defensive technologies.

Moreover, the metrics should be contextualized against industry benchmarks where available. While the unique nature of ICS environments often makes direct comparisons difficult, understanding how an organization's response times or impact mitigation efforts stack up against peers can provide valuable perspective. This is particularly relevant for critical infrastructure sectors where regulatory bodies may impose specific performance expectations or reporting requirements. Companies can leverage threat intelligence reports and cybersecurity maturity models to set realistic targets for their KPIs.

The process of defining and tracking these metrics also plays a critical role in fostering a culture of accountability and continuous improvement. When teams understand that their performance is being measured against defined objectives, they are more likely to prioritize and optimize their efforts. This data-driven approach moves incident response from being a perceived cost center to a demonstrable value driver for the organization. For instance, a well-articulated report showing how effective incident response averted significant financial losses due to a simulated phishing attack that targeted OT personnel can provide a compelling business case for further investment in security awareness training and technical controls.

It is imperative that the metrics chosen are not only measurable but also actionable. A metric that cannot inform a decision or drive a change in behavior is of limited practical value. For example, simply tracking the total number of security alerts generated by a system without analyzing their false positive rate or their correlation with actual incidents provides little insight. Instead, focusing on metrics like the **rate of actionable alerts** (i.e., alerts that require human investigation and are confirmed as legitimate security events) allows for a more precise assessment of the effectiveness of detection rules and the efficiency of the alert management process.

Furthermore, the evolution of ICS environments, with their increasing connectivity and convergence with IT, necessitates a continuous review and adaptation of these metrics. As new technologies are adopted, such as IoT devices or cloud-based control systems, the potential attack vectors and operational impacts change, requiring a corresponding adjustment in the measurement framework. For instance, if an organization begins leveraging cloud services for data analytics from its ICS, new metrics related to cloud security incident response times and data integrity within the cloud environment would need to be incorporated.

In summary, establishing a comprehensive system for measuring the effectiveness of ICS implementation, particularly concerning incident response and resilience, is a non-negotiable requirement for modern operational technology security. By meticulously tracking metrics such as response times, containment success rates, impact reduction, resource utilization, and overall cost-efficiency, organizations gain the objective insights necessary to validate their strategies, identify weaknesses, and drive continuous improvement. This data-informed approach ensures that investments in cybersecurity are optimized, operational resilience is demonstrably enhanced, and the organization is better positioned to withstand the sophisticated and persistent threats that target critical industrial control systems. The ability to quantify performance transforms incident response from a reactive necessity into a proactive, value-generating capability.

The aftermath of an incident, whether it's a minor security event or a full-blown cyber-attack targeting the Industrial Control Systems (ICS), presents a critical juncture for organizational learning and strategic refinement. Merely restoring operations and patching vulnerabilities is insufficient; a comprehensive and systematic approach to post-incident analysis is paramount. This process transforms a negative event into a catalyst for enhancing future security postures.

The objective is not to assign blame but to dissect the incident meticulously, understanding precisely what transpired, how the response unfolded, and what lessons can be extracted to strengthen defenses, improve response capabilities, and ultimately bolster the overall resilience of the ICS environment.

Conducting a post-incident analysis (PIA), often referred to as a "lessons learned" session, requires a structured methodology to ensure all relevant aspects are covered. It begins immediately after the incident has been contained and recovery efforts are well underway, or ideally, once full operational status has been achieved. The core of the PIA is a deep dive into the entire incident lifecycle, starting from the initial detection. This involves reconstructing the timeline of events with as much accuracy as possible. Key questions to address include: When was the first indication of an anomaly observed? What systems or logs provided this initial alert? Who was the first responder, and what were their immediate actions? This phase is critical for understanding the efficacy of existing monitoring and detection mechanisms. Were the alerts timely and relevant, or were they buried in noise? Was the alert signature or behavioral anomaly detection tuned appropriately for the ICS environment, or did it trigger excessively high false positive rates that could have masked the real threat? Furthermore, examining the chain of alerts leading up to the confirmed incident can reveal precursor activities that might have been missed or misinterpreted. This meticulous reconstruction helps identify weaknesses in visibility and the ability to discern genuine threats from benign events, a particularly challenging aspect in the often noisy and dynamic world of industrial operations.

Following detection, the analysis must scrutinize the **alerting and notification procedures**. How quickly was the relevant security team notified? Was the notification process clear, direct, and did it reach the appropriate personnel without delay? In complex ICS environments, this often involves multiple communication channels and stakeholders, including IT security, OT engineering, plant management, and potentially external cybersecurity experts. The effectiveness of these communication pathways is a frequent area for improvement. Were there any breakdowns in communication? Did the information conveyed accurately reflect the severity and nature of the incident? Were contact lists up-to-date? The analysis should identify any communication bottlenecks or failures that could have prolonged response times or led to misinformed decisions. For instance, if an alert was generated on an OT network segment but the notification failed to reach the on-call OT engineer for several hours due to an outdated contact list or a poorly configured alert forwarding system, this represents a significant gap in the response process. This examination extends to the clarity and completeness of the initial incident reports and the subsequent updates provided to stakeholders. A well-documented and efficiently communicated incident status is crucial for coordinated action and stakeholder confidence.

The **investigation and analysis phase** is another cornerstone of the PIA. This involves examining the evidence collected to understand the root cause, the scope of compromise, the attack vector, and the adversary's tactics, techniques, and procedures (TTPs). For ICS, this requires specialized forensic capabilities that respect the unique protocols, hardware, and operational constraints of OT environments. The analysis should delve into: What specific vulnerabilities were exploited? Were they known vulnerabilities, or zero-days? Were they in the control system software, hardware, network devices, or supporting IT infrastructure? How did the adversary gain initial access? Was it through a phishing email, a compromised remote access point, a vulnerable web interface, or a supply chain compromise? The PIA should also meticulously document the lateral movement of the threat within the ICS network. Where did the attacker go after the initial compromise? What systems did they interact with? What data did they access or modify? Understanding the TTPs employed by the attacker is invaluable for improving defensive strategies, updating threat intelligence, and refining detection rules. This often involves correlating logs from various sources, including network intrusion detection systems (NIDS), endpoint detection and response (EDR) solutions in the IT domain, historians, programmable logic controllers (PLCs), human-machine interfaces (HMIs), and security cameras, if applicable and accessible. The challenges of obtaining and preserving forensically sound evidence from operational systems, which may have limited logging capabilities or be difficult to take offline, must be acknowledged and addressed within the PIA. This might involve leveraging specialized OT forensic tools or techniques that minimize disruption.

The **containment, eradication, and recovery procedures** are also subject to rigorous examination. During containment, how effective were the actions taken to prevent further damage or spread? Were the correct systems isolated? Were there any unintended consequences of the containment actions, such as disrupting critical operations beyond what was necessary? The PIA should assess the speed and accuracy of containment. For example, if a critical operational process was shut down as a precautionary measure but was later found to be unaffected by the incident, this represents an opportunity to refine containment playbooks to be more targeted and less disruptive. Eradication involves removing the threat completely. Was the threat fully removed from all affected systems? Were all backdoors closed? Were any compromised credentials reset? Recovery is the process of restoring systems to full operational status. Were the recovery procedures well-defined and tested? How long did it take to restore full functionality? Were the restored systems verified for integrity and security? The PIA should also look at the impact of the incident on operations. Were there any unplanned downtime events? How long did they last? What was the actual production loss or service disruption? Were safety procedures maintained throughout the incident response? Quantifying these impacts, even with estimates, provides a crucial link between cybersecurity and operational outcomes. This phase often reveals the importance of having robust backup and restore capabilities, and importantly, regularly testing these capabilities in a simulated environment that mirrors the complexity of the actual ICS.

Beyond the technical aspects, the PIA must also evaluate the **effectiveness of the incident response team and its management**. This includes assessing the team's composition, skill sets, training, and coordination. Were the right people involved? Did they have the necessary expertise in both IT security and OT operations? Was there a clear command structure and decision-making authority? How effective was the collaboration between IT and OT teams, which often operate with different priorities and cultures? The PIA should identify any skill gaps, training needs, or structural issues within the response team. This could range from needing more specialized OT cybersecurity training for IT personnel to requiring clearer delegation of authority for OT engineers to implement critical containment actions. Furthermore, the PIA should examine the decision-making processes during the incident. Were decisions made based on available information, or were they delayed due to uncertainty or lack of consensus? The availability and effectiveness of **incident response playbooks and procedures** are also scrutinized. Were the playbooks followed? Were they adequate for the incident encountered? Were they up-to-date and accessible? Often, playbooks are developed for common scenarios, but real-world incidents can present unique challenges that strain or break these predefined procedures. This highlights the need for playbooks that are flexible and adaptable, and for response teams that are empowered to deviate from the script when necessary, provided such deviations are documented and justified.

The conclusion of the PIA should result in a comprehensive report that not only documents what happened but also outlines concrete, actionable recommendations for improvement. These recommendations should be prioritized based on their potential impact and feasibility. They might include updating security policies, enhancing network segmentation, deploying new security technologies, improving logging capabilities, conducting additional training, revising incident response plans, or establishing new communication protocols. Crucially, these recommendations must be assigned owners and deadlines, ensuring accountability and driving implementation. The follow-up on these recommendations is as important as their generation. A system should be in place to track their progress and verify their effectiveness. This iterative process of analysis, recommendation, implementation, and verification forms the bedrock of **continuous improvement** in ICS cybersecurity and resilience.

Complementary to the post-incident analysis, regular **audits of the ICS framework** are indispensable. While a PIA focuses on a specific event, audits provide a systematic, ongoing assessment of the entire security program's health, compliance, and effectiveness. These audits should be conducted periodically, independent of specific incidents, and cover a broad spectrum of security controls, policies, and procedures. The primary goal of an audit is to verify that the implemented security measures are functioning as intended and that the organization is adhering to its own security policies and relevant regulatory requirements.

Audits can take various forms, including internal audits conducted by dedicated internal audit teams or external audits performed by third-party cybersecurity firms. The scope of an ICS security audit is extensive, encompassing not just the technical security controls but also the organizational and procedural aspects. Key areas of focus include:

Firstly, **Policy and Procedure Review**: Audits examine whether documented security policies and procedures are current, comprehensive, and effectively communicated to all relevant personnel. This includes reviewing access control policies, incident response plans, change management procedures, data backup and recovery policies, and employee security awareness training programs. The audit will verify that these policies are being consistently applied and that they align with the organization's risk appetite and regulatory obligations. For instance, an audit might discover that while an access control policy dictates the principle of least privilege, in practice, many privileged accounts have been granted broader access than necessary, increasing the attack surface.

Secondly, **Technical Control Effectiveness**: This involves an in-depth assessment of the deployed security technologies and configurations. For ICS environments, this could include firewalls and intrusion detection/prevention systems (IDS/IPS) at network perimeters and within segmentation zones, antivirus and endpoint protection solutions on workstations and servers, secure remote access solutions (e.g., VPNs with multi-factor authentication), data loss prevention (DLP) systems, security information and event management (SIEM) systems for log aggregation and analysis, and vulnerability management tools. The audit will verify that these controls are properly configured, actively monitored, and regularly updated. It will also assess their effectiveness in preventing, detecting, and responding to threats. For example, an audit might reveal that firewall rules have not been reviewed or updated in years, potentially allowing outdated or unnecessary communication paths to remain open, or that the SIEM is not configured to ingest logs from critical OT devices, thereby hindering comprehensive threat detection.

Thirdly, **Access Control and Identity Management**: A critical component of any security framework is ensuring that only authorized individuals have access to ICS resources, and that their access is appropriate for their roles. Audits will review user account provisioning and de-provisioning processes, password policies, the use of multi-factor authentication (MFA), role-based access control (RBAC) configurations, and the periodic review of user access privileges. In OT environments, this also extends to physical access controls for control rooms, server rooms, and critical equipment locations. The audit will aim to identify any instances of unauthorized access, excessive privileges, or weak authentication mechanisms. For example, an audit might uncover that dormant accounts have not been disabled, or that shared accounts are being used for critical operations, making it impossible to attribute actions to specific individuals.

Fourthly, **Vulnerability Management and Patching**: The proactive identification and remediation of vulnerabilities are fundamental to maintaining a strong security posture. Audits will assess the organization's vulnerability scanning programs, penetration testing activities, and its patch management process for both IT and OT systems. This includes evaluating the timeliness and effectiveness of patching, especially for critical vulnerabilities. In ICS, patching can be particularly complex due to the need to avoid operational disruptions and ensure compatibility with legacy systems. Audits will examine the organization's risk-based approach to vulnerability remediation, including the use of compensating controls when patching is not immediately feasible. For instance, an audit might find that critical vulnerabilities in OT components have been outstanding for months without adequate compensating controls in place, or that the patching process for OT systems is ad-hoc and lacks proper testing and rollback procedures.

Fifthly, **Security Awareness and Training**: Human factors remain a significant element in cybersecurity. Audits will evaluate the effectiveness of security awareness training programs for all employees, with particular attention to personnel who directly interact with or manage ICS. This includes assessing the frequency, content, and delivery methods of the training, as well as methods for measuring its impact. The audit will verify that employees understand their security responsibilities and are aware of common threats like phishing, social engineering, and malware. For OT personnel, specific training on the unique cybersecurity risks and procedures relevant to their roles is essential. The audit might reveal that training is superficial, not regularly updated, or not tailored to the specific risks faced by different job functions within the ICS environment.

Sixthly, **Incident Response Preparedness**: While PIAs follow incidents, audits proactively assess the readiness of the incident response program. This involves reviewing the incident response plan, conducting tabletop exercises and simulations, verifying the availability and functionality of incident response tools and resources, and ensuring that response teams are adequately trained and have clear roles and responsibilities. Audits can identify gaps in the plan, weaknesses in team coordination, or insufficient resources that could hinder an effective response during a real incident. For example, a tabletop exercise conducted as part of an audit might reveal that the OT and IT incident response teams have conflicting procedures for network isolation, or that critical communication tools are not readily available or functional.

Seventhly, **Compliance and Regulatory Adherence**: Many industries operating ICS are subject to specific regulatory frameworks (e.g., NERC CIP for the electric power sector, TSA directives for pipelines, NIST cybersecurity frameworks). Audits play a crucial role in verifying that the organization's ICS security program meets these mandated requirements. This involves reviewing documentation, interviewing personnel, and testing controls against the specific stipulations of relevant regulations. A failure to comply can result in significant penalties, reputational damage, and operational restrictions. The audit process helps to identify any compliance gaps well in advance of regulatory examinations.

The findings from these audits are critical for identifying deviations from established procedures, areas where security controls have weakened, and potential risks that may not have been apparent. The audit report should clearly articulate the identified findings, assess their risk level, and provide specific, actionable recommendations for remediation. Similar to PIAs, audit recommendations must be assigned owners, have clear timelines for implementation, and be tracked to ensure completion. This process creates a structured feedback loop, ensuring that the ICS security framework is not static but is continuously reviewed, validated, and strengthened in response to evolving threats and organizational changes.

By integrating both post-incident analyses and regular audits, organizations establish a powerful, cyclical mechanism for continuous improvement in their ICS cybersecurity and resilience. The PIA offers immediate, event-driven insights, allowing for rapid adjustments based on real-world occurrences. Audits, on the other hand, provide a broader, more systematic, and proactive view, ensuring that the overall security posture remains robust, compliant, and aligned with best practices. This dual approach is essential for navigating the complex and ever-changing landscape of industrial control system security, transforming potential threats into opportunities for enhanced operational safety and reliability.

Benchmarking against industry best practices serves as a critical compass for navigating the complex terrain of Industrial Control System (ICS) cybersecurity. It moves beyond internal introspection, offering an objective lens through which to evaluate the efficacy of an organization's incident response (IR) capabilities. This process of comparison is not about replicating what others do; rather, it is about understanding established benchmarks, identifying areas where performance may lag, and pinpointing opportunities for strategic enhancement. By aligning with recognized standards and best practices, organizations can systematically elevate their resilience, ensuring their defenses and response mechanisms are not only adequate for current threats but also adaptable to future challenges. This subsection aims to guide organizations in effectively leveraging benchmarking to achieve a higher state of security maturity for their ICS environments.

The initial and perhaps most crucial step in benchmarking is the identification of relevant industry best practices and standards. The landscape of cybersecurity frameworks is vast, but for ICS environments, certain standards offer particular relevance due to their focus on operational technology, critical infrastructure, and the unique challenges they present. The National Institute of Standards and Technology (NIST) Cybersecurity Framework (CSF) is a prime example. While not exclusively for ICS, its risk-based approach, comprehensive set of controls, and flexible implementation tiers make it highly adaptable. The CSF's five core functions – Identify, Protect, Detect, Respond, and Recover – provide a structured way to assess and improve an organization's cybersecurity risk management. Within the 'Respond' and 'Recover' functions, specific guidance on incident response planning, communication, analysis, and remediation can be directly applied to ICS scenarios. For instance, NIST SP 800-61, "Computer Security Incident Handling Guide," offers detailed procedures for incident handling that, with appropriate adaptation for OT constraints, can form the basis of an organization's incident response plan.

Beyond NIST, the International Organization for Standardization (ISO) provides globally recognized standards that are fundamental to cybersecurity management. ISO 27001, "Information Security Management Systems," establishes requirements for an information security management system (ISMS). While often perceived as IT-centric, its principles regarding risk assessment, policy development, control implementation, and continuous improvement are universally applicable. Annex A of ISO 27001 lists a comprehensive set of security controls, many of which have direct relevance to ICS security, such as access control, cryptography, physical security, and incident management. Furthermore, ISO 27035, "Information security incident management," offers a more detailed framework specifically for managing security incidents, providing guidance on incident response processes, roles, and responsibilities, which can be tailored for OT environments.

For organizations operating in specific critical infrastructure sectors, sector-specific regulations and frameworks are indispensable. For instance, the North American Electric Reliability Corporation (NERC) Critical Infrastructure Protection (CIP) standards are mandatory for the bulk electric system in North America and impose stringent security requirements on cyber assets, including those within ICS. These standards dictate requirements for identification, security management controls, electronic security perimeters, incident response, and recovery plans. Similarly, the Transportation Security Administration (TSA) has issued directives for pipeline and railroad cybersecurity, which include mandates for incident response planning and execution. Benchmarking against these regulatory requirements is not just good practice; it is a legal necessity.

Moreover, industry-specific consortia and working groups often develop best practices tailored to particular operational environments. For example, the ISA/IEC 62443 series of standards is specifically designed for Industrial Automation and Control Systems security. This series provides a robust framework for security in ICS, covering requirements for security program management, risk assessment, system design, and life cycle management.

Benchmarking against the principles and security levels (SLs) defined in IEC 62443 can provide a highly relevant and technical baseline for ICS security capabilities.

Once relevant benchmarks have been identified, the next crucial step is to assess the organization's current performance against these standards. This assessment should be thorough, objective, and involve key stakeholders from both IT and OT domains. A common approach is to conduct a gap analysis. This involves systematically reviewing the organization's existing incident response policies, procedures, technologies, and personnel against the requirements and recommendations of the chosen benchmarks. For example, if the benchmark (e.g., NIST SP 800-61) mandates a specific timeline for incident detection and notification, the organization must evaluate how its current detection systems and communication protocols measure up. Are alerts timely? Is the escalation process efficient? Are the correct personnel notified promptly and accurately? The gap analysis will highlight areas where the organization's capabilities fall short of the benchmarked standard.

To facilitate this assessment, organizations can leverage various tools and methodologies. Self-assessment questionnaires, based on the chosen frameworks, can be a starting point. These questionnaires guide teams through a series of questions designed to evaluate adherence to specific controls and practices. However, for a more robust evaluation, independent assessments are highly recommended. These can include:

Internal Audits: As discussed in the previous context, internal audit teams can be tasked with evaluating ICS security and incident response capabilities against selected standards. This requires that the internal audit team possesses adequate expertise in both cybersecurity and ICS environments.

External Audits and Consultancies: Engaging third-party cybersecurity firms specializing in ICS security can provide an unbiased and expert perspective. These firms often have extensive experience with various benchmarks and can offer detailed assessments, identify subtle gaps, and provide actionable recommendations. They can perform:

Vulnerability Assessments: While not solely an IR benchmark, understanding the vulnerability landscape is foundational. A benchmarked vulnerability assessment will compare the organization's vulnerability management program against best practices for identification, prioritization, and remediation, especially concerning ICS-specific challenges.

Penetration Testing: Simulating real-world attacks against ICS environments, tailored to industry-specific threats, can reveal how effectively current defenses and incident response plans hold up under pressure. Benchmark comparisons here focus on the adversary's ability to achieve objectives and the defender's success in detection, containment, and eradication within defined timeframes.

Tabletop Exercises and Simulated Incidents: These exercises are invaluable for testing the IR plan and team coordination. By posing realistic ICS incident scenarios (e.g., ransomware targeting HMIs, denial-of-service on control networks, manipulation of sensor data), organizations can evaluate their response in a controlled environment. Benchmarking here involves comparing the speed, effectiveness, and adherence to procedures observed during the exercise against documented best practices for incident handling and decision-making. For instance, how quickly was the incident classified? Were the correct diagnostic steps followed? Was communication effectively managed between IT, OT, and management?

Maturity Model Assessments: Many cybersecurity frameworks, including NIST CSF and IEC 62443, can be mapped to maturity models. These models typically define different levels of maturity (e.g., initial, repeatable, defined, managed, optimizing). Assessing the organization's IR capabilities against such a model allows for a more nuanced understanding of its current standing and the incremental steps required to reach higher levels of maturity. For example, an organization might find its IR plan is "defined" (documented and understood), but its actual response execution is only "repeatable" (basic capabilities exist but are inconsistent), indicating a gap in practical application and training.

When assessing against industry best practices, it's crucial to consider the specific context of the ICS environment. Not all IT security best practices can be directly applied to OT without modification. The stringent uptime requirements of industrial processes, the use of legacy systems, proprietary protocols, and the potential safety implications of security actions necessitate a tailored approach. Therefore, when benchmarking, the focus should be on how well the organization has adapted standard practices to the unique constraints and risks of its ICS.

For example, a benchmark might emphasize rapid patching of all critical vulnerabilities. In an IT context, this is straightforward. In an ICS environment, however, patching might require extensive testing, vendor approval, coordination with production schedules, and potentially the use of compensating controls if patching is not immediately feasible. An effective ICS security program, when benchmarked, would demonstrate a risk-based approach to patching that balances security needs with operational continuity and safety, rather than a blanket application of IT-centric patching policies. This involves documenting the risk assessment for unpatched vulnerabilities and the compensating controls in place.

Another area of benchmarking is the effectiveness of the incident response team itself. This goes beyond just having a plan; it includes the skills, training, and coordination of the individuals involved. When comparing against benchmarks like ISO 27035, an organization would assess:

Team Composition and Expertise: Does the team include personnel with the necessary knowledge of ICS architecture, protocols, and operational processes, alongside cybersecurity expertise? Benchmarking would look for evidence of cross-functional teams or strong collaboration mechanisms between IT and OT.

Training and Drills: Are team members regularly trained on incident response procedures, including ICS-specific scenarios? Are simulated drills conducted regularly to test and refine skills? Benchmarks often stipulate frequency and types of training and exercises.

Roles and Responsibilities: Are roles and responsibilities clearly defined, documented, and understood by all team members? During an incident, is there clear leadership and decision-making authority? Benchmarks provide guidance on establishing clear chains of command and communication lines.

The outcome of this benchmarking and assessment process is the identification of specific gaps and weaknesses. These might range from the lack of a comprehensive IR plan to insufficient logging capabilities on critical control devices, or inadequate training for OT personnel on cybersecurity threats. The true value of benchmarking, however, lies not just in identifying these gaps, but in using them to drive strategic improvements.

Once gaps are identified, the organization must develop a roadmap for improvement. This involves prioritizing remediation actions based on risk and feasibility. For instance, if the benchmarking reveals that the organization lacks robust detection capabilities for certain OT-specific attacks, the priority might be to invest in specialized ICS intrusion detection systems or enhance network segmentation to better isolate critical assets. If training is identified as a weakness, the priority could be to develop and implement a targeted ICS cybersecurity awareness and incident response training program for both IT and OT staff.

The benchmarking process should be continuous, not a one-time event. The threat landscape is constantly evolving, and new vulnerabilities and attack techniques emerge regularly. Therefore, organizations should schedule regular benchmarking exercises, perhaps annually or biennially, to ensure their ICS security posture remains aligned with evolving best practices and emerging threats. This iterative approach ensures that incident response capabilities are not static but are dynamically improved over time.

Furthermore, benchmarking provides a valuable mechanism for demonstrating due diligence and organizational maturity to stakeholders, including regulators, insurers, and executive leadership. By showing that the organization actively compares its capabilities against recognized standards and is taking concrete steps to address identified gaps, it builds confidence in its ability to protect critical operations. It transforms incident response from a reactive necessity into a proactive, strategic component of overall operational risk management. Ultimately, rigorous benchmarking against industry best practices allows organizations to move beyond simply "hoping for the best" and toward a state of assured resilience, where their ICS environments are demonstrably prepared to withstand and recover from cyber incidents effectively and safely.

The dynamism inherent in the cybersecurity domain necessitates a proactive and adaptive approach to the implementation of any framework, especially within the critical context of Industrial Control Systems (ICS). The threat actors are not static; they continuously refine their methodologies, exploit novel vulnerabilities, and leverage emerging technologies to achieve their objectives. Consequently, an incident response (IR) framework, no matter how robust at its inception, risks obsolescence if it does not incorporate mechanisms for continuous evolution. This subsection delves into the critical processes required to ensure that the ICS cybersecurity framework remains agile, responsive, and effective in the face of an ever-shifting threat and technology landscape. It underscores the importance of moving beyond a "set it and forget it" mentality to one of perpetual vigilance and strategic adaptation.

A cornerstone of adapting the framework to new threats and technologies lies in establishing a robust, ongoing threat intelligence program. This program should not be a mere passive consumption of external reports but an active, integrated process that feeds directly into the organization's risk assessment and IR planning. Proactive monitoring of emerging threats involves subscribing to reputable threat intelligence feeds, participating in industry-specific information sharing and analysis centers (ISACs), and fostering relationships with cybersecurity researchers and peer organizations. The focus should be on identifying not just

what threats exist, but *how* they are evolving, particularly those that specifically target ICS environments. This includes tracking new malware families designed for OT, novel exploitation techniques for industrial protocols, and the growing sophistication of nation-state-sponsored attacks that often involve persistent, low-and-slow methodologies to infiltrate and disrupt critical infrastructure.

Furthermore, it is crucial to understand that threats are often enabled or amplified by technological advancements. The proliferation of Internet of Things (IoT) and Industrial IoT (IIoT) devices in ICS environments, while offering significant operational benefits, also introduces new attack surfaces and potential vulnerabilities. These devices, often deployed without the same rigorous security considerations as traditional ICS components, can become entry points for adversaries. An adaptive framework must therefore include processes for evaluating the security implications of new technology deployments. This involves conducting thorough security assessments of any new IoT/IIoT devices or platforms before integration, understanding their communication protocols, authentication mechanisms, and potential for exploitation. The incident response plan must be updated to reflect potential incident scenarios involving these new technologies, such as compromised IIoT sensors leading to inaccurate process data or the exploitation of unsecured IoT gateways to gain access to the control network.

The rise of Artificial Intelligence (AI) and Machine Learning (ML) presents a dual-edged sword. On one hand, AI/ML can be leveraged to enhance defensive capabilities, enabling more sophisticated threat detection, automated response actions, and predictive analytics for identifying potential security weaknesses. On the other hand, adversaries are also increasingly employing AI/ML to develop more potent and evasive attack tools. They can use AI to automate vulnerability discovery, craft highly convincing phishing campaigns, or develop polymorphic malware that constantly changes its signature to evade detection. An adaptive IR framework must therefore not only explore the integration of AI/ML into its defensive arsenal but also anticipate and prepare for AI-powered attacks. This might involve developing AI-driven anomaly detection systems that can identify subtle deviations from normal operational behavior, which could indicate a sophisticated attack. It also means understanding how AI might be used to orchestrate complex attacks across multiple systems, requiring a coordinated and swift response that leverages automation where possible.

The process of adapting the framework should be systematic. When a new threat or technology emerges that has potential implications for the ICS environment, a structured risk assessment should be initiated. This assessment should consider:

1. **Relevance:** How directly does this new threat or technology impact our specific ICS assets and operations?

2. **Likelihood:** What is the probability of this threat being realized or this technology being exploited within our environment?

3. **Impact:** What would be the potential consequences for safety, operations, environment, and business if this threat were to manifest or this technology were compromised?

4. **Existing Controls:** What current security controls and IR procedures are in place that might mitigate this risk?

5. **Gaps:** Where are the deficiencies in our current defenses and response capabilities concerning this new risk?

Based on the outcomes of this risk assessment, specific updates to the IR plan, procedures, playbooks, and training materials should be developed. For instance, if threat intelligence indicates a rise in attacks targeting specific types of programmable logic controllers (PLCs) used in a facility, the IR team needs to develop or update playbooks detailing how to detect, contain, and recover from such an attack. This might involve ensuring that specific diagnostic tools capable of analyzing PLC traffic are readily available, that OT personnel are trained on recognizing the indicators of compromise for these devices, and that there are established procedures for isolating or safely shutting down affected PLCs if necessary, while minimizing operational disruption.

The adaptation process also requires continuous review and refinement of existing IR capabilities. This is where the concept of "learning from experience" becomes paramount. Every incident, no matter how minor, provides valuable lessons. Post-incident reviews should not just focus on the immediate technical remediation but also on identifying any shortcomings in the IR plan, procedures, or team execution that were exposed during the event. Were there delays in detection? Was communication inefficient? Were the containment strategies effective? Were recovery procedures tested and reliable? These insights are critical for iterative improvement.

Beyond actual incidents, organizations should actively pursue opportunities to test and validate their adaptive capabilities through exercises. This includes:

Scenario-Based Exercises: Developing exercise scenarios that incorporate the latest threat intelligence or emerging technologies. For example, an exercise could simulate an attack that uses AI to bypass traditional signature-based intrusion detection systems, forcing the team to rely on behavioral analysis and anomaly detection. Another scenario might involve the compromise of an IIoT device that has been recently deployed, testing the organization's ability to identify and isolate the affected device quickly.

Red Team/Blue Team Engagements: Increasingly sophisticated red team exercises can be designed to mimic the tactics, techniques, and procedures (TTPs) of advanced persistent threats (APTs) that leverage novel attack vectors. The blue team, tasked with defending the ICS environment, must then adapt its detection and response strategies in real-time to counter these evolving TTPs. This adversarial approach is invaluable for uncovering unforeseen vulnerabilities and testing the agility of the IR team and its tools.

Technology-Focused Drills: Periodically conducting drills that specifically test the response to incidents involving new technologies or protocols. For example, if the organization has recently integrated a new SCADA system that uses a different communication protocol, a drill could focus on how the team would detect and respond to an incident involving that specific protocol.

The evolution of attack vectors also demands constant attention. Adversaries are no longer confined to traditional network-based intrusions. The attack surface has expanded to include supply chains, third-party service providers, and even the physical security of operational facilities, which can sometimes be a precursor to cyber-physical attacks. An adaptive framework must therefore encompass the security of the entire ICS lifecycle and its associated ecosystem. This means scrutinizing the security practices of vendors who supply hardware and software, ensuring that software updates and patches are verified for integrity and malicious content, and establishing clear incident response protocols for supply chain compromises. If a critical component supplier is found to have been compromised, the organization needs to understand the potential impact on its own systems and have a plan to verify the integrity of received components or implement alternative solutions.

Furthermore, the regulatory and compliance landscape is also in flux. New regulations or updates to existing ones often emerge in response to evolving threats or high-profile incidents. An adaptive framework must stay abreast of these changes to ensure continued compliance. This might involve incorporating new reporting requirements into the IR plan, updating data retention policies to meet new legal obligations, or ensuring that specific security controls mandated by regulators are properly implemented and auditable. For example, if new regulations require more granular logging of access to critical control systems, the IR plan and its associated technical controls need to be updated to meet these enhanced logging requirements.

The human element remains a critical factor in adapting to new threats and technologies. Continuous training and awareness programs are essential. As new threats emerge, the IR team, IT staff, and OT personnel must be educated about them. This includes understanding the new TTPs, recognizing novel indicators of compromise, and being aware of the potential impact of emerging technologies on cybersecurity. Training should evolve to incorporate new scenarios and technologies, moving beyond generic cybersecurity awareness to focus on ICS-specific threats and vulnerabilities. For instance, training for OT engineers might now include modules on how to identify and report suspicious activity related to AI-driven malware or how to secure newly deployed IIoT devices.

A key aspect of fostering adaptability is cultivating a culture of continuous improvement and open communication. Silos between IT and OT, while often a reality, can hinder the rapid adaptation required in the face of dynamic threats. Encouraging cross-functional collaboration, regular information sharing sessions, and joint planning exercises can help bridge these divides. When IT security teams understand the operational constraints and priorities of OT, and when OT personnel feel empowered to report potential security concerns without fear of reprisal, the organization becomes far more resilient. This collaborative environment is essential for effectively translating intelligence about new threats and technologies into actionable changes within the ICS IR framework.

In essence, adapting the ICS cybersecurity framework is not a discrete project but an ongoing organizational commitment. It requires a proactive intelligence-gathering capability, a structured risk assessment process, a willingness to update plans and procedures, robust testing and validation mechanisms, and a focus on continuous learning and development for personnel. By embedding these principles, organizations can ensure that their incident response capabilities remain a relevant and effective defense against the ever-evolving landscape of cyber threats and technological innovation, safeguarding the critical operations that depend on their ICS environments. The framework must be viewed as a living document, subject to constant scrutiny, testing, and refinement to maintain its efficacy in protecting industrial operations against the challenges of tomorrow.

Senior management and executive leadership are the linchpins for ensuring that an Industrial Control Systems (ICS) cybersecurity incident response (IR) framework not only exists but thrives and remains effective over time. Their commitment is not merely about providing a budget, although that is undeniably crucial; it extends to actively championing the importance of robust IR preparedness as a strategic imperative for the organization. Without this visible and unwavering support from the top, even the most meticulously crafted plans and technologically advanced defenses risk becoming neglected, under-resourced, or de-prioritized when faced with competing business demands or budget constraints.

The role of leadership begins with recognizing that ICS cybersecurity and the ability to respond effectively to incidents are not solely technical concerns for the IT or OT departments. Instead, they are fundamental to operational continuity, safety, regulatory compliance, and the overall reputation of the enterprise. When leaders understand and communicate this, they set the tone for the entire organization. This involves articulating a clear vision for cybersecurity, one that explicitly includes readiness for disruptive cyber events within the ICS environment. This vision should be integrated into the organization's broader strategic objectives, demonstrating that cybersecurity is an enabler of business resilience, not a barrier to operational efficiency. Leaders must consistently advocate for the necessary investment in people, processes, and technology that underpin a state of sustained preparedness. This includes ensuring that IR plans are not just theoretical documents but are actively supported by the resources required for their implementation, maintenance, and regular testing.

A critical function of leadership in sustaining ICS IR preparedness is the proactive allocation of resources. This encompasses not only the financial capital necessary for acquiring and maintaining security tools, training personnel, and conducting exercises, but also the allocation of human capital and time. Leaders must ensure that dedicated personnel, with the requisite skills and expertise in both IT and OT security, are available to develop, implement, and execute IR plans. This might involve hiring new staff, providing specialized training to existing employees, or establishing partnerships with external cybersecurity service providers. Furthermore, leadership must empower these teams by granting them the authority to make timely decisions during a crisis and by ensuring that their efforts are recognized and valued. This includes allocating sufficient time for regular training, exercises, and post-incident reviews, understanding that these activities, while potentially seeming to detract from immediate operational tasks, are vital for long-term resilience. For instance, a commitment to sustained preparedness might manifest as a dedicated line item in the annual budget for IR-related activities, ensuring that funding is not subject to ad-hoc cuts when other financial pressures arise. It also means authorizing overtime or dedicated project time for IR team members to update playbooks, conduct tabletop exercises, or participate in threat intelligence briefings.

Fostering a security-aware culture is another paramount responsibility of leadership in maintaining a high level of ICS IR preparedness. This involves embedding a mindset throughout the organization where cybersecurity and incident response are considered everyone's responsibility, from the frontline operator to the executive suite. Leaders achieve this by consistently communicating the importance of security policies, promoting best practices, and leading by example. They must champion training and awareness programs that are not just generic cybersecurity refreshers but are tailored to the specific risks and operational realities of the ICS environment. This education should highlight the unique vulnerabilities of industrial systems and the potential catastrophic consequences of cyber incidents, such as safety failures, environmental damage, or prolonged operational downtime. When leadership actively participates in security awareness campaigns, visits control rooms to discuss security protocols, or publicly commends teams for diligent security practices, it signals that security is a core organizational value. This cultural shift is instrumental in encouraging employees to report suspicious activities, adhere to security procedures, and contribute to a vigilant environment where potential threats are identified and addressed before they can escalate into full-blown incidents. The ripple effect of this cultural reinforcement means that an anomaly detected by an operator on the plant floor, or a misconfiguration spotted by an engineer, is more likely to be reported promptly, providing the IR team with crucial early warning signals.

Moreover, leadership plays a decisive role in ensuring that the ICS IR framework remains a strategic priority and drives continuous improvement. This means establishing clear metrics and key performance indicators (KPIs) for IR readiness, such as mean time to detect (MTTD), mean time to respond (MTTR), and the frequency and effectiveness of IR exercises. These metrics should be regularly reviewed by senior management, providing tangible evidence of the organization's preparedness levels and identifying areas that require attention. Leaders must then act on this information, initiating corrective actions, investing in new capabilities, or refining existing processes based on performance data and lessons learned from exercises or actual incidents. This commitment to continuous improvement is what differentiates organizations that are merely compliant from those that are truly resilient. It involves establishing a formal feedback loop where insights gained from IR activities are systematically integrated back into the IR plan, training programs, and security controls. For example, if tabletop exercises reveal that communication protocols between IT and OT teams are slow or inefficient during simulated breaches, leadership should mandate improvements to these communication channels, perhaps through joint training sessions or the implementation of dedicated IR communication tools.

Leadership's active involvement also ensures that the organization's response capabilities are aligned with its risk appetite and business objectives. Different organizations, and even different business units within the same organization, will have varying levels of tolerance for cyber risk. Senior leaders are responsible for defining this risk appetite and ensuring that the ICS IR framework is tailored to meet these specific requirements. This might involve prioritizing investments in protecting the most critical assets and processes, or establishing different levels of response readiness based on the potential impact of an incident. For instance, a chemical plant might have a zero-tolerance policy for any cyber incident that could compromise safety protocols, requiring the highest level of IR preparedness for those specific systems. Conversely, an administrative system might have a higher tolerance for downtime, allowing for a less immediate but still robust response. Leaders must champion this risk-based approach, ensuring that resources are deployed strategically to address the most significant threats and vulnerabilities. They are also the ones who ultimately approve the IR plan and its associated budget, thereby signifying its importance to the organization.

The concept of accountability, driven by leadership, is also fundamental to sustained IR preparedness. Leaders must ensure that roles and responsibilities within the IR process are clearly defined and that individuals and teams are held accountable for their assigned tasks. This fosters a sense of ownership and responsibility, ensuring that all parties understand their contribution to the overall resilience of the organization. Accountability extends to the review of incident response performance, where leaders can identify individuals or teams that excel and those that may require additional support or training. This can also involve establishing consequences for negligence or a failure to adhere to established security protocols, thereby reinforcing the seriousness with which the organization treats cybersecurity. When leaders consistently emphasize the importance of each individual's role in maintaining security and response readiness, it cultivates a culture where proactive measures are valued and a high standard of performance is expected across the board. This might involve incorporating security-related performance objectives into individual employee reviews, or implementing recognition programs for exceptional contributions to the organization's cybersecurity posture.

Furthermore, leadership is instrumental in navigating the complex and often evolving regulatory landscape that impacts ICS security. Many industries are subject to stringent regulations regarding the cybersecurity of critical infrastructure and industrial systems. Leaders must ensure that the organization's IR framework not only meets these regulatory requirements but also anticipates future changes. This involves staying informed about new legislation, engaging with industry bodies, and advocating for policies that support robust cybersecurity practices. Their involvement can also extend to ensuring that the organization's IR capabilities are regularly audited and that any identified deficiencies are promptly addressed. This proactive approach to compliance, driven by leadership, minimizes the risk of significant fines, legal liabilities, and reputational damage. It also positions the organization as a responsible operator, which can be a competitive advantage.

In summary, the sustained effectiveness of an ICS incident response framework is intrinsically linked to the commitment, vision, and active involvement of senior leadership. Their role is multifaceted, encompassing the championing of cybersecurity as a strategic priority, the allocation of essential resources, the cultivation of a pervasive security-aware culture, the establishment of clear accountability, and the ongoing drive for continuous improvement and regulatory compliance. By embedding these principles into the fabric of organizational governance and operations, leaders ensure that the organization is not only prepared to respond to cyber incidents but is also building enduring resilience against the dynamic and ever-present threats to industrial control systems. This steadfast leadership ensures that the investment in preparedness is not a one-time effort but a continuous, evolving journey, safeguarding critical operations for the future.

www.ingramcontent.com/pod-product-compliance
Lightning Source LLC
LaVergne TN
LVHW052210200926
848481LV00001B/69